POLEMOS:
THE DAWN OF PAGAN TRADITIONALISM

Askr Svarte
(Evgeny Nechkasov)

Translated and Edited by Jafe Arnold
With a Foreword by Richard Rudgley

2021

PRAV Publishing
www.pravpublishing.com
pravpublishing@protonmail.com

Originally published in Russian by Veligor Publishing House (Moscow, Russian Federation) under the title *Polemos: Zaria iazychestva*, text copyright ©2016 Askr Svarte (E.A. Nechkasov).

Translation copyright © 2020, 2021 PRAV Publishing

1st edition, 2020, copy-edited by Lucas Griffin
2nd edition, 2021, copy-edited by Michele Olzi

All rights reserved. No part of this book may be reproduced or distributed in any form or by any means, electronic or mechanical, including photocopying, recording, or by any information storage and retrieval, without permission in writing from the publisher.

Cover image: "Perseus with the Head of Medusa" by Benvenuto Cellini, 1554.

ISBN 978-1952671-00-5 (Paperback)
ISBN 978-1-952671-01-2 (Hardcover)
ISBN 978-1952671-02-9 (Ebook)

TABLE OF CONTENTS

	FROM THE TRANSLATOR AND PUBLISHER	7
	FOREWORD	11
	AUTHOR'S PREFACE TO THE ENGLISH EDITION	19
I.	**PROLEGOMENA**	**25**
	Dawn?	25
	Paganism: Doctrines, Names, and Symbols	28
	Traditionalism	37
II.	**TIME AND INITIATION**	**49**
	Cyclical Time	49
	Linear Time	58
	The Golden Age	62
	The Silver and Bronze Ages	67
	The Profane	71
	The Heroes	74
	The Iron Age	77
	The Ontology of Estates	82
	Pagan Initiation	101
	Initiation as Death	102
	Initiation as a Social Phenomenon	105
	Initiation and Education	107
	The Historical Heritage	108
	The Horizontal and the Vertical	114
	Language and Thinking	117
	Two Languages	121
	Translation and Rite	125
	Vertical Initiation	128
	Aspects of Initiations in Contemporary Paganism	133
	The Problem of Counter-Initiation	136
	The Triumph of the Titans	140

III. PAGANISM, MODERNITY, AND POSTMODERNITY — 155

- Dharma and the Due — 155
- Dharma in the Kali-Yuga — 157
- Modernity and Estates — 159
- The Constructs of Modernity — 169
- The Human — 172
- Humanism — 174
- The Material View on Traditional Societies — 182
- Reflection — 184
- Reality — 185
- Primitiveness — 188
- Gnoseological Racism — 190
- Technology — 196
- Freedom — 202
- Postmodernity — 203
- Post-Ontology and Post-Gnoseology — 207
- The Post-Human — 216
- Post-Society — 221
- The Consumer Society — 225
- Revolt, Anomie, and Death in the Consumer Society — 229
- The Rhizome — 232
- Post-Space — 232
- Post-Time — 235
- Post-War — 237
- An Intermediate Summary — 241
- The Horizons of Counter-Initiation — 243
- Post-Religion — 244
- The Fate of Europe - the Destiny of the World? — 251
- The Place and Time of Postmodernity — 253
- The Potential of Russia — 255

IV. THE CONTEMPORARY PAGAN EXPERIENCE — 263

   The Authentic and the Foreign — 264
   A Typology of Pagans — 270
   Subcultural Infiltrations — 272
   The Contemporary Experience — 282
   Personalities — 287
   Critical Remarks on Practice — 304
   Simulacra and Sects — 330
   The West — 334
   Russia and the Post-Soviet Space — 345
   The East and Asia — 368
   Compromises — 371

EPILOGUE — 379
BIBLIOGRAPHY — 381

FROM THE TRANSLATOR AND PUBLISHER

That 2020 would be the year in which a rising Russian intellectual would make the leap from Siberia into the realm of English-language literature, for no less than to herald a "new dawn" of pagan philosophy and spirituality, is likely a turn of events which even many of the thinkers, movements, and visions invoked in this book hardly could have forecasted. This is not even mentioning the impression of the unsuspecting, curious browser who, upon picking up this tome, will probably be struck as if they have suddenly peered into a whole other world, one populated by beings, forces, and ideas long thought to have disappeared into the mysterious depths of ancient history. Yet, as readers will surely soon learn for themselves, this book, *Polemos: The Dawn of Pagan Traditionalism*, is at once long overdue and ahead of its time, both timeless in the eternal subjects which it embraces and most timely in the trends and problems which it identifies and addresses. Part study and part manifesto, part prose and part poetry, both a courageous exposition of complex theories as well as a sober guide to wide-ranging experiences and practices, Askr Svarte's (Evgeny Nechkasov) *Polemos* can safely be called one of those works defying the Modern divisions between fields, perspectives, genres and styles. The book before you now engages such an immense span of times and spaces, ideas and personalities, and metaphysical heights and sociological depths that we do not dare to offer an introduction here - for that, readers can turn to the foreword provided by the renowned English author Richard Rudgley, to the preface to this edition by Askr Svarte himself or, if one so wishes, take the plunge immediately into *The Dawn of Pagan Traditionalism*. Here we wish to present only a few details about the translation and publication of this book in the English language.

Polemos: The Dawn of Pagan Traditionalism is the English translation of the Russian book *Polemos: Zaria iazychestva* (*Polemos: The Dawn of Paganism*), the first of the two-volume work *Polemos: Iazycheskii traditsionalizm* (*Polemos: Pagan*

7

Traditionalism) released in Russia in 2016 by the publishing house Veligor. Aspiring to remain faithful to the original Russian edition, as well as in anticipation of the future translation and publication of the second volume, *Polemos: Perspektivy iazychestva* (*Polemos: Pagan Perspectives*), no major conceptual additions to or subtractions from the content of the original text have been made. The only subjects of exclusion were the appendices to the Russian edition, which consisted of a short essay by Askr Svarte, "*Dobroslav: vzgliad traditsionalista*" ("Dobroslav: A Traditionalist View", the subject of which is introduced and briefly discussed in Chapter IV here) and a short review of the present work by Ilya Cherkasov (Veleslav), both of which are available online. Otherwise, the text presented here has been edited in only four respects: (1) some of the tenses have been changed to reflect the passing of various events and lives, as mentioned in the author's preface to this edition; (2) the author has taken the opportunity to correct a small handful of inaccuracies, misprints, and confusions discovered in the Russian edition; (3) the titles of the third and fourth chapters, originally "Paganism and Modernity" and "On the Contemporary Experience", have been amended to be "Paganism, Modernity, and Postmodernity" and "The Contemporary Pagan Experience" so as to more clearly reflect their content; (4) the author has agreed to minor supplemental explanations of Russian-peculiar terms for English-language readers. Indeed, as highlighted in Askr Svarte's preface, one of the valuable, special aspects of this work is its Slavic-Russian perspective - a vantage point so often desperately lacking in the Anglophone sphere - with the corresponding formulaic and linguistic fashions unique to this language's modes of expression. The present translation has thus sought not only to preserve the author's own voice and style, but also, to the extent such is possible, its culturo-linguistic "accent." Hopefully, readers will appreciate this as they encounter the author's discussions of "linguistic paradigms" and "initiation into language" and especially, already in the first chapter, the explanation that the very Russian word for "paganism", *iazychestvo (язычество)*, is derived from the Old Church Slavonic *iazyk (iдзык)*, which meant "people", "folk" or "tribe", whose descendant, identical cognate in modern Russian and all other extant Slavic languages, *iazyk (язык)*, is the word for "language." Perhaps the only considerable textual difference between the present book and its Russian edition - and we would say a most positive one for readers and researchers - is the more consistent citation of quotations and sources, including the presence of an updated, refined, better organized, and translated bibliography.

Finally, a few words on PRAV's publication of *Polemos*. PRAV Publishing's mission statement articulates:

> As the illusions of the waning period of ideological and geopolitical unipolarity fade, and as the planet's diverse cultures are faced with the many complex realities and possibilities of multipolarity and the return of "rejected knowledge", PRAV sees the growing need and aspirations for critical reconsiderations of histories, ideas, and currents which transcend the Modern, predominantly Western frameworks which have "divided and conquered" in recent times and spaces. Through the publication of diverse authors, ideas, and perspectives, PRAV strives to contribute to a Polylogue of Civilizations, unfettered by the reductions and prejudices of what has passed for the "progress of knowledge" under the paradigm presently in decline. This means not only recovering the diverse histories and intellectual exchanges which have been excluded, mistreated, and disconnected in mainstream discourses, but also moving beyond these inadequate paradigms towards perspectives which reintegrate the old and new in relations befitting of the world's plurality of cultures and experiences from the depths of prehistory to the horizons of the contested future.

In light of these recognitions, motivations, and orientations, it is difficult to imagine a more fitting book than the one at hand to emerge as one of PRAV's first published titles. For this reason and many more, PRAV is most pleased to present readers and researchers with *Polemos: The Dawn of Pagan Traditionalism*.

- Jafe Arnold
PRAV Publishing
19 March 2020

FOREWORD

by Richard Rudgley

"Looking at the sky, the person initiated into the Divine will see the blue cloak of the God Odin through the holes of which the stars shine."[1]

When approached by Jafe Arnold of PRAV Publishing to write this foreword, I immediately accepted with great pleasure, as the present work is undoubtedly of major significance in its field for a number of reasons. Most obviously, it brings an in-depth exposition of a notable Russian pagan thinker to the Anglophone world. It also provides fascinating material on the revival of Slavic paganism in late Soviet and post-Soviet Russia, much of which will probably be as unfamiliar to most readers as it was to me. Askr Svarte (Evgeny Nechkasov) also provides a multi-dimensional critique of the Western (most notably Western European and North American) understanding, or lack thereof, of neo-paganism and its authentic forms. The book is also a major landmark in establishing the spiritual compatibility of neo-paganism and Traditionalism.[2]

POLEMOS: THE WAR OF IDEAS

Let us begin with the final statement of the present book, which reminds us that Heraclitus stated that War (*Polemos*) is the "father of all things." Askr Svarte comments that this war takes place in the twin arenas of the heart and mind – i.e. it is both a holy, spiritual war as well as an intellectual and metapolitical one.

---

1   Askr Svarte, *Polemos: The Dawn of Pagan Traditionalism*, p. 148.

2   Here 'Traditionalism' refers not to 'traditionalism' in the conventional understanding, but rather the particular school of esoteric thought that arose in the twentieth century. Among its key thinkers are René Guénon, Julius Evola and more recently Alexander Dugin, all of whom have had a profound effect on Askr Svarte.

The transformational power of ideas involves the unfolding of strategies to realign the intellectual and spiritual firmament. In this regard, the present work is an exposition of how paganism is currently perceived both within the neo-pagan movement and beyond it, by those adhering to different worldviews, be they secular, religious or spiritual. It is also a multidimensional polemic with targets on the spiritual, metapolitical and intellectual levels. As such, it is as much a destructive process as it is a creative one. Hence *Polemos*.[3] The author is spiritually oriented to the Northern Tradition (Germanic neo-paganism) and more specifically a practicing Odinist, a follower of the Norse God Odin (a.k.a. Woden, Wotan).[4] As the god of battle, magic, disguise and words, Odin is a very fitting role model for engaging in such strategies and tactics in the war of ideas. Stephen McNallen, the founder of the Asatru Folk Assembly (formerly the Asatru Free Assembly), one of the most prominent and long-lived neo-pagan organizations in the U.S., wrote of the followers of Odin: "in the military sphere, they gravitate to military intelligence and covert operations of all sorts."[5]

Readers will discover for themselves what the author fights for and against. They will come to know who his comrades-in-arms are and what ancestral fallen warriors he invokes from the other world.[6] And who his enemies are in this war of ideas.

It is often remarked in common parlance that there is both a war of words and a war of ideas in the obvious sense – competing and incompatible worldviews vie for dominance through the media, propaganda ('hearts and minds') and

---

3 This should hardly surprise, as the word polemic derives from the Greek word *Polemos*.

4 For an in-depth exposition of what this means to him, see Askr Svarte, *Gap: At the Left Hand of Odin* (multiple translators; Fall of Man, 2019).

5 Stephen A. McNallen, *Thunder from the North: The Way of the Teutonic Warrior* (Nevada City: Asatru Folk Assembly, 1993), p. 8.

6 The Einherjar are those who have been removed from the earthly battlefield by the Valkyries and transported to Valhalla to be with Odin.

various other means.[7] Many of these social and ideological forces, such as Christianity, Islam and secularism are, of course, dramatically larger than neo-paganism both in terms of political power and in the number of active adherents and relatively passive followers they have in their ideological armies. Paganism is often misrepresented by outsiders variously as a fad of the counterculture (be it associated with hippiedom, black metal or the like) or an offshoot of Satanism. Such fabrications are in significant part built on the actions and writings of so-called pagans of the New Age variety themselves. These etic and emic caricatures have led to a certain credibility problem for neo-pagans which, when taken in conjunction with their current relative demographic insignificance, could be perceived as making the task at hand seem overwhelming. However, the battle is far from lost. If the military theory of the generations of warfare (1GW through to 5GW) is transplanted into the metapolitical sphere of the war of ideas, then the rise of fourth generation warfare and fifth generation warfare does not require superior numbers to be highly effective.

It must also not be forgotten that the philosophers of Greece and Rome, from the time of Heraclitus down to the Neo-Platonists were, almost without exception, pagans, and that both Christian and Islamic theology would be threadbare without drawing on the intellectual and spiritual traditions of this ancient paganism. The foundations of paganism are profound in both senses of the word and its history is deeper than that of the Abrahamic faiths. The arsenal of the ancient pagans may have been looted by Christians and others, but it is a veritable cornucopia overflowing with an inexhaustible stockpile of weapons that may be used by neo-pagans in the war of ideas.

A number of serious neo-pagan and Traditionalist thinkers have emerged to orient metapolitical and theological strategies, and *Polemos: The Dawn of Pagan Traditionalism*

---

7   There is also a hidden level to this conflict. For an in-depth description, see "Occult War - Weapons of the Occult War", the 13th chapter in Julius Evola, *Men Among the Ruins: Postwar Reflections of a Radical Traditionalist* (trans. Guido Stucco, ed. Michael Moynihan; Rochester, Vermont: Inner Traditions, 2002).

draws inspiration from Alain de Benoist, the leading figure of the French New Right, the French Traditionalist Dominique Venner, the Russian philosopher Alexander Dugin, the American philosopher Collin Cleary, and Julius Evola among others. Evola, perhaps the most influential of these on our author, was one of the founding fathers of Traditionalism, a modern school which through its perennial philosophy seeks to restore ancient wisdom, but without the superficial primitivism with which neo-paganism is often associated.

THE ENEMIES WITHIN THE NEO-PAGAN MOVEMENT

Ever since the neo-pagan revival in the nineteenth century, many external or tangential elements (Theosophy, Kabbalism, the Faustian grimoires, yoga, Thelemic Magick, Wicca etc.) have been used to augment the available knowledge on the beliefs and practices of the old pagans. Taking a leaf out of Evola's book, Askr Svarte provides an in-depth critique in order to weed out what he sees as the extraneous elements. Evola was highly critical of many prominent figures in the neo-pagan movement, including Guido von List (the father of neo-pagan Runosophy) and his followers, whose teachings and use of symbolism he summarily dismissed as "without roots or connections with a true tradition and with a mixture of personal idiosyncrasies of every sort."[8] He was also equally skeptical about the claims of the modern proponent of witchcraft Gerald Gardner (whose own cult turned into what is now known as Wicca) that his covens represented a genuine and ancient tradition.[9]

---

8   Julius Evola, *Notes on the Third Reich* (trans. E. Christian Kopff; London: Arktos 2013), p. 66.

9   See Julius Evola, *The Witches' Coven* (trans. Sergio Knipe, ed. John B. Morgan) in *The Initiate: Journal of Traditional Studies* #2 (Fall 2010). This article by Evola was based on his meeting with Gerald Gardner in Rome in the late 1960s when the latter paid him a visit. An amusing aside is that Evola remarks that his guest was carrying books in a type of bag used by housewives, which seems to have offended his hyper-masculinity. Gardner had formerly been a member of the Ordo Templis Orientis (O.T.O), an occult organization that had been taken over by Aleister Crowley, and it has been suggested that Crowley had a hand in helping Gardner concoct the original documents for his modern witch cult.

Yet Evola, despite his typically caustic approach to most occultists, was for some reason much less dismissive of Aleister Crowley, even though Crowley and his Thelemic teachings are highly antagonistic to the Traditionalism espoused by the Baron. This is particularly significant when thinking about Pagan Traditionalism, as Crowley, for a number of reasons, was no more a genuine pagan than he was an authentic Traditionalist. Nevertheless, Crowley's influence on Anglo-American neo-paganism is very pervasive.[10] Crowley's influence is also plain to see among the Northern Tradition's neo-pagan subcultural offshoots of antinomian groupuscules such as Rokkatru, Thursatru and those of the Loki-worshippers, all of which represent radical departures from historical paganism in that there is no precedent for the worship or veneration of these beings.

On the metapolitical and political levels, the author also takes issue with both Universalism and White Supremacism within the neo-pagan movement. Whilst the former suffers from that malaise which the French thinker Guillaume Faye has dubbed "ethnomasochism"[11], the other clearly endorses what can be called "ethnosadism." These two ideologies are not only at odds with each other, but also with the multipolar worldview advocated by Askr Svarte, his perspective being that there are as many paganisms as there are ethnic groups, and not just one universal paganism or any one superior paganism.

---

10 A particularly notable example is the occult links between the 93 current (the term refers to the magical energy emanating from Crowley's religion of Thelema, the number 93 being derived by isopsephy from key passages in his *Book of the Law*) and the Rune Gild founded by Edred Thorsson (Stephen Flowers), whose watchword *Reyn til Runa* ('Seek toward the Mysteries!') also adds up to 93 according to the runic numerology formulated by Thorsson. For further details see my "Edred Thorsson: Runa and the Rune-Gild" in Troy Southgate (ed.), *Runemasters: Mystics and Teachers of the Heathen North* (Black Front Press, 2018). It is worth noting that the aforementioned neo-pagan thinker Collin Cleary is a member of the Rune Gild.

11 Faye defines this term as "the masochistic tendency to blame and devalue one's own ethnicity, one's own people." For further detail see his "Metapolitical Dictionary" in *Why We Fight: Manifesto of the European Resistance* (trans. Michael O'Meara; London: Arktos, 2011).

THE WAR ON REALITY

Last, but by no means least, there is another level of conflict, perhaps the most pressing of all and one that not only threatens paganism and Traditionalism but also every spiritual tradition. It may not be overdramatic to characterize it as the final conflict - The End of Days, the culmination of the Kali-Yuga, the Ragnarok. This is the War against Reality. The dramatic acceleration of technology involves not only the alteration of the biological integrity of the human organism (biorobotics, transhumanism etc.)[12], but also another postmodern project – that of a virtual reality so all-encompassing that it seeks to displace reality itself by means of an infernal alchemy by which the cults of matter transmute their dominion onto a higher plane, namely, that of the imagination. The merely imaginary seeks to override the Imaginal realm.[13] The geopolitical conflict is now accompanied by a war in the realm of the imagination, where the geography of simulacra does battle with sacred geography – the horizontal and poisonous rhizomes versus the vertical *Axis Mundi*.[14] There is no question as to which side Askr Svarte takes in this spiritual conflict, as he remarks: "Wherever an initiatory path reaches its culmination, where the language of a people and language of a tradition end, where the Divine Silence sets in - the achievement of this state can be spoken of as initiation into the One that is beyond names and forms, languages and the effable. This is the upper pole of the sacred vertical, the axis of the cosmos..."[15]

---

12 In the postmodern late stage of liberalism the literal integrity of its subject - the individual - is no longer sacrosanct and the process of dividuation opposes that of the holistic traditional goal of individuation.

13 For the distinction between these terms see Henry Corbin, *Mundus Imaginalis, or the Imaginary and the Imaginal* (Ipswich: Golgonooza Press, 1976).

14 See Richard Rudgley, "The Polar Tradition: Ancient Myth, Boreal Geography and Modern Metapolitics", *Journal of Eurasian Affairs* 4:1 (Moscow: International Eurasian Movement, 2016), p. 117-122.

15 Askr Svarte, *Polemos: The Dawn of Pagan Traditionalism*, p. 137.

AUTHOR'S PREFACE TO THE ENGLISH EDITION

It is no coincidence that the book which you are holding in your hands has as its main title the word *Polemos*. This, along with the subtitle, "The Dawn of Pagan Traditionalism", should be understood as an open question and invitation to be immersed and participate in numerous parallel, intersecting, and surrounding studies and debates on the contemporary state of (neo-)paganism in the world.

It is also important to note that this book stands on the shoulders of many other important predecessors and their works. Particularly noteworthy is the approach of Alain de Benoist and his book, *On Being a Pagan*, with the consideration of the critiques of the latter offered by Collin Cleary. Of no less importance are the general contributions of René Guénon, who throughout his works, both before and after his symbolic conversion to Islam, relied on the doctrines of the Vedas, the most detailed expression of pagan metaphysics in the space of India and Asia.

At the very core of this work lies the spirit of the Italian thinker Julius Evola, who comprehensively substantiated the possibility of Traditionalism in an active form and brought to this philosophy's field of consideration numerous other traditions and schools. Although we may not agree with the Baron in some places on matters of specific details and evaluations, nevertheless, his volitional spirit in affirming the truth, no matter what and against all odds, inspired many of the lines of this work.

Nor should we overlook such a purely Russian phenomenon as the Yuzhinsky school of metaphysics that emerged out of a circle of radical philosophers, mystics, and poets who, in the late 20th century USSR, discovered the philosophy of Traditionalism for Russia, corrected some of René Guénon's misconceptions, and proved capable of posing more radical metaphysical and existential questions. Without a doubt, the poetic and creative myth-making influence of the works of Evgeny Golovin, as well as references to the works and methodologies of Alexander Dugin and his sociological paradigm of Traditionalism, can be found in this book - with, of course, due recognition of our opposite views on the metaphysics of the Abrahamic religions.

We see a unique, positive point in the fact that this work was written in Russia and in Russian. First of all, this adds to pan-European Traditionalist discourse the great Slavic-Russian field of thought and its corresponding linguistic specificities. Secondly, in modern Europe and North America the development of paganism in the 20th century bore the effects of numerous false and erroneous doctrines and positions, whereas in Russia, for example, the Russian-speaking branch of Asatru has based itself on more reliable historical, archaeological, folkloric, and linguistic data than the flights of fantasy of late 19th and early 20th century European occultists. In other words, for objective reasons some European misconceptions concerning Tradition have not been perpetuated here, which makes our view somewhat purer. Thirdly, in connection with the latter point, the emergence of pagan movements in the late USSR and in the new Russia was also to a fairly notable extent tainted by our own local pseudo-pagan movements, which have speculated on Slavic-Russian and European mythologies and mixed them with New Age doctrines and the outright lies of newly-minted gurus. These pseudo-Slavic cults subsequently began to be exported to Europe and other countries, thus yielding a paradoxical situation in which Slavic-Russian paganism has been presented to and across the world through those same pseudo-pagan speculations which adequate and competent representatives of *Rodnoverie* (Native Faith) here in Russia have been struggling against for many years. Hence why our book devotes so much attention to the analysis and history of these pseudo-pagan currents, so that Western readers may have the minimally necessary starting orientations to be able to distinguish lies from truth for themselves.

The latter question is related to the even greater problems explored in this book, such as the relation of paganism to

Modernity with its whole complex of sciences, technologies, and arguments, the ironic suggestions of Postmodernity with its propositions of universal mixing and the final dissolution of meanings and hierarchies, as well as, importantly enough, the polemicizing and deconstruction of Abrahamic influences on pagan traditions and Traditionalism in general.

The two-volume work *Polemos* was finished in the spring and published in the fall of 2016. In the time which has passed since then, some situations have changed. Some movements and prospective currents of thought have come to a halt, while other, previously unnoticed ones have begun to manifest themselves. Moreover, several of the iconic personalities discussed in this book have since passed on to other worlds, such as Nikolai Speransky, a.k.a. Velimir, in 2018, the ideologist of Greek paganism Vlassis Rassias in 2019, and the writer Lev Prozorov, a.k.a. Ozar Voron, in 2020. If rewritten now, this book would stand to gain from paying more attention to new authors, figures, theologians, and poets of contemporary paganism. It would behoove us to dwell in more detail on contemporary instances of Pagan Traditionalism, such as the Roman Traditional Movement (MTR) in Italy, the Supreme Council of Ethnic Hellenes (YSEE) in Greece, on neo-paganism in the Caucasus, particularly Armenia, on the survival of the last pagans of the Hindu Kush in the Chitral valley, on the situation of contemporary shamanism, the complex palette of traditions among the indigenous peoples of Russia, such as the Ossetians, Mari, Buryats, and others, as well as, finally, on covering the religious situation in Latin America, Africa, and Oceania. We have already filled some of these gaps in our other, more recent interviews, articles, journals, pamphlets, and books.[16]

---

16 See: Askr Svarte, *Priblizhenie i okruzhenie. Ocherki mysli o Germanskom Logose, Traditsii i Nichto* [*Forthcoming and Encirclement: Thoughts on the Germanic Logos, Tradition, and Nothingness*] (Novosibirsk: Svarte Aske, 2017; Moscow: Gnosis, 2020); *Identichnost' iazychnika v XXI veke* [*Pagan Identity in the 21st Century*] (Moscow: Veligor, 2020); *Gap: At the Left Hand of Odin* (Fall of Man, 2019); "The Kalash People and their Identity" (Novosibirsk: Svarte Aske, 2019). See also the volumes of the Traditionalist almanac *Warha* (Russian edition) and *Warha Europe* (English edition) published by Svarte Aske since 2015.

Of course, every author is condemned to face such a situation when addressing and relying on illustrations and examples from the transient contemporary world. Thus, in our opinion, of the greatest importance is understanding the methods and procedures which we have declared here to be the foundations of Pagan Traditionalism. It is important to understand the thinking and nuances of paganism in the conditions of the Postmodern world and the existential nerve of paganism's struggle for purity and authenticity. This is the matter to which the greater part of this book is devoted. We have since developed many of the individual topics raised in the first chapters in detail in our other works, but the foundations were and are laid here.

As we said at the very outset, this work is an invitation to cooperative reflection and practice. Pagan Traditionalism is potentially fertile soil for all those pagan traditions in all the different corners of the world which are struggling for their identity, purity, and their very existence and being.

- *Askr Svarte*
Novosibirsk
18 March 2020 (Era Vulgaris)

I
PROLEGOMENA

Paganism is a Song, a beautiful Song of Eternal Wisdom and Unity. A forgotten, but not lost Song. Today, in the era of Modernity, in the Dark Age, one can evermore often hear the tune and melody of this Ancient Song - a tune which, although faint, nuanced, and fragmentary in its memory, is certain in its deep element. If you are reading these lines, then you have likely in one way or another been touched by this melody.

Dawn?

Paganism today is both alive and an indelible part of the lives of numerous people across the whole world. Paganism was an absolute reality in ancient times, but, as is well known, between the past and the present which currently surrounds us, the dominance of paganism was interrupted first by the monotheistic religions (Judaism, Christianity and Islam) and then by the Enlightenment and the rise of the scientific, secular view of the world, which denies in its very foundations not only monotheistic Sacrality and mysticism but Sacrality as such. The main polemic - or war - then ran between the Christian churches and scientific society, as a result of which the scientific, atheistic view of the world came to dominate, as it does to this day, casting all those who uphold a Sacred orientation of being into the marginal periphery.

Scholarly interest in the pre-Christian, pagan traditions of Europe began to rise in the 19th century, where we encounter such in Romanticism, in reactions to the Enlightenment, in paintings, poetry, literature, philosophy, and occult societies. Some of the first in Russia to devote any attention to pre-Christian folk traditions and motifs were the 19th century Slavophile populists, who passed on the baton to the brilliant Silver Age of Russian poetry.

If the first scholars of paganism in Europe and Russia were Christians (Catholics or Orthodox respectively), philosophers, theorists, or simply esotericists, then the 20th century can rightfully be considered the heyday of the practical reincarnation and reconstruction of paganism in life, the era of the reemergence of pagan communes and communities, and the age of active practice in the social, political, cultural, and philosophical fields.

In Europe, the first proto-pagan communities arose only in the late 19th century and were punctuated by the emergence of pro-Eastern circles amidst Europe's discovery of the philosophy and doctrines of the East, especially India. In Russia, the practical incarnation of paganism, the rebirth of the native pre-Christian tradition of the Slavic peoples, began in the second half of the 19th century and would be the result of broad historical, archaeological, and ethnographic studies (such as those of Vladimir Dal', Vladimir Miloradovich, Alexander Afanasyev, Boris Rybakov, and Evgeny Golovin) alongside the fact of the uninterrupted practice of the pagan traditions of the Volga region (such as among the Udmurts and Mari) and the peoples of Siberia (shamanism). By the end of the 20th and the beginning of the 21st century, numerous prohibitions - both religious and secular - were abolished in Russia, as a result of which the number of pagan communities, branches of different traditions, and the volume of literature on the subject have steadily amassed and penetrated the masses to the point that many people have been drawn to see the present period as that of the long-awaited Dawn following the Iron Age. Among contemporary Russian pagans, we might discern some of the most interesting to be Alexey Dobrovolsky (Dobroslav, 1938-2013), Ilya Cherkasov (Veleslav) and Bogumil Gasanov of the constituent communities of the Veles Circle, and Vadim Kazakov and his Union of Slavic Communities of the Slavic Native Faith. While in the present book we do not aim to describe the whole history of the rebirth and formation of pagan traditions in Modernity, let us remember the 19th century as the beginning of the pagan dawn, as the era of reaction to the Enlightenment, and as one of the reference points of our account.

In the modern world, the paganisms of all different peoples, including the traditions continuously preserved among small peoples and the traditions of pre-Christian Europe, Russia, and the East which are being revived and reconstructed, are all faced with a number of risks and problems pertaining to the influence of monotheistic and scientific-atheistic ideas. Enormous layers of the exoteric manifestations of traditions have lost relevance and actuality amidst shifts in lifestyles and paradigms of thinking. For example, the foundational folk cycles associated with agriculture and fertility have lost relevance to the inhabitants of cities, and largely even for the populations of the countryside themselves. Moreover, there is a distinct absence of mythological explanations being advanced to characterize the new customs and situations of the industrial and post-industrial world.

In the present work, we will appeal to the heritage and legacy of India, which boasts both a rich accumulation of texts and an admirable capability of synthesis and integration; to the reborn Slavic-Russian traditions, and the potential of Russia in particular; as well as to the reborn European pagan traditions that have developed in the specific conditions of post-Christian Europe. This main axis of European, Slavic, and Hindu traditions encompasses the greater part of the Eurasian continent in all its breadth and is representative of the civilizational diversity of the Indo-Europeans.

We set before ourselves the task not so much of covering all of paganism in a historical and spatial perspective - which in principle would be a colossal task - but rather of grasping the principal meanings and structures hidden in the depths of paganism, like the roots of the World Tree, so as to offer a fully-fledged description of the situation of paganism and pagans in which we find ourselves today. We also seek to outline the contours of a strategy for fighting against this profane world so foreign to us, so that the "pagan dawn" about which so many are speaking today might be prevented from deforming into the spectacle and games of a "weekend pastime."

Paganism: Doctrines, Names, and Symbols

DOCTRINE

Paganism is manifestationism. Manifestationism, from the Latin *manifestatia* and the verb *manifestare*, i.e., "to manifest", is the doctrine of manifestation. According to manifestationism, the whole world is an embodiment of the Divine, a revelation of the aspects of the Divine. In a word, the world is the self-discovery of God. In manifestationism, there is no gap between "creator" and "creation", for both the world and God are identical - they are ontologically equal in their primordial nature. In paganism, this is most vividly expressed in the affirmation "We are the children and grandchildren of the Gods", or in other words: man is kindred to the Gods. In the same way, pagan Gods and especially the supreme ones are frequently given the epithets "Father" and "Mother", such as All-Father (as is Odin), Mother-Earth (e.g., the Slavs' Mother Mokosh), and so on. In India, where the doctrine of manifestationism is most broadly presented across texts, a widely common greeting is *namaste*, which means: "The Divine in me greets the Divine in you." In other words, the Divine manifests itself in the world, including even when different Gods act as Demiurges ('creators') of the Cosmos or man.

This principle underlies the ubiquitously attested myths of the murder and dismemberment of a primordial being and the construction of the world out of his parts. For instance, in the case of *Puruṣa* in Hinduism (*Rigveda* X.90 (916), *Puruṣa*, 13-14)[17]:

17　*The Rigveda: The Earliest Religious Poetry of India* (Oxford: Oxford University Press/University of Texas South Asia Institute, 2014), p. 1540.

मुखादिन्दुरश्चाग्निनश्च पराणाद
वायुरजायत ॥
नाभ्या आसीदन्तरिक्षं शीष्णोर्
दयौः समवतर्त ।
पद्भ्यां भूमिदिर् शः शरोत्रात तथा
लोकानकल्पयन ॥
सप्तास्यासन परिधयस्ितरः सप्त
समिधः कतारः ।

mukhādindraścāghniśca prāṇād
vāyurajāyata ǁ
nābhyā āsīdantarikṣaṃ śīrṣṇo
dyauḥ samavartata ǀ
padbhyāṃ bhūmirdiśaḥ śrotrāt
tathā lokānakalpayan ǁ
saptāsyāsan paridhayastriḥ
sapta samidhaḥ kṛtāḥ ǀ

The moon was born from his [Puruṣa's] mind.
From his eye the sun was born.
From his mouth Indra and Agni, from his
breath Vāyu was born.
From his navel was the midspace. From his head the heaven developed.
From his two feet the earth, and the directions
from his ear. Thus they arranged the worlds.

In the Scandinavian tradition as well, there is the creative dismemberment of Ymir (*Poetic Edda*, Grímnismál 40[18]):

Ór Ymis holdi
var jörð of sköpuð,
en ór sveita sær,
björg ór beinum,
baðmr ór hári,
en ór hausi himinn.

The earth was formed
from Ymir's flesh,
And the sea from his blood,
The rocks from his bones,
The trees from his hair,
And the sky from his skull.

We also know of myths describing the unions of the Gods and primordial elements - e.g., Sky/Fire and Earth/Water - as well as the many types of beings spawned by them. Examples of this include the myth of Uranus and Gaia in the Greek tradition, or in the Scandinavian tradition the myth of how the primordial contact between the Fire of Muspelheim and the Ice of Niflheim gave birth to Ymir. This manifestationist principle is sometimes referred to as *creatio ex Deo*, i.e., "creation out of God", as opposed to *creatio ex Nihilo*, or "creation out of nothing", which is characteristic of the Abrahamic religions.

However, this fundamental ontological identification of God with the world does not exclude a hierarchical structure

---

18 *The Poetic Edda* (trans. by Jackson Crawford; Indianapolis: Hackett, 2015), p. 68.

of the world. The world is filled with older and younger Gods and different spirits and animals, yet this hierarchy does not generate a rupture between the world and the Principle. It should be clarified that this non-duality does not imply a oneness of God, and on this matter we could cite the saying of Slavic Native Faith (*Rodnoverie*) to the tune of: "[The] *Rod* is one and manifold." The word *rod* means at once "kin", "family", "clan", "tribe", and "folk" or, more broadly, "type", "genus" or, in some modern translations, "race." Inseparable from this, *Rod* is the Slavic God embodying the primordial, eternal manifestation of cosmic order. In other words, the many Divinities are equal both between each other and the world. *Rod*, in this case, refers to the very principle of the non-duality of manifestationism. Manifestationism is the primordial doctrine of the living, direct perception of reality as it is, not deformed by the rift between God and the world which punctuates the Abrahamic traditions.

NAMES

The question of the definitions and determinations of the names and terms with which we shall operate in this work cannot be avoided, insofar as such immediately immerses us into the very problems and questions peculiar to our subject. In the preceding, we have already offered what we propose to be the main, definitive principle and term: manifestationism.

The Russian term for paganism which we have employed in the title of our work, *iazychestvo (язычество)*, is derived from the Old Church Slavonic language, in which the word *iazyk (ιάзыκ)* meant "people", "folk" (in modern Russian: *narod*) and "tribe" (in modern Russian: *plemia*), translated as such was to correspond to the Greek *ethnos (ἔθνος)*. In modern Russian and other Slavic tongues, the word *iazyk* means "language." The practice of calling other, non-Christian peoples "pagans" (*iazychniki*) dates back to the translation of the Bible into Slavonic, following which the term retained negative connotations for many centuries. From the point of view of Christians, "pagans" meant all non-Christians and other-believers - although Judaism and

Islam would later be rehabilitated - while "paganism" itself came to refer to any form of worshipping creation as opposed to the Creator, i.e., idolatry. Any cursory overview of this history can be said to forebode how the term "paganism" has been even further demonized to the point that today the term "paganism" is attached to any and all kinds of materialism, liberalism and consumerism (e.g., the worship of the "Golden Calf"). All of this must be understood as derived from the point of view of Christianity and, more broadly, the Abrahamic religions.

Yet we can also see an analogous situation in Europe in the case of the Latin word *paganus*, which originally meant a "person of the countryside", and was derived from the word *pagus*, meaning a "countryside district" or "village" (as opposed to the term urbanus, i.e., "urban", "city-dwelling"). The word *paganus* can be found in the writings of Livy in its original meaning, devoid of the negative color with which it would be painted later. The very meaning of *paganus* as referring to a "pagan" was codified as a legal term under Emperor Theodosius I in the 380s when the latter introduced a prohibition on pagan cults.

In the Middle Ages, including in Rus', Christianity spread mainly through the elites, whereas ordinary peasants remained reluctant to break with their "superstitions", customs, and omens, hence the emergence of the term *religia pagana* or "village faith", which also bears derogatory semantics.[19] Besides *paganismus* and *pagani*, Christian authors used another characteristic term, *ethnici*, from the Greek *ethnikoi* (ἐθνικοὶ), which is closest of all to the original sense of *iazychniki*, i.e., "members of specific folks." The Greek term was a literal translation of the Ancient Hebrew term *goyim*, which referred to all non-Jewish peoples alleged to "worship idols instead of the one true God."

Despite the differing etymologies of these words, the terms *paganus* and *iazyk* both harbor one fundamental similarity: this originally derogatory name for folk beliefs and traditions,

---

19 The closest analogue to *iazychestvo* widespread among pagans is the German term *völkisch* ("folkish"), which might also be translated (in Russian) as *narodnichestvo*, i.e., as "populism" or "folkism."

preserved as a designation for the "other" of the baptized elites, was eventually "cleansed" and introduced both into scholarly language and as a self-designation of pagans themselves, i.e., those who follow these ancient traditions.

In contemporary Russian-Slavic paganism, there is the popular saying "as many paganisms (*iazychestv*) as peoples/languages (*iazykov*)", which means that every *ethnos* has its own tradition. The correspondence between ιᾱзык and ἔθνος suggests an indissoluble connection between a faith and the people which maintains and preserves such. This contrasts with the "world religions", which are not bound to *ethnoi*. In the Bible, for instance, we encounter the famous passage: "There is neither Jew nor Gentile, neither slave nor free, nor is there male and female, for you are all one in Christ Jesus" (Galatians 3:28). In other words, the Christian religion introduced an absolute equality of all believers in Christ: they are no longer Jews nor Gentiles (e.g., Hellenes), but Christians. This established a break with ethno-religious unity in favor of a strictly religious identity. We will return to this matter later on.

In contemporary scholarship, "paganism" is frequently understood as referring to either all "polytheistic religions", all the cults, rites, and beliefs of archaic peoples before their conversion to one of the Abrahamic religions, or sometimes is even used as a synonym for the even more contested term "neo-paganism." The latter refers to modern reconstructions and new doctrines of a syncretic character. One such definition proposed by the scholar of religion Alexey Gaydukov holds that neo-paganism is "the totality of all religious, para-religious, socio-political, and historico-cultural associations and movements which aim in their activities to turn to pre-Christian beliefs, cultures, ritual and magical practices, and to engage in their rebirth and reconstruction."[20] Neo-paganism is a strictly modern phenomenon which, in its positive range, strives to

---

20 Alexey Gaydukov, *Ideologiia i praktika slavianskogo neoiazychestva* [*The Ideology and Practice of Slavic Neopaganism*] (Saint Petersburg: Herzen State Pedagogical University of Russia, 2000).

overcome the effects of Modernity and monotheism but which, in its negative range, degenerates into profane, totalitarian sects which mix the external forms and *membra disjecta* of different traditions and promote such as "ancient knowledge" with the aim of personal gain. Unfortunately, we are compelled to state that most neo-pagan movements gravitate towards this negative trajectory, and therefore the use of this term is unsatisfactory.[21] For these reasons, we have decided to use the term "paganism" (*iazychestvo*), and we shall consistently understand such as referring not only to the tradition of a given people, their faith, but also as a synonym for "manifestationism."

In addition to the general terms "paganism" and "neo-paganism", we can also encounter more narrow names for individual traditions, such as *Rodnoverie*, "Odinism", *Forn Siðr*, or Ásatrú. In these cases, we are dealing with the contemporary self-designations of traditions, communities, and sub-cultures which are, as a rule, ethnocentric. *Rodnoverie*, which is Russian for "Native Faith", is the modern self-designation of those pagans who trace their traditions back to the beliefs of the ancient Slavs[22], while Ásatrú, which means "true to the Aesir", is the paganism proper to the Scandinavians which can also be encountered among other Germanic pagans. The term "Odinism" is not so unambiguous, as today it is often taken to refer to the doctrine of the racial-religious supremacy of white pagans over all other peoples, which is in the final analysis false, and will be examined later. In the Scandinavian tradition, we find two authentic variations of self-designation: *Forn Siðr*, which means "Ancient Way"[23], and *Forneskja*, which in Old Icelandic means "Ancient [pagan] Times." The term "Hinduism" is a neologism from the early 19th century, whereas the territory of modern Hindustan is home to an incredible number of currents, schools, sects, and

---

21 In Dobroslav's works, we find the even more organic and beautiful term *mladoiazychniki*, "young pagans."

22 In its present form, this term was coined by Volkhv Veleslav (Ilya Cherkasov) in the 1990s. See chapter IV, section "Personalities."

23 Forn *Siðr* is also the name of the religious organization registered in Denmark in 2003.

offshoots of different traditions which can only be united under one name with significant, conditional reservations. In India, we can find Shaivites, Ganapatites, Vaishnavites, Vedantists, and even currents situated somewhere between Islam and Indian traditions. In other words, India is an astounding example of the diversity of cults devoted to different divinities and castes, and we will clarify each of the concrete schools or currents which we will reference on particular matters.

The essence of self-designation lies in the necessity of identification and self-identification in the modern world. The pagan of the pre-Christian era would not say, for instance, "I am a *Rodnover*", but rather "I am a grandchild of Dazhdbog", "a glorious son of Odin", or, in the case of a Shaivite, "a faithful follower of Shiva", and in the case of a Ganapatite, an "adept of the cult of Ganapati/Ganesh." The main question underlying self-identification is that of the authenticity of terminology, and the capacity of the latter to cover what it should define; a name ought to encompass a phenomenon and convey its meaning to others. Thus, the term Asatru today is used more often to describe one current among neo-pagan reconstructions of the Northern tradition, and the members of various organizations using this word in their names, for instance, the American Asatru Folk Assembly. The original term *Forneskja*, meanwhile, refers to Icelandic paganism, as does, in our opinion, the simple yet weighty term "Odinism" (with the caveat of cleansing the latter of its negative connotations mentioned above).[24] Here it would be appropriate to recall that the last pagan Emperor of Rome, Julian the Faithful (361-363, more famously known in Christian historiography as Julian the "Apostate"), called his religion *Hellēnismós*, or "Hellenism." The latter is an example of the organic manifestation of the name of a tradition in relation to the name of a people. Another curious case is the self-designation of modern Anglo-Saxon pagans as professing "Theodism", which is derived from *þeod*, meaning folk, tribe,

---

24 In the West, there is the widespread theory that the term "Odinism" was first used by Orestes Brownson in his 1848 work, *A Revival of Odinism, or the Old Scandinavian Heathenism*.

society, or village. Here once again we find the well-established motif of the village, the countryside, society, and tribe as a religio-ethnic self-identification familiar to us from the cases of *iazyk, ethnos (ethnici), Volk,* and *paganus* (as well as the related term *odal,* i.e., the indigenous land-allotment among the Scandinavians, as referenced in the name "Odalism"). In the case of Slavic-Russian Native Faith, we have seen how a new name can sink into the level of an archetype, finding resonance with deep, ancient grounds. Indeed, this term is encountered more often than other, more contested names, such as *prav'[o]slavie, staroverie* ("Old Faith"), and others.[25]

SYMBOLS

An altogether similar situation, and one which the sharpest critiques of paganism more often than not take aim at, is posed by the question of the authenticity and legitimacy of different traditions' symbols. The Abrahamic traditions have historically been stably associated with such symbols as the Star of David in the case of Judaism, the cross for Christianity, and the moon for Islam. Paganism, meanwhile, is most frequently attributed two main symbols: the Swastika and the Celtic Cross (or Solar Cross), both of which express the solar element and sun-worship. Both symbols reflect the fundamental principles of practically all Indo-European traditions. The Swastika, representing the course of the Sun in the sky, is widespread as a symbol among numerous, even non-Indo-European cultures. The Celtic Cross is the symbol of the Year and the four most important solar festivals: the Summer and Winter Solstices and the Spring and Autumnal Equinoxes.

---

25 *Prav'[o]slavie* is a "play on words" intended to appropriate the Slavic term for Orthodox Christianity, *pravoslavie,* whose etymology indicates "the right (*prav*) [way of] glorification (*slavie*)." The apostrophe after the "v" in the pagan term shifts the reference from "prav" in the sense of "right" to the Slavic Native Faith concept of the higher level of reality, *Prav'* (which is discussed further below), thus rendering "The Glorification of *Prav'*". This term is used with respect to paganism primarily by pseudo-pagans, especially Ynglists, as part of their pseudo-linguistic notions (see chapter IV, "Simulacra and Sects"). Rodnovery and scholars of paganism do not consider the etymology of *pravoslavie* to mean "glorification of *Prav*."

In recent times, Slavic Native Faith, Odinism, and Hinduism have raised as their banners other particular symbols, primarily the Kolovrat, Mjölnir, and Om.

In the Hindu and Vedic traditions, Om (or "Aum") is the sacred mantra and primordial sound, and it is ubiquitously employed across many schools, *darśana*, and teachings. While raising such to be the symbol of Hinduism would be a rather organic gesture, it should not be forgotten that among Hinduism's diverse range of sects we can find other, more narrowly-charged symbols belonging to individual schools, such as Shiva's trident, *Triśūla*, brandished by Shaivites and Aghori. As follows, we should qualify that we use the word "Hinduism" as an umbrella term to encompass the endless diversity of traditions of ancient and modern India. In ancient times, Mjölnir, or Thor's hammer, was believed to be a talisman effective against impure forces, worn in the form of a pendant or a drawing schematically depicting the hammer with which the Guardian God Thor battled the giants. A less well-known but by no means less organic symbol is the rune Odal ᛟ, which means "native land", "family lot", "estate", or "inheritance."

Among these symbols, the Kolovrat is the most problematic, insofar as archaeological and ethnographic findings confirming that the Slavs used such a symbol are lacking. From the standpoint of ethnography, the earliest and most charged depiction of the Kolovrat is to be found in the book of the Polish artist Stanisław Jakubowski, *Old-Slavic Motifs in Architecture* from 1923. Jakubowski claimed that this symbol had been carved onto wooden monuments and presented a graphic reconstruction. The symbol closest of all to the Kolovrat, the solar circle framed by numerous rotating rays, is fairly widespread on wooden buildings, but might be only a distant prototype of the Kolovrat. The Kolovrat or "Kolovorot" as the symbol of Native Faith, frequently portrayed in yellow against a red background, was introduced in the 1980s by Alexey Dobrovolsky, better known as Dobroslav. In this case, we are dealing with the tapping of an archetype, i.e., a case in which an author's work is vindicated to the extent that the deep layers of ancient tradition are therein manifested in new, organic form. Hence why the Kolovrat symbol has so quickly and firmly taken root to become the inalienable symbol of Slavic-Russian paganism today.

Bringing this examination to a conclusion, we can assess the results of the process of the creation of symbols and terms for self-identification by these traditions which interest us, with the indication of caveats and remarks regarding their authentic and organic qualities, as overall positive.

Traditionalism

The philosophical current known as Traditionalism, which arose in early 20th century Europe and which is associated with such names as René Guénon, Julius Evola, and Mircea

Eliade, is of enormous significance and potential to us. Traditionalism arose as an ideology advocating a complete and uncompromising return to the values of the traditional era and treating the modern world as an absolute negation of higher, traditional principles, i.e., the reign of the profane and the quantitative as the main criteria. Traditionalism is not a religion and is neither new nor old. Traditionalism is not Tradition. Rather, Traditionalism is rooted in the notion of perennialism, also known as Sophia Perennis (*Sanātana dharma* in Hinduism) or the "Eternal Wisdom", i.e., the common foundation of all religions, the metaphysical Source. The philosophy of Traditionalism revolves around the following key postulates:

- The notion of one Primordial Tradition, that is to say the Tree or common root of all individual ethnic traditions and religions. In other words, in their esoteric (inner, hidden) dimensions, all traditions and religions of the world, in the forms of their own folk cultures, uniquely reflect the one, unified Principle.

- The obtainment of esoteric knowledge is accomplished through chains of initiation. The very word "tradition" is derived from the Latin *tradere*, meaning "to hand down", and is thus concerned with the direct transmission of initiation from teacher to student, from elder to youth, and so on.

- The primordial, the original, is attested to by all cosmogonic myths which tell of the creation of the world and the primordial, eternal experiences and elements. Such are eternal not because they "last forever", but because they exist outside of (above) time with no beginning and, as follows, no end. Asserting the historical existence of one primordial religion among the ancients which over time disintegrated into the many different traditions which we know today would be an altogether controversial argument, although such was indeed advanced not only by René Guénon himself but also by another seeker who sought to reconstruct the language of this ancient tradition, Herman Wirth. The very word "primordial", meaning "original", "first", or "primal", evokes the ideal state of the Golden Age, characterized by the absolute sacrality of the whole cosmos and by the existence of the sacredly substantiated, natural hierarchy of duties and human being.

On this basis, we argue that the primordial root of all traditions is the indivisible unity (synthema) of the Sacred, the Dutiful, and Hierarchy, which are manifest in different forms in the social and human being of different peoples. We argue that the reality of the metaphysical Tradition, of the transcendental level of being, is superior to the modern, profane, degenerate world. Man, his individual and social life, and society and the state itself ought to be arranged in clear agreement with the sacred order. Julius Evola wrote: "For us, 'Tradition' is the victorious and creative presence in the world of that [mystical force] which is 'not of this world,' i.e., that of the Spirit, understood as a power that is mightier than any merely human or material one."[26]

In the era of Modernity, the chain of transmission has been broken. Tradition has been condemned to death by secular, positivist science and has been profaned by rogues who reduce Tradition to the entertainment of secular society, or to mere "manners" or "habits." In other words, today we live in an anti-traditional time, one which the founding fathers of the philosophy of Traditionalism quite justly called the Iron Age or the Kali-Yuga. If previous European societies lived according to their folk traditions, which is to say that they lived in tradition along the chain of transmission of the Eternal Wisdom of the Golden Age, then in the era of Modernity this chain has been broken. And it is in this era

---

26 Julius Evola, "On the Secret of Degeneration", *Deutsches Volkstum* 11 (1938). The Russian translation includes the substantive "mystical force."

that Traditionalism manifests itself. Traditionalism declares war against the de-sacralized, godless, and disorderly world of Modernity and calls for a radical reconsideration of values, for orienting oneself towards higher ideals and higher order for the organization of society, the state, and the whole world.[27]

Today, one can encounter a widespread, confused conflation of the terms "Tradition" (with an uppercase "T") and "tradition" (with a lowercase "t"), in which the latter is taken to refer to one or another religion or tradition of a given people, a single branch on the one tree of Tradition. Hence takes root an essentially differing, fundamentally wrong understanding of the term "Traditionalism" as a new euphemism for ethnocentrism or, more broadly, nationalism and racism, in which "Traditionalism" means merely loyalty to a people's religion, culture, and language. In this context, the widespread characterizations of "traditionality" and "traditionalness" ascribed to a given phenomenon or author in the context of one or another tradition, are oxymorons. "Traditional" rather, refers to a specific tradition, while "Traditionalist" refers to the philosophy of Traditionalism.

How do these three elements - Tradition, tradition, and Traditionalism - correspond to one another? Tradition with an uppercase "T" is the Primordial Principle, the Source, and the common foundation of all traditions with a lowercase "t", which constitute the natural faiths of given peoples and the manifestations of the Sacred in forms unique to a given *ethnos*, the very *iazyk* in which the Divine reveals itself to the people (the *ethnos*) and through which, in the form of myths, rituals, cults, dutiful behavior, customs, cultural forms and, finally, language (*iazyk*) itself, peoples engage in contact with and return to the one Sacred and participate in the transmission (*tradere*) of this Knowledge.

---

27 In the opinion of the French historian and Traditionalist René Alleau, by virtue of its fundamental radicality Traditionalism is comparable to Marxism and can even be deemed "the most revolutionary trend in philosophy in the modern era." See: René Alleau, *De Marx á Guénon: d'une critique «radicale» a une critique «principielle» des sociétés modernes* (Les dossiers H, 1984).

Traditionalism arises when the chain of transmission, of tradition, is interrupted, when descriptions of the world in the terms of the sacred language of myth and ritual are missing. Traditionalism, as noted above, is not a tradition itself, but is rather an orientation towards traditional principles and the philosophical expression of their prioritization in the conditions of the modern world. In its radical maxim, Traditionalism ought to transcend its context and lead to tradition. But, from the point of view of the Traditionalist classics, today there is no such tradition to be led to, and therefore Traditionalism (and not any one tradition) is the path for those seeking Sacrality in our days.

The founding father of Traditionalism was undoubtedly the French mystic and philosopher René Guénon, who in his many works laid out the foundational postulates of this philosophy and described in detail the situation in which mankind finds itself today. A second, no less significant figure of Traditionalism was the Italian thinker, Baron Julius Evola. While Guénon represented a contemplative, passive form, Evola was a warrior who actively fought against the modern world. This can be noted in the very titles of these thinkers' works: if Guénon's major work was *The Crisis of the Modern World*, then Evola responded with the work *Revolt Against the Modern World*. Julius Evola and his philosophy are of the greatest interest to our path, especially as one of his first books was entitled *Pagan Imperialism* (also translated as *Heathen Imperialism*), and as his later works covered altogether diverse dimensions of Traditionalism and the conceptualization of a strategy of action towards the surrounding world. Unlike Guénon, who emigrated to Egypt, adopted Islam, and became a Sufi, Evola showed the way of a different path, that of fidelity to higher ideals and contempt for the degenerate world, and in his philosophy Evola unveiled a number of postulates which we shall find necessary to apply to pagan traditions, to both strengthen and enrich them.

Firstly, however, we must venture to address some of the rather controversial aspects of Traditionalism, especially with regards to our intention to apply the Traditionalist method to paganism. In his later period, Baron Evola expressed a certain regret over the use of the term "paganism" in the title of one of his earliest works and even prohibited the re-publication of *Pagan Imperialism*. In 1942, Evola published an article under the title "Against the Neo-Pagans", in which he criticized the attempts of certain radicals to resuscitate pagan cults on the basis of Christian descriptions and a kind of primitive naturalism which closes the individual off from immanent Nature. Somewhat rushing ahead, we shall say, firstly, that Evola's criticism was largely justified with regards to "neo-pagans", a point which will be examined in detail in the fourth chapter, "The Contemporary Pagan Experience", and, secondly, many of the theses of *Pagan Imperialism* nonetheless found fuller development in the Baron's subsequent works.

Another perhaps more important aspect of Traditionalism which deserves qualification is the fact that the works of its founder, René Guénon, bear traces of being already (or perhaps still?) affected by Abrahamic dualism. In other words, despite his deep interest in the Indian Vedanta and Advaita (the doctrine of non-duality), Guénon nevertheless reduced the categories of the Sacred, the Profane, Initiation, and Counter-Initiation to the level of absolute significations and described their relations in Christian tones as a battle between Absolute Evil and Absolute Good, a perspective which ultimately led to his conspiracy-theorizing over "counter-initiatic forces." The argument that "Guénonism" was punctuated by Abrahamic dualism is indirectly confirmed by the fact that Guénon himself emigrated to Egypt and adopted Islam, thereafter becoming a Sufi master who would at a later point recommend that Traditionalists seeking a living chain of initiation into Tradition should turn to the Alawiyya Sufi order headed by another Traditionalist, Frithjof Schuon. To be fair, the main reason behind Guénon's interest in Islam was his conviction that Sufism still retains a chain of genuine, living initiations, and along the path to this conclusion the French philosopher denied that the Catholic Church and Masonic and occultist circles harbored any initiatic qualities. Frithjof Schuon's words offer confirmation of this perspective:

> The question has been asked why Guénon "chose the Islamic path" and not another; the "material" reply is that he really had no choice, given that he did not admit the initiatic nature of the Christian sacraments and that Hindu initiation was closed to him because of the caste system; given also that at that period Buddhism appeared to him to be a heterodoxy. The key to the problem is that Guénon was seeking an initiation and nothing else; Islam offered this to him, with all the essential and secondary elements that must normally accompany it.[28]

This original exposition of Traditionalism would give way to the reconsideration and overcoming of a number of errors and mistakes peculiar to "orthodox Guénonism" by other representatives of this philosophy. While recognizing the authority and role of René Guénon as the founder of Traditionalism, for our purposes we must strive to overcome the Abrahamic impacts on Traditionalism, an endeavor which has already been partially accomplished by our predecessors, and on which we will dwell in greater detail over the course of our account. Overall, however, as one of the most radical philosophies of the 20th century, and as one which calls upon us to turn to the great heritage of humanity and the transcendent levels of being as the only true reality, Traditionalism is an indisputable, necessary source of aid on the path to grasping the metaphysical principles of paganism.

Additional perspectives close to our subject and related to Traditionalism have been developed by the French philosopher Alain de Benoist, first and foremost in his work *On Being a Pagan*, as well as by the French historian Dominique Venner.[29] The latter proposed to move away from the classical Traditionalist commitment to analyzing all traditions - including both pagan

---

28 Frithjof Schuon, "A Note on René Guénon", *Studies in Comparative Religion* 17:1-2 (1985).

29 Dominique Venner committed suicide by gunshot on 21 May 2013 in the Notre Dame Cathedral as an act of protest against mounting campaigns which Venner saw as destroying traditional values in France. See Chapter II, section "Revolt, Anomie, and Death in the Consumer Society".

and Abrahamic - as equals, in favor of a more narrow, organic pursuance of European pagan tradition. Venner proposed to call this approach "traditionism" and emphasized: "For Europeans, as for other peoples, the authentic tradition can only be their own. That is the tradition that opposes nihilism through the return to the sources specific to the European ancestral soul."[30] Departing from Venner's position, we will examine a more complex system of interrelations between manifestationism, creationism, and the modern atheistic world (Modernity) instead of the classical Traditionalist dichotomy between Tradition and Modernity. While giving absolute priority to the ancient Eternal Wisdom, the philosophy and views of paganism's situation today which we will expound in this work can be called "Pagan Traditionalism."

One final point on which we would like to dwell is the division of Traditionalism into two currents: so-called "hard Traditionalism" and "soft Traditionalism."[31] "Hard Traditionalism", undoubtedly represented by Guénon and Evola, maintains a radical opposition between the traditional world and the modern world, and their respective values. René Guénon and Baron Evola presented two variations of this radical path against the world of Modernity: the path of withdrawal from this world and seclusion within a living tradition and religious society (as Guénon did), or the path of radically opposing the modern world in its very center by challenging such widespread institutions as, for example, the Catholic Church, whose initiatic capacity was also doubted by Evola. Hard Traditionalism means choosing the side of the divine, of the traditional worldview, rejecting social status, public opinion, economic demands and consumption, and other such criteria for life. Instead, the main values and criteria are those of the tradition into which one is initiated. Compromises with the modern world are either altogether impermissible, or are extremely minimal both qualitatively and quantitatively, and such

---

30 Dominque Venner, "Living in Accordance with Our Tradition", *Counter-Currents* (8/10/2013).

31 See: Mark Sedgwick, *Against the Modern World: Traditionalism and the Secret Intellectual History of the Twentieth Century* (Oxford: Oxford University Press, 2004).

are not afforded any significance or given the opportunity to bind or condition one's being.

Soft Traditionalism is more "loyal" to the modern world and permits certain compromises. This is the path of "soft power" in changing the surrounding world. One most vivid representative of soft Traditionalism was the great Romanian historian of religions and author Mircea Eliade. In his many works, this philosopher and scholar of religions formulated and implemented a new approach to the study and description of the world's religions, one which departed from the previously predominant approach that treated all non-monotheistic religions either as "heresies" or "primitive" cults of "barbaric" peoples. Instead, Eliade examined religions as representing the self-sufficient, self-valuable, organic and important traditions of specific people or peoples. Eliade rejected some of Guénonism's postulates, including the idea of the Primordial Tradition, and himself remained a faithful Christian, but many of his works were dedicated to the unbiased study of the pagan traditions of the world, the History of Religions, and the metaphysics of sacred mysteries. Eliade's soft, academic approach and his insistence that traditional values and the sacred world were not only a higher value for ancient peoples, but are also relevant and valuable today, such as in the 21st century, have yielded much fruit in the scholarly world and have earned fame for this scholar as the founder of the modern history of religions. Eliade's perspectives were a catalyst for fundamentally revising prevailing attitudes and approaches towards archaic cults and beliefs among both the scholarly world and the public.

Soft Traditionalism, as we have said, is a kind of "soft power" which does not urge revolution or radical revolt against the modern world, but rather wages struggle within the "system", striving to consistently, steadily develop its own space with its own orientations within academic disciplines, culture, literature, and public life. In Russia, two vivid representatives of this soft approach are the Traditionalist philosopher Alexander Dugin, who is recognized to be one of the founders of the Russian school of Traditionalism, and Veleslav Cherkasov, who is one of the most important pagan thinkers in contemporary Russia.

These two paths, in our opinion, can only complement one another. Soft Traditionalism establishes alternative space, vectors, and centers of attraction within the system and develops questions and knowledge in the fields of philosophy, the study of culture, and the study of religion which, without a doubt, can be of use to the path of hard Traditionalism. Hard Traditionalism, for its part, can translate such "soft" theories into religio-communal, social, and political practice (ranging from systemic to radical) and can serve as the source of fiery inspiration for "soft" scholars and thinkers.

While there may at times arise distortions which lead to confrontation between the "hard" and "soft" paths (such as in disputes over "insufficient" or "excessive" radicalism), we believe such to be counter-productive within the greater cause. Within the scope of the present study, we are drawn more towards the positions and experience of the hard Traditionalists, although we by all means pay tribute and homage to the soft Traditionalists for their immense works and contributions to the common cause.

***

II
TIME AND INITIATION

Being a pagan today means leaping into the Abyss, the Gap. This is a purely voluntarist act, void of any guarantees of anything from anyone in any way. You jump and stand the test, either to soar up from the very "bottom" or to crash into titanic debris. All or nothing.

The question of Time and our location in history decides everything. Our position is our tower from which we look upon history as it unfolds in our direction, towards the place which we occupy in it. Time defines our position relative to Eternity. Eternity is to be understood not as a constant repetition or presence or place in time - as in "there was yesterday, there is today, and there will be tomorrow" - but as above time, without beginning and end. Thus, history is part of time and is its "filling."

The two most widespread and broadly recognized conceptions of Time are those of "cyclical time" and "linear time." Cyclical time corresponds to manifestationsm (paganism), while linear time is peculiar to creationism (Abrahamism). We can examine the relations between Eternity and Time in terms of these two ontologically different doctrines.

Cyclical Time

We can express this concept of time with the ancient and concise symbol of a circle with a point in the center - circumpunct. The point in the center is Eternity, the metaphysical Center, the One and the Sacred; this is the point of absolute quality, the absence of Time and Space. The surrounding circle, conversely, is the realm of quantity, history, Time, and Space. Time moves around the circle, and cycle replaces cycle on all levels: from the cycle of day and night to the cycle of the year, rising up to the cycle of Life and Death and the metaphysical cycles of the becoming and destruction of the Cosmos. Each individual cycle bears a likeness to the greater cycle and includes another cycle, such as how the cycle of day and night forms the cycle of the year, and the cycle of human life and death forms the cycle of the life and death of the *rod*. This likeness is a manifestation of the one, paradigmatic principle, the manifestation of Eternity in Time. The circle is the realm of the becoming and dissolution of phenomena and things in time, and in this world of time the revelation of the Gods (theophany) is of a momentary nature, a manifestation "here and now." The Gods manifest themselves in the world in the form in which they wish. They can create or destroy things instantly, passing over time.

If through the center of the circle, i.e., the metaphysical Center, we run two direct lines (vertical and horizontal), then we have before us a most ancient symbol: the Celtic Cross. The resultant cross-inscribed circle is the universal key to the pagan understanding of history, the relation between Time and Eternity, and the rise, decline, becoming, and aging of phenomena and things.

The lowest point of the intersection of the circle and the vertical line is the source, the beginning-point of movement along the circle on the right. This is the point of birth, the beginning of the new cycle, the year, the pivot of the sun towards rising out of winter (Yule, Koliada, the Winter Solstice). The highest point of the vertical line is the supreme height of development, force, maturity, and the pivot of the sun towards falling after the peak of summer (Midsummer, Kupala, the Summer Solstice). Between these two points is the horizontal line of the Spring and Autumnal Equinoxes, which divide the circle into two equal halves - such as the transitions between the dominance of day over night and vice versa. Following the Autumnal Equinox, the dark time of days is expanded, the year wanes, and the sun descends towards the lowest point, which in the cycle of life corresponds to death. The circle of life and the Celtic Cross can, therefore, be correlated in the following manner: Birth (sunrise, Winter Solstice) -> Youth (Spring Equinox) -> Maturity (Summer Solstice) -> Old Age (sunset, Autumnal Equinox) -> Death (Winter Solstice). Let us take note of the particularly mysterious significance of the Winter Solstice, as the point of transition from end to a new beginning, the time of the metaphysical Night and winter. In essence, all solar festivals are reflections of this Yule/Kupala, its metaphysical saturation at different stages of the cycle, and it is precisely the Winter Solstice that is the genuine New Year. Sacred festivals and holidays punctuate the duration of cyclical time, thereby constituting Sacred Time, which is the projection of Eternity itself. Related ritual acts and rites produce the myths and the deeds of the Gods. The sacred festival, therefore, unfolds Time, while its own time is Eternity - in the circle and in the present.

Mircea Eliade pointed to the fact that in many of the languages of the indigenous Native Americans, the Yakuts, and the Iukki, the word for "World" or "Cosmos" is identical to the meaning of "Year." In Yakutian, "The world has passed" means that a year has passed, and the Dakota call the Year the "circle around the World."[32] We can find such symbolism of the year and the circle in the structure of dwellings, settlements, shrines, altars, and temples. The circle which surrounds a magus, and their orientation within the circle during the performance of a ritual, as well as the fencing and orientation of structures within a temple or shrine are all embodiments of this ancient metaphysical archetype. The Brahmins of India also knew that Prajapati is the Year.

Returning to the symbols of paganism, we can note that the Swastika, especially in versions with rounded ends, is therefore

---

32   See: Mircea Eliade, *Myth and Reality* (Long Grove: Waveland, 1998).

not only a solar symbol, but also more broadly a symbol of the year, one which directly refers us back to the Celtic Cross, the normative symbol of all calendric and cosmological conceptions. In other words, such a symbol is the ideal representation or "map" of the year and time, and one which can have nuances and variations across different traditions.

Beyond its rich temporal symbolism, the Celtic Cross is also a map of Space. North and South are situated at the top and bottom of the vertical line respectively, while East and West are situated on the right and left of the horizontal. It should be understood that the prehistoric people of the North saw the year differently than people living below the 22nd parallel of Northern latitude. Above this latitude, a day lasted half a year, and the polar night lasted another. This phenomenon can be observed in the Arctic North to this day. South of this range, however, one can observe the division of the year and day into four parts, i.e., into spring, summer, autumn, and winter, and into morning, day, evening, and night, all of which also fit into the crossed circle.

The intersection of the horizontal and vertical axes in the Celtic Cross coincides with the point of the Sacred Center, the unmoved axis which moves, turns the cosmos. Like rays of light, the Sacred emanates from the good of the bountiful center towards the periphery of the circle and returns. One mythical expression of this circle is the Scandinavian Jörmungandr coiled around the World Tree of Yggdrasil (which represents the circle and the axis) and eating its own tail. The latter is related to the famous symbol of Ouroboros, frequently depicted as biting on to its tail either at the lower or at the upper point, corresponding to the Winter and Summer Solstices. Also of undoubted relevance are the myths of Jörmungandr's confrontation with the solar Guardian God, Thor, who acts as the divine, sacred center against the chthonic serpent-circle. All the beautiful tension of life unfolds in the space between them, in their struggle, and dies with them.[33] In Hinduism, the circle is represented by the

---

33 Heraclitus's famous fragment declares: "War is father of all and king of all; some he has shown as gods, others men; some he has made slaves, others free."

wheel of *Saṃsāra*, or the snake Anantashesha, curled into a ring and symbolizing the Cosmos swimming in the ageless waters of Chaos. Representations of the World Tree, Pillar, or Mountain as the Axis, or the Egg as the circle or sphere, reflect this structure.

Comparing the temporal, spatial, and qualitative, i.e., matter and the spirit, the periphery and center, we arrive at the picture of a saturated, beating cosmos encompassing the microcosm of man, the community, society, the state, the Gods, and the macrocosm. The Celtic Cross is the Cosmos: it is Time, Space, and Eternity of the One. The time from birth to death, the space from South to North and East to West constitutes the qualitative map of the world, thereby leading us to the application of the Celtic Cross as the key to the chest of history.

According to Hesiod, just as the Gods have gone through several generations, so are there five generations of mortals: the generations of the Golden Age, the Silver Age, the Bronze Age, and the generation of the Heroes and the Iron Age. In his poem *Works and Days*, Hesiod presented the first conceptualization of history in development and affirmed such a regressive character: the world degenerates from the Golden Age to the Iron Age. Hesiod describes the Golden Age as the time of the rule of Kronos, the first generation of Gods and people who lived in celebration and prosperity as long as Kronos remained in power. Subsequently, the Gods created the generation of people of the Silver Age, but Zeus destroyed them for their sins (such as ceasing to sacrifice to the Gods) and created the fierce warriors of the Bronze Age. The transition from the Bronze to the Iron Age coincides with the Generation of Heroes who gained fame in the battles for Thebes and Troy, the survivors of which Zeus sent to the Blessed Islands at the end of the earth where Kronos rules. The Heroes were revealed to be capable of transcending Time and its declining quality, of returning to the state of the Golden Age of Kronos' rule. Next begins the Iron Age, about whose people Hesiod succinctly exclaimed: "I wish that I were not among this last, fifth race of men."[34]

---

34 Hesiod, *Theogony and Works and Days* (Ann Arbor: University of Michigan Press, 2007), 174 / p. 62.

Describing the theology of the Etruscans, Mircea Eliade presented their vision of history in the *Libri Fatales*, according to which the Etruscans held human life to consist of 12 periods of seven years, after which people lose their souls and their connection with the Gods: "Men 'go out of their minds' and the gods no longer send them any sign."[35] Eliade took particular note of the archaic and paradigmatic character of this concept, which can also be found among many other peoples.

Hesiod's version of history as fall and decline from best to worst, over time and over generations of people (the anthropology of the degradation of people), is in many ways similar to the Indian doctrine of the four Yugas. According to Hinduism, the largest cycle of the world's manifestation and existence is the *kalpa*, which means "order" (Cosmos) and is symbolized by Prajapati, the Lord who Begets All, and the circle. One kalpa consists of 14 sub-cycles, or *manvantaras*, derived from Manu, or "man." The Hindus believe that each manvantara is ruled by one Manu, the King of Kings and the highest of all people, and Manu was thus also held to mean the time of existence of one earthly humanity in his and its material manifestation. One manvantara, in turn, consists of four Yugas: the Satya-Yuga, the Treta-Yuga, the Dvapara-Yuga, and the Kali-Yuga. Thus, the manvantara can be envisioned as a great year with four seasons: the Satya-Yuga lasts 4/10 of the whole manvantara, the Treta-Yuga 3/10, the Dvapara-Yuga 2/10, and the Kali-Yuga 1/10. These Yugas also have a corresponding set of colors: white, red, yellow, and black. The Satya-Yuga corresponds to Hesiod's Golden Age, to spring on the circle of the year, and the color white and pure light. The Golden Age lasts the longest of all cycles, as it is qualitatively void of Time, instead being filled with sacred beings and the Gods' cohabitation with people in celebration. As follows, the Silver Age corresponds to the Treta-Yuga (the red), the Bronze to the Dvapara-Yuga (yellow), and the Iron Age to the

---

35 Mircea Eliade, *A History of Religious Ideas, Vol. II: From Gautama Buddha to the Triumph of Christianity* (Chicago: University of Chicago Press, 1982), p. 130.

Kali-Yuga, the black age. The Kali-Yuga is named in honor of the Goddess Kali, the wife of Shiva, whose name can be translated as both "black" and "time." Kali is the Goddess who destroys the degraded world. Despite the fact that the Kali-Yuga or Iron Age lasts only 1/10 of the manvantara, it is so fully immersed in Time that it may seem to have no end. If we correlate the continuity of the Yugas with the five elements of the Hindu tradition, then we can see the manifestation of the principle of degradation and decline in history. The Satya-Yuga, as the longest, covers the two cycles of the lightest elements: Ether and Air. The shorter Treta-Yuga covers the cycle of Fire and half of the cycle of Water. Here we can note the qualitative dimension of the compaction of time. The even shorter and more compact Dvapara-Yuga covers half of the cycle of Water and half of the cycle of Earth. The Kali-Yuga, of the shortest duration, covers half of the cycle of Earth. As becomes evident, the qualities of Time and Space coincide in the Golden and Iron Ages, with the etheric-areal timelessness of the beginning of the cycle and the inertial, earthly time of the end.

Visions of the Golden Age as an era of prosperity and direct closeness to the Gods can be found in practically all traditions alongside an eschatological idea of the End of the World, the final fall of the world, the battle of the Gods with monsters, and the Gods' destruction of the world. The idea of eschatology draws the line of the process of the degradation of man and the world, expressed in the metaphysical principle of the change of Yugas. Two passages from the Prophecy of Völva in the *Elder (Poetic) Edda* illustrate such eschatological views in Odinism and the vision of a new beginning following Ragnarök (*Völuspá* 44-46, 57, 59, 62):[36]

---

36   *The Elder Edda: A Book of Viking Lore* (transl. by Andrew Orchard, New York: Penguin, 2011), p. 11-14. The Old Icelandic *Ragnarøkkr* is composed of *ragna*, the genitive of *regin*, meaning "lords" or "the great ones", and *røk*, meaning "doom" or "fate." *Ragnarøkkr* is thus not only the battle of the Aesir and the Giants (*Jötnar*) but also the doom/fate of the Gods and the world (rendered in this translation as "powers' fate"). The common translation of *Ragnarøkkr* as "Twilight of the Gods" is, albeit of poetic appeal, incorrect.

Geyr Garmr mjök
fyr Gnípahelli;
festr man slitna,
en freki renna.
Fjöld veit hon frœða,
fram sé ek lengra,
um ragnarök
römm sigtíva.
Brœðr munu berjask
ok at bönum verðask,
munu systrungar
sifjum spilla;
hart er í heimi,
hórdómr mikill,
skeggjöld, skálmöld,
skildir 'ru klofnir,
vindöld, vargöld,
áðr veröld steypisk;
man engi maðr
öðrum þyrma.
Leika Míms synir,
en mjötuðr kyndisk,
at inu gamla
Gjallarhorni;
hátt blæss Heimdallr,
horn er á lopti;
mælir Óðinn
við Míms höfuð...
Sól tér sortna,
sígr fold í mar,
hverfa af himni
heiðar stjörnur;
geisar eimi
ok aldrnari
leikr hár hiti
við himin sjálfan...
Sér hon upp koma
öðru sinni
jörð ór œgi
iðjagrœna;
falla forsar,
flýgr örn yfir,

Garm howls loud before the
Looming-cave,
the bond will break, and the
ravenous one run;
much lore she knows, I see
further ahead
of the powers' fate, implacable,
of the victory-gods.
Brothers will struggle and
slaughter each other,
and sisters' sons spoil kinship's
bonds.
It's hard on earth: great
whoredom;
axe-age, blade-age, shields are
split;
wind-age, wolf-age, before the
world crumbles
no one shall spare another
Mim's sons sport, the wood of
destiny is
    kindled
At the ancient Sounding-horn.
Heimdall blows loud, the horn
is aloft,
Odin speaks with Mim's head...
The sun turns black, land sinks
into sea;
the bright stars scatter from the
sky.
Flame flickers up against the
world-tree;
fire flies high against heaven
itself...
She sees rising up a second time
the earth from the ocean, ever-
green;
the cataracts tumble, an eagle
flies above,

sá er á fjalli	hunting fish along the fell…
fiska veiðir…	All unsown the fields will grow,
Munu ósánir	all harm will be healed, Baldr
akrar vaxa,	will come;
böls man alls batna,	Höd and Baldr will inhabit
Baldr man koma;	Hropt's victory-
búa þeir Höðr ok Baldr	halls,
Hropts sigtoptir	sanctuaries of the slain-gods, do
vel valtívar.	you know yet, or what?
Vituð ér enn eða hvat?	

This notion of qualitative decline is also reflected in Russian folktales and legends of various kingdoms, such as the Golden, the Silver, and the Copper. The theme of regress is also to be noted in the *Byliny* (East Slavic oral epic poetry), in which the time of the heroes is followed by decline and degeneration. One interesting reflection of this idea of regress is encapsulated in the words of Vladimir Dal': "Earlier there were *voloty*, [now] we are *tuzhiki*, and next there will be *pyzhiki*." Here *voloty* is a reference to the ancestral giants of Slavic myth, and *pyzhiki* means "dwarves." In the past, people, i.e., "we", were mighty and handsome, whereas now "we" are "straining" (*tuzhimsia*), that is to say we are already exerting effort, only to be succeeded in the future by altogether weak dwarves.

Insofar as change comes cyclically, it is impossible to reverse the wheel of Time. The new Satya-Yuga will necessarily arrive in due time, after the Kali-Yuga, just as a new kalpa will dawn following the Mahapralaya, the "Great Dissolution." Hesiod's generation of Heroes, to which were later added the initiated wisemen and chosen ones of the Gods, does not turn Time backwards, but breaks out of Time to Eternity. Returning to the symbol of the Celtic Cross, we can symbolically correlate each of the four different sectors of the circle with one of the Yugas, taking into account their differing durations, and we are, once again, revealed the saturated life of the Divine Cosmos. The Golden Age corresponds to the metaphysical center, whereas the Iron Age corresponds to the circle of Time. All the tensions of history unfold between the Beginning of the cycle and its End, like the course between birth and death.

Thus, we are more focused on examining history and time in tripartite form: from the Golden Age to the era of decline, i.e., the Silver and Bronze Ages, to the Iron Age (the Koshchny Age or Ragnarök), in the very heart of which, according to Hesiod, the Hindu darśanas, Traditionalists, and modern pagans, we live today. Let us note in particular that, according to Hinduism, humanity presently finds itself not only in the heart of the Kali-Yuga, but this Kali-Yuga is of the seventh manvantara out of 14, i.e., the final of the seven manvantaras of removed distance (the exhalation of Brahma), that is to say the maximal possible distance from the center out in the periphery. Only in the next cycle will the seven manvantaras of return (the inhalation of Brahma) begin.[37]

It may seem that we are walking on earth with the sky above us, but in fact this "sky" is water, and we are on the very bottom, on the lower levels of earth, bogged down in the muddy sediment of the river of Time. We are in the very center of the Heart of Night.

Linear Time

Before we turn to examining the above-introduced ages in greater detail, let us briefly examine the particularities of linear time, which emerged in creationism and found continuation in the scientific, atheistic view of the world.

In paganism, despite the tension in the qualitative and quantitative difference between the center and the periphery, there is no ontological rupture between their nature: Time is a manifestation of Eternity, the Archetype, and unfolds around it always at an equal distance. In paganism, historical content is subordinated to metaphysical cycles. The Gods and

---

37 See: Alexander Dugin, *Absoliutnaia Rodina* [*Absolute Homeland*] (Moscow: Arktogeia, 1999).

people participate in the joint fate of the Cosmos. The model of linear time proper to creationism, however, establishes a fundamental ontological difference between God and the world. In creationism, as expressed in the Abrahamic religions of Judaism, Christianity, and Islam, Time is not a manifestation of Divine Eternity, but is a creation of God and, like the world, is not identical to him in nature. In Abrahamism, Time is uniform, consisting of only one segment with a beginning and an end, and is situated below God, who wields full being and Eternity.

Creationism manifests a clear division between the transcendental (from the Latin *transcendens* or "surpassing", "overcoming") and the immanent (from the Latin *immanens*, meaning "remaining, being within"). As a higher being who is different in nature from the world, God occupies the transcendent level of being. The world, meanwhile, occupies the immanent level which is closed upon itself in a negative sense. For people, God is transcendent and unknowable, and due to his differing ontological nature man cannot become God and is not God in any sense. By virtue of his transcendence, height, and might, God is capable of descending to the world to bestow his voice, deeds, and will. In creationism, man can only aspire to strive towards God, and communicating with God is only possible if He wills such from above, from the transcendent to the immanent. In his upward ascent, man is always limited by the ontological gap between natures, and his ascent is frequently prevented by God himself, as demonstrated in the myths of the exile of Adam and Eve from Eden and of the Tower of Babel.[38] Assertions of immanence and the oneness of God and the world fell under the third canon of anathema proclaimed by the First Vatican Council.

Paganism differs from creationism on this count insofar as the Divine is immanent in the world in a positive sense: everything is an embodiment of the light *eidoi* (ideas), all things are imbued with spirits and Divinities, and all things are a symbol of or reference to the higher dimension, towards essence. In manifestationism, transcendence emphasizes the

---

38   See: Alain de Benoist, *On Being a Pagan* (North Augusta: Arcana Europa, 2018).

aspect of hierarchy, not ontological difference. The philosopher, the ascetic, the *volkhv*, the monk, and the wisemen, through the practice of rituals and sacrifices, through philosophizing and contemplation, realize transcendence, i.e., the ascent of their mind to the Divine One. Thus, transcendence in paganism does not bear a divergent character and can even be illusory (as in the Indian *maya*), at times most convincingly illusory, but there is always the possibility of removing the veil of illusion to the transcendent-immanent view of the world, wherein is present the necessity of emphasizing hierarchical and powerful difference, the process of spiritual becoming and realization of one's own Divine Nature.

If the relation between the transcendent and the immanent can be traced in the illustration of cyclical time as a circle with a point in the center, then linear time can be depicted as a segment with a point above it.

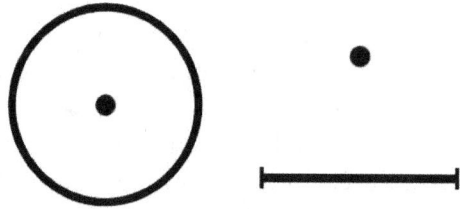

In manifestationism and cyclical time, Time is a manifestation of Eternity and is participative in the latter. Just as things contain grains of the Divine, so does Time encase Eternity in an immanent-transcendent manner. In creationism, transcendent Eternity is not co-participative in Time, as man is thrown out onto the segment of time and, just as man himself cannot be deified, so can he not tear himself out from Time to Eternity.

In Christianity, the Golden Age corresponds to Adam and Eve's time in the paradisal garden of Eden. Time emerged after the exile of these first humans from Paradise. In other words, Time is the punishment of mankind for primordial sin; Time is an indelible attribute of the world to which people have been exiled, to which Adam and Eve were sent in "clothes made of skin" (representing the hardening and worsening of the environment). Thus begins Christian history, which goes from this beginning to the final resolution of this burden - the Apocalypse, the Final Judgement, and the salvation of the faithful.

The only Abrahamic tradition which does not conceive of history as a process of degradation from better to worse but, on the contrary, from worse to better, is Judaism. According to the Jewish view, all historical burdens, hardships, and wanderings will pay off with the future coming of the Moshiach, the Messiah, who will liberate the people of Israel and humanity from adversity and establish peace on Earth.

The established Christian neglect of the "created" world, of Nature as something of "clay" devoid of being, affects Time as well. The linear, disposable, and finite nature of Time in creationism underscores the non-co-participation of Eternity, unlike in the cyclical time of manifestation. Time is the punishment that one must get rid of and escape, not heroically overcome. The end of Abrahamic time is resolved by the hoped-for salvation of the faithful. A positive trajectory of history can be traced in Christianity, but such intersects with the decline of the Church on Earth, the reign of the Antichrist, the Apocalypse, and Judgement, which bear a rather vividly regressive character.

In the era of the Enlightenment and amidst the decline of Christianity, this view of linear time was taken over and developed by the philosophers and scholars of Modernity, who reversed the notion of changing ages in the opposite direction, declaring humanity to be progressing from the "dark ages" of its "childhood" towards the "golden age" with new discoveries and social and scientific achievements. Final eschatology was replaced with new myths of a beautiful, prosperous future, a world of order and technological development, and myths of utopias, one of the most famous of which was the "golden age" of Communism. One of the main myths of Modernity, thus, was that of progress, of development towards a better state.

However, following the denial of final eschatology, even the myth of an immanent "golden age" was discarded as well. In the end, any kind of transcendent level or dimension of being was denied, metaphysics was cast from being the main lifeline of human development into the periphery. The final segment was turned into an open ray. History loses any ultimate goal - whether pessimistic or optimistic - and acquires the form of an arrow of progress and quantitative development launched not into Eternity, but into infinity. The suffocating and heavy immanence of the world unto itself assumes reign, without any transcendent dimension (much less any immanent-transcendent). Man no longer sees things as symbols referring to the higher dimension, and loses the kernel of Divinity. This view of Time and history as endless quantitative development - the fragmentation of quality - corresponds to the Iron Age of the cosmos - the black age of *Kali*-Time. An even denser view of history and such unbearable ductility of Time found its conclusion in the notion of the "End of History."[39] Pierre Chaunu remarked on this matter: "The rejection of history is a temptation for civilizations that have emerged from the Judeo-Christian tradition."[40] This "End of History" is not an eschatological finale in the likes of Pralaya, Ragnarök, or the Apocalypse, but entails the maximal uniformity of life, its solidification in place. This is the endless "today prolonged into tomorrow." This view does not contradict the quantitative multiplication of material things but rather crowns such as the absolute senselessness and hardening of the Kali-Yuga.

The Golden Age

Offering a detailed description and characterization of the Golden Age is practically impossible or, in the very least, extremely

---

39 For example, Francis Fukuyama's 1992 *The End of History and the Last Man* associated the "End of History" with the establishment of the global hegemony of the United States of America and liberal democracy.

40 Pierre Chaunu, *Histoire et foi: deux mille ans de plaidoyer pour la foi* (Paris: France-Empire, 1980), quoted in Alain de Benoist, *On Being a Pagan*.

difficult and complex. Each tradition has its own cosmogonic myths, its own myths spelling out the ideal order of the Golden Age, and its own myths of decline and a new beginning. The Golden Age of Tradition, it might therefore be said, was the time when the Golden Ages of different traditions were reality, when man dwelled in, corresponded to, and suited such.

Visions of the Golden Age, the Satya-Yuga, bear an idealistic and utopian character, but this does not mean that their subject never existed, nor that such myths are fantastical fictions derived to regiment the socio-political and everyday life of society. This de-sacralized, functionalist, sociological approach, which severs the possibility of more sublime interpretations of myths, is foreign to us.

Above we presented a sample of characteristics which can be attributed to the Golden Age: the saturation of the life of the whole Cosmos with the qualitative rays of the Divine, the immanence of God *vis-à-vis* the world, and the due behavior and Sacred-inspired hierarchy of society. Many of the characteristics of manifestation were primordial in the Satya-Yuga, thereafter undergoing the metamorphoses and trajectories by which they unfold in their temporal and historical path towards the Kali-Yuga.

Sacrality (from the Latin *sacrum*) is an important characteristic of the Golden Age, as the latter is its concentrated expression. The Latin adjective *sacer*, from which is derived the modern English word "sacrifice", means "consecrated", "initiated", "hieratic", "magical", or "great." The English word "bless" is derived from the Proto-Germanic *blopisona*, meaning "to sprinkle with / to consecrate with blood", blood being from *blopa*. The link between the Sacred, blood, and sacrifice is well known and enshrined in many traditions. According to Hesiod, the cessation of sacrifices to the Gods drew their ire, causing conflict and the diminishing of the Sacred presence of the Divinities.

In essence, in the conditions of primordial prosperity, man could not say that he lived in a Sacred world, insofar as he knew no other, profane dimensions of life, and thus Sacrality was seen as the natural given and fullness of life, the goodness of the Gods. We encountered a similar situation above in our analysis of the self-designations of modern pagan traditions, where we noted the absence of the very need for such reflections in antiquity. The world was holistic.

Holism, from the Ancient Greek ὅλος, meaning "whole" or "integral", is the view of the totality of phenomena and things in which the whole precedes the individual. The primordial precedes finite, differing variations, just as the Eternal precedes the Temporal. If a thing can be examined as a mechanism, as a "totality whose elements constitute a functioning automation, then holism stands on the opposite pole and affirms that the organic wholeness of a thing precedes its division into its component elements. The whole is something greater than the mere sum of component details of a thing. A thing is a hint, an indication towards something greater than itself. It is from this greater whole that a phenomenon derives its being and its components which indirectly point towards this higher identity.

The Greek word ὅλος is related to the English "whole" and the German *Heil* ("good", "health") as well as *heilig* ("sacred"). Holism is good, healthy, and sacred wholeness. The holistic method of knowledge captures all phenomena, all things, not simply as a totality of parts and functions, but captures that which a thing indicates or gestures towards. In holism, a thing is never equal to itself but is always in addition to something, an instruction towards something. In this lies the manifestation of the Sacred symbolism of any pattern, thread, thing, word, kenning, verse, or phenomenon - such is always not merely what it is, but along the chain of indications towards something else the Mind can ascend to the Gods themselves, to divine symbols, and to the Ineffable One, that which is the Primordial Whole whose parts are the Gods, spirits, demons, people, phenomena, and things.

Holism is Sacrality. The holistic principle reveals the threads and subtle rays of the Divine light that reach everything and along which are arranged the hierarchies of spirits, *Bereginia*, guards, angels, and Gods, as well as, going down, Leshy, devils, demons, and titans. If someone says that they are a blacksmith, then they are not speaking only of the fact that, within the community of humans, they engage in the working of metals. This is indeed the last thing that such a statement says. First and foremost, the holistic threads of blacksmithing lead us back to the divine demiurge, the Creator God that is known as *Svarog* among the Slavs and Hephaestus among the Greeks. Or it can refer to chthonic elements, such as the dwarves and gnomes which the Northern tradition holds to be skilled blacksmiths. Thus, the statement "I am a blacksmith" speaks to the fact that a person is involved either with higher creative forces, martial forces, or subterranean and dangerous forces. Across folklore, the forge is widely associated with the abode of demons and devils, and the blacksmith himself and his smith were commonly located on the outskirts of the village. A similar unfolding of holistic lines can be pursued with anything. A fisherman is not simply a fisherman, but could just as easily be the God Thor, and instead of fish he could be catching Jörmungandr himself and shaking the whole world. A fisherman might be a most dangerous Deity and a villager. A horse encountered in a field might very well turn into Pegasus, and a poor visiting stranger might turn out to be Odin himself.

In holism, there is no strict division into the customary and seemingly "natural" pair of "subject-object." Following holism, the subject, the beholding and knowing, is always linked to the object (the observed, the known), and vice versa: the object is always connected with the subject and has a subjective dimension. Hence the ubiquitous motifs of transformations, metamorphoses, and enlivening of seemingly "inanimate" objects, or the turning of living beings into "stones."

The question of historically dating the Golden Age is a complex and difficult one in the pagan sphere. Traditions habitually speak of days and years of the Gods as equal to whole eras in the world of humans, thereby emphasizing the remoteness of the blessed era from the modern world. The most common place in time where the Golden Age is placed by both scholars of religions (such as Mircea Eliade and Herman Wirth) and contemporary pagan figures (Veleslav, Dobroslav, and others) is the Paleolithic and Neolithic (the Stone Age) of hunting lifestyles and corresponding cults. The exact dating of the Paleolithic and Neolithic ages is a difficult question, although it might be suggested that we are dealing with times preceding us by several dozen thousand years.

The end of the Golden Age is frequently deemed to be the Neolithic revolution, i.e., the transition to settled life and agriculture with the increasing role of culture (the Latin *cultura,* from the verb *colo, colere* meaning "cultivation" and later "upbringing" or "education") and the emergence of an ever greater contrast between culture, man, community, and Nature. The duration of the Neolithic revolution is estimated to be close to 7,000 years, ending approximately in the third century BCE. According to this dating and its correlation to known times of the formation of spiritual heritages, material artifacts, and the texts of great civilizations, we can suggest that the latter were created either during the time of transition or after the Golden Age. The emergence of writing and books on the territory of modern Hindustan was regarded by the Ancient Hindus and Tibetans to be signs of decline, which is to say that they had already reflected on the diminution of Sacrality in the world and saw the need to and sought to record, preserve, and transmit sacred knowledge, teachings, and philosophy (*darśana*).

Yet the consensus on the Golden Age is the fact that it will necessarily come again in a new, future cycle. This certainty has nothing in common with the perversions of the "Golden Age" of progressives and the Enlightenment but is entirely organic to the doctrines of the cyclicality of time and the changing of epochs.

The Silver and Bronze Ages

The Silver Age can be considered the space of time between the Golden Age and the emergence and strengthening of the creationist religions. The Silver Age of Tradition was the time when traditions entered the period of decline, of the erosion of rituals and mysteries, and of the reduction of tradition to customs and laws. The process of decline does not occur evenly for all of humanity. Indeed, it should be said that the European part of mankind was the first to enter these denser and darker times. In different regions and different cultures, obvious signs of decline can be recorded in different centuries and even millennia, although on the whole, the tempo of regression has overall increased.

Historically, in Europe, Plato already recorded a definite decline in the religiosity of his fellow citizens and attempted to breathe new life into rituals and to reform society in accordance with his ideal state and philosophy. The Greeks' increasingly pessimistic view on life and the afterlife in the underworldly realm reflected an increasing distance between the transcendent and the immanent, as the light of the Gods slowly yet surely began to fade. Mircea Eliade cited on this note the statements of Theognis, Pindar, and Sophocles that man is better off not being born - and if he has been born, then to die as soon as possible. Homer saw the afterlife as painful and miserable[41], and a similar view of Helheim, one of the lower worlds of the dead, was common among the Scandinavians. Herodotus told of a case in which a devout Greek woman implored Apollo to reward her children with the highest gift, and Apollo fulfilled her wish: her children died instantly, without torment.

The Greeks also more acutely felt the predestination of destiny and fate, as in the threads of the three Moirai (the Norns in Odinism), and such views of fate as suffering were widespread and even more dramatically developed in

---
41 See: Eliade, *History of Religious Ideas*, Volume I.

Hinduism's doctrine of karma and suffering. In late Rome, as well, the degeneration of tradition reached the level of reducing the Gods to legal figures who could be called as witnesses to courts, thus rendering the Gods elements of Republican law. The results of fortune-telling before battle during sacrifice were recorded in a special book to, in the case of defeat, be used as a legal "reference" in Senate hearings. Also dubious were the cults of syncretic deities, such as Serapis, introduced by Alexander the Great to unite the Egyptian and Greek traditions in conquered lands; the same could be said of the cults of some Roman emperors who imagined themselves as Gods in fits of hedonism, such as Nero, Heliogabalus and the latter's cult of his Syrian solar God Elagabalus, which undermined Roman religion. In Rus, evidence of decline is attested in Vladimir's reform of the Kievan pantheon, which saw Perun raised to the rank of dominant Deity. Despite the logicalness and certain justifiability of such a reform, its precariousness and the subsequent baptism of Rus annulled any potential of this initiative.

The ensuing situation, in which tradition lost might and light, where the Gods were reduced to edifying prayers or court witnesses, and in which men began to create "gods" for worldly, earthly needs, eased the ground for the imposition of Christianity which, arriving from the Eastern part of the Roman ecumene, at first encountered no proper opposition. Creationism marked the Bronze Age of Tradition.

The doctrine of creationism asserts a principal ontological difference between God and the world. This assertion is clearly illustrated by the metaphor of the master and the clay pot. Of course, the pot bears the imprint of the master, but between them is an insurmountable difference of levels. God is transcendent, while the world is immanent. Correlating creationism with the Bronze Age of Tradition is substantiated by the fact that after creationism nothing fundamentally new has appeared in the history of religions which might manifest itself on the field of battle between paganism, Abrahamism, and Modernity. Modernity, in turn, set itself in opposition to everything traditional. Since creationism, no fundamentally new traditional ontologies, metaphysics, or new traditions have been born. Contemporary forms of new religiosity ("New Religious Movements") are either perversions of old religions, sects and speculations, or are smaller fragments of traditions which have been mixed in a syncretic manner and seasoned with the cheap tricks of spiritualism and scraps of medical, psychological, and psychiatric facts and myths ("soft religion" and "soft ideology"). Posing the question as follows, no matter what religiosity or lack thereof, the answer is always unequivocally in favor of the higher principles of Divine order. Therefore, creationism is located at the lower border of the Bronze Age, maximally close to the Iron Age.

But creationism did not "plug" the epoch of Tradition, like the bottom of a ship, from Modernity. The situation of creationism is intermediate: on the one hand, it contains Sacred dimensions and a number of pagan relics; on the other hand, it is the key, the source from which the river of the Modern World originates. Creationism manifests the very prerequisites that will find full expression and development in the Kali-Yuga.

According to Lactantius and St. Augustine, the very word "religion" - from the Latin verb *religare*, meaning "to connect, to reunite" - speaks to the nature of relations between God and man. It is quite characteristic that *religia* appeared in Ancient Rome before Christianity took root, as such testifies to the above-indicated growing distance between the Sacred and the worldly. It is precisely with creationism that the term "religion" is most strongly associated, as such reinforces the gap in levels and need for "reunion." In its worldly expression, this separation, this craving for *religare* manifests itself in the rigid division of the aspects of life into "sacred" and "profane", which suits the opposition between God and the world: e.g., the sacred time of liturgies, the sacred space of the church, and the Heaven / Heavens as the abode(s) of God are contrasted to the creatures and creations of Earth.

The historical boundaries of the Bronze Age are more clearly delineated. This time stretches from the development of Judaism, the emergence in the latter context of Christ in the first century CE, through the accomplishment of the formal baptism of Europe at the turn of the 10th-11th centuries, up to the Renaissance. The Bronze Age is also associated with the issues of the dating of Christian, secular, and pagan calendars. The Christian chronology of before and after Christ and the secular measurement of "before and after common era" are identical, both taking their starting point to be the Birth of Christ. The problem is that determining the precise year of Christ's birth is impossible according to chronicles and myths, and therefore in the secular record of the "common era" the timeframe of Christ's birth can vary up to 12 years. For example, in Russia before the introduction of the new calendar by Peter I on 1 January in 1700, the chronology of the Constantinople era was used which counted the year 7208 "since the creation of the world" according to Christian theology. In Islam, the starting point of the calendar is Hijrah, or Muhammad's move from Mecca to Medina in 622 CE; thus, the year 2014 corresponds to the year 1435 in the Islamic chronology.

Among pagan traditions in existence today, there is no single reference point for chronology and calendar. Each tradition and various currents, sects, and communities within it have their own calculations of different dates, whether for the founding of settlements and cities, glorious battles, victories or defeats, the establishment of dynasties, the coronation of monarchs, or mythical events. Russian Native Faith commonly dates its calendar from the fall of Arkona (Jaromarsburg on the island of Rügen, modern Germany) in 1168 CE to the Danish King Waldemar I. The choice of this date is based on the postulation that Arkona was the last pagan center of the Slavs (Rus had already been baptized), and thus its fall meant the onset of the dark age. According to this dating, the modern year 2014 is 846 since the fall of Arkona or "A.A."

Some Norwegian Odinists similarly date their calendars to the beginning of the dark age of Christian domination, i.e., to the baptism of Norway. One can also find dating to the unification of Norway by its first King, Harald Fairhair, in 872. Within only a century, Harald's descendent, Olaf II, succeeded in seizing the high ground over the pagans resisting Christianization. According to this starting point, the year 2014 is 1142 since the unification of Norway.

There also exists a manner of dating based on the use of the modern, secular calendar, but with the qualification "era vulgaris", which means "commonly recognized." In this format, the year 2014 is 2014 e.v., and here "vulgaris" can also bear the connotation of "vulgar", referring to the broader, lower masses of the era and dating. Overall, the growing relevance of dating calendars and introducing consistent calendric systems of years directly refers us to the idea of the descending shift of epochs, immersing us ever deeper into Time.

The Profane

A special place in the process of decline is occupied by the phenomenon of the profane, the secular. "Profane" is from the Greek prefix *pro-*, meaning "before" and the Latin *fanum*, meaning shrine or temple. Thus, the "profane" is that which is before the church or temple, outside of its walls. More broadly, the profane is everything that is not part of the sacred, all those who are not initiated into the mysteries or cult, and all things and phenomena which are not marked by Divine grace and signs. Given that in creationism God descends from above into the world, such phenomena are perceived as miracles and Sacred experiences, and everything surrounding them is attributed to a sacred meaning and inscribed into the cult. The world of creationism, unlike the pagan world, is not absolutely sacred but is periodically sacralized by Divine phenomena, by visits of the Master to his creation.

In the "sacred vs. profane" map of the world, a special place is occupied by the temple or shrine. The delineation of ritual space into a special space was known long before Christianity, but it is precisely in creationism that the space of the temple reaches its culmination. Before, forests, groves, rocks, and rivers could all be sacred places: a forest could be considered the home of a God, a nearby river might be the river of the world (a motif in Slavic mythology), just as a boulder could be a sleeping giant or a hero turned into a rock. In his *Germania*, Tacitus wrote: "from the grandeur and majesty of beings celestial, they [Germanics] judge it altogether unsuitable to hold the Gods enclosed within walls, or to represent them under any human likeness. They consecrate whole woods and groves, and by the names of the Gods they call these recesses; divinities these, which only in contemplation and mental reverence they behold." [42] Taken together, this yields an uninterrupted ensemble of manifestations of the sacred space of the whole cosmos. The sacrality of space was ceaseless but could be especially marked by heights or depths, mountains or swamps, dark coniferous forests or light meadows of flowers.

In the non-pagan view of the world, the Sacred also occupies a central space but is localized in certain places distinguished by myths, such as Golgotha Hill, where Christ was crucified, or the place of the Sermon on the Mount for Christians, Mecca and Medina for Muslims, the Temple of Solomon for Jews, and so on. In addition to mythical places, there is also the temple whose architecture is distinguished by its representing the *imago mundi*, i.e., the "image of the world" of Abrahamic myths, which repeats the same principle as in paganism of the likeness of the little to the great and the structure of the sacred space (in paganism everything is sacred) in accordance with cosmogonic myths. Christianity is also known for architectural motifs in which a temple repeats sacred places, such as Golgotha, the birthplace of Christ, his tomb, and so on. Such are departures from the *imago mundi* towards individual sacred places and related myths.

---

42 Tacitus, *Germania* (transl. by Thomas Gordon), 1910.

In the structure of the sacred temple, the *fanum* occupies a qualitative place, insofar as it represents the intersection of the *tempus* and *templum*, or Time and Space.[43] The liturgical ceremony (eucharist) in the church is also a special place and time in which *religare* is established with God, as the church is considered to be the house of God in the world. We can see similar symbolism in the *imago mundi* of the Celtic Cross during the solar holidays, but here such is localized in space and time, is discontinued, and is intermittent. As follows, everything that does not intersect Time and Space in such a special structure is *profanum*, i.e., "outside of the church", outside of revelation, outside of God. The community and man meet with God inside the church at liturgy, but not as God.

As noted above, in paganism sacrality is continuous in both space and time. In paganism, the "profane" does not express a rupture - as in "here is Holy and God (in the Church) and beyond there is the nothing and void of the (non-Divine) world" - but rather reflects the hierarchical structure of the *sacred* which is on all levels (ontologically) participative in the One in nature as a manifestation of such. Different estates/castes engaged in different levels of the hierarchical pyramid are characterized by different mythical plots, preferred Deities and manifestations corresponding to the nature of each caste. The profane is treated as "less better", such as in the view from a higher caste rung of a lower one. The profane can be any representative of a different sect or cult that is not initiated into the specific doctrine of whatever might be "our" cult or mystery; thus, he is "less good" but can become "more good." For example, in the case of the forest dedicated to Baldr, the forest is the *fanum*, the temple of Baldr, it is his land and is tied to his cult. As follows, standing at the edge of the forest or in the field in front of the forest, one finds himself *pro-fanum*, outside of or before the sacred forest of Baldr. Yet if the forest is the space, the house of this God, then the field in turn belongs to other

---

43 See: Mircea Eliade, *The Sacred and the Profane: The Nature of Religion* (New York: Harvest, 1959).

spirits, nymphs, elves, Bereginia, and rivers passing through the field, or the field might belong to a God of fertility and be sown. This is realized by the continuity of the Sacred. Man is always *profanum* with regards to something, to some given space of spirits or Gods, but he is simultaneously always within a *fanum*, temple, or space of some other God or spirits. Thus, we have a picture of saturated, natural space (sacred mountains, rivers, forests, and fields) and saturated sacred, social space (mysteries, cults, caste rituals, the myths of guilds or craft artels, etc.). In paganism, the world is one thorough, continuous hierophany, a manifestation of the Sacred. In essence, this is sacred geography: the landscape of mountains and valleys, chasms and peaks, forests and seas, and different currents and nuances within at once a given tradition and Tradition as a whole.

In conclusion, let us take note of the convergence between the notions of "profane" and "impure" as opposed to the sacred as expressed with such epithets as "high", "pure", "white", or "light." In its more rigid forms, such an opposition reflects the inequality of space and landscape which ultimately leads to divisions into pure and impure ritual activities and paths of spiritual practice. Particular attentiveness has been devoted to the notions of "pure" and "impure" with regards to the Sacred by the Tibetans and Hindus, who have resolved this problem of opposites by revealing the illusoriness of its nature (as in the notion of *maya*).

The Heroes

In the foregoing, we mentioned Hesiod's description of the generation of Heroes, those who gained fame in the battles of Thebes and Troy, the survivors of which Zeus settled on the Blessed Islands at the edge of the Earth. Julius Evola offered a similar description of the era of Heroes, calling such the "cycle of Aryans" of such figures as Theseus, Perseus, and Hercules. The Heroes, in whose ranks would later be included initiated wisemen (see the Indian example of the Jivanmukta), went against the descent of cycles and represented a special type of people exhibiting a colossal exertion of will in the spirit of the "Nordic" ideal of Hyperborea. Such heroes committed to a burst of will towards the Divine amidst the most unfavorable existential and ontological conditions on the eve of the Iron Age.

The Greek poet Pindar said that Hyperborea cannot be found or reached by land or sea, and this remark emphasizes the transcendental remoteness of Hyperborea in an adverse epoch. The paradigm of the hero is always closely associated with war or battle and extreme volitional and physical tension, a characteristic which strictly corresponds to the classical heroes of antiquity, such as those named above. The figure of the wiseman, monk, or ascetic who is enlightened amidst the dark age is also associated with such incredible volitional and intellectual intensity. The hero, the sage, and the ascetic consciously destroy their "comfort zones" and leap "neither by land nor sea" but by will, rushing towards wars, feats, and overcoming the resistance of the titanic masses of the surrounding reality. The wiseman, the thinker, and the ascetic take shot at the modern world and its comfort zones in the Mind, refusing to recognize the values and meanings of the degenerate reality and thereby committing to a fundamental gesture of not merely challenging the monster, but rejecting and declaring war against everything that has brought this monster into being. Heroes and wisemen, albeit engaged in different modes of war, always choose the highest ideals and dimensions of life.

The fate of the hero is always dramatic, as an example of which we can recall the sad lot of Heracles and the Heraclids. In the Russian *Byliny* epics as well, the fate of the warrior-heroes (the bogatyrs) is also tragic: in the end, they are turned into stones or, in one version, become the figures of the Kiev fortress. A similar myth of petrification can be found in the Scythian legend of the hero Bartakl, who shoots an arrow (or in another version throws his bow to the ground) and is turned into a mountain.[44] The heroes represent the final rays of the setting sun,

---

44 The modern Altaic peoples, i.e., the Kyrgyz who arrived in the 17th century, ascribe this myth to their own culture.

whose flash offers a final orientation for the ensuing darkness. Against the thickening inertia of the Earth, degradation, and the dissipation of the Sacred in society, they light the path to the Sun, to the metaphysical North. Here we can recall the words of Ernst Jünger: "In history there will always repeat eras demanding paradigmatic acts and sacrifices from the individual - such is necessary for restoring the measure according to which people are born and raised."[45] Finally, to emphasize the nature of the environment surrounding the generation of Heroes, let us cite the words of Nietzsche and Alain de Benoist in their discussions of heroism and Christianity. Nietzsche, in his *The Antichrist*, wrote:

> Renan, that mountebank in psychologicus, has contributed the two most unseemly notions to this business of explaining the type of Jesus: the notion of the genius and that of the hero ("héros"). But if there is anything essentially unevangelical, it is surely the concept of the hero. What the Gospels make instinctive is precisely the reverse of all heroic struggle, of all taste for conflict: the very incapacity for resistance is here converted into something moral: ("resist not evil!"—the most profound sentence in the Gospels, perhaps the true key to them), to wit, the blessedness of peace, of gentleness, the inability to be an enemy.[46]

And in the words of Alain de Benoist:

> In antiquity, the exemplary figure of the hero constituted the intermediary between the two levels. The hero is a demigod - an idea that seemed completely natural to the Ancients, whereas in the Bible it is obligatorily blasphemous. Among the Greeks and Romans, when an individual was heroized, they found that proper and good. But in the Bible, when the 'serpent' suggests to Eve that she 'become as a god' (Genesis 3:5), it is an 'abomination.' More recently, Erich Fromm has shown how the figures of the hero and the Christian martyr are antithetical: "The martyr is the exact opposite of the pagan hero personified in the Greek and Germanic heroes...For the pagan hero, a man's worth lay in his prowess in attaining and holding onto power, and he gladly died on the battlefield in the moment of victory."[47]

---

45 See: Ernst Jünger, *The Adventurous Heart: Figures and Capriccios* (Candor: Telos, 2012). Quote translated from the author's Russian.

46 F.W. Nietzsche, *The Antichrist* (New York: Alfred A. Knopf, 1924).

47 De Benoist, *On Being a Pagan*.

The Iron Age

Dating the beginning of the Iron Age is an easier matter: such began in the Renaissance in the 15th century and gained strength over the course of the Enlightenment (starting in the 17th century). During this period, history was divided into three parts: ancient, medieval, and new, and thus arose "New Time" (Modernity), or the era lasting up to the 20th century, succeeded by "Newest Time" from 1918 to the present.

Despite the heightened interest in antiquity which has at times been interpreted as a renaissance of the pagan (primarily Greek) Gods, the Renaissance was first and foremost characterized by man's final turning away from the Divine - at that time Christian and Catholic - and turning towards man and his activities. Secularism, anthropocentrism, and humanism grew as the very notion of "spiritual" was substituted by "science" and "culture", thus ultimately driving the Sacred dimension out. Following the Renaissance and beginning with the scientific revolution in England in the 17th century, the Enlightenment and its French philosophers pushed forward the trend of de-sacralization and the "debunking" of myth, raising their banner to be the "free-thinking" and "rational" mind of French thinkers. The American Declaration of Independence and the French Declaration of the Rights of Man and the Citizen marked an important milestone of the turn towards man, his "liberation" and "equalization" (read: the destruction of hierarchy).

The Christian Church was successively denied the right to power, and God was debunked with physics, mathematics, and natural science. Positivist scientists, and following them secular society, logically incurred the wrath of the Church, which branded their self-proclaimed free-thinking in the scientific and social spheres as manifestations of "paganism", or "excessive devotion to Nature and infatuation with its structure." In turn, they accused the Church of obscurantism - from the Latin *obscurum*, meaning "dark" and in opposition to their "enlightened", "enlightening" rational minds. Thus began the (in)famous confrontation between religion and science, on the battlefield of which paganism itself was not yet able to clearly comprehend its own position and side. On the one hand, the Enlightenment overthrew the tyranny of creationism, thus manifesting a surge of interest in demonology, alchemy, and the poetry and prose dedicated to the ancient Gods; on the other hand, the secular scientific community, becoming the locomotive of social thought, did not hesitate to impose onto consciousness its new network of physical laws and interpretations of Nature and reality in which no room for the Divine was found. At secular gatherings and receptions, it became fashionable to exhibit the achievements of such science, such as the camera obscura, the burning lamp, mechanical components and machines, and to fervently expose and denounce the magic of magicians and illusionists on the basis of technology, which they evermore began to use towards their ends. On the other hand, spiritualistic seances and communicating with spirits and ghosts came into fashion along with the opening of salons and "gurus" for contacting the other world. Such a profane approach was vigorously criticized by René Guénon in his book dedicated to these phenomena, *The Spiritist Fallacy*.

It is important to clarify just which God these first natural philosophers and scientists were speaking of - as is well known, many of the first scientists were representatives of the priesthood or had religious upbringings (such as Newton). After all, the scientific milieu did not appear out of thin air and immediately oppose God. The gradual diminution of the Divine in the natural-philosophical description of the world, and later in positivist science, was expressed in the emergence of the following, most emblematic conceptualizations:

- Theism, which affirms belief in God or Gods and their direct or indirect participation in the life of the world. The essence of theism lies in its recognition that the world could not have arisen by coincidence or accident, but must have been created with intention and reasonability expressed by a Deity. Theism allows for both mystical and rational knowledge of God, and overall represents a simplified, unifying arch for all who recognize such a position, i.e., by and large the creationist religions.

- Atheism, which asserts the absence of any Divine element and beginning of the world. Atheism's radical form of actively denying the Divine structure of the world (whether mono- or pan-theistic) is anti-theism. The Russian Traditionalist, pagan, and alchemist Evgeny Golovin most expressively explained atheism thusly:

    Atheism is simply a form of negative theology assimilated uncritically or altogether unconsciously. The atheist naively believes in the omnipotence of reason as a phallic instrument capable of penetrating as far as one likes into the intimacy of 'mother nature.' Alternating between admiration for the 'amazing harmony prevailing in nature' and indignation at the 'elemental, blind forces of nature', atheism, like a spoiled son, wants to have everything without offering anything in return. In recent time, frightened by environmental disasters and the prospects of moving to hospitable lands on other planets in the near future, it calls for mercy and humanism. But the 'sun of reason' is only a wandering swamp light and its phallic instrument is only a toy in the predatory hands of the 'great mother.' The generative and just as active killing feminine principle cannot be approached. 'Lady Nature' demands distance and worship. This was well understood by our patriarchal ancestors who, being careful not to invent the car or the atomic bomb, adored roads with the image of the god of the Terminus and inscribed on the Herculean pillars *non plus ultra*.[48]

- Deism is a philosophical trend which recognizes the principle of God and his creation of the cosmos, but argues that God has since not manifested himself and does not participate in the life of the world. Deism rejected supernatural phenomena and descriptions. The widespread metaphor of deism is the watchmaker, who creates and sets the watch mechanism only to no longer touch it afterwards. At the same time, deism presupposes

---
48 See: Evgeny Golovin, "*Era ginekokratii*" [The Era of Gynecocracy], *Elementy* 6 (1996). The Latin *Non plus ultra* means "nothing further beyond" or "nothing beyond measure."

that reason, logic, and the observation of nature are the only means for knowing God and his will. Desiring to reconcile religion and science, deists openly "castrate" the sacred dimension of being for the sake of their natural-scientific interests, by virtue of which it would be more correct to define deism not as "reconciling" but as "subordinating" religion to the interests of science. The most colorful representatives of deism were the Scottish philosopher, agnostic, and positivist David Hume, Voltaire, Jean-Jacques Rousseau, Thomas Jefferson, Isaac Newton, and Mikhail Lomonosov.

– Agnosticism, closely related to deism, asserts the unknowability of the world by means of the subjective contemplation of metaphysical principles (ideas), arguing that God is unknowable and, as follows, so is the divine meaning (and purpose) of the world.

– Apatheism is the culmination of the emasculation of God in the secular modern worldview. Apatheism, in the words of the French Enlightenment philosopher Denis Diderot (1713-1784), proclaims an apathetic, indifferent attitude to the question of the existence of God, as explicated in Diderot's famous phrase: "It is very important not to mistake hemlock for parsley, but to believe or not believe in God is not important at all." The step from this dark, ironic maxim to the complete denial of God was only a natural act, and was indeed undertaken.

Thus, in the Iron Age, myth and the mythological perception of the world have been annulled as "overcome", as a previous "infantile" stage of underdeveloped humanity. The French positivist sociologist Auguste Comte (1798-1857) formulated the idea of progress as contrasting the theological phase of "childish naivety" to the contemporary scientific phase of mankind which has realized the materiality of the world.

To the masters of Renaissance and Enlightenment thought, any metaphysical superstructure over empirically knowable reality was adverse, and the methods of speculative rational cognition and conclusions are subordinated to strict logic and scientific verifiability. Physics, mathematics, and logic, founded on the strict mathematical identification of A=A, became the "holy trinity" of knowing the world. The apparatus of physics and mathematics and their logic were projected onto the humanitarian and social spheres, demanding strictly determined and mathematically predicted results, theories, and descriptions. Everything "superfluous" to the human and physical was "cut off" by Ockham's razor, which proclaimed: "Entities should not be multiplied beyond necessity."[49] Ockham's razor, in essence, determined the procedure for considering descriptions and hypotheses. If a hypothesis explains the nature of a phenomenon on the basis of the known laws of physics, body mechanics, etc., then it is satisfactory and there is no need to involve metaphysical entities in the likes of spirits or Gods. If a hypothesis does not explain a phenomenon, then the reference of new entities does not mean the introduction of the supernatural (supra-Natural or supra-physical instances), but the deepening and expansion of knowledge of the natural. Such "new entities" can be taken from the horizontal and material dimension, but not the higher and transcendent. This principle can be recognized as a denial of the Divine element and participation in the life of the world, or can be seen as the substitution of the "higher" with the quantitatively "more complex" for any "new entities."

In the Renaissance period, a window of opportunity opened up for paganism as the Christian church was subjected to fundamental doubt and removed from supreme authority over society, in which many poets, writers, and various mystics and philosophers found inspiration. Yet the latter were driven into the periphery of social thought, blackened as irrationalists by the new anti-theistic positivist scholars acting against the sacred, expressed at the time in the form of Christianity. Therefore, we can conclude that the war of the godless view of the world which we know today as the war of science against religion, the field of battle of which includes other, non-Christian religions as well,

---

49 William of Ockham (1285-1349) was an English Franciscan monk and pioneer of nominalist philosophy.

has been waged not only against Abrahamism but against the Sacred as such. This is a fundamental war of principle by the lower against the higher: if pagan pantheons had historically stood in the place of the Christian churches against the Enlightenment, they would have been questioned, ridiculed, and cast out as well. In this confrontation, we can define our pagan front as strictly opposed to Modernity and all its institutions and worldview. We will examine the tactics and infiltrations of Modernity in the pagan world-outlook and philosophy throughout the succeeding chapters, and in the second volume, we will consider in greater detail the relationship of paganism to the "third party" of this conflict, i.e., creationism in its three basic religions.

The Ontology of Estates

Having repeatedly evoked the topic of hierarchy, let us turn to examine the normative views of hierarchy of traditional societies, which held such to be the earthly expression of Divine laws. The main principle of the hierarchical system of Tradition was that of "casteness" or "estateness." One frequently encounters the name "caste system", although such is improper, as "castes", properly speaking, were a phenomenon specific to India and are not identical to estates, even if they coincide in a number of terms. The difference between the two can be briefly formulated in the following manner: within one estate there can be different castes, e.g., in the estate of Producers there might be the closed castes of potters, fisherman, and hunters. Castes might also exist among outcasts, such as castes of thieves, robbers, and murderers. The chief sign shared by both castes and estates is the relationship of one or another caste or estate towards its patron Divinity. The analogue to the estate in India is *varna*. René Guénon wrote of Indian caste doctrine:

> In actuality, caste corresponds to each person's own nature, to their deep calling…No one will doubt that in the same family there exist clear differences between children which are demonstrated very early. One, for example, might demonstrate facility with singing and the mastery of musical instruments. Another will prefer mechanical or manual tasks. Still another with an introspective nature will

readily devote to study. These differences are determined essentially and demonstrate each one's makeup, constituting what we would call their natural "vocation" or "calling."[50]

To disclose the hierarchical structure of traditional Indo-European societies, we can turn to the works of the French mythologist Georges Dumézil. In the 20th century, Dumézil revealed Indo-European societies (and in his opinion, only Indo-European societies) to have been characterized by a particular tripartite or, in his terminology, trifunctional structure.[51] According to this view, society is divided into three estates in accordance with functions: the first and highest estate is the priestly one; the second, close to the highest, is the martial or warrior; and the third, final estate is that pertaining to fecundity or, more specifically, agriculture. Dumézil correlated the functions fulfilled by these estates with the Gods who fulfilled (or were patrons of) the very same functions on the metaphysical level. The following is a generalized table of the correspondences between estates and Divinities:[52]

People	Priestly Estate	Martial Estate	Agricultural Estate
Greeks	Zeus	Ares	Demeter
Romans	Jupiter	Mars	Ceres / Quirinus
Scandinavians / Germanic peoples	Odin / Wotan	Thor / Tyr	Freyr
Slavs	Svarog	Perun	Veles
Iranians	Mitra	Bahrom	Anahita
Indians	Varuna	Indra	Vishnu
Celts	Teutates	Taranis	Esus

50 René Guénon, "Indiiskaia kastovaia doktrina" [Indian Caste Doctrine], in Julius Evola, Frithjof Schuon, René Guénon, Kasty i rasy [Castes and Races] (Tambov: Ex Nord Lux, 2010).

51 In Dumézil's opinion, the purest form of the tripartite structure of society was preserved by the Ossetians of the Caucasus in the Nart saga.

52 Dumézil deemed Perun to be the supreme God of the Slavs, but Perun's figure corresponds rather to the second, warrior estate and is considered by contemporary Russian pagans to be such, which is tied to the elevation of Perun resultant of the warrior-prince Vladimir's reform of the pantheon. In contemporary Native Faith, the supreme God, the God of the Sky, is held to be Svarog.

In Hinduism, the three estates were those of the Brahmins, the Kshatriya, and the Vaishya, with a fourth, subordinate group sometimes being distinguished: the Shudra. Here we can also sense the echoes of the patron deities: the Brahmins of Brahma, the supreme God; the Kshatriya from the Sanskrit *kṣatra*, meaning "ruling, noble", or *rājan*, meaning "lord" or "king"; and the Vaishya from Vishnu, the God of the third estate, with the Vaishya sometimes being referred to as Vishnuites or Vaishnavi. In Hindu myths, the origin of the castes is described in accordance with the laws of Manu: the Brahmins are born from the mouth, the Kshatriyas from the hands, the Vaishya from the thighs, and the Shudra from the legs of Brahma. A sacred and holistic substantiation of the social system is therefore presented: the whole world, in its totality, is a manifestation of the Divine, as every *varna* has its place reflecting the most ancient principle of justice to each his own.

Already from the preceding, it can be seen that the traditional view of society is holistic and directly opposed to the modern individualist view of man and the atomic society as a sum of individuals. In the world of Tradition, there is no such modern self-identity between the "I = I", but rather the holistic dimension of man is equivalent to the I being an estate and, higher, a Divinity/God. Instead of a sum of individuals constituting society, the Divine is manifest in estates, and these estates, at once representing Divine functions, live through man, who is thereby in principle non-individual. In Russian Native Faith, the *varnas* correspond to the *vervi* ("ropes" or "lines"): the *verv'* of priests and magi (the *volkhvy*), warriors and rulers (princes, *kniazy*), and the *verv'* of producers. On the ancient estate structure of Slavic society, Volkhv Veleslav writes:

> The Sacred Tradition of the Slavs knows another, more ancient system of societal divisions related to the time preceding the division of unified Indo-European society into different ethnoi. Like the Ancient Indian structure, it consisted of four vervi: the white, symbolically related to the element of Air and corresponding to the priests and magi (*volkhvy*); the red, related to Fire, of rulers

and warriors; the yellow, related to Water and corresponding to artisans and traders; and the black, related to the element of Earth, of herdsmen and farmers. The four vervi symbolically corresponded to the four symbolic positions of the Sun in the year and, as follows, the four times of the year. The Winter Sun was symbolically considered Black (or *Nav*), the Spring Yellow, the Summer Red, and the Autumn White.[53]

In the Indo-European tripartite system, the supreme place in the hierarchy was by right occupied by the Priest (the Scandinavian *goði* or Slavic *volkhv*), as the person closest to God engaged in realizing their divine nature. Next, a rung below, stood the kingly-ruler, the warrior, who could be at the height of the social and state system insofar as the priestly estate could realize itself ascetically. Indian texts preserved the already legendary, mythical memory of the ancient *varna* of priest-kings, the Hamsa, which over time came to be divided into the two *varna* of Brahmins and Kshatriyas. Julian the Faithful attempted to restore a similar order in the figure of the priest-emperor with his restoration of Hellenic religion which, unfortunately, was not crowned with triumph. In the 20th century, Julius Evola would propose a more adequate view of the figure of the warrior-priest unifying the two functions in the absence of adequate intitiatic institutions for Priesthood and Kingly/Imperial power. In Traditionalism, the organic manifestation of the union between the Brahminic and Kshatriyan elements was that of René Guénon and Julius Evola. Guénon manifested contemplation of the decline of the world, while Evola manifested uprising against this decline and the vehement Kshatriyan spirit of the warrior-priest. Below warriors are the subordinates of the state, the lay people or commoners. Indian myth offers the following explanation for this distribution of the *varna*:

> Verily, in the beginning this world was Brahma, one only. Being one, he was not developed. He created still further a superior form, the Kshatrahood, even those who are Kshatras (rulers) among the gods: Indra, Varuna, Soma, Rudra, Parjanya, Yama, Mrityu, Isana. Therefore there is nothing higher than Kshatra. Therefore at the

---

53 Veleslav, "*Obshchestvo i kasty*" [Society and Castes], *Svarte Aske* (2012).

Rajasuya ceremony the Brahman sits below the Kshatriya. Upon Kshatrahood alone does he confer this honor. This same thing, namely Brahmanhood (Brahma) is the source of Kshatrahood. Therefore, even if the king attains supremacy, he rests finally upon Brahmanhood as his own source, So whoever injures him [i.e., Brahma] attacks his own source. He fares worse in proportion as he injures one who is better. (*Brihadaranyaka Upanishad* 11)[54]

With regards to the Germanic peoples, Dumézil wrote:

> Above all, the second function - the needs and morals of war - deeply penetrated the first, high function. The former neither suppressed nor joined the latter, despite the competition, as Tacitus would express it, between the *dux* and the *rex*, but rather pierced and drove it in its direction...The example of the Vedic Indians and the Ancient Romans, on the contrary, would leave us to expect a pair of supreme gods which, although equal in principle, would be more or less drawn in favor of one member (Varuna, Jupiter) to the detriment of the second (Mitra, Dius Fidius). *Wōdanaz (Wotan) and *Tiwaz (Tyr) fully correspond to this structure.[55]

We encounter confirmation of the ruling and legal role of Tyr in the *Elder Edda*, in the *Lokasenna*, "Loki's Quarrel" or "Loki's Taunts", in which Loki pointedly reprimands and reproaches Tyr at Aegir's feast thusly (*Poetic Edda, Lokasenna* 38)[56]:

Þegi þú, Týr,	Silence, Tyr!
þú kunnir aldregi	You don't know how to
bera tilt með tveim...	settle disputes between men...

In his dialogue *The Republic*, Plato wrote: "the god who made you mixed some gold into those who are adequately equipped to rule, because they are the most valuable. He put silver in those who are auxiliaries and iron and bronze in the

---

54 *The Thirteen Principal Upanishads* (transl. by Robert Hume, Oxford: Oxford University Press, 1921), p. 84.

55 Georges Dumézil, *Verkhovnye bogi indoevropeitsev* [*The High Gods of the Indo-Europeans*] (Moscow: Nauka, 1986), p. 137, 146. The *Dux* and *Rex* refer to spiritual and state authority, respectively. In Germanic historiography, such is recognized to correspond to the Heerkönigtum (warrior-kingly power) and Sakralkönigtum (sacred kingship, religious at its core). See also: Georges Dumézil, *Gods of the Ancient Northmen* (Los Angeles: University of California Press, 1973).

56 *The Poetic Edda* (transl. by Jackson Crawford), p. 108.

farmers and other craftsmen."⁵⁷ Therefore, rulers (in Plato's view, philosophers were compared to priests) are the most valuable, closely adjacent to which is the silver estate of warrior-guards. According to Plato, those who strive for material wealth are those who lack such inwardly, and thus merchants are always allotted to the third estate. Plato laid this tripartite system at the foundation of the ideal state, archetypal for Indo-European societies. Plato also emphasized the openness of the estates, contrary to the common misconception of an impassable, closed nature of groups and lack of mobility between estates (derived from the example of degraded Indian castes). Thus, Plato wrote:

> For the most part you will produce children like yourselves, but, because you are all related, a silver child will occasionally be born from a golden parent, and vice versa, and all the others from each other. So the first and most important command from the god to the rulers is that there is nothing that they must guard better or watch more carefully than the mixture of metals in the souls of the next generation. If an offspring of theirs should be found to have a mixture of iron or bronze, they must not pity him in any way, but give him the rank appropriate to his nature and drive him out to join the craftsmen and farmers. But if an offspring of these people is found to have a mixture of gold or silver, they will honor him and take him up to join the guardians or the auxiliaries, for there is an oracle which says that the city will be ruined if it ever has an iron or a bronze guardian.⁵⁸

The openness of the *vervi* in Slavic society has also been mentioned by Veleslav. As for the three types of life, we find in Aristotle's *Nicomachean Ethics*:

1. βίος θεωρητικός - contemplative life for the essence of the human in itself and truth;
2. βίος πολιτκός - political life, for glory;
3. βίος ἀπολαυστικός - life for pleasure, hedonism.

These types can be compared with the estates:

1. The complete man achieves full self-rule through philosophy and contemplation.

---

57 Plato, *Complete Works* (Indianapolis/Cambridge: Hackett Publishing, 1997), p. 1050.
58 Ibid., 1050-1051.

2. The heroes strive to do good that is internal and indelible through glory, but nevertheless are dependent, if not on nature, then on society.
3. Ordinary people worry about the economy and are fully dependent on the external world, on society and nature.

Despite the differences between Plato and Aristotle, the archetypal tripartite structure remains identical. In addition to the three estates within society, there are also those who exist beyond "castes": these are the enlightened sages liberated over the course of life (*Jivanmukta*), which is to say that the magi or volkhvs are *ativarna*, or literally "above *varna*", while formally being in the highest estate. Outcasts, untouchables, pariahs, the *chandala*, criminals, and naughts are *avarna*, or literally "outside of *varna*."

Similar to Georges Dumézil's theory is the tripartite structure of Divinities projected onto history and the Celtic Cross. According to this model, triads of Deities can be discerned as corresponding to the three life stages of Birth/Creation, Becoming/Culmination, and Aging/Destruction. The following Divinities correspond to this structure:

People	Creator Gods	Guardian Gods	Destroyer Gods
Indians	Brahma	Krishna	Shiva
Germanics	Odin	Thor	Odin (and Loki)
Slavs	Svarog	Perun	Veles
Greeks	Zeus	Athena	Dionysus

Within this structure, attention can also be drawn towards the feminine pair of destroyer Gods, as in Tantric Shakti - the life energies embodied in their wrathful aspects by the Goddess of Death. More broadly, the matter at hand is the Goddesses of Death which frequently act as the consorts of the Gods of Death and Destruction. We should emphasize the principal difference between the statuses of the God of Death and the God of the afterlife, as these functions do not always coincide in the figure of one Divinity, and indeed at times are administered by non-divine entities. Being a governor of a realm, a world, and being the gateway and guide to another world are two different things. Any God - and not only a God - can end the life of a creature, but this function and patronage over it is inherent to the Gods of Destruction.

God of Death	Consort
Shiva	Kali / Durga
Bhairava	Bhairavi
Loki	Sigyn
Odin	Freya
Veles	Morena / Mara
Dionysus	Ariadne

Let us examine each of these triads and dyads of Divinities in greater detail. Creator Gods often occupy the highest rank in pantheons, and at times yield to Warrior and Guardian Gods, while Destroyer Gods are frequently in confrontation with Guardian Gods. In India one can find the well-known myths of the disputes between Shiva and Vishnu and the conflict over supremacy between Shiva and Brahma. In the *Puranas*, we find the model Trimurti of the Gods: Brahma, Vishnu, and Shiva, as indicated in our above table. In the Bhagavad Gita, Shiva is the patron God of the Kaurava tribe at war on Kurukshetra field with the Pandavas, whose patron is the God Krishna. The end of the latter battle marked the onset of the Kali-Yuga. Shiva's wife, the blessed Parvati, is in her wrathful hypostasis known as the Goddess Kali, and in her most wrathful incarnation as Durga. The God Shiva's most wrathful form is that of Bhairava, the Destroyer of Worlds and Gods, the husband of Bhairavi.

In the Scandinavian epics, Loki acts against all the Gods (as in *Lokasenna* and Ragnarök). The question of Loki's "Godlike" status is disputed: on the one hand, Loki hails from the Jötnar (giants), and this nature consequently plays a key role in the fate of the Gods who accept him into their family. As the father of giants, Loki is functionally hostile to Thor, but also is frequently found traveling in companionship with him just as often as Loki can be seen causing trouble for the Divine family. In Ragnarök, Loki and his children, Fenrir and Jörmungandr, are destined to fight against the Aesir and Vanir in the final battle. Loki's wife, the Goddess Sigyn, accompanies him after his punishment by the gods: Loki is chained to a rock under a snake exuding burning poison, which Sigyn collects in a vessel. Whenever Sigyn turns away to empty it, the poison drips onto Loki, causing earthquakes. On the other hand, Loki is a typical Trickster God adopted into the family of the Aesir as a brother of Odin. Frequently causing troubles, Loki nonetheless frequently resolves them himself, helps to save the Gods and Goddesses, and stands on their side against the giants. Loki, therefore, stands on the side of the Gods, corresponding to the proper behavior of the Aesir, only to, in the decisive moment, slide from this status to stand against the Aesir and Vanir. In his myths and figure, Loki is therefore close to the figure and myth of Prometheus.

Odin's correspondence to the Gods of Death is also complicated. Odin's figure integrates many functions; he is non-dual. In search of wisdom, Odin frequently finds himself on the other side of Life, descending into the world of the dead to speak to Völva (as in the *Völuspá*) and sacrifices himself to reveal the mystery of the runes. Odin is thus the God of the Hanged and, finally, in the form of the mortal man Oda, is Freya's husband who disappears without a trace (dies). Freya is henceforth considered a widow and it is Freya, not Hel, who is the Goddess of Death in the guise of the mad widow, the masteress of *seiðr*. Like Odin's supreme wife Frigg, Freya (whose name literally means "*Lady*") is responsible for the hall of deceased lovers, i.e., she is one of the recognized patrons of the dead.[59] Hel, in turn, is the mistress of Helheim, the world of the dead, but is not a Goddess, being rather the daughter of Loki and the giantess Angrboða, the governor of territories who is associated with various mysterious and magical myths.

In a footnote above, we mentioned our amendment to Dumézil's classification of Perun's place in the pantheon of

---

59 The representation of Freya as an initiatic Goddess and escort to Valhalla is analyzed by Maria Kvilhaug in her *The Maiden with the Mead: A Goddess of Initiation Rituals in Norse Mythology?* (VDM Verlag, 2009).

Slavic Native Faith, namely that Perun should be moved from the dominant position to the guardian function, replaced instead by Svarog as the head of the Divine family. Perun's confrontation with Veles in the figure of the snake (the serpent or lizard) is so deeply reflected in Russian folklore to the point of finding expression even in the Orthodox iconography of George the Victorious slaying the dragon. The situation with Veles is similar to that of Odin, as he is a "bipolar" Deity. Native Faith distinguishes between Veles Skoty, the patron of cattle and fertility, i.e., the hypostasis of Veles described by Dumézil, and the other Veles - Veles Koshchny, the Divinity of the Koshchny Era (the Iron Age) who is the God of Wisdom and the escort to Death. The role of Veles' partner is ascribed to the dark-haired Goddess of Death Mara-Morena, from whose name are derived the words *mor* ("pestilence"), *zamorit'* ("to starve", "to abuse", "to work to death"), *umorit'* ("to kill"), and *moroz* ("frost").

In the strictly solar Greek tradition, the figure of Dionysus is problematic by virtue of his openness to the lower worlds: Dionysus descends to Hades and returns, and his retinue includes chthonic creatures such as fauns, pans, and satyrs. Dionysus-Bacchus is the patron of the "deadly" orgiastic mysteries, the Bacchanalia. Dionysus himself dies at the hands of the titans who dismember, boil, and eat his flesh, but his Heart, his divine essence, is saved by the Goddess Athena. Dionysus' wife, originally the mortal woman Ariadne, the bride of Theseus, receives immortality from Zeus, but does not find deeper reflection in Greek myths. In Hellenism, the place of the Guardian God is occupied by the Goddess Athena, in whom we encounter the complex paradox of a woman in a man's place and stereotypically male function. This paradox was resolved in the structure of Hellenism by Athena's wielding of such masculine attributes as the helmet, armor, and spear. Athena is born out of Zeus' head, making her fundamentally intellectual, which is also an emphatically masculine trait. In fact, Athena is maximally masculine and minimally feminine: she is a man fulfilling a masculine function, the one who saves Dionysus, patronizes the polis of Athens and the Greeks in their wars. From the name of her armor - or, in another version, from Zeus' shield, Aegis, sometimes wielded by Athena - is derived the famous expression "to be under the aegis of", which is to say "under the protection or patronage of."

Imagining the Celtic Year-Circle, we can note the position of the Creator Gods and Guardian Gods on the righthand and upper halves of the circle, and the Destroyer Gods' place on the lefthand and lower positions. Most immediately striking are the overlappings of functionalities and pivotal moments in the historical cycles and life path. In the year, the Guardian Gods and martial Deities strictly correspond to summer, the upper part of the circle, and the Summer Solstice, i.e., the peak of light and the sun in the sky. The Destroyer Gods correspond to winter, the lower part of the circle, and the Winter Solstice, i.e., the low point of the sun's course through the sky. Many festivals and dates for commemorating deceased ancestors fall in the autumnal-winter season. The Creator Gods and Divinities of fertility correspond to Spring and Autumn, the colorful agricultural and fertile periods of the sowing of fields and harvesting. These are the points of the Spring and Autumnal Equinoxes.

At the same time, there is a noticeable difference and some kind of displacement of the patronizing Divinities of the upper estate. This is explained by the fact that Dumézil described the ideal state of Indo-European myths pertaining to the Golden Age without taking into account regressive cyclical fall. The emergence to the forefront of the Deities of Destruction and Death in the Kali-Yuga is related to the fact that in this time the problem of initiation becomes critical, and initiation is always associated with death. In essence, the question of initiation is always partly a matter of death and is always relevant for the upper estate. Below is a summative table of Deities in accordance with the models of Dumézil and the Celtic Cross correlating to the estates and their revered, patronizing Gods:

Estate	À la Dumézil	On the Celtic Cross
Priestly	Zeus, Odin, Svarog, Brahma	Dionysus, Odin, Veles Koshchny, Shiva, Freya, Mara, Kali
Martial	Ares, Thor, Perun, Indra	Athena, Thor, Tyr, Perun, Krishna
Productive	Demeter, Freyr, Veles, Vishnu	Demeter, Freyr, Veles Skoty, Vishnu

The reason for the differing veneration of different Divinities between estates lies in the latters' differing natures, ontological views, and world-descriptions. Above we noted Plato's remark on the differing natures of the varna in which he saw the presence of different metals: gold, silver, bronze, and iron. Each estate raises a certain God to the first, most revered place in the pantheon, constructing around them a hierarchy of all the other Gods by degrees of significance. For example, for farmers the most relevant Gods are those of fertility, life, the new sun and spring (the beginning of sowing), Gods of the hunt and patron-Gods of herds, as well as the Guardian Gods to whom they turn for help and defense from natural inclement weather, the falling of cattle and predators, as well as for protection from the external enemies of other societies. The supreme God is perceived in the likes of a demiurge, a formidable, intimidating creator and ruler of the universe.

Warriors put first the Gods of War, justice, and of blacksmiths (for weapons and armor). Heightened attention is also devoted to the great Gods, the legendary heroes who are seen as ideal, as equal to the Gods. The Gods of farmers recede into third place, as the supreme Divinities are worshipped as Fathers and greater, more skilled warriors: for instance, the God of Wars and Victories Odin (the supreme God) and his son the Warrior and Guardian god Thor, whose representation in the form of the hammer Mjölnir was worn as a pendant and became a widespread folk talisman.

In the priestly view, the demiurgic Gods who created the ordered Cosmos, the All-Fathers (one of Odin's names is Alföðr) and the Deities of Death, are at the forefront. The peculiarities of the fulfillments of priestly functions, and the distinctions between priestly-conducted rituals and rituals for priests, are explained by Veleslav in the following manner: in different situations, the role of the priest performing a rite can be assumed by an elder or dignified member of society, the clan, or the family. But the ceremonies and practices of priests can be performed only by the *volkhvy* in a closed circle of initiates, insofar as they can seem incomprehensible and even alien to the worldview of unprepared eyes. In the *Bhagavad-Gita*, we find the following lines (*Bhagavad-Gita* XVIII.41):[60]

ब्राह्मणक्षत्रियविशां शूद्राणां च परंतप। कमारणि प्रविभक्तानि स्वभावप्रभवैगुरणैः ॥	The work of Brahmans, Kshatriyas, Vaisyas, And Sudras, O thou Slayer of thy Foes! Is fixed by reason of the Qualities Planted in each.
brāhmaṇakṣatriyaviśāṃ śūdrāṇāṃ ca paramtapa ǀ karmāṇi pravibhaktāni svabhāvaprabhavair guṇaiḥ ǁ	

Thus, each estate has its own inherent set of initiations and rituals related to and mythically explaining its activities, beliefs, symbols, tools, and clothing. Every estate constructs its own picture of the world in which everything is considered and explained. The stability of society is achieved through each estate having its common set of myths out of which tradition is composed, and through each group interpreting their content and drawing various conclusions. The variety of interpretations is leveled out by the sacred hierarchy, at the top of which are the enlightened sages (priests, philosophers, volkhvs), joined by the close and "allied" warriors, with the "body of Brahma" closed by the producers with their own, earthly sets of beliefs

---

60 *The Song Celestial, or Bhagavad-Gita from the Mahabharata* (transl. by Sir Edwin Arnold, New York: Truslove, Hanson & Comba, 1900).

and myths. Outcasts either did not have their own myths and rituals or tried to imitate those of all estates at once, thus giving rise to dysfunctional mixtures of all sorts of rites and rituals and satisfaction with lower magic and domestic witchcraft. The priesthood perceives God non-dually (*advaita*, immanence), while warriors rely on limited duality (*dvaita-advaita*, immanent-transcendence), and while artisans perceive God primarily as a creator (transcendence).

The non-dual view of the *ativarn* dismantles the imaginary contradiction between the praise and veneration of the creative Gods in the Satya-Yuga and the destructive ones in the Kali-Yuga. To each corresponds his own, just as less pure estates are at greater risk of falling into confusion, illusion, losing connection with the Divine, even destroying the organic, sacred hierarchy, and falling into ignorance of the sacred dimension of being (as in the Indian *avidya*, literally meaning "ignorance of one's divine nature").

Based on these differing estate ontologies, we can examine the historical decline in terms of the degradation and historical shift in the domination of different *varna*. The Golden Age is the time of the sacred order headed by the priestly estate (in Plato's ideal state, philosophers). The Silver Age is the time in which order is conserved, but by means of relying on force and the authority of the martial estate, often entailing the exclusion of the priesthood from supremacy. The Bronze Age is the time of the revolution of the third estate of producers, artisans, farmers, and especially merchants and traders against the two higher estates or, more broadly, any form of aristocracy or estate-based inequality. The Iron Age is the time of the complete liberation of all remaining categories of people from any kind of estate pressure or oppression, the time of the liberated and now dominating pariahs, chandala, and outcasts incapable of perceiving the sacred in a hierarchical and holistic form, instead only mixing or rejecting the higher dimension according to which these groups themselves belong on the very bottom of the hierarchy.

Thus, historical regression appears as a series of revolutions of the lower estates against the higher ones. The pushing out of the priesthood from its supreme position is caused by the regression of this estate, its degeneration from communion with the Eternal Divine and its translation of the will of the Gods into dry-bone conservatism. The fully-fledged military estate therefore rightfully usurps power for the sake of maintaining due order. Evola called this the replacement of the power of the Spirit with the authority of Blood, time, leaders, judges, and absolute rulers. These too, however, are subject to corrosion and the infiltration of the interests and representatives of the third estate in the form of the mercantile, trading "elite." Vivid illustrations of this period can be seen in ancient imperial-martial Rome and the triumph of the "slave and plebeian" faith of Christianity, or in Prince Vladimir's reform of the Kiev pantheon, soon after which he abandoned the Slavic native faith for Christianity altogether.

In his *The Worker in the Thought of Ernst Jünger*, Evola wrote on this matter in the contemporary era:

> The era of the third estate is ignorant of the unity of freedom and service and the unity of freedom and order; the age of the third estate never recognized the wonderful power of this unity, for pleasures all too human and all too affordable seemed to deserve its efforts. The counterpart to the abstract and individualist notion of freedom is the social concept, the system defined by the social contract. It is precisely thanks to this abstract notion of freedom that the nature of the bourgeois is to eventually dissolve all organic unity, to transform all ties of mutual responsibility into contractual relationships which can be dissolved.[61]

The revolution of the third estate reached its peak with the emergence of Christianity and the logically ensuing rejection of the latter in the age of the Enlightenment, which thereby opened the way for the fourth estate, a point also addressed by Evola. The revolutions of the third and fourth estates lack any ties to preserving and supporting sacred hierarchy and instead are

---

61 Translated from the Russian: Julius Evola, *Rabochii v tvorchestve Ernsta Jüngera* [*The Worker in the Thought of Ernst Jünger*] (Saint Petersburg: Nauka, 2005).

concerned only with their own estate and individual interests and liberation from authority for the sake of their own aims. Let us note that Jean-Jacques Rousseau, whose ideas inspired the French Revolution that overthrew the monarchy, described the ideal human as the "noble savage" living in harmony with nature according to the laws of equality and justice. Rousseau's ideal was the peasant, a representative of the third estate, freed from the "oppression" of aristocracy, Church clerics, warriors, and priests. It is telling that one of the symbols of the French Revolution was the Phrygian cap - the symbol of slave uprisings in Rome. Furthermore, let us emphasize that the question at hand is the greater process of the degradation of estates. In and of themselves, the second and third estates are not "evil." Occupying their due places in the sacred hierarchy of society, each of them is engaged in revealing aspects of the Divine and in fulfilling their functions. The problem begins with the regressive degeneration of the consciousness of estates, which leads to decline and to the liberation of the lowest forces that take precedence over such consciousness. As Plato said: "for there is an oracle which says that the city will be ruined if it ever has an iron or a bronze guardian."

Let us draw attention to the connection between the estate structure of society and the ethnosociological theory of the allogenic origin of the state. According to this theory, the majority of states have been created by the conquest of a local (autochthonous) population by more martial, warlike nomads. Most often, this means the conquest of settled agriculturalists by nomads and pastoralists and the raising to the level of the higher estates the priests and warriors of the dominating, conquering ethnos, while the conquered population largely remains the producer estate. The victorious ethnos introduces its mythology, language, and culture. Thereafter, the ethno-dualism between the two upper estates of the one ethnos and the lower estates and castes of the other gradually softens, and elements of the popular beliefs and myths begin to penetrate and mix with the religion of the incomers to the point of shaping a new cultural type. A detailed tracing of the formation of the Hindu tradition by means of the synthesis of pre-Aryan and Aryan elements has been offered by Mircea Eliade, and an attempt to project the same logic onto the formation of the Scandinavian tradition has been undertaken by the contemporary pagan philosopher Collin Cleary.[62] The arrival of Aryan nomads in the Balkans saw the Achaeans' conquest of the Minoans and Mycenaeans, while the traces of the Dorians were left in heroic Sparta. In Hinduism, the incoming nomadic conquerors were the Devi, who attacked the indigenous Asuras. Cleary also cites the synthesis of the pre-Aryan God Rudra and the later God Shiva into the Shiva cult. In the Scandinavian tradition, the conquerors of the Vanir were the Aesir. One particularly characteristic gesture in the ensuing establishment of social peace was the exchange of Gods between the Vanir (second-order Gods) and the Aesir (first-order Gods), such as the introduction into the first order of Freya and Freyr. Freyr, from the Vanir, the son of Njörðr, became the adopted son of Odin. Elsewhere we have already mentioned Freya's marriage to Odin in the person of Oda. As collateral Asgard in turn sent to the Vanir Odin's esteemed giants Mimir and Hönir, after which Hönir became the leader of the Vanir and Mimir was beheaded by hex. One possible ethnosociological interpretation of this myth suggests that Mimir was a revered figure in the upper estates, as evidenced by Odin's heightened concern with his afterlife up to the point of self-mutilation, but was considered an unworthy exchange (or misunderstood?) by the indigenous people. The appearance of the God of Wisdom, Kvasir, who arose out of the saliva of the Aesir and Vanir, represented a positive moment of normalization between the two ethnoi which resolved the formation of a common culture.

In his work *The Sociology of Russian Society*, Alexander Dugin examines in detail the formation of Russian culture and society in the context of the conquests of heterogeneous Slavic tribes. In particular, Dugin discerns the structure of Russian

---

62 See: Collin Cleary, "What God did Odin Worship?" in *Summoning the Gods: Essays on Paganism in a God-Forsaken World* (San Francisco: Counter Currents, 2011).

society as consisting of the following layers: the pre-neolithic culture of the Finno-Ugric tribes which, according to Vladimir Propp, has been preserved in the broadest layer of Russian fairy tales; the peasant layer of the sedentary Slavic tribes engaged in slash-and-burn agriculture; and the heroic layer punctuated by the call of the Varangians to Rus, the time of the formation of the Kievan Principality, and the active conquest of neighboring tribes. About these layers, Dugin writes:

> The heroic layer of the unconscious and the peasant and pre-neolithic layers did not disappear over time, but have periodically emerged on a nationwide scale, especially during wars, uprisings, and revolutions. Despite the fact that the Russian state has, throughout all of its history, been compelled to constantly fight, this type has not become predominant or exclusive. It has been superimposed onto the agrarian, peace-loving strata, blending into but not displacing or suppressing them.[63]

Thus, employing its own language, sociology recounts the mythical organicity and unity of society as the body of Brahma. Another vivid, later example of the nomadic influence on Russian culture is that of the Mongols, whose influence saw the change of the tree most revered by the people. Today it seems self-evident that the birch tree is the symbolic tree of Russia, but in fact, the birch was held to be special by the Turks, while the Slavs especially revered the willow. This difference can be clearly noted as one crosses Russia from the West (Kiev and Moscow) to the East (Siberia and the Far East): birches gradually begin to dominate forests after the Ural mountain ridge, and in the North-East are replaced by the coniferous Taiga.

On the basis of these views, we can interpret the deep reasons underlying the advancement by traditions of different symbols in the present period as presented in the introduction. Out of the Scandinavian tradition, the most steadfast attention

---

63 Alexander Dugin, *Sotsiologiia russkogo obshchestva. Rossiia mezhdu Khaosom i Logosom* [*The Sociology of Russian Society: Between Chaos and Logos*] (Moscow: Academic Project, 2011). See also: Alexander Dugin, *Etnosotsiologiia* [*Ethnosociology*] (Moscow: Academic Project, 2011). In English: Alexander Dugin, *Ethnos and Society* (London: Arktos, 2018); *Ethnosociology: The Foundations* (London: Arktos, 2019).

and distribution have been enjoyed by the warrior archetypes of the Norse: the Vikings (the nomads of the sea), the berserkers, and the wolfserkers. Thor's Hammer, the Valknut, and the Odal rune as symbolizing Odin directly refer us back to the second estate, and in second and third place relating to the priestly-magical and agricultural aspects respectively. The Kolovrat as the symbol of Slavic-Russian paganism has always been interpreted as a solar symbol and symbol of the year, the *kologod* ("wheel-year") or annual circle, which directly refers us back to the agricultural theme and archetype of the third estate. This is especially emphasized by the fact that few pagan texts have survived from Rus, and thus one of the main sources of the reconstruction of paganism in the 20th and 21st centuries has been the reservoir of folk beliefs, superstitions, folklore, and ethnography. This has had a particular impact on the difficulty of the revelation of *volkhv* wisdom, which has to a greater extent been the result of the mystical insights of modern Native Faith figures. Om, the sacred syllable and mantra of Hinduism, succinctly emphasizes the archetype of the upper estate which is most clearly manifest in this tradition. Such also rightfully points to the enormous quantity of texts and the second-rate importance of the martial and productive *varna*, which are often interpreted through the prism of their peculiar ritual-spiritual practice and aspects of their liberation from samsara.

Finally, we should also recall Mircea Eliade's important observation that the majority of religious texts which have been preserved across cultures are those which were created by, intended for, and kept by the upper estates of society, i.e., the priests, kings, and warriors. This most vividly summates the significance of the heritage and doctrines of the higher castes, such as knowledge of cosmogony, hierarchies of Deities, metaphysics, correct ritual practice, state administration, achieving the liberation or realization of one's Divine nature, and so on. In antiquity, the higher estate of philosophers supplied the teachers of future kings and emperors (e.g., Aristotle was the teacher of Alexander the Great). In India, reading the Vedas was accessible to the third estate of artisans so that, in creating new things, they could be conscious of the manifestation of the demiurgic function of Creator Gods in their estate.

Pagan Initiation

The question of initiation is a cornerstone theme of the philosophy of Traditionalism, and especially Pagan Traditionalism. The importance of initiation can be briefly stressed in the following words: without initiation, any (re)-constructions of the paganism of the past, even more so in the present, and any ritual and ceremonial practices would be no more than hot air and vain gestures. Initiation is the wine in the vessel of forms and the essence of the esoteric, which is clothed and attained through exoteric, culturally and temporally dependent rites, rituals, and practices. If tradition is a chain of transmission which, according to Guénon, originates outside of man on the metaphysical level, then initiation is that which at once binds and is transmitted through this chain.

As an action, initiation means that a person transitions to a different mode of existence. All coming-of-manhood rites for boys or womanhood rites for girls mean transitioning from one form - through dying - to another form of life in society. The initiation of a person makes them complete, into a real human being. Before initiation, a person exists merely on the "natural" level of existence, is not independent, and does not participate in the affairs of society on equal footing. Mircea Eliade wrote of initiation:

> Initiation usually comprises a threefold revelation: revelation of the sacred, of death, and of sexuality. The child knows nothing of these experiences; the initiate knows and assumes them, and incorporates them into his new personality. We must add that, if the novice dies to his infantile, profane, nonregenerate life to be reborn to a new, sanctified existence, he is also reborn to a mode of being that makes learning, knowledge, possible. The initiate is not only one

newborn or resuscitated; he is a man who knows, who has learned the mysteries, who has had revelations that are metaphysical in nature. During his training in the bush he learns the sacred secrets: the myths that tell of the gods and the origin of the world, the true names of the gods, the role and origin of the ritual instruments employed in the initiation ceremonies…Initiation is equivalent to a spiritual maturing. And in the religious history of humanity we constantly find this theme: the initiate, he who has experienced the mysteries, is he who knows.[64]

We might also quote the *Shatapatha Brahmana*, which contains the following lines on initiation: "He who is consecrated [initiated], truly draws nigh to the gods, and becomes one of the deities."[65]

Initiation as Death

In speaking of initiation, we are always speaking about death. If initiation is the cornerstone of Tradition, then death is the cornerstone of initiation itself. In initiation rituals, death can be expressed in different guises, ranging from the literal burying of the initiate underground, descending into a cave or chasm, to the withdrawal of the initiate from the village or locking the neophyte underground or in a separate shack. In Eliade's *The Sacred and the Profane*, we find the example of the Mandja and Banda tribes of Africa practicing initiation through playing out the myth of the monster Ngakola, which devours people and regurgitates their blood. In such a ritual, the neophyte enters a hut symbolizing Ngakola's womb, where he is whipped and tortured as he "enters the womb of Ngakola." Following this ordeal, the initiate is declared to have been reborn, and the monster releases him.

Death plays a twofold role in initiation. He who is suitable for initiation and who seeks and longs for such will be met with death. The person who begins the ritual and the one

---

64   Eliade, *The Sacred and the Profane*, p. 188.

65   *Shatapatha Brahmana* (transl. by Julius Eggeling, Oxford: Oxford University Press, 1894), 3:1:1:8.

who comes out after the end of the ritual are different people. The imperfect, inexperienced, uninitiated person perishes for worldly life finally and irrevocably. On the other side is death, the guide, the transition into the world of the initiated, the new, fully-fledged human being. In this regard, initiation consists of the inseparable unity of three elements: birth, death, and rebirth. Ritual seclusion of the initiate symbolically reproduces cosmogony: being removed from society for the necessary time, the neophyte is left outside of the life of the community. When the young are taken away, they are considered dead and can be bewailed or mourned. For the neophyte, such means exclusion from the state of the ordered Cosmos and return to matter, to the Great Mother, approaching the Primordial Chaos from which he, through the ritual of initiation, passes through his own personal demiurgy to return to the community in a new capacity. Thus, one of the main motifs of initiation is the return to the womb, the neophyte's acceptance of the embryonic position, and his hiding in such a position, for instance, in the basement of a dwelling, to be closer to earth. The return to the womb is also an allusion to death, tempered by the pronounced aspect of transition and then rebirth.

Detachment from the dead "I" is emphasized by the fact that the initiate acquires a new name, duties, and privileges. Initiation is often marked by ritual scarring, tattooing, shaving hair (or, vice versa, the right to a beard) or changing clothes. The tragedy of ritual and the newness of the initiate is vividly illustrated in the case of shamanic initiations widespread among the many peoples professing shamanism. The shamanic initiate, in a state of intoxication (whether by alcohol, mushrooms, or herbs) is invited to a feast of all spirits, at which the main dish-offering to the spirits is the body of the shaman himself. The spirits flock to the call, tear the shaman apart, devour him and collect and assemble his bones into a new body. If the spirits position any bone wrongly, or if the spirits of diseases come to the feast, then in rebirth the shaman may find himself with corresponding ailments or the so-called "shamanic illness."

Often enough, after returning from the "feast", the shaman becomes a "crazy" madman or "blissful shaman."[66] A similar motif is present in the Chöd ritual of Tibetan Buddhism. For the sake of the highest initiation, the adept, using a drum made out of two arches of a human skull *(damaru)* and a horn made out of a human femur *(kanglin)*, summons to a secluded place the terrifying spirits of the three worlds, offering them his body and his blood in a skull cup. He who survives this most difficult test becomes free from all fears and is awakened.

Heightened attention to aspects of fertility and vitality was paid in the female initiations of the *Weinerbunde*, or women's unions. The initiation of girls into women was carried out following the beginning of menstruation. Many motifs of seclusion in a hut, forest, or ritual defloration by a priest point towards the ritualized death of the preceding person.[67] Women are thus initiated into the main sacred mystery of being a woman, a creator of life. This is a specific experience that cannot be transplanted into male initiations. In Rus, the mysteries of the *rod*, death, and the *Weinerbunde* intersected in communities of midwives, which are still be found in some remote villages. In these instances, the elder midwife takes a child away after birth, heats the bathhouse - which, in the life world of the Ancient Slavs, was a disturbing, dangerous, and even deadly place associated with many superstitions and folkloric episodes - and rests with the infant, rubbing their head with hands for hours with accompanying charms and songs.[68]

Reference to death in this context is harbored in Julius Evola's term *la rottura del livello*, or "the rupture of levels." In the latter, it

---

[66] We understand the term "crazy" here without the modern negative, clinical and social connotations. Eliade called the state of the disintegration of the personality during initiation "psychic chaos." We might call such "approaching" or "nearing Chaos."

[67] Some African tribes practice what would, from the point of view "civilized, modern" man, be "savage" customs, such as ritual defloration by the father or all the men of a community. This emphasizes the patriarchal nature of such societies' endowment of a woman with vitality.

[68] The profane dimension of this act suggests that, in so doing, the midwives shaped the correctly rounded vault of the infant's skull.

is easy to sense the ritual of passage from the mundane (profane) world to ascension towards higher wisdom. The rupture of levels is when a person sharply and clearly realizes that the whole sphere of everyday life is not all, but merely an illusion claiming to be all. This fundamental suspicion "collapses" the whole previous, incomplete view of the world as man discovers that above the immediate world there are still other "floors" or "levels." This discovery, this "collapse", and this opening of higher dimensions - the "rupture of levels" - is initiation. If one were to attempt to describe the states experienced during this "rupture of levels", then the most accurate and generalizing beyond all secondary experiences which might be merely different expressions of the same element, would be horror, terror, or fright. The experience of initiation, of death, is the experience of pure, purifying terror. Evola especially emphasized trauma and existential tension as criteria of initiation.

Increased attention and reverence of the Gods and Goddesses of Death and Wisdom on the part of the upper estate in the Kali-Yuga is also related to the problem of initiation, which we will examine further on in this chapter. In this regard, it is noteworthy that in Hinduism the God of Wisdom, Ganesha, appears as the son of the God of Destruction, Shiva. In Odinism, Odin's search for wisdom leads to his frequent encounter with death, such as the head of Mimir, whose wisdom is honored by the All-Father and which is, in a certain sense, dead. In the words of Volkhv Veleslav: "The Path to Wisdom is the Path to Death."

Initiation as a Social Phenomenon

As a social phenomenon, initiation is also associated with imparting to neophytes new social functions, rights, and duties. The initiation of boys into men gives them the right to fully participate in the life of the male half of society, such as in the discussion of questions affecting the life of the community, the right to start a family, and so on. After their initiation into women, girls can join women's unions (midwives, fortune tellers, herbalists, etc.) and give the signal that they are ready to marry and produce offspring.

An important role in initiation is also played by estates, whether the acceptance, as Plato suggested, into a higher estate of a child raised with a predominantly "gold" nature, or the surrendering of a "silver" child to the military estate. There are also initiations into different castes under the patronage of various Deities within the same estate, such as, in later times, among hunters or blacksmiths. One colorful example of initiation into various forms of armies and warrior groups can be seen in the "duels of dignity", as well as in the widely known rituals of fighting a bear or wolf in an altered state of consciousness, victory in which meant attaining the title of *berserker* or *wulfserker*. Closely related to such are the intra-estate, hierarchical initiations akin to ranks in armies, hierarchs in the priesthood, or in terms of master and apprentice. On the estate role of initiation, Baron Julius Evola wrote the following:

> Thus, from the traditional point of view, not-having-ancestors distinguishes the plebeian from the patrician less than not-having-rites. In Aryan hierarchies, a single characteristic differentiated the higher castes from the lower: rebirth. The *arya*, as opposed to the *shudra* (the one who serves), was the *dvija*, the born again. The assertion of the *Manavadharmashastra* (II, 172), that the *brahman* himself, if he left out initiation, would no longer be differentiated from the one who serves, the *shudra*, is indicative. Analogously, what characterised the three higher castes of the Iranians was that each of them corresponded to a determinate celestial 'fire'. The Nordic nobles were noble because, in their blood, they carried the blood of the Aesir, of the 'celestial' forces in continuous struggle with the elemental beings. The nobility of the great medieval orders of chivalry - among which the most significant were the Templars - was also tied to initiation.[69]

The converse to social initiation can be seen in the act of exiling someone from their estate and society, which is to say their ritual "killing", and echoes of this phenomenon could still

---

69 Julius Evola, *Pagan Imperialism* (Gornahoor Press, 2017), p. 82.

be seen in the 20th century in the breaking of one's sword, the cutting of their estate-related clothing, and their branding with fire, paint, or apparel (such as bells).

Initiation and Education

Let us briefly touch upon another dimension of initiation, namely, access to knowledge and the transmission of this knowledge. We can discern two aspects here: the acquiring of knowledge about one's own and other traditions from literary sources, and the organized education of children within a tradition amidst the conditions of Modernity.

With regards to the first, René Guénon took the harsh stance that being merely formally erudite means next to nothing. One can read numerous books, observe rituals, and so on, but if there is no "rupture of levels", then there is nothing at all to boast beyond a baggage quantitative of facts. In this lies the complementarity between Guénon and Evola: the first dedicated his life to describing Tradition and identifying the front against Modernity, while the second practiced and described operative aspects of Tradition in different situations. Initiation is not the reading of books, but the changing of one's mode of existence. It is an experience, the experience of the sacred terror which is subjective and obligatory for any genuine realization.

The second aspect concerns the more institutionalized, mundane sphere of the transmission of knowledge about the Gods, myths, and customs adopted within a tradition to the children of the community whose parents adhere to the pagan tradition. In this sphere, we are compelled to admit a state of profound crisis. Contemporary pagan communities are attempting to create a common education course for children, albeit on the level of a recommendation. The American Asatru Folk Assembly has released educational booklets for children that resemble modern children's books. The Russian Native Faith community has also seen the publication of educational tales for children who, besides the already existing cultural heritage, have been immersed in pagan upbringing.[70] Close attention to "pagan schooling" has also been paid by Velimir (Nikolai Speransky), although in his case such is of an artisanal and folkloric character. A pagan school also exists within the Union of Slavic Communities of the Slavic Native Faith. Yet these examples remain exceptions to the greater picture. More complex and pedagogically subtle projects aimed at educating children have not yet been realized within pagan communities. In Russia, against the backdrop of past education reforms, two vectors have been consolidated in teaching, namely the secular-scientific and religious-creationist (such as lessons in Orthodox Christian culture and Islam), while the proper education of children in the line of the pagan worldview, not to mention proper preparation for initiatic rituals, remains faced with complications.

The Historical Heritage

Under this section, we could recount the enormous heritage which paganism has left in texts and cultural artifacts and point to the great number of authors who have drawn on paganism since the very first years of Christianity up to the present day, but such would require more than a dozen volumes for sufficient presentation and examination. Instead, we will limit ourselves to the indication of some general lines which clarify the direction of our thought.

It is indisputable that Christianization took place in different countries in Europe at different times and in different manners. The higher estates, which were the first to adopt the Christian faith, still preserved their rites of burials, lamentations, and their very ways of doing business and courts of honor for a long time. Among the third estate of producers, the process of assimilating the new religion proceeded even slower, and the new rules,

---

70 This initiative has been supported by the editorial board of the journal *Rodnoverie* and the Union of Slavic Communities of the Slavic Native Faith.

dogma, and culture coexisted with the old pagan traditions in complex relations of enmity, synthesis, complementation, or even without openly intersecting. In the Russian context, this phenomenon acquired the name *dvoeverie*, i.e., "double-belief" or "dual-faith."

Dual-faith began to take shape in Russia starting with the very baptism of Rus in the 10th century, developed in the 11th, and would continue, according to various sources, up to the 14th and 15th centuries. However, the discovery of an Old Believer icon of the Burning Bush featuring a runic inscription of the divine name *Radegast*, dated by experts to the early 17th century, lengthens the possible period of dual-faith by at least two centuries. In addition to the preservation of the pre-Christian tradition in remote and silent places, about which we cannot claim to assert that the line of transmission has been either uninterrupted or merely come to light today, we can say that paganism was altogether organically intertwined into the fabric of Orthodoxy and has very much lived on among the people. The interesting fact should be noted that these two cultures coexisted in their purest forms on the peripheries of society: in the works of Byzantine thinkers and artists invited to Rus, on the one hand, and in the folklore barely touched by the Church on the other.[71] In addition, it is worth taking note of the customs of winter *koledari* (carols) and the burning of the stuffed straw figure of winter (Morena) on the occasion of Maslenitsa, which official Christianity is still struggling against to this very day.

It is also known that the Russian *skomorokhi*, the "actors" or "jesters" who appeared in the 11th century, owe their origins to the volkhvs who were persecuted by the Tsar and the Church until their repertoire was emasculated across the glumy (social satirical sketches), the *byliny*, and fairy tales, leaving only empty fairground entertainment as their legacy. The *skomorokhi*

---

71 See: A.D. Sukhov (ed.), *Vvedenie khristianstva na Rusi* [*The Introduction of Christianity in Rus*] (Moscow: Institute of Philosophy of the Academy of Sciences of the USSR/ Mysl, 1987).

singers were present at the tower of St. Sophia of Kiev during the time of Yaroslav. Many pagan symbols, beliefs, superstitions, and folkloric figures were kept alive in the people and in folk art, such as fairy tales, songs, poetry, carvings, and embroidery, where pagan motifs are not only ubiquitously present but are often the only depictions to be found. Examples of such include double-sided amulets, on one side of which one finds a depiction of the Virgin Mary, while on the other the "serpent-haired Goddess", as well as the "thunder arrows" made of stone with crosses inscribed on them. In Scandinavia, Thor's Hammer was also modified to imitate the Christian equal-armed cross. Even today, Siberian shamans use Orthodox Church candles as suitable for certain rituals of purification.

Another illustrative example of dual-faith is the developed cult and special veneration of the Virgin Mary, the mother of the earthly incarnation of Jesus Christ conceived immaculately by the Holy Spirit. No such special attention to the mother of Muhammad, or female figures in Judaism, is to be found as vividly as in Christianity, especially in Orthodoxy. This emphasis conceals a popular pagan foundation typifying the worship of Mother Earth in various aspects, such as the mother of the earthly *rod*. The mother is frequently associated with fertile earth, and with the depths and the dark (the hidden, the implicit). In creationism, Heaven and God are opposed to the created Earth and the world, whereas in Orthodoxy we see a very strong cult of the Virgin Mother of God. In the scriptures, the Mother of God is also called the Ever-Virgin, i.e., she retains purity and integrity before and after the birth of Christ, which is to say that, compared to Earth, the Mother of God is pure before both God and the world. This corresponds to the positive pagan understanding of earth. Another female who accompanied Christ, Mary Magdalene, a saint and myrrh-bearer, represents another important female emphasis in Orthodoxy, as she is equal to the apostles and, together with the Virgin Mary, retires with John the Theologian. Nikolay Voronin has drawn attention to the fact that the cult of the

Mother of God in Vladimir has very little Christianity in it: "The Vladimir icon firstly preserves semi-pagan features of the female deity: in essence, she acts as a pagan amulet."[72] Such an attitude towards the Mother of God reflects the motif of intercession and the fertility of land so widespread among the Slavs with their pronounced third-estate thinking.

Other Gods, meanwhile, "dissolved" into the large "pantheon" of Orthodox saints, whose reverence among the people it would be difficult to call anything other than "pagan". Perun and Yarilo found reflection in Ilya, Boris, Gleb, and George the Victorious. Perun-George battles the Snake/Veles in the famous Christian motif, and Veles himself was nearly identified with St. Blaise, the patron saint of cattle. Makosh merged with Paraskevi's Friday. According to scholars, it is based on this conceptualization by the people of native and foreign Divinities that the Marcian heresy, which "distorted" the trinity in the spirit of polytheism, developed in the 14th century.[73]

Moreover, nearly all important Orthodox holidays directly coincide with or are close to the pagan solar festivals, and some saints are obvious analogues of pagan Deities. One vivid example of such is the Christian holiday of Ivan Kupala (John the Baptist/Theologian), which is celebrated with a difference of about a month from the pagan Summer Solstice, Kupala. A brief table of the correspondences between pagan festivals celebrated by Native Faith and Orthodox holy dates looks the following:

Date	Old and Modern Pagan Festival	Orthodox Holiday
January 6	Festival of the God Veles	Christmas Eve
January 7	Koliada	Christmas
February 24	Day of Veles patron of cattle)	Day of St. Blaise
March 2	Day of Marena	Day of St. Marianna

---

72 Sukhov (ed.), *Vvedenie khristianstva na Rusi* [*The Introduction of Christianity in Rus*].
73 Ibid., p. 272.

Date	Old and Modern Pagan Festival	Orthodox Holiday
March 21 (pagan) / floating date	Spring Equinox	Easter
May 6	Day of Dazhdbog	Day of St. George the Victorious
June 21 (pagan) / July 7 (Orthodox)	Kupala	Day of Ivan Kupala (John the Baptist)
September 21 (pagan) / October 1 (Orthodox)	Autumnal Equinox	Intercession, or Festival of Harvest in some regions

Indeed, an enormous contribution to describing paganism in Rus was afforded by Christianity itself, especially in Christian descriptions of pagan rites. For example, one case of Christianity's heightened attention to paganism was the *Sermon on Law and Grace of Hilarion* (11th century).[74] However, there is a certain problem with Christian sources that Julius Evola emphatically pointed out: the subjectivity of their descriptions of pagan beliefs and their active engagement in denigrating popular faith towards their own ends. The blind use of church sources, according to Evola and many other authors, can lead to the creation of ridiculous constructs which, being far from paganism, in fact, are embodiments of the caricatures devised by Christian apologists. Therefore, Christian sources should be treated with great caution and attention.

One unique phenomenon in Russia is that of the Old Believers or Old Rite. Without delving into the theological and political details of the church schism in the 17th century (which, let us note in passing, also touched on the important topic of the *iazyk*), we believe that the Old Believers, in breaking away from the church and retreating, fleeing to Siberia and the Taiga to autonomous, closed villages, preserved to a certain extent not only pre-Nikonian-reform Christianity, but also the pagan components of Ancient Rus woven into such. In his book, White Doves, Melnikov-Pechersky offered a description

---

74 Sukhov (ed.), *Vvedenie khristianstva na Rusi*, p. 266.

of the ecstatic circle-ceremonies of the *khlysty*[75] as reflecting the veneration of Mother Earth:

> The main, annual ecstatic circle-ritual (radenie) takes place... around Trinity Day. During this time, in other altogether small arks (communities), the khlysty, in their circle, sing songs addressed to "the mother of raw earth", which they identify with the Virgin Mary. After some time, the Mother of God rises out of the ground wearing a colored dress and wearing on her head a cup with raisins or other sweet berries. This is the "mother of raw earth" with her gifts. She communes with the khlysty with raisins, sentencing them: 'Eat by the gift of the earth, enjoy the Holy Spirit, do not waver in your faith.' Then she anoints them with water, and commands: 'By the gift of God wash yourselves, enjoy the Holy Spirit, and do not waver in your faith.'

Mentions of the beliefs of the Slavs can also be found in the chronicles of Arab and Greek authors and historians. In modern times, the study, description, and reconstruction of the pagan worldview of the ancients has been the work of prominent scholars such as Carl Gustav Jung, Mircea Eliade, James Frazer, Boris Rybakov, Alexander Afanasyev, and others. As mentioned in the introduction, a significant number of written sources and architectural artifacts of the pagan heritage have been preserved in Europe, such as the Elder Edda, the skaldic ballads of heroes, *Beowulf*, the *Song of the Nibelungs*, the Finno-Ugric *Kalevala*, and others, not to mention the megalithic monuments of Stonehenge, Externsteine, and the Scandinavian runestones (found even in North America). An enormous written heritage along with what could be said to be an uninterrupted tradition has survived in modern Hindustan. In the North, in Iceland, even today the ancient and Christian religions coexist simultaneously, both with official, equal recognition. The situation there with the dating of pagan and Christian festivals is analogous to the Russian case.

---

75 The *khlysty* were an underground sect among the so-called "folk-spiritual Christian" currents which split from the Russian Orthodox Church in the mid-17th century. While referring to themselves as *khristovovery* ("Christ-believers") or *khristy* for short, this group came to be known as *khlysty* from the word *khlyst* for "whip", associated with ritual practices of flagellation. One famous figure alleged to have been involved with the *khlysty* was Grigory Rasputin.

The French sociologist and cultural theorist Georges Bataille, in his analysis of Jules Michelet's *Satanism and Witchcraft*, wrote: "The mediaeval rites were undoubtedly a continuation of the religion of the ancients, though there is a certain confusion as to the identification of the deities: in a sense, Satan was a Dionysos *redivivus*. They were the rites of the *pagani*, of peasants and serfs, victims of a dominant order, and a dominant religion." [76] The latter passage is a direct reference to the phenomenon of dual-faith in Europe, the traces of which we can find in folk culture just as among the Slavs.[77] Pagan relics were harshly persecuted by the Inquisition under the guise of "witchcraft" and "Satanism", all the while as, according to many scholars, the medieval view of the knight was but a splash of the pagan warrior ethic, and it is this model of chivalry that occupied a most important place in Evola's philosophy. A great number of examples could be reproduced here; however, given the fact that European civilization in time and space remains the single most studied culture in the world, the list could be continued indefinitely - for this reason, we restrict ourselves merely to the preceding indication of possible vectors of research for those who wish to seek further.

The Horizontal and the Vertical

The above remarks on initiation and historical survivals of paganism concern more external and social forms, which we might call the horizontal dimension of initiation. This horizontal dimension is related to forms of rituals varying in time and space, intra-estate emphases, and the educational and status-related facets of rites of passage and initiation. In their most profane forms, we can find echoes of the horizontal aspect of initiation in modern society as well, in its stereotypes and myths about what one "should" know and be able to accomplish

---

[76] Georges Bataille, *Literature and Evil* (New York: Penguin: 2012). *Dionysos redivivus* - "Dionysus resurrected."

[77] On Icelandic dual-faith on the eve of the Enlightenment, see: Leonid Korablev, *Jón Knizhnik-Charodey* [*Jón's Book of Sorcery*] (Ignis, 2009).

by a certain age, and what one "should" experience and be tested for. But these views are of a purely conventional and optional character, which negates any of their significance to the topic under consideration.

The affirmation that initiatic centers exist to this day in the form of churches or branches of various organizations which, having reached Modernity, have degenerated, ossified, and had their links in the chain of the transmission of Tradition broken, is a matter of horizontal initiation. It would be too optimistic to count on genuine initiation in the vast majority of contemporary pagan and Abrahamic organizations. On the other hand, as the English thinker Nigel Pennick has optimistically written about the resumption of pagan rites:

> Even if a ritual is revived after a long discontinuation, as in the case with the Rochester chimney sweeps on the First of May, this means that the break between celebrations was longer than usual. That's it. There always exist stable layers of Tradition which can be restored in force at any moment. They are de facto reborn, returned to life anew after a long time spent in oblivion.[78]

On this note, we can recall Alain de Benoist's words on Hölderlin: "If the divine once existed, said Hölderlin in essence, then it would return because it is eternal."[79] In terms of "horizontal" initiation, we should also take note of the indisputable positive role of the still healthy third estate in the preservation of the pagan heritage in the body of the folk, both in Rus and Europe. As we mentioned in the beginning, the very terms "paganism" and "paganus" have their roots in the "countryside" and "village."

To further define what we discern in addition to the horizontal aspect of initiation as vertical initiation, we can employ the following allegory: if horizontal initiation is the chain of initiates stretching over the centuries, then vertical initiation is the establishment of the connection between the

---

[78] Nigel Pennick, *Practical Magic in the Northern Tradition* (Loughborough: Thoth Publications, 2005). Translated from the Russian.

[79] De Benoist, *On Being a Pagan*.

initiated and the higher transcendent element, initiation into the Sacred Knowledge and Eternal Wisdom. Speaking of initiation in terms of the ascent from the profane periphery to the Spiritual Center, René Guénon remarked that the closer an adept reaches the center, the more the differences between paths fade.[80] The One removes many differences, just as rays ascend to the source, reducing the distances between them to the point of merging. It is important to emphasize that we are not talking about merging on the level of the periphery, on the level of different external forms of traditions, but about their common source whose essence is inexpressible in formal language. In this light, it can be said that the pagan tradition of a people is the language of this people's communication with the Divine, which is revealed through the experience of the Sacred, through rapture, terror, and silence which seize all of the nature of man.

The historical continuity of initiation, the line of "ordination", might be preserved in the world, but such just as well might be emasculated of its vertical dimension, and therefore be merely a repetition of forms exerting no impact on the neophyte. Horizontal initiation can exist when vertical initiation is absent. The problem of vertical initiation in our current era is that which has most of all concerned Traditionalists and pagans reviving their ancient traditions today. Indeed, the question of initiatory quality is one of the main fronts for criticisms of paganism today. Above we showed how an enormous legacy of pagan forms and artifacts has been preserved and remains alive to this very day; now we might add that while such may ensure the horizontal aspect of initiation, this is not without the problems which we have pinpointed. We will turn to the inner, vertical dimension of initiation in the coming pages. Before turning to the question of vertical initiation, however, we must consider an important topic that might be attributed to the intermediary level which connects the horizontal and vertical levels of initiation into a single whole.

---

80 René Guénon, *Perspectives on Initiation* (Ghent: Sophia Perennis, 2004).

Language and Thinking

The great philosopher of the 20th century, Martin Heidegger, said: "Language is the house of Being."[81] René Guénon distinguished negative changes in human thinking as cause for degradation and the onset of Modernity. In examining the problem of the transmission of the pagan worldview and initiation into this view, it is impossible to avoid the most important dimensions of language and thinking. In Russian, the "play on words" of *iazyk* meaning "language" and the Old Church Slavonic *iazyk* meaning "folk" leads us to the analogy of: "language and thinking" = "folk and [its] thinking." While we briefly touched upon the question of language in the introduction to this work and in the section on names and symbols, now we will dwell on this topic in greater detail.

On this matter, of great interest are the studies of the Russian philologist and folklorist Vladimir Viktorovich Kolesov.[82] Kolesov distinguishes three orders of language arising over the course of the Christianization of Rus, whose historical point is dated to 988, and the translation of key Christian texts from Greco-Christian into archaic Old Slavic. The result of the latter was not so much a translation as a most complex new language, Old Church Slavonic, entailing the construction of new notions, words, and terms lacking in both Old Slavic and Greek. The three orders of language distinguished by Kolesov are: "equipolence" (*ekvipolentnost'*), "graduality" (*gradualnost'*), and "privativity" (*privativnost'*). Kolesov explains these:

> Equipolence helps to highlight specific objects and data in their specificity (e.g., man-woman, day-night, top-bottom, etc.). Graduality introduced into consideration ideas (views, conceptions) about things and the possibility to envision altogether fantastical objects, faces, and creatures in the infinity of their manifestations.

---

81 See: Martin Heidegger, "Letter on Humanism" in Martin Heidegger, *Basic Writings: From Being and Time to The Task of Thinking* (London: Harper, 2008); *On the Way to Language* (New York: Harper, 1982).

82 See Kolesov's collected series of books under the name *Drevniaia Rus': nasledie v slove* [*Ancient Rus': The Legacy in the Word*], cited in the bibliography.

Privativity serves not the image or symbol, but the concept as the most scientifically rigorous, precise content of a verbal sign...Equipolence exists in the mode of similarities and identicalities, graduality in likenesses and similarities, and privativity in substantive similarities and differences.[83]

According to Kolesov, the pagan worldview corresponds to the equipolent order of language. The latter term, equipolence, is formed by the Latin *equi-*, meaning "equal" or "to be strong", and *pollens*, meaning "to be able." In Kolesov's words:

> The simplest way to identify a thing which falls into our field of vision is to compare it to another type of thing of the same kind...Such is the 'pagan' understanding of the classification of the material world by means of the pairwise comparison of 'bodies' of common ground. Man and woman are both a "person", and top and bottom are both a space and expanse, and so on... The Old Russian era of Christianization, and long afterwards, nearly to the 14th century, was the time of the dominance of the equipolent opposition, which conditioned many peculiarities of our history and culture...Light and darkness are contrasted to one another and are perceived as equivalent, uniformly existing, irreducible entities. They are explained through one another.[84]

This means that present poles (e.g., top-bottom, day-night) equally belong to being; they are equal and determined by one another. The absence of a man does not mean a "non-man", but a woman. The absence of life is death, but death not as oblivion, but as a different life. Hence the developed cult of ancestors and descriptions of the afterlife in pagan traditions. Kolesov points out that the dominance of this order of language was preserved up to the 14th century, which corresponds to the dating of the era of dual-faith.

The dominance of the equipolent order of language was later replaced by another order. Kolesov holds that Russian

---

83 V.V. Kolesov, *Drevniaia Rus': nasledie v slove, tom 4 - Mudrost' slova* [*Ancient Rus': The Legacy in the Word, Volume IV - The Wisdom of the Word*] (Saint Petersburg: Faculty of Philosophy of Saint Petersburg State University, 2011). See also the discussion of Kolesov in Alexander Dugin, *V poiskakh temnogo Logosa (filososkobogoslovskie ocherki)* [*In Search of the Dark Logos: Philosophico-Theological Outlines*] (Moscow: Academic Project, 2013).

84 Ibid.

society entered the Middle Ages in the 9th century and that this transition was accompanied by the transformation of language. The Old Church Slavonic language was created, developed, and mixed with the popular equipolent language, but remained proper to the political and social elites. In other words, the clergy and elite began to speak, and as follows, to think along a different rationality than the ordinary people. Kolesov believes the turning point of linguistic dominance to be the 15th century, when Rus saw the wide circulation of translations of Dionysius the Areopagite produced by the monk Isaija the Serb. The structure of the medieval Russian language was that of graduality. Graduality is a tripartite system fundamentally differing from equipolence in three major ways: (1) the distinguishing of three articles instead of two; (2) the arrangement of articles acquires a vertical hierarchy instead of a horizontal one; and (3) entropy descending from the upper term. For example, we can take the chains of God-man-beast (or God-Angel-man) and crown-trunk-roots. God occupies the upper position of grace, while man is the middle and good, and the beast is lower and evil. With the figure of the Angel, the logic remains the same, but shifts to a level higher: God is supreme and good, the Angel is pure, light, close to God, and mediates between God and sinful man. The same is the case with the tree: the crown is the top and bears fruit, while the trunk is in the middle and strong, and the roots are at the bottom, somewhere in the earth where there are no fruits, no wood to be cut, and therefore no use.

We can correlate the equipolent language system with pagan immanence, and graduality with the immanent-transcendence of pagan hierarchy, self-development, and self-knowledge, or with the Platonic emanations of the One from top to bottom and returning from bottom to top. In other words, in the gradual language system we witness the possibility of Divine manifestations in the world and man's ascent to the Gods. The gradation emerges from light and good to dark and evil, from more good to less good. The equipolent and gradual structures of language also fit into the principle of holism. In equipolent logic, designation is immediate, here and now, from the thing to what it points towards (and it can point to several things at once). An example in Russian is that of *klyon*, meaning a maple tree, and *neklyon* which, literally consisting of the components "not" and "maple", refers to a field maple. In the topography of graduality, there is the gradual unraveling and moving along the thread of indications and hints towards what is up or what is down. Yet here we can also see the preconditions for the realization of the gap between levels in the likes of the ontology of creationism.[85]

The Iron Age corresponds to the privative order of language. The latter is built on the radical opposition of 1 and 0, or one and the other, where the first is positive, is being, while the other is not, is negative, is nothing. If the gradual system breaks into absolute poles in which the higher completely denies any being of the lower (properly or tangentially), then the privative order simplifies language, discarding that which is complex and loaded with archaic, gradient meanings and notions. Alexander Dugin writes in his discussion of Kolesov's approach:

> If in an equipolent pair "no" or "not-" points towards another being which is endowed with autonomous being and deductively connected to the given being (let us recall the example of *klyon* and *neklyon*), and if this very "not-" means "not all the way" or "not entirely" in the gradual topography, then in the privative grammatical system the "not-" automatically means "zero" as "nothing", as "abyss", as a "hole" in the fabric of a being, thus launching into the fabric of language the "terrifying power of the negative" (*à la* Hegel).[86]

On the one hand, the privative structure of language is the structure of all modern science, automation, robotics, electronics, and modern digital thinking in terms of simple pairs. The most vivid representative of the positivist approach to language was

---

85 We dare to propose that the instantaneous leap from a thing to what it indicates, and the gradual passage from the thing to higher/lower/other is related to the gradual change in the quality of time and/or environment, i.e., the compacting of Space and the thickening of Time over the course of the fall from the Golden Age.

86 Dugin, *V poiskakh temnogo Logosa* [*In Search of the Dark Logos*], p. 25.

the Austrian philosopher Ludwig Wittgenstein (1889-1951). In his earlier works, Wittgenstein firmly argued that a thing exists only as an empirical unit, which is to say only as a signifier/sign with a corresponding single signification.[87] Meaning and the symbolic and holistic dimension are thereby cut off from the thing, and thus, according to this Austrian philosopher, philosophy should arrive at a system of precise correspondences. Only the "atomic fact" is reality. Therefore, all ontology, mythology, and archaic layers should be discarded (Ockham's razor), and philosophy must be built on a mathematical and strictly logical basis. This is the choice not of the "unit", but of "zero." On the other hand, in selecting a conventional unit, we can find religious fanatics within any tradition or without, whether in modern neo-paganism, spiritualism, and New Age sects. But it is the creationist religions which, by virtue of their metaphysics, are especially drawn towards this system, and within these religions today one can name some of the most lucid representatives of this binary thinking, such as Zionists in Judaism, Uranopolites and Protestants in Christianity, and Salafists and Wahhabists in Islam.

Based on this overview of Kolesov's concepts, it could be said that the pagan worldview dominated through language up until the 15th century, and thereafter went into the "underground" of consciousness. The orders of language corresponding to the Golden and Silver Ages of Tradition were preserved even longer until they were superseded by the distilled order of privativity.

Two Languages

Closely related to the question of the structure of language are the historical dimensions of official state language, and, along this line, of the formation of ritual language in contemporary paganism. Modern languages have been excessively subjected to globalization and, as a consequence, to the strong influence of the dominant "global" language of English. Globalization is linguistically reflected

---

87 See: Ludwig Wittgenstein, *Tractatus Logico-Philosophicus* (London: Routledge, 2006).

in the increased, immoderate growth of borrowings from foreign languages, the phonetic borrowing of words, and the latter's displacement of indigenous, similar notions. Insofar as language is a bearer of culture, in the latter case of a foreign one, the question of the penetration into an indigenous language of foreign words, or the question of the purity of a language, practically becomes a matter of national interest.

In Russia, the borrowing of foreign words increased rapidly starting under the reign of Peter I, who was oriented towards Europe in "modernizing" the Russian Empire along the templates of the former. Already during the reign of his successors, the question of borrowings was raised at the state level. Mikhail Lomonosov, while striving to introduce "globally accepted" scientific terms into the Russian language, added Russian counterparts and re-conceptualizations. Since the era of the Enlightenment and the reign of Catherine the II's "Enlightened Absolutism", three powerful waves of linguistic borrowing can be distinguished in Russian: from French, German, and English. English arrived only in more recent times, and its conductor was by and large not scholars and the aristocracy, as was the case with French and German before the Revolution, but merchants, marketers, and mass media. In order words, we are dealing with aggressive cultural expansion on the lowest level of semantics. As a consequence, pagan milieux exhibit a natural dislike for the new fashionable anglicisms and borrowings and appeal instead to the purity of language.

An interesting experience of preserving language can be found in modern Iceland. As an island state that initially had little contact with its neighbors, the Icelandic language has been preserved virtually unchanged with regards to Old Icelandic and Old Norse.[88] Iceland's national linguistic policies do not allow the introduction of borrowings and minimize their number in the language. A special commission is mandated to examine new

---

88 Icelandic was subjected to the heavy influence of Danish under Danish rule over Iceland, but the subsequent writers' movement engaged in purifying the language from borrowings.

words and to select their equivalents within the native language, often with reference to mythological motifs and kennings. This is, without a doubt, a positive experience.[89]

In the Russian pagan milieu, the construction of a ritual language has been undertaken with elements of reconstruction drawing upon folkloric materials (fairy tales, chronicles, folk songs), Old Church Slavonic which has to a certain extent preserved pre-reform Slavic words, and by employing the data of philology and linguistics. We will not delve into the question of how convincing the reconstructions of the "pagan" Russian language have been; rather, on the contrary, let us note that the problem lies in the fact that this language exists apart from everyday language and is far from the modern literary and everyday Russian language. Unlike in Iceland, where the old language has been preserved and been continuously "present", in Russia the proposed versions of the "Slavic language" are returning (even if reformed) after a long historical stretch of absence. Hence why today this language is limited to ritual practices, pagan literature, and to a lesser extent communication and guidance forming a counterweight to the influence of globalization.[90] This situation raises the following questions: How relevant are the words and linguistic constructions proposed in the "pagan" language for the contemporary pagan? Is not the option of internally reforming the modern Russian language, based on Kolesov's classifications with a preference for the equipolent and gradual systems, and with the introduction of adequate terms, more productive than opposing "modern Russian" with reconstructed "Slavic-pagan"?

It can be said that for contemporary, predominantly urban pagans, the proposed ritual language is alien. They might repeat these words during rituals and reading texts,

---

89 It is worth noting that the movement of Icelandic purists has made Thor's hammer the symbol of their fight for linguistic purity.

90 A most simple example: instead of the universally widespread American "OK", Russians can say *ladno* or *dobro*, and instead of "photo" (*fotografia*), *svetopis*, etc.

but this language still consists of "anachronisms" and "obsolete words." In other words, this language is beyond their everyday experience. The being of this language and the being of the pagan insufficiently intersect, and when they do, then only in the restricted circumstances of ritual practice. The mere repetition of words after a priest without understanding their meanings and being does not yield any spiritual experience beyond illusions. Therefore, more productive, albeit longer-term, would be the tactic of "soft power", or the gradual return into circulation of "obsolete" words, purifying language from borrowings, attaching priority to using Russian analogues and, if possible, moderating the use of "everyday" words in ritual practice in order to convey through rites not the external forms of beautiful words, but their meaning and the essence of the activity. Understanding the meaning of ritual acts and the importance of authenticity should ultimately, to close the circle, inspire greater interest in such authenticity and linguistic purity or, in other words, drive one to reveal for themselves the necessity of purifying their native language for the sake of advancing along their spiritual journey.

In light of the above, it is easy to consider the differences in approaches to things and phenomena both in their historical perspective (in terms of deterioration over the centuries and the degradation of estates) and in their qualitative, synchronic perspective. As noted above, the language of Tradition, the language of paganism (in its equipolent and gradual variations) is "next door" to everyday privative language, intersecting, contacting, and conflicting with it under various conditions. In this light, we can speak of the need to approach language as initiation, or initiation into language. Initiation into language is a qualitative passage to another thinking. Taking a stand to oppose the digital privative system means taking a step towards beautiful antiquity and accomplishing the work of transferring the ordinary language of communication into another structure.

Translation and Rite

The subject of initiation into language is relevant to the Russian-speaking followers of other pagan traditions (such as Hinduism, Odinism, and others) in another, non-structural sense. While for indigenous pagans (the small peoples professing shamanism) the preservation of language and connection between younger and older generations through language and culture in the situation of bilingualism (between formal Russian and their own folk's native language) is a more relevant problem, for representatives of other traditions in Russia the question of ritual language is just as relevant. This concerns the choice of language or the relation between the language authentic to tradition and the language authentic to the adept.

Among Russian-speaking followers of the Northern tradition, a variant has been put forth on the formation of two types of rite: Northern and Eastern.[91] The essence of the Northern rite lies attaching priority to one of the languages of this tradition's areal distribution, i.e., Old Icelandic, Danish, or Swedish and, with certain reservations, Norwegian, Proto-Germanic, Gothic, and so on. Rituals, rites, spells, amulets, and magic are to be conducted using the language of the tradition. The Eastern rite, for its part, bases itself on the use of the Russian language in ritual activities, partially with the employment of translations of similar terms from the source language into Russian, and partially with the use of transliterations of basic concepts. For example, the Scandinavian *draugar* (or *aptrgangar*) has, in the Eastern rite, become *nezhit'e* (the "undead"). One of the factors behind the emergence of the Eastern rite, besides the natural factor of its birth within the Russian-speaking environment, might be said to be the incredible complexity involved in translating Eddic and Skaldic songs, poems, and tales into a similar structure and form in Russian. The alliterations, kennings and heiti of the Gods originally constructed along the patterns of Icelandic or Old Germanic are practically

---

91 This account is based on the author's conversations with members of this tradition.

structurally untranslatable into Russian. It is possible to translate the literal meaning, but impossible to preserve the specific form of alliteration and magical component of the text so frequently associated with terms' runic writing.

To offer one example, we have chosen the Proto-Germanic language, as the basis of the branches of Germanic languages. If we take Old Icelandic, then the latter offshoot language takes us to the North, with all the corresponding specifics. In this linguistic context, the very term "Northern tradition" acquires strict meaning. Yet Anglo-Saxon takes us to the West, Gothic to the East, and Old High German speaks for itself. Proto-Germanic remains their common base, while its offshoots form a broad picture of the variations among traditions.

Proto-Germanic	Russian	English
Wiratīwaz wīsīþi,	Тиу людей учит,	Tiw teaches people,
Walamōdēr wikkōþi,	Мать павших ворожит	The mother of the fallen divines
Wiha-Þunraz warōþi.	Освящающий-Тунар защищает.	Sanctifying Thunar protects.

PROTO-GERMANIC IN RUNIC:[92]

ᚹᛁᚱᚨᛏᛁᚹᚨᛉ:ᚹᛁᛋᛁᚦᛁ:
ᚹᚨᛚᚨᛗᛟᛞᛖᛗᚱ:ᚹᛁᚲᚲᛟᚦᛁ:
ᚹᛁᚻᚨᚦᚢᛜᚱᚨᛉ:ᚹᚨᚱᛟᚦᛁ:

In Proto-Germanic, we can see the alliteration of all the first letters of each line with Wi- and the rhythm of endings on -þi, which we can see in the runes ᚹ and ᚦᛁ, whereas the Russian translation only indirectly echoes the rhythm of endings with -it / et.

---

92 Rowo Rekwaz, *Hwitaz Hrabnaz* (Svarte Aske, 2015). "Tiw of people", "mother of the fallen", and "sanctifying Thunar" are heiti for Wotan, Freya, and Thor, respectively.

The development of the Eastern rite was strongly influenced by the Northern, as the endeavor of translation demands knowledge of the language, understanding the meaning of the terms used, the names of the Gods, animals, and spirits. Otherwise, the situation would consist of the empty repetition of words or one or another kenning/heiti for the general description of a God without understanding their significant roles. This problem has partially been solved by the use of the Russian language and versification techniques, which guarantee understanding of the form and content of praises, hymns, spells, and addresses in practice. One example of the successful formulation can be seen in the line "The mother of the fallen [who] divines", i.e., Freya, the masteress of *seiðr*, divines. The Russian line does not use borrowings, but conveys the meaning and is maximally understandable to a Russian-speaking adherent of the Northern tradition. However, let us repeat, knowledge of this *Walamōdēr*, or Mother of the Fallen, Freya, is obtained only through the study of the language of the original, and this study is capable of enriching any Russian-language variants of sacred texts and praises with the specific forms of Germanic and Scandinavian stylistic devices and metaphors. Thus, the combination of the two languages can yield harmonious double contemplation of phenomena allowing one to overcome the limitations of modern language with regards to ritual praises and discursive constructions.

Russian Hindus find themselves in a situation similar to that of Russian Odinists. Instead of various Germanic and Scandinavian languages, they use Sanskrit, Nepali, and their variations. Russian Hindus preserve the use of original terms as much as possible by transliterating them. Meanwhile, the question of translating the Tibetan traditional teaching of Bon into the language of the Russian tradition has recently become a stumbling block between Tibetan and Russian followers. According to one hypothetical translation, the core of the Bon tradition, upon coming to different lands, was "dressed up" in different forms: for instance, upon arrival in Japan, Bon adopted Japanese characters and Chinese in China. In Russia it has been proposed to express the teachings of Bon in the images and names of Russian Gods, the God of Wisdom being Veles, the sacred bird Garuda being Gamayun, etc., with the aid of ethnography and linguistics. But such an approach, despite its logic and interest for comparative mythology, has found its opponents among some Lamas and their Russian followers.[93] The idea of such translations has been supported by Volkhv Veleslav, but at the present there is no active development of Bon in the language of the Russian tradition.

The ancient linguistic forms in which the Germanic Eddas, the Skaldic sagas, the Indian Vedas and Upanishads, as well as the Russian annals and tales were recorded have long since been lost, or simply are not a part of everyday life, thus remaining the domain of linguistics and dedicated followers of these traditions. Even the single most preserved language, Icelandic, has not saved Icelanders themselves from modernizing their thinking, abandoning the sacred-mythical worldview in favor of the secular-scientific one, even while their local linguistic space has names for modern technology and phenomena.

Thus, for Russian pagans, initiation into language, into the ancient form of language for the bearers of a tradition on their native land, initiation into equipolent and gradual structures, and Russian Odinists' or Hindus' study of the authentic languages of their traditions, remain especially important elements which influence both the external forms of adhering to tradition and thinking itself.

Vertical Initiation

Above we showed how the exoteric (outer) forms of pagan traditions have been preserved and passed on up to our times, that numerous everyday and "small-magical beliefs", rites, and other elements have persisted into the modern world. We have

---

[93] The author learned of this from conversation with Alexander Khosmo, the founder of the Bon Shen Ling education center in the Altai Republic, Russia, 2014.

also considered the question of initiation into the language and thinking of the pagan worldview and outlook. Now of importance is the question of the connection between the Divine and the worldly, the filling of the external vessel with the wine of Wisdom. It is at this point that we must examine the type of initiation which we referred to in the preceding as "vertical."

Unlike horizontal initiation, which René Guénon called "metamorphosis" (identified with Sanskrit *samskaras*) and which is available to every member of society, vertical initiation refers to the higher metaphysical dimensions, the knowledge of the higher estates, the links and transmissions between the Divine and the world and man. This concerns precisely the higher estates, the elite.[94] René Guénon and Julius Evola evaluated the possibility of such initiation in the modern world, to put it mildly, very critically. Guénon put in first place absolute continuity in the chain of initiation from person to person within an initiatic organization. Even if such an organization degenerated, the very fact of uninterrupted, inter-generational "overlapping" and "handing-off" was deemed capable of exerting initiatic influence on the adept in preparation. Evola, for his part, paid more attention to what we mentioned above to be the "rupture of levels" and the readiness of a person for initiation. On this preparedness for initiation and initiatic organizations, Evola said:

> In order for initiation to be possible, a center with people "capable of initiating" is necessary. This is especially clear today, given all the mystifications and hoaxes of all kinds: apparently in San Fransisco there is even initiation by mail, which cannot be spoken of without laughing. The obstacle lies precisely in the presence or absence of an individual or group capable of carrying out such action over the initiate. Two conditions are necessary for this: firstly, the initiate must be capable of initiation and, secondly, the initiating must be genuinely such. The former is associated with certain tests which the initiate must pass. In antiquity, before being honored with initiation, a person was subject to trials which largely affected the realm of instinctive reactions. There were tests by fire, by water, etc.

---

94 See: Guénon, *Perspectives on Initiation*.

In addition, it is necessary for these actions to affect the individual so that he is in some way predisposed to them and can feel within him what could be defined as the "thrust."[95]

Thus, vertical initiation is dependent upon one's inner state, the readiness of the initiate, external competence, and the initiatic quality of the organization (the community which is initiating the adept). The possibility of contact with living tradition is called into doubt, although, even in today's circumstances, it is not fundamentally denied.[96] Evola provides the illustrative example of the profanation of initiation through "initiation via mail", similar profanations to which can be encountered today in so-called "pagan priest schools" which teach over the Internet. These phenomena vividly illustrate the presence of privative thinking, which cuts off the "extra" archaic levels and legitimizes modern, profane means of "transmitting" sacred knowledge. In Evola's philosophy, reliance upon initiatic organizations (external environment or group) pales in comparison to the dominance of the principle of the rupture of levels, which Evola allowed for outside of initiatic milieux to the point of allowing for self-initiation in principle, about which Evola nonetheless critically said the following:

> If initiation is understood to be a departure to a level that is different from purely human, individual consciousness, then in this sense there are two possibilities: the first is the shortest path of so-called self-initiation, which has led no few minds to error. For example, the Anthroposophists, the Steinerists, claim self-initiation and, moreover, oppose the ancient initiations, which they consider obsolete compared to modern initiation of an individual, active, independent character. But this is a pure concoction, insofar as initiation of this type is conceivable only in exceptional cases. On the whole, initiation of a purely individual character, that is, without the intervention of a higher power, would be like Baron Munchausen's attempt to pull himself by his own hair. In order for initiation to

---

[95] From Julius Evola's final interview, conducted in his apartment in Rome (Corso Vittorio 197) on 27 December 1973 by Gianfranco de Turris and Sebastiano Fusco, available on YouTube.

[96] Seyyed Hossein Nasr, the philosopher and religious scholar who is held to be the leading Muslim philosopher today, does not rule out contact with living tradition in the East. See: Natella Speranskaya, "Interview with Seyyed Hossein Nasr", *Medium* (2013).

be effective, it is necessary to have an intervening factor which is transcendent with respect to the individual, and that can happen spontaneously only in extremely exceptional circumstances. Such initiation might be called wild, just as Rimbeau was called a "mystic in the wild state." It may happen that existential trauma itself leads to such an opening of horizons even if the one to which this happens is not cognizant of this. This might happen in the modern world, although in view of the ever-growing materialization (and we will add closing-ness) of the modern individual, such a possibility is becoming increasingly doubtful. This is what could be said to answer your question about "initiation in the modern world."[97]

Agreeing with the Baron in his conclusions that "self-initiation" is often the fruit of delusions and enthusiasm for fairly simple miracles, accidents, or simply unusual states of mind and the discovery of new facts, let us dwell on the two aspects which Evola considered key to self-initiation.

The first factor is the intervention of a higher force, without which there can be no initiation. If Guénon saw this expressed in the earthly continuity of chains of initiates, then we can point to this chain as in fact consisting of one link: that of the Divine within man. The Divine is on the top link of the chain, while man is on the bottom. The matter at hand is the direct initiation of man from God, the bestowing of insight or epiphany (Sanskrit *samadhi*). This is known in Kashmiri Shivaism as liberation spontaneously bestowed upon the adept by Shiva.[98] The metaphor of one link directly hints to the unity of the nature of the Gods and people, as well as to the fact that there exists between them merely a difference of levels. Such forms an obvious example of direct vertical initiation.

The second aspect is existential trauma, which ensures the inner readiness of a person and the "rupture of levels" which the adept might not suspect himself.[99] A most glaringly evident

---

97   See footnote 95.

98   Viktoria Dmitrieva (ed.), *Kashmirskii shivaizm. Naslazhdenie i osvobozhdenie* [*Kashmiri Shivaism: Pleasure and Liberation*] (Moscow: Ganga, 2010).

99   It is important to note that René Guénon strictly distinguished between initiatic tests and the profane "harsh experiences" which confront man in everyday life.

illustration of this principle can be seen in the alchemical metaphor of acquiring the philosophical fire. The first means of obtaining this fire is the immersion of a substance into a fire of such force that it burns everything, even the dampest of wood. This is the society of Tradition, in which the sacred is absolutely everything and every soul drawn to it is also sacralized. The second means is immersion into absolute ice, into the void. In this case, the fire burns within, as a radical divergence with the identity of the surrounding environment. This is the consciousness of oneself within the thickest of ice, in the darkest of nights, in the heart of Hell, and consciousness of one's difference from their surroundings. As Heraclitus said: "When night sets in, man lights a fire."

One important peculiarity of the Kali-Yuga, according to Veleslav, is that the path to Insight (Higher Initiation) is the shortest and at once the most dangerous and risky. Many of today's initiatic groups and societies are not genuine and do not constitute a qualitative environment in which adepts can be transformed. The accent of initiation and Spiritual Deed thus moves within man as he is submerged into the thick of the ice of Modernity. True initiation, Veleslav notes, is now possible only within. The shift in prevalence between initiatic groups (initiation within a community) and internal readiness (self-initiation) is illustrated in the following words of Veleslav: "True Tradition is the transmission of Living Fire, not the preservation of ashes. True Wisdom is Spiritual Insight HERE and NOW, not a memory of the past, no matter how great and glorious it was." A similar thought on the individual path was expressed by Evola:

> Therefore, those who, once they have assumed the karma of this civilisation, in which they wanted to be born, being most certain of their vocation, want to move forward, by means of their own power, to seek to reach metaphysical contacts, instead of making mere horizontal attachments to organisations which claim to offer them support in their search - those are naturally on a dangerous road, something which we want to underline explicitly here: they will be traveling in wild country without 'credentials' nor an exact geographic map. But, basically, if, in the profane world, one considers that it is natural that a

person of noble origin risks his own life when the goal is worthwhile, there are no grounds for thinking differently with respect to the one who, given the circumstances, has no other choice when it comes to the conquest of initiation and of liberation from human bounds.[100]

From the foregoing it follows that in the modern world the highest and genuine initiation is the destiny of inquisitive and selflessly dedicated individuals, more often than not loners on their own path. On the exclusivity and rarity of initiated individuals representing an elite (a higher estate), Guénon issued the following remark: "In the final analysis, we could say that the elite as we understand it represents the totality of those who possess the qualifications required for initiation, and who naturally are always a minority among men; all men are in a sense 'called' by reason of the 'central' position the human being occupies among all the other beings found in the same state of existence, but few are 'chosen', and in the conditions of the present age there are indeed surely fewer than ever."[101]

The existence of initiatic societies, as Guénon saw them, seems to us to be either dubious, or possible only in remote areas of Asia or, perhaps, among the shamanic peoples of Russia. This absolutely excludes all so-called New Age groups. It would be a great blessing if a pagan community or association were headed by an initiated person capable of guiding others on their own paths. But this is a rather optimistic view. Unfortunately, many stop on a certain, far from highest level achievable through horizontal initiation and in their corresponding inner work.

Aspects of Initiations in Contemporary Paganism

For clarity, let us examine a set of examples of contemporary pagan practices of initiation pertaining to initiating a new

---

100 Julius Evola, "The Limits of Initiatory Regularity", *Hercolano 2 English Library* (2005/2010).

101 Guénon, *Perspectives on Initiation*, p. 271.

member, whether from birth or older age "from without." Rites of initiation into traditions were not so widely relevant in antiquity insofar as children were already born into a tradition and, even before their birth, divinations were made about their fate and name, midwives divined over mothers during childbirth, and so on. Even before birth, a child underwent traditional rituals and influences. Later followed training in customs, the names and glorifications of the Gods and different spirits, and specific estate-related rites and skills, which were combined with age-related initiations and status changes (Sanskrit *samskaras*). Nor was initiation into tradition relevant for slaves, the subjects of empires on conquered lands, and other foreigners. For them, rather, the matter was of rituals of purification, offering first sacrifices and gifts to the Gods, and changing names. It is to this complex that the rites of initiation into the tradition of contemporary pagans are connected today.

A newborn member of a community is presented to the elements, the community itself, and is given a name. For example, there is the practice of carrying the child through a split rowan, in which the father splits the young shrub down the middle, but not to the end, and pushes the cleft sufficiently open. The mother shows the child to all the spirits, announces them as "small and weak, having done no harm to no one" and passes the child through the split tree to the father. Saying "there is no more child, for he is stuck in the tree", the father takes the child to the fire with the assurance that the spirits no longer terrify him. A similar ritual involves carrying a child through a door with a break in the threshold and, after nailing the threshold into place, announcing "the child has been brought to *Domovoi* [to the household god, into the home]." Both of these rites are designed to symbolically hide the child from impure forces and evil spirits, to present it to good spirits, the elements (fire, earth in the form of the tree) and to the household deity, so that the latter will not disturb him.

An important element of the first initiation of a child (their presentation to the spirits, elements, and the Gods) is the bestowing of name and presenting them to the Gods and *rod* by their name in the native language, i.e., the language of the tradition. In contemporary Native Faith, there is a separate ritual for granting people their name.[102] On the one hand, this ritual is consistent with the fact that traditions have long sustained various initiations for different ages associated with changing one's name. On the other hand, today this rite of naming is often the first step of entering a tradition and, often enough, into a specific community of fellow believers. In its structure and meaning, this modern ritual is often practiced with the so-called rite of "de-baptizing", i.e., the removal of the binding and influence of the previous, for instance, Christian, tradition. In essence, the rite of de-baptizing is an act of cleansing preceding the naming rite. Some Russian Native Faith priests distinguish one of the main significances of this rite to be the withdrawal of the person from the "pendulum of Christianity and anti-Christianity", which is to say the lifting of inner tensions and fanatical conflictedness, their liberation from spiritual burden for the sake of their further path. One historical example of such was cited by Henry of Latvia, who observed mass cases of de-baptizing among the populations of the Baltic states in the late 17th century, where Christianity had been the religion of the Saxon conquerors: "lo! The treacherous Livonians, emerging from their customary baths, poured the water of the Dvina River over themselves, saying: 'We now remove the water of baptism and Christianity itself with the water of the river. Scrubbing off the faith we have received, we send it after the withdrawing Saxons.'"[103]

Volkhv Veleslav has proposed a simple - and in this simplicity, incredibly pure and strong - rite of purification and naming: the initiate is to go out into the field in the morning, wash themself with dew from the grass, greet Nature and the

---

[102] Contemporary Native Faith more often uses later, two-component Slavic names such as Vladi-mir, Vele(s)-slav, Bogu-mil, Dobro-slav, etc., and less often Scandinavian ones, such as Olg/Olga, Ragnar, etc.

[103] Henricus Lettus, *The Chronicle of Henry of Livonia* (transl. by James A. Brundage, New York: Columbia University Press, 2003), p. 34.

Sun, and introduce themself by their new Russian name. In this variant proposed by Veleslav, we at once see references to self-initiation, openness to Nature during this simple rite, and to the importance of one's native language for communicating with the Gods, a point on which we have dwelled in the preceding.

The Problem of Counter-Initiation

One of the single most controversial and problematic points in the philosophy of Traditionalism as developed by René Guénon is the question of "counter-initiation." Guénon understood "counter-initiation" to be altogether specific forces and organizations which consciously lead one away from the path of initiation and knowledge of the Eternal Wisdom of Tradition. The notion of secret organizations leading people away from the good of initiation, and the assertion that such is universal, has given fertile soil for the development of various occult conspiracy theories which, to us, seem to be but shaky ground. The universalism of initiation vs. counter-initiation, similar to the absolutism of the categories of good and evil, is a creationist element within Traditionalism. It is telling that Guénon himself called counter-initiatic forces by the Islamic term *Awliya es-Shaytan*, i.e., "saints of Satan." In Guénon's version, representatives of counter-initiation stand behind all the negative phenomena and aspects of the modern world: degradation, materialization, and the disappearance of spirituality.

Yet in speaking of universal counter-initiation and initiation in such a manner similar to creationist absolutism, it is necessary to issue an important clarification of meanings and terms. On this matter, there is a certain confusion in "classical" Traditionalism which we have already mentioned in agreement with Dominique Venner. We have established the fundamental difference between two metaphysics, two ontologies: creationism and manifestationism. Insofar as pagan traditions primordially exist within ethno-religious ties, as is suggested by the very terms *iazychestvo* and "paganism", we cannot project universal categories onto them. From people to people, language to language, and tradition to tradition, there exists a variety of forms, subtle nuances, and patterns of Divine manifestation. In the case of manifestationism, the truth is that of the One Source which manifests itself in numerous manifestations, traditions, languages, and peoples. Speaking of universal initiation and counter-initiation, therefore, does not follow. Every people has its own ritual forms of initiation, names for the Gods, and caste and estate divisions, with the overlapping of many nuances that make people unique in their own paths. All of them express the one sacred structure as described in detail by Plato and his followers. In the social dimension, this structural constant was revealed and described by Georges Dumézil. Wherever an initiatory path reaches its culmination, where the language of a people and language of a tradition end, where the Divine Silence sets in - the achievement of this state can be spoken of as initiation into the One that is beyond names and forms, languages and the effable. This is the upper pole of the sacred vertical, the axis of the cosmos, whose manifestations we can see in the vertical (pyramidal) hierarchy, in initiations, and the patriarchal *Logos*.

The ontology of creationism asserts the quantitative oneness of the Creator and the singularity of his creation - the world and man. The Abrahamic religions of creationism are emphatically not folkish, i.e., not tied to ethnic belonging and language.[104] The people of Christ or Allah are not a specific ethnos, but first and foremost a religious identity independent of ethnic belonging. Here we can mention the universalism of Abrahamic norms for the whole world, i.e., for all who adopt their faith and symbol. The universal categories of good and evil, God and Satan, and their confrontation over the human soul are proper to creationism. In this lies Guénon's conceptualization of universal forces of counter-initiation, along with a mixing of the metaphysics of paganism and Abrahamism and the generalization of initiation as a common, universal phenomenon. As we have already pointed out, universalism is typical of creationism, whereas

---

[104] A partial exception to this is posed by Judaism which, although still fundamentally open, imposes serious restrictions on non-Jews who have adopted the faith.

the unity of a multiplicity of traditions in the Supreme Divine corresponds to manifestationism.

The notion of universal counter-initiation falls apart in the face of pagan traditions and their numerous currents, paths, estate- and caste-related sects within any given tradition. Would one initiatic path within one sect be counter-initiatic from the standpoint of another? Given the possibility of worshiping different Gods within one pantheon, which are emanations and faces of the Divine One, one can only speak of different forms and paths of initiation, just as there are different patron Gods for different estates and corresponding cults.

A much more complex question is the relation between one tradition and another: is a foreign faith "dignified" or not? In Ancient Greece and Rome, we can find examples of historians, travelers, and philosophers describing the traditions of other peoples and finding analogues within their own, determining matches between, for instance, Egyptian and Greek Gods, featuring the very same estate characteristics, functions, and attributes to recognize the dignity of worshipping them as their own Gods, albeit under different names. Attributing absolute counter-initiatic quality to another tradition is right only within creationism, just as Christianity rejects Judaism as an old, no longer valid testament, and Muhammad as a false prophet. Islam, in turn, recognizes genuine initiatic quality only for itself, considering Judaism and Christianity to be preceding, distorted versions. Judaism does not recognize Christ and Muhammad as prophets at all and considers Christianity and Islam to be sects. All three of the Abrahamic religions, for their part, deny any initiatic quality on the part of the non-Abrahamic traditions. This situation is, overall, the root of the purely creationist phenomena of religious wars. Colorful confirmation of this can be seen in the following lines from Deuteronomy:

> If anyone secretly entices you - even if it is your brother, your father's son or your mother's son, or your own son or daughter, or the wife you embrace, or your most intimate friend - saying, "Let us go worship other gods," whom neither you nor your ancestors have known, any of the gods

of the peoples that are around you, whether near you or far away from you, from one end of the earth to the other, you must not yield to or heed any such persons. Shem them not pity or compassion and do not shield them. But you shall surely kill them; your own hand shall be first against them to execute them, and afterwards the hand of all the people. Stone them to death for trying to turn you away from the LORD your God, who brought you out of the land of Egypt, out of the house of slavery.[105]

Pagan traditions, on the other hand, postulate a fundamental plurality of paths, qualitative by virtue of polytheism: the veneration and serving of one or another God is not a contradiction in relation to other Gods. The imagination of "counter-initiation" becomes most lucidly irrelevant in the case of the veneration of light Creator Gods and dark Gods of Death. It may seem that Tantrists and Aghori, meditating in cemeteries and eating raw meat, are far removed from Divine initiation in comparison to Brahmins and Kshatriyas, but in reality, this difference is a gross illusion. The Russian Traditionalist philosopher Alexander Dugin, commenting on the notion of counter-initiation in relation to the Abrahamic traditions, declares a similar view of "heresies": "More often than not, religious non-conformists ('heretics', 'Satanists', etc.) are seeking the totality of sacral experience which the representatives of orthodoxy cannot offer them."[106] On this basis, it can be concluded that intra-traditional differences, currents, and sects can be understood, for instance by Hindus, without negative connotations and not as "counter-initiatic."

More substantive phenomena impeding the initiatory path are blind repetition (formalism), such as following a teacher or guru, or copying and mixing diverse forms and practices, as well as what is called "following what is not one's own path." To paraphrase a famous expression, it is better to badly follow one's own initiatory path than to follow someone else's well. Imitating the external, romantically alluring path of a teacher or holy

---

105 *New Oxford Annotated Bible*, Deuteronomy 13:6-10.

106 Alexander Dugin, "Counter-Initiation: Critical Remarks on Some Aspects of the Doctrine of René Guénon (1998)", *Eurasianist Internet Archive (1998/2019)*. See also: Dugin, *Puti Absoliuta* [*The Ways of the Absolute*] in *Absoliutnaia Rodina* [*Absolute Homeland*].

volkhv leads essentially nowhere and gives nothing but illusions, whereas making mistakes on one's own path imparts the adept with experience and development. Living life according to foreign patterns, the adept in a certain sense always remains before the gates of initiation without ever stepping over the threshold. Inability to restrain one's emotions and passions, falling into certain states such as depression, exaltation, or apathy, excessive infatuation with novelty, external appearance, and attaching primacy to changes of status, knowledge and, finally, power - all of this forms an obstacle on the initiatory path, but can also be utilized as challenges which must be overcome in the likes of an existential test. As is well known, the first stage of initiation is fraught with the great danger of falling into temptation and the illusion of supposed omniscience, when an adept, seeing the first ray, imagines himself to be the light. These reflections on counter-initiation are more of a personal character and can be seen as fairly common human vices and lower principles which draw a person away from the Spirit to matter.

Thus, the search for counter-initiatic elements in tradition leads us to that which hinders, erodes, threatens, and attacks the Divine world order, the sacred hierarchy, the Gods and heroes, kings and toilers, Empires and communities.

The Triumph of the Titans

In speaking of the opposition between Modernity and Tradition, the secular and the sacred, the initiatic and the counter-initiatic, we fall into a situation of duality, in which there is the "sacred all" and "non-sacred all." This is the logic of privativity: 1 and 0. This view offers two pictures of a world in a state of war. We correlate the pole of the sacred with the Divine, with Olympus, Nordic Asgard, and the interpretation of the whole cosmos from this topography. The language of myth is more than sufficient for describing the whole cycle of time and history, including those modern ideas proclaiming to reject myth and the Divine. This means that in order to determine who or what is operating behind the mask of Modernity, we need to attentively look at those who have always and everywhere been the opponents of the Gods.

The matter at hand is the chthonic element, the titans at war with the Gods, the monsters threatening men and the cosmos who are opposed by the Gods and heroes. In Greek mythology, the Titans try to seize Olympus. The hundred-handed giants, cyclops, the snake Python, and other chimeric beasts act as the evil threat to all the living and sacred. When speaking of the "non-divine", we, in fact, have in mind something imbued with its own particular life and logic - titanic in nature. With some caution, we can also propose that their own thinking, worldview, Logos, and views harbor their own sacred value.

In Greek myth, the titans persecute and dismember the God Dionysus. In the Scandinavian tradition, Thor is the eternal opponent of the giants, the *jötnar* and *þursar*, and in the eschatological battle at Iðavöllr field, the Gods and men clash with the wolf Fenrir, the snake Jörmungandr, and the dead from Naglfar led by the liberated Loki. Fenrir swallows Odin, and the snake is killed by Thor, but only after managing to fatally poison him. The end of the battle is marked by the most ancient fire-giant of Muspelheim, Surtr, chopping down the world tree Yggdrasil, with which the sacred hierarchy collapses and the Gods disappear from the world. In Hinduism, the Devas are opposed by the Asuras, the warrior demons at times of part-bestial forms, and the hordes of *Rakshasas* (the undead) threaten man, who asks for defense from the Gods. In Slavic myth, Perun, like many other Slavic heroes, battles the snake Gorynych, Likho, and various evil spirits, the undead, demons and beasts.

The adversaries of men, the heroes, and the Gods are therefore the chthonic creatures whose origins date back to the genesis of the cosmos. They can be found present in myths as relatively neutral primordial beings (such as Gaia, Kronos, and Ymir), and as respected with a certain awe by people as ancient and mighty, often being attributed the status of Gods. The snake-mother Gaia, the giants, and the titans are among the first to appear out of the pre-eternal Chaos. From the abyss of Ginnungagap, the first worlds to appear are those of the frost and fire giants, Niflheim and Muspelheim. Across many traditions, the cosmogonic event is described as the dismemberment of one of the first, most powerful titans and the creation of the world out of his remains. Thus the Northern Gods created the world out of the body of Ymir. This act is the affirmation of Divine order and the dominance of the sacred expressed in a hierarchy in which the Gods occupy the top. Henceforth the world is ordered, tripled by the Divine hands and their laws and built according to them. The remaining titans are cast down into Tartarus or pushed into the periphery of the cosmos, into lower and distant worlds. Monsters are chained or defeated and go into hiding from the Divine light within the folds of matter. To be more exact, they have been in hiding, until today.

With this point, which demands our utmost attention and effort, we are taking a step forward in Traditionalism. From the point of view of "orthodox Guénonism", perhaps such would appear as a step to the side. But let us repeat that we by no means seek to detract or diminish the merits and authority of the first Traditionalists. Rather, we aim to reveal the further directions laid out by them. Our step forward consists of arguing that the notion that Modernity is an anti-traditional, non-mythological, non-mythical, profane world is a misconception. The world has never stopped developing according to traditional, mythical patterns and trajectories.

When we characterize our time as 'anti-traditional' or 'secular', as a time in which all that is 'archaic' has supposedly been overcome as 'infantile human delusion', then we are depriving ourselves of the right to call this era by its name in terms of tradition - the Kali-Yuga, the Iron Age. If we speak of Modernity as the Age of Koshchei (the "Koshchny Age"), as the epoch of Ragnarök, then we impart it with traditional characteristics and a traditional description. If it is the Iron

Age that indeed surrounds us, then this is no mere matter of 'anti-traditionality.' We are within Tradition here and now. We always have been. The surrounding situation of collapse rather fully fits into traditional eschatological prophecies. Metaphysical laws are still in effect and the wheel of the Celtic Cross continues to turn. We are in the very heart of the night. We live in a traditional world in which the Gods have retreated and been concealed. We live in a traditional world in which the titans and chthonic material monsters are gaining the high ground in the battle with the Gods. The titans, chthonic as their Great Mother, are always antagonistic to the Gods. This is a continuation of the very first war, as a result of which the victorious Gods organized space into an ordered cosmos. The Greek tradition named this war *Titanomachia*.

Thus, we can look at tradition and the modern world not only through the historical view of degradation, the gradual change of eras in time but also as synchronicity. We are dealing not with the cyclical and linear time of Tradition of Modernity, but with vertical time. In vertical time, Golden, Silver, and Iron mankind exist always, simultaneously. They are closely intertwined. Today the Iron element dominates, and the bearers of the Gold of the Spirit are driven into the marginal periphery alone. The modern world, being a success of the titans in their war with the Gods, has its very roots in and is embedded in Tradition itself. This world is that of the titans, the worlds of Hell, iron forests, swamps, and oblivion. These are the numerous Vedic worlds of hell, Naraka. This is the Helheim of the Scandinavians, the Tartarus of the Greeks. In the Golden Age, the heroes went to these distant worlds and lands for glory and battles or expunged their native lands of incomers from these realms.

These are the cults and sects of the Great Mother of matter, the adepts of the titanic figures, the natural philosophers, Epicureans, and atomists in the lines of Democritus and Xenophanes. Democritus developed the doctrine of atomic materialism, laying at its core the being of the indivisible atom of which there is an innumerable quality and void in-between. According to legend, Plato bought up all of Democritus' books and burned them. Xenophanes attacked Homer and Hesiod, urging others to not pay attention to the *Titanomachia*, and presented the Gods as the fruits of people's fantasies (on which point he was close to Euhemerus). Xenophanes believed the beginning of all to be land and water, that is to say the chthonic and hypochthonic elements.

In the *Chandogya Upanishad*, the difference between the perceptions of the high Brahman and the prevailing cults of the Devas and Asuras was described very clearly, as can be seen in the following passage:

Seventh Khanda

1. 'The Self (Atman), which is free from evil, ageless, deathless, sorrowless, hungerless, thirstless, whose desire is the Real, whose conception is the Real - He should be searched out. Him one should desire to understand. He obtains all worlds and all desires who has found out and who understands that Self' - Thus spake Prajapati.

2. Then both the gods and the devils (*deva-asura*) heard it. Then they said 'Come, let us search out that Self, the Self by searching out whom one obtains all worlds and all desires. Then Indra from among the gods went forth unto him, and Virocana from among the devils. Then, without communicating with each other, the two came into the presence of Prajapati, fuel in hand.

3. Then for thirty-two years the two lived the chaste life of a student of sacred knowledge (brahmacarya). Then Prajapati said to the two: 'Desiring what have you been living?' Then the two said: 'The self (Atman), which is free from evil, ageless, deathless, sorrowless, hungerless, thirstless, whose desire is the Real, whose conception is the Real - He Should be searched out, Him one should desire to understand. He obtains all worlds and all desires who has found out and who understands that Self. Such do people declare to be your words, Sir. We have been living desiring Him."

4. Then Prajapati said to the two: 'That Person who is seen in the eye - He is the Self (Atman) of whom I spoke. That is the immortal, the fearless. That is Brahma."'But this one, Sir, who is

observed in water and in a mirror - which one is he?'" The same one, indeed, is observed in all these", said he.

(*Seventh Khanda*, 1-4), p. 268.

Eighth Khanda

1. "Look at yourself in a pan of water. Anything that you do not understand of the Self, tell me." Then the two looked in a pan of water. Then Prajapati said to the two: "What do you see?" Then the two said: "We see everything here, Sir, a Self corresponding exactly, even to the hair and finger-nails."

2. Then Prajapati said to the two, "Make yourselves well-ornamented, well-dressed, adorned, and look in a pan of water." Then the two made themselves well-ornamented, well-dressed, adorned, and looking a pan of water. Then Prajapati said to the two: "What do you see?"

3. Then the two said: "Just as we ourselves are here, Sir, well-ornamented, well-dressed, adorned - so there. Sir, well-ornamented, well-dressed, adorned." "That is the Self", said he, "That is the immortal, the fearless. That is Brahma." Then with tranquil heart (santa-hrdaya) the two went forth.

4. Then Prajapati glanced after them and said: "They go without having comprehended, without having found the Self (Atman). Whosoever shall have such a mystic doctrine (upanisad), be they gods or be they devils, they shall perish." Then with tranquil heart Virocana came to the devils. To them he then declared this mystic doctrine (upanisad): "Oneself (atman) is to be made happy here on earth. Oneself is to be waited upon. He who makes his own self (atman) happy here on earth, who waits upon himself - he obtains both worlds, both this world and the yonder."

5. Therefore even now here on earth they say of one who is not a giver, who is not a believer (a-sraddadhana, who is not a sacrificer, "Oh! Devilish (asura)" for such is the doctrine (upanisad) of the devils. They adorn the body (sarira) of one deceased with what they have begged, with dress, with ornament, as they call it, for they think that thereby they will win yonder world.

Ninth Khanda

1. But then Indra, even before reaching the gods, saw this danger. "Just as, indeed, that one [i.e. the bodily self] is well-ornamented when this body (sarira) is well-ornamented, well-dressed when

this is well-dressed, adorned when this is adorned, even so that one is blind when this is blind, lame when this is lame, maimed when this is maimed. It perishes immediately upon the perishing of this body. I see nothing enjoyable in this."[107]

Further, the Chandogya Upanishad tells of Indra's return and comprehension of the teachings of Prajapati on the higher Brahma (Para Brahma, Nirguna Brahma), while the Asuras remain satisfied with Virocana's answer and teaching. Today, these gloomy words and reverence for the body have spread everywhere, becoming global. Space has been squeezed with transportation networks and entangled in the network of their interpretations and meanings which exclude their sworn enemies, the Gods and their order, from the legitimate worldview. The titanic saints are the scholars of the Enlightenment. Departments of the physical-mathematical sciences are the altars of the monsters from which *Jörmungand* spits his venom. The infamous opposition of the science of the Enlightenment to traditional institutions represents one of the most vivid manifestations of this war.

The chthonic element of the Great Mother, who gives birth to the chimeras, monsters, and titans, is multifaceted and manifests itself in the most diverse, at times very subtle forms, enveloping and replacing with doubles and copies that which seems to be Divine and sacred. A literal interpretation of the myths of Fenrir's devouring of the sun as an event in which a wolf of large physical proportions is to swallow the sun-star is one such ploy preventing the enlightened layman from doubting the truth of its tale. "For this does not happen", he will say. Thus, the meridian threads leading to many meanings and interpretations of a higher order are cut off from myth. In this way, it is easy to discern the privative system of modern language.

Modern paganism has been more focused on opposing formal Christian institutions and culture, thus largely

---

[107] *The Thirteen Principal Upanishads* (trans. by Robert Hume) (Oxford: Oxford University Press, 1921), p. 268-270

existing within a dualist logic. But the picture of the world has more than two dimensions. Paganism largely ignores the influence of Modernity on itself and on Christianity, Islam, and creationism in general. It lets in the subtle, evermore obvious infiltrations of titanic elements and ideas, which eventually replace the forms and orientations of the sacred Gods. The world is more complex than the confrontation between pagans and Christians and the religious and scientific worldviews. Focusing only on this front diverts us from the puppeteer behind the whole situation, that of the winning (but not victorious) titanic element. Truly, setting one's opponent against another, diverting attention from oneself, is one of those wonderful techniques of war which, according to Heraclitus, is the father of all things.

We are faced with two languages for describing reality which absolutely encompass the entire cosmos and which offer explanations and interpretations for all phenomena and things in all times and corners of the world. The first language is the Olympian, Divine language, the language of the Sacred. This is the language of the Nordic Gods of Asgard, the language of the Aryan Devas of India. Its description of the world is revealed by each people in their traditions, languages, epics, legends, and culture. We have given a concise, structural definition of this language in the preceding sections. This language describes Modernity as the offensive of monsters, the lower, gloomy, melancholic worlds, those ruled by the giants (*jötnar*) and the Asuras, the dwelling places of the *draugar* (or *aptrgangar*) and *Rakshasas*, the (un-) dead. These are the oceanic abysses, dungeons, the chthonic, dense layers of matter. This is Lokasenna, or Loki the Titan's assault on all the Gods as he questions their goodness and status, just as the learned men of Modernity lay the principle of doubt at the foundation of knowledge.

The second language is the language of matter itself, the Great Mother and her offspring. This language treats Heaven, the Gods, all of their order, and everything which they ennoble with their light as negative. The titans have neither forgotten nor forgiven their expulsion to Tartarus and have kept their hate and desire for revenge on the Gods. Their language is that of strict correlations devoid of Sacred, higher dimensions. This language emerged in Modernity and became the language of science and secular culture. It is Wittgenstein's atomic fact, the privativity of 1 and 0, the displacement, derision, and disregard of religiosity as a marginal, naive, infantile, unscientific worldview. Looking at the sky, the person initiated into the Divine will see the blue cloak of the God Odin through the holes of which the stars shine. Looking at a tree, they will see Yggdrasil, the cosmos, and themselves. But the person initiated into science and materialism, when looking at the sky, will recall that science has enlightened him as to the fact that the sky is blue because of the refraction of light in the atmosphere and by virtue of the retina's perception of waves. They do not see Odin's cloak. These two languages are antagonistic. Each of them contains a compressed state of the other clothed in corresponding meanings. Each language denies the logic and thinking proper to the enemy's opposing language.

For men, heroes, and Gods, matter is that which must be transformed with Sacred templates and ideas to be given form. The Gods bestow upon people tools and teach them the skills of gathering, plowing, hunting, blacksmithing, ceramic-making, parenting, the way of the warrior, the artisan, and other callings. From the point of view of the Gods, the Earth is a field that must be cultivated in order to bear fruit. The earth bears fruit from the Divine seed, thus crowning their union as reflected in the Gods of Sky and Earth's granting of fertility from both earth and sky. But for the Great Mother and her spawn, Divine interference is pain, invasion, usurpation, and overthrow. They disturb her self-sufficient slumber, her oblivion, and she therefore enters into a confrontation with them. The Gods tear apart her children and establish order, creating the world out of their remains.

The Sacred view of history reveals to us the process of fall into the Iron Age, the diminishing of the Divine presence, the violation of the sacred hierarchy, the blurring of the estates and their relations, the abandonment of traditions and customs, the problematization of initiation, and the profanation of doctrines. The chthonic view reveals the triumph of progress, development, the expansion of the spaces conquered by the titans, and the thickening of time. Such is the return to calm monotony, the absence of genuine events, and the gentile repetition of the same, the "today, prolonged into tomorrow." Evolution, progress, and development ultimately discard the unnecessary, archaic ideas "about some gods" so that man, enlightened and freed from the "dictatorship" of traditional norms, can do whatever he wants, whether play with religious toys, study the structure of an atom, or go see a movie at the cinema. With universal equality, rights, and opportunities, he can fill his stomach and fall asleep in front of the TV. The Great Mother absorbs him into her womb of materiality.

In the modern era, the pagan worldview and pagan philosophy have been dealt many blows and infiltrations by the creationist traditions, and have become even more vulnerable and wounded by the influences of the titanic element. The chthonic element constructs its own set of illusions for each estate, in a special way blurring their own natures, the directions and spiritual paths in life proper to them. The widespread opinion that the conflict at hand is between the modern, physical, scientific, mechanical view and world and the religious one (expressed in the tradition of creationism and most lucidly represented by European Christianity), and that therefore this does not concern or affect pagans, is incorrect. Moreover, from the point of view of pagan thought, the assumption that it is possible to support science in debunking Christianity and the latter's authority is one of the greatest misconceptions. For science, as understood in the illustration of Modernity, there is no difference between the Gods of manifestationism and the God of creationism. Science, as an instrument, as one of the weapons of the titans, is aimed against any and all hierarchies and Divinities. The principles of physics, mathematics, and positivist-rationalist science are transplanted into the sphere of the humanitarian and social sciences, into ideology and politics, and thereby infect the active estates (*à la* Plato) of auxiliaries, warriors, heroes, and all passionary people realizing their nature as rulers.

Yet another tool is used to erode traditional institutions, to emasculate the sacred depth of traditions, to occupy the abandoned throne of the supreme God and pose as him: the chthonic element can produce religious forms. In antiquity, we can see such in the suppressed cults of the Great Mother (not to be confused with Mother Earth, the Goddess of Fertility), the cults of the titans, the castrates of Hekate-Cybele, etc. This front still requires careful and risky immersion.[108] Today, the religious toys of the titans are lite, shallow, and mixed out of various components (syncretism) and "soft-theology" in the likes of New Age religions, cheap spiritualism, and entertainment. "Tradition" thus becomes another commodity for consumption.

Infiltrations have also affected the purism of language. In keeping one's language maximally pure, translating borrowed and new terms, and using analogies from one's native language and culture, a subtle substitution of values and worldview can be revealed by just which field the analogies for a new word are chosen. By translating the term "Internet" as *Niti* ("threads"), like those which helped the heroes find their way or escape, we see the endowment of a new word with a positive connotation associated with heroic myths. At the same time, it would be apt to attach to such demonic tones. The use of technology is pure black magic, the deceptive gifts of the subterranean dwarves which should be used within a whole complex of protective magic and verbal determinations through the demonic element. The value of linguistic purism can be called into question if one merely quotes words and does not pay attention to the importance of negative interpretations of the translations of new terms.

---

108 A foundational examination of the titanic element from antiquity to the modern era has been offered by Alexander Dugin in his *Noomakhia* volumes, for which see the bibliography below and the English-language previews available at *Eurasianist Internet Archive*.

It may seem that such a strict and radical delineation of a dichotomy between the Divine and Titanic is a metaphysical feature of the creationist bent, which would, therefore, be misleading. Yet war always requires rigidness and decisive strategies. Even the absence of absolute, much less moral categories of good and evil does not annul the heat of battles and the necessity of fulfilling fate and the due. In the mythological picture of the world, there are now two camps, each of which has its own ontology, whether metaphysical or strictly physico-mathematical. In myth, the former is normative, while the second is denied even the possibility of expression. When the Gods look at matter, they see only matter, the Platonic khora. Alongside ontology, two languages for describing the world are affirmed. The language of myth is inclusive, including the titanic and chthonic and calling it as such, as a dangerous enemy. The language of the titans, in its modern apogee, declares its exclusivity and exceptionality. It says that it is not titanic, for "there are no more Gods and titans, those relics of the childhood of mankind." It hides such all the while as it, in its privative system, expresses its element. The sacred picture of time says "the further the worse", while titanic linear time reassures: "the further the better, the more developed." The language of the titans, their logic, their values, and their philosophy - let us not be afraid of admitting such - are revealed and opened up in Hesiod's final ages. The gates of Tartarus are wide open. Tartarus is now everywhere.

Modernity and creationism can be placed in the pagan worldview: in the language of paganism and pagan traditions, we can describe our reality and history as the ongoing battle of the Titanomachia. In the language of paganism, we can describe all the theories of Modernity, all its black miracles and subterranean gifts. Modernity, for its part, claims that the language of Tradition cannot describe all of its social, biological, and scientific-technological progress. Modernity postulates only the total exclusivity of its language, its gnoseological racism and the privativity of its point of view alone. In the binary equation of 1 and 0, the titanic element denies the Divine dimension its very existence. It "drowns" it into nothing. As Nietzsche wrote on European nihilism, its sweeping away of everything traditional and its reduction of everything to naught, to Nothingness: "The desert grows: woe to him who harbors deserts within!"

The examination of various aspects of the influence of Modernity on paganism, its influence on creationism, and the relation between manifestationism and creationism in this revealed optic will be the subject of our further chapters. Carefully but strictly untangling the cunning designs of ideas, metaphysics, and influences, we will purify the pagan foundations, the Essence, and more clearly define its perspectives and prospects. Further, in speaking of Modernity, "anti-traditionality", and counter-initiation (or "initiation" into the cults of matter through the rejection of the Divine), we will understand as a matter of course that we live in Tradition here and now, and that we are fully living through its eschatology. We are participating in it.

It is necessary to think of Traditionalism and Modernity in a different perspective, not in the diachronic view which presupposes that Tradition was, that within it Ragnarok already happened, and thereafter came Modernity in which there are neither Gods nor titans, but in the synchronic view, in which *Ragnarök* is being fulfilled here and now, in order to reveal that the phenomena of Modernity are the new faces of the titans, the jötnar, the Asuras. In this regard, we believe that the insight that we are living in precisely this era and situation today is, without a doubt, an important and necessary step which every pagan seeking the Divine in our days must take.

***

III
PAGANISM, MODERNITY, AND POSTMODERNITY

By taking the side of the eternal beyond Time, the side of the Divine element, and by affirming the heroic type in the era of Modernity, no choice remains but to declare and wage war - in difficult and confusing circumstances in which the enemy is strong, cunning, ignoble and, at first glance, everywhere and nowhere. But we shall remember that the Gods always defeat the titans, and the heroes will gain glory and find immortality. Thus, it is necessary to boldly oppose low modernity with high antiquity and to fulfill the due.

Dharma and the Due

The notion of the due is one of the foundational, eternal elements of paganism which affirms sacred hierarchy and order. The creationist traditions rely on morality as a component that links and binds people, the sources of this morality being fear of punishment in the afterlife, public censure for sinfulness, and the need for suffering and repentance. This principle found maximal expression in the Catholic insistence on the first sin of Eve and Adam, which renders all people a priori the heirs of the original sin of the first people. Paganism, being fundamentally pure and innocent, is based not on moral fear but on the natural Divine order. The sacred hierarchy is expressed on the level of the community and the state in the pyramid of social estates, on the level of the estates themselves, and through such in each and every person, in proper, due behavior. Man is not an individual, but the estate and caste of his inner, deep nature - the gold, silver, or iron of his soul. Abiding by the due of one's estate binds and maintains the whole body of society (the body of *Brahma*) and the cosmos. The Sanskrit root *dhṛ* means "to hold, to maintain", and it is from this that the word Dharma, meaning the universal law of being, duty, and moral pillars, is formed. This interpretation of *Dharma* traces the development of the three estates as the Sacred Law of the Gods, the main law of being for all living beings, as duty akin to military service and will, and as moral law for the broad strata of society. *Sanātana dharma* ("eternal order") is the self-designation of Hinduism in India.

The analogue of Dharma in Russian Native Faith is the notion of *Lad*. As the order of *Rod* is present in everything, *Lad* is the orientation for pagans. Living in *Lad* with nature, society, kin, and oneself is achieved through *Lad* in the soul and the world. The words *naladit'* ("to arrange"), *uladit'* ("to settle, to order"), *ladno* ("fine", "alright"), *skladno* ("smoothly, harmoniously") and others are derived from the etymological root of *Lad*. Volkhv Velimir proposed an alternative designation for *Lad* with the term Darna, borrowed from the contemporary Lithuanian pagan community of Romuva founded by Jonas Trinkūnas (1939-2014). Trinkūnas admitted such to be a borrowing from the Hindu "*Dharma*", but justified this with the fact that the idea of a universal cosmic law maintaining world order is common to all Indo-European traditions. In Velimir's view, Darna is complemented with ritual practices and social, ethical, and moral dimensions. However, this form has not become widespread among pagan communities.[109]

In Odinism, a close analogue of Dharma is Wyrd, or higher destiny and fate. Close to Wyrd is Rok, whose meaning is close to that of fate. We can see the latter in the word Ragnarokr, which can be translated as "Fate of the Gods" (or "Lords"). Here we can see a close interweaving of the Divine order, the due, and fate. The pagan understanding of fate is not tragically and pessimistically understood as total predestination in the likes of the physical determinism of material laws. In fact, following

---

109 Velimir's version of Darna is recognized by his Koliada Vyatichi community and the Circle of Pagan Tradition (see chapter IV, section "Personalities" below) which are close to the periphery of pagan philosophy and life in contemporary Russia. See: Roman Shizhensky, *Pochvennik ot iazychestva: mirovozzrechenskie diskursy volkhva Velimira (N.N. Speranskogo)* [*A Pochvennik from Paganism: The Ideological Discourses of Volkhv Velimir (N.N. Speransky)*] (Nizhnii Novgorod: Volga Typograph, 2014).

Dharma, *Lad*, Wyrd, or Rok means realizing one's own nature. Fate is thus the realization and consciousness of the nature of one's path, its mileposts, and the path which a person must traverse independently.[110] As already said above, following one's path, one's nature - which is to say observing Dharma and the due - is the highest good, honor, valor, and pledge of spiritual advancement. It is better to follow one's own path poorly than another's well. In the epic of Beowulf, the fusion of duty and fate finds culmination in the maxim: "Fate will unwind as it must!"

Non-observance of the due, of Dharma, is called *adharma* and leads to *avidya*, which is "ignorance" and "delusion."[111] In the *Devi Mahatmya*, Kalika urges Raktabija to give up discourses unbecoming of a warrior and to fulfill his *dharma* - to duel with her and die. Fidelity to one's nature is the Latin *semper fidelis* ("always faithful") and can be compared to the Sanskrit *bhakti*, meaning devotion to the Divine in different forms. The Divinity is the higher element of an estate, and so the Gods of priests, the Gods of warriors, and the Gods of tillers and artisans are the theological expressions of the due and internal nature of man. These propositions find expression in the ancient *maxims suum cuique* and *nosce te ipsum*, "to each his own" and "know thyself."

Dharma in the Kali-Yuga

We have already described the views of the due peculiar to each estate in general terms. Artisans, farmers, and producers are more focused on the family, the clan, the continuation of the life of the *rod*, agriculture, and handicraft. A wide clan and large family means more stability and guarantees survival. Accordingly, the magic of the third estate is predominantly concerned with spells and charms for wealth, harvest, and health. The valor of

---

110 The Union of Slavic Communities of the Slavic Native Faith's 2013 pamphlet, *Slavianskaia Rodnaia Vera* ("Slavic Native Faith") terms the immutable laws of Rod "*Prav*'".

111 The term *dharma* would later be replaced in Indian philosophy by the earlier, similarly-meaning term *rita*.

a warrior, *fides*, consists of deeds of power, war, dominion, and heroism. Relations with family and kin are treated dynastically and defined by the due honor and dignity of future sons for the name of the father, and on the part of the father himself for the God. The value of life is defined by death in battle, as opposed to the death "in the manger" which does not frighten farmers. While some may believe that others are defending ordinary people and the folk in wars, warriors treat wars, both offensive and defensive, as occasions for the affirmation of their sovereignty, their will, and the establishment of order in society and state borders. The duty of a warrior is to be a warrior. This does not mean defending merely one commandment and seeing the world in the light of moral dualism, but none other than to follow their nature. Warriors on both sides of the field of battle are equally fulfilling their warrior *dharma*. Neither side is morally evil or unfulfilling of the due. The priestly *nosce te ipsum*, which was inscribed in the forecourt of the Oracle of Delphi (in Greek: γνῶθι σεαυτόν, *gnōthi seauton*), maximally expresses the duty of this estate. Knowing oneself to be Divine is an inner work. Its external manifestation is the performance of priestly functions, instructing, teaching, communicating with the Divine, fulfilling cosmic myth together with all the other parts that constitute the one whole body of *Brahma*, and the transmission of the light (and order) of the Gods to men. We can see the motif unifying the estates to be following the Divine and strict adherence to its respective sides. In different estates, devotion to Divine forms (*bhakti*) finds different expressions which must be seen not as a sum of three elements, as parts, but as one expression in multiple ways.

In relation to Modernity, the Dharma of the farmer, the warrior, and the volkhv can be expressed briefly as *fidelis est Deus*, which can be interpreted in a general, high sense as consistent and peremptory insistence on the Sacred view of the world against its profanation and denial. On the estate level, this means following the God-archetype (*à la* Dumézil), nature, and Wyrd of one's estate. In other words: living maximally in correspondence with *Lad*. In the words of Wulf Grimsson: "I would call on fellow pagans and Traditionalists to consider the true Radical nature of our path. It is not enough to be "weekend pagans", we must transform our whole lives, every minute detail. We need to limit our exposure to the pernicious influence of fundamentalism, monotheism, and materialism and reprogram ourselves to be true pagans."[112]

On a practical level for any pagan community or organization existing today, this means the community's obligation to observe the divisions and reverence of hierarchy. The small reflects the greater, in this case, the archetype. In this view, for example, the practice of democratic administration based on equal voting by all members of a community is a profound self-contradiction. The community should be, or should strive towards being, one organism (as in the image of Brahma), and its parts should follow their nature and be subordinated hierarchically. Let us emphasize that this approach is not an apology for tyranny or dictatorship, a point which we will certainly discuss further later on. Rather, fidelity to the Divine, estate-nature, and the God-archetype which it expresses is the pledge of a healthy organization in which the head of the community, whether a person of Kshatriyan or Brahmanic nature, leads and guides the community towards its goal. In this case, the pretensions of artisans, and more generally people of the third estate, to mandate the reckoning of their opinion (by which is implied that their opinion should always be realized) are groundless. The will of the higher estates excludes the dictatorship of the minority that is democracy within communities.

Modernity and Estates

Continuing our examination of history as degradation across eras and corresponding estates, let us dwell in more detail on the estate basis of Modernity. We have already said that over the course of regression from the Golden Age to

---
112 Askr Svarte, "An Interview with Wulf Grimsson", *Svarte Aske* (19/6/2013).

Modernity, the Bronze Age comes under the dominance of the third estate consisting of farmers, artisans, and merchants. If we analyze the Indo-European estate system, we can discern that merchants, as a particular type of people, belong to the Semitic realm and were a newcomer element among Indo-European peoples. As a foreign element belonging neither to the estate of warriors nor priests, the merchant is placed at the very bottom of the hierarchy, being marginal even among the third estate of producers. Not formed into a fully-fledged estate or intra-estate caste, merchants came to represent "professional" enclaves with ethnic specificities. A vivid example of such organization and incorporation into the Indo-European system throughout history is the case of communities of Jews. The intolerance that has accompanied them across history has its roots in their fundamental foreignness to the Indo-European structure of society. Another historical example of the rigid confrontation between mercantile civilization and Indo-European estate-based society was the Punic Wars between Carthage and Rome. The outcome of the Three Punic Wars was the destruction of Carthage from the face of the earth and the cursing of the places where it stood. As demanded by the Plebeian politician Marcus Porcius Cato the Elder, Carthage was destroyed.

With the growth of cities and the gradual disintegration of the upper estates in the era of the Enlightenment, the disparate and unformed groups of merchants and servants of the aristocratic strata began to form a fundamentally new identity, that of the urban bourgeoisie. In his Republic, Plato distinguished a particular type of governance, timocracy, in which decomposed warriors begin to behave like merchants. We can see in this the shift of the source and nature of power towards the monetary, mercantile element, towards oligarchy. The bourgeoisie finally took shape in Europe in Modernity, which led to a series of bourgeois revolutions, the overthrow of monarchies, and the establishment of a new social formation at whose heart were laid secular, Enlightenment concepts of equal choice (*à la* John Locke). The bourgeois revolutions overthrew the sacred-estate hierarchy (although the quality of such by that time remains up for question) and established the positivist view of society as a sum of equal individuals. The vertical was thus abolished in favor of the horizontal. Julius Evola characterized this shift as the coming to power of the unbridled Shudras, who in the long run opened the gates for the liberation and power of estateless elements in the likes of pariahs, chandalas, and *avarna* outcasts.

The bourgeoisie's assault was aimed against all three estates, in principle being fundamentally anti-estate and not merely a criticism of specific, temporary decline in defense of the estate ideal. In other words, as we have repeatedly emphasized, fierce modernist criticisms aimed against Christianity should not be seen as apologetics for pagan values. We shall not speculate on just which forms of criticism might have manifested if paganism was in the place of Catholicism in Europe, but we will merely stress that such bear a fundamentally anti-sacred character independent of tradition and metaphysics. As things were, the secular values of autonomous morality and scientific atheism as a form of knowledge (*à la* Ockham's razor) were established against the priesthood, and the Church was deprived of authority. From the feudal warrior aristocracy, the renunciation of privileges and the extortion of legal taxes on the peasantry were demanded. Yet from the point of view of the enlightened bourgeoisie, the peasants themselves were "ignoramuses" akin to ditch mud who still believed in "religious relics" and were incapable of accepting the light of scientific facts. Here we can recall that despite the active Christianization of the elites, the peasantry preserved double-faith, a special alloy of pagan and Christian culture, for a long time.

The estates, already marked by degeneration and the adoption of the Abrahamic tradition, took a step towards betraying healthy adherence to their nature. The poisonous ideas of the Enlightenment slowly penetrated the ranks of Christian clerics, and the Catholic and Orthodox Churches bowed to the authority of enlightened monarchs. In the Russian Empire, the radical turn to the West which would define

Russia's fate up to the Revolution of 1917 was committed by Peter I, who abolished the patriarchate and created the Holy Synod. In Europe, the dominance of Papal authority fell along with the monarchs. The power of the military aristocracy was attacked alongside the monarchs, being as they were inseparable - the Emperor, after all, was the supreme commander in chief. In Russia, where the Tsar's entourage consisted of his generals and admirals, Peter I undermined the closed character of the estates as expressed in the dynastic form of the transmission of heritage, and introduced tables of ranks which would be reformed and survive up until 1917. Peter's Table of Ranks professed the aim to "give honor to those willing to serve, not to insolents and parasites", i.e., to enable those of talent from among the lower classes to "become people" and gain access to the higher hereditary nobility. This initiative eventually turned into an invasion of the top by the bottom which, as an exception to be recognized, included those who were outstandingly honest representatives of their nature.

It was in the third estate that pagan remnants were longest of all retained, brought all the way up to the modern era, woven into the context of Christianity and thereby powerfully affecting such. But outside the estate hierarchy, the third estate disintegrated and found new expression in such an artificial formation as the proletariat. The proletariat is the concentrated chthonic class construct of Modernity. If the third estate of farmers was the lower boundary of estate society which scooped its being into an organic whole (the body of Brahma), of which it remained part and at once under the patron Gods of its estate, then the proletariat represents an artificially assembled community of free workers liberated from the Divine, holistic dimension and seeking only employment and hire. The proletarian was below the third estate, being the configuration of marginal and fragmented elements. This class was torn away from the earth and "chained" to the machine and production through technology, which is to say that which in the mythical view of the world is not described at all. Pagan antiquity knew no machines, assembly lines, hydroelectric power stations, or other such inventions. The closest such known image was the figure of the blacksmith, traditionally belonging to the zone bordering the lower worlds. The forge was located far from the village, and the mining of metal was associated with descending into the underworld and harsh physical labor which, with the help of tools and training from the Gods, resulted in the incarnation of ideas and things out of formless matter. The proletarian is a step away from the blacksmith inspired by the Gods to the soulless operator of a machine, the turner of monotype mechanical parts according to a precise drawing meaning nothing more than its given dimensions. In forging a sword, the blacksmith performed a demiurgic act, transforming matter and creating a weapon for a warrior - an act which connected estates. The sword itself was not merely worked metal, but was something unique which revealed the myths, legends, tales, and beliefs pertaining to this Sacred weapon of war, from tribal and folk stories of heroes and battles to the very final battle between the Gods and monsters. In forging a sword, the blacksmith participated in the war that generates all (à la Heraclitus). Hence why the creation of such products was accompanied by the reading of spells, charms, the performing of rituals and praises, and smiths themselves were allowed to read sacred texts. On the difference between artists and artisans, Evgeny Golovin remarked:

> I have already said that the Greeks paid little attention to matter. Of course, they paid some attention to it, but far from the attention it receives now. This was because the ancient world was incredibly 'formal.' Form was the main thing and matter was nothing. If an artist, for example, found an outline, silhouette of an amphora, he was immediately called a great artist; he didn't have to embody any idea in a work or anything. If a sculptor said "I see a statue of Zeus so-and-so" and sketched a few lines in the air or in the sand, he was already considered a great sculptor, and people would say to him "Yes, you found the outline of a God which suggests a soul." Some other people could make a sculpture or an amphora and would not be considered artists, but artisans, that is, in the ancient world the artist and artisan never coincided. A painter would not put himself through the labor of taking up brushes and painting a canvas. He would

simply say: "I want to do this, this is my idea. "And if you are a fool", he would say to the artisan, "if you don't understand, then give me the stylus, give me the brush." He would very casually show something and say "Here's what should be done, like this and that" (all gesture-drawn in the air). The artisan or the poet, as he was called (because "poet" in Greek meant a "man of work" and *poete* meant "that which is done", "work", or "craft") would grasp these instructions and take off with them...Thus the "poet" would take the brush, the materials, and fellows like him and they would make it happen. So when they say "Oh, the statue of Phidias, the statue of such-and-such", it is necessary to consider that this was, frankly speaking, the idea of Phidias or the idea of the architect of the Parthenon. These people played no role in construction and concretization. This contempt for matter on the part of creative people reached the point that even the great engineer and inventor Daedalus never built anything himself - neither the labyrinths nor Icarus' wings. All of this was simply done according to his plans, according to his instructions. Nothing more, because it was believed that such people are close to the gods and will never stoop down to work with matter. That's what matter was in the ancient world.[113]

The situation is different with the proletarian turner, woodworker, painter, electrician, or builder, who receives a piece of metal into his hands and grinds clear detail out of it according to a drawing. This is the detail of the conveyor, identical to the previous and the resultant, precisely coinciding with the dimensions indicated in the drawing, which represents a pure profanation of knowledge by engineering-mathematical calculation. A real product is an imprecise, uneven work bearing the traces of the human hand of its maker. As long as the turner rotates the part and adjusts the blade, he does not have to think about anything - thoughts about millimeters and sizing have nothing to do with the serious dimension of thinking whatsoever. Moreover, the accurate creation of individual parts does not mean that the proletarian participates in anything greater than the process of production and the fulfillment of a plan. Surrounded by matter configured according to the templates of physics, engineering, and electronics, he produces the very same

---

113 Evgeny Golovin, *"Dionis-2"* [*Dionysus* 2] (Moscow: New University, 2005).

matter given in these plans. The apogee of this production is the creation of machines using the very same machines. This is the pure multiplication of matter, devoid of spirit, any Sacred dimension, and any connection to other estates and classes.

If the bourgeoisie consisted of newcomers, foreign elements, elevated commoners, the servants of warriors, and townspeople, and thereby still retained some idea of the due, albeit in the form of an empty vessel of wine which still gives off an aroma, then the proletariat consisted of the collapsed, failed third estate, of foreign incomers, slaves, Shudras, and so on. Proceeding from the fact that the fall into the Iron Age entails the growth of materiality, the displacement of spirituality and the qualitative by the quantitative, we can see how in the philosophy described by Karl Marx the chain of revolutions brings with each new turn evermore liberation from the spiritual (the Sacred) in favor of the material. When the bourgeoisie took shape and the bourgeois revolutions were accomplished, the still reproducing estate hierarchy was destroyed. A most striking example of this was the execution of Louis XVI even though he originally granted considerable concessions and abandoned many of the attributes of the upper estate. According to Marx, the bourgeois revolution should be followed by the revolution of the proletariat. The proletarian rises up against the bourgeois who is insufficiently material in comparison to the proletariat, i.e. gives off the aroma of aristocracy, is smarter, more educated, and has manners and pedigree.

The era of Modernity, of the bourgeois geniuses of the Enlightenment and the proletarian masses, unfolds under the enrapturing reign of the titan Prometheus. Whereas hitherto this figure had never drawn so much attention and never became a model or orientation, Modernity becomes the time of Prometheus unbound. Examining Modernity as the manifestation of the titanic element, the German conservative thinkers and brothers Friedrich Georg and Ernst Jünger pointed out the following characteristics of Titanism: "Titanism makes itself known wherever life is understood only as labor and the world as a world of labor...The titans do not need prayers, they are worshipped through labor."[114]

Prometheus is the offspring of the titan Iapetus and the brother of the titan Atlas, who stood on the frontline of the Titanomachia. Prometheus inherited their logic, their nature, and their drive to assert their power. Hesiod described Prometheus' creation of people out of clay, subsequently endowed with soul and spirit by Athena and Zeus. In this myth, we can see the animation and spiritualization of the purely material creations of the titans and people of a particular nature, that of red clay. In sterile form, the mankind created by Prometheus was spiritless and thoroughly material. Prometheus himself is a special figure who is in some sense higher than the other titans. He is close to the Gods of Olympus and acts on their side during the Titanomachia, and is also close to man. However, at the same time, Prometheus is neither God nor man. In fact, he would become the reason for the Gods' withdrawal from people and, ultimately, the reason for the Gods' punishment of people and modern decline. Prometheus' first deceit of Zeus took place in Mecone, where he rearranged the different parts of humans' first sacrifice of a bull, as a result of which Zeus ended up choosing the worst part of the sacrifice, the bones instead of the meat, and therefore deprived people of fire. The cunning Prometheus stole the fire and returned it to the people. For revenge, Zeus sent Pandora, "beautiful evil", down to Earth, who was married to the simpleton Epimetheus. With the opening of her box, Pandora released into the world all existing misfortunes. Yet the main "exchange" was Prometheus' "returning" - instead of the Fire of the Spirit burning in the heart of man - an ordinary light, an incandescent lamp, which he claimed to be fire itself. Thus, instead of lighting a fire from within themselves and returning to their ever-present divine nature, people are deceived by imaginary material light. It is in this spiritual vein

---

[114] Friedrich Georg Jünger, *Griechische Mythen* [*Greek Myths*] (1947); *Die Titanen* [*The Titans*] (1944). Translation from author's Russian.

that the myth of Zeus' seizure of Fire and its replacement by Prometheus, as well as the above-cited saying of Heraclitus on man lighting a fire at night, should be understood.

In Ancient Greece, one could meet supporters of Prometheus, particularly Aeschylus, who saw history not as degradation, but as ascent. Aeschylus praised Prometheus as the giver of fire, heat, and light who defended people from the jealous tyrant Zeus. Since this titan was close to man (that is to the humanity which he created) and since man accepted his gifts, Zeus responded to this threat to the sacrality of Olympus with the decision to rid this generation of people with a flood. This instance can be seen as the erasure of the potential of an ancient proto-proletariat, a godless people of clay. Zeus, as the father and a good, strict, just God, accepted a sacrifice from Deucalion, the only survivor of the flood. Deucalion sacrificed in the manner his father, Prometheus, did. In other sources, such as Aeschylus's account, it is said that Zeus forgives Prometheus and the titans. Yet the version of this myth which became most widespread and received the most attention was that in which Prometheus was punished by being chained to a mountain in the Caucasus, where an eagle feasted on his immortal liver daily. In the consciousness of modern man, this plot is supposed to emphasize the despotism and violence emanating from the Gods. Prometheus was freed by Hercules, who thereby wished to demonstrate his power (as a typical act of a hero asserting his will) and, according to Hesiod, convinced Zeus to calm his wrath.

We can observe a similar scenario in Scandinavian mythology in the figure of Loki, who is born from the *jötunn* (giant) Fárbauti. According to several versions, Loki participates in the creation of men, acting in the trinity of Odin-Hoenir-Lóðurr under the latter's name, and bestows upon man warmth, human feelings, and passion. Loki was accepted into the family of the Gods and frequently accompanies Thor on his campaigns, only to later betray the Aesir following a number of troubles of which Loki himself is the cause. Loki was also punished by being chained to a stone and tortured by animals, in particular a snake that sprinkled venom onto his face.

Prometheus is the cult figure of the thinkers of Modernity. He becomes the hero of time. Napoleon, Marx, Freud, Byron, and Wilson were all fascinated by Prometheus, whom they thought to be a figure representing radical liberation. Indeed, his rebellion against the Gods is consonant with the scientific "discoveries" of the secular zones of the physical world. Prometheus is the bearer of the light of reason (*ratio*), of civilization, and represents progress. This trickster titan, according to Oswald Spengler, liberates technology and revokes senses of proportion. Prometheus' gifts in the Modern era are Ford's assembly line and Edison's artificial light. In Modernity, the children of the stolen fire create the ideal humanity of their father: a spiritless, material society. The unbound titan is the unbound man left to himself as an individual. It is telling that the Rockefeller Center in New York is the site of a bronze statue of Prometheus covered with gold gilding. The light of Prometheus, his "divine" gold, and the "golden age" of the progressivists are deceitful fakes.

Prometheus penetrated the pagan world as an element from Greek myths and epics and through the culture of the Enlightenment. He was smuggled in as an element of myth lacking proper reflection. Prometheus is indeed a part of myth, but how he is treated in myth itself (and not only him, but any chthonic figure) must be taken into account. Thus, we arrive at the necessity of attentively - even painfully for modern paganism - examining the constructs of Modernity which have become the "natural" and "objective" given basis of mankind. It may seem that "thus it has always been" or that this is the "natural state of affairs and the course of things", but this is a blind delusion that negatively affects paganism in its rise.

The constructs of Modernity are the titans' constructs, and the strategies of Modernity are their strategies.

The Constructs of Modernity

Modernity sets itself up in total opposition to traditional society on all fronts. For each and every thesis of the world of Tradition, Modernity puts forth a contrasting antithesis.

Modern paganism is beset by the mixing of these two pictures of the world, two languages, and two fundamental paradigms of worldview and world-description. This gives rise to conflict and an unhealthy situation in which, over the course of the unfolding of pagan philosophy at the present stage, the turn to the Sacred and the Gods has not proceeded without the use of the constructs, ideas, and language of those very opponents of the Gods, the language of the modern world. Insofar as these two languages are total, it is impossible to simultaneously and equally operate with them both. Wherever there are elements of the structure of the language of Modernity, the structure of the language of Tradition has been displaced. This can be aggravated by the deployment of these structures when, to describe the same thing, a corresponding adequate idea and construct from the language of Tradition could be used. For example, we can say that the sky is blue for it is Odin's cloak, or we can put a person in their place by seeing their nature, their estate. On the other hand, for instance, in polemics with Abrahamism criticisms of the latter's dogmatism have been based on scientifically debunking its myths, e.g.: the sky is not created by the God Yahweh or Allah, but is a gas shell surrounding the earth, the atmosphere of which, by virtue of the refraction of light, takes on a blue hue. In its very structure, society - like man in his unique reality - is incapable of accommodating the two total interpretations of the languages of Modernity and Tradition, as society is able to maintain only a finite number of connections. There is also the span of public attention. Modern people can easily name a hundred different commercial brands but cannot distinguish ten different herbs. A child can figure out the intricacies of a virtual world or a computer, but meeting a real pig in a village would incite culture shock, not to mention that understanding that a wild boar is not simply an animal, but a sacred one which is daily consumed by the Einherjar in Valhalla, is unthinkable. The child may hear of such formal knowledge but can remain distant from and ultimately forget it. On such profanation of knowledge, Julius Evola wrote:

> The foundation of the imperial hierarchy must be based on knowledge: "The wise should govern", Plato already said - and this is a central, absolute, definitive point in every rational order of things. But nothing would be more ridiculous than to associate this knowledge with some technical competence, positive science, or philosophising speculation: instead, it coincides with what, from the outset, we have called Wisdom, a traditional expression used by both the classical West and the East. Wisdom is as much aristocratic, individual, real, substantial, organic, and qualitative, as the knowledge of the 'civilised' is democratic, social, universalistic, abstract, leveling, and quantitative. Here again, there are two worlds, two eyes, two different visions, opposed against each other without any abatement.[115]

The same is true for society, especially modern industrial and urban society. Philosophers, scholars, politicians, and other actors of the Enlightenment drew the attention of society away from the higher, qualitatively rich ideals then expressed in creationism to lower, material, quantitative ones. Cyclical time became too "difficult" and overloaded with archaic motifs and meanings, and the attention of society came to be seized by linear time and progress which promises prosperity in the future once and for all. At its peak, this has yielded hundreds of different types and varieties of coffee on the shelves of hundreds of retail chains, in which the rule is: if you want it, take it; if you don't like the red design of the store, step into the one decorated in blue or yellow and buy the coffee in the purple jar. Man ends up being incapable of thinking about the meaninglessness and unnecessariness of such diversity. His attention is directed horizontally: one hundred TV channels, a million websites, two or more candidates in elections, etc. Rising up and paying attention to the vertical dimension, looking to the Gods or inward to one's nature, which

---

115 Evola, *Pagan Imperialism*, p. 98.

is one and the same, becomes impossible and unnecessary. The clutch of material totality is iron-strong. The bear is turned from the beast of Veles into a member of the bear family of the order of carnivores, merely a bear as a unit of biological diversity. This comparison could be continued indefinitely to reveal the totality of ubiquitous contradictions.

Man as Estate and God	Man as an Individual of Biological Origin
Society as the body of Brahma, structured according to Sacred hierarchy	Society as a contract of equal, free individuals with differing capacities
The origin of the world and beings as the manifestation of creation of the Gods (myth)	Physico-biological view of the world and the evolution of matter and species (science)
Knowledge through holistic grasping of an "object"	Knowledge through determined causal-effectual theories
Sacro-centrism	Materialism

Here we can recall Jünger's remark that the titans do not need prayers, only labor for the production of goods. This is the service of the titans, their praise through the multiplication of the number of products. Thus is accomplished the oblivion of the Gods in the waterfall of the development of the production of commodities and knowledge of the material level of the world.

Over the course of the breakdown of the identity of medieval Europe and Christianity, a window opened up for paganism in the form of an opportunity to escape the pressure of the dogmas of creationism. This partially happened, but the heralds of the titans, the sons of the Great Mother, broke free more rapidly and successfully. Although partially free from Abrahamic oppression, paganism has still found itself in the periphery of the world's major ideological and philosophical disputes and fronts.

Therefore, the exposure and rejection of the language of Modernity and its constructs is of categorical importance to the development of pagan philosophy. Paganism, being part of the periphery to which it has been consigned in the historical period of the past several centuries, has partially encountered this language and its constructs proposed in the philosophical and social spheres. It would be impossible to cover the horizons of this topic even in a series of works, so we shall point towards merely the most principal and axial lines, in the direction of which it is necessary to continue systematic and attentive work in the future.

The Human

One maxim which expresses the holistic perception of man in traditional societies is the Hindu formula "Atman is Brahman." Atman is the inner "I" of man, while Brahman is the absolute being, embracing both object and subject. In Brahman, in holism, the divergence between "object" and "subject" is resolved through unity. Man has never been equal to himself alone, he is always a man and something else. Hence the mysticism of masks and persona, i.e., personalities and guises.

The humanity of the Iron Age combines the elements of Earth and Sky, the chthonic clay of Prometheus, and the soul and spirit of Athena and Zeus. In Odinism, the first people, Ask and Embla (the Ash and the Willow), represented logs thrown ashore, the wood which Odin-Hoenir-Lóðurr imparted with soul, spirit, and warmth (emotions). It is noteworthy that the Greeks also called matter *selva*, i.e., "wood", which emphasizes that the material element of the human being is antecedent and primary. Man is the marriage between the Sky (the paternal element, God, the soul and spirit) and Earth (the maternal element, matter, and flesh), and as such can be imagined as a circle with a point in the center in which the surrounding periphery is structured around the center of the spirit. Around the Sacred axis which passes vertically through this center, matter is constructed, spiritualized, and cleansed of the strictly material, chthonic element. Today this center has been confiscated, just as Zeus took Fire away to Olympus.

Every tradition claims its own myth of the origins of man. Modernity asserts the evolutionary theory of the origin of species based on the theories of Lamarck, Cuvier, and the culmination of Darwin and his follower's theories which complemented and refined this concept. Today this theory is generally accepted and predominant, while all others have been pushed into the marginal periphery of scientific attention. The theory of the biological origin of species and evolution from simple to complex forms is the direct translation of the idea of progress into the animal world and anthropology. This theory replaces myths on the origins of animals as sacred beasts of the Gods (e.g., the *vāhana* of the Gods in Hinduism) with explanations of adaptation to environment, the principle of natural selection, the accumulation and transmission of traits (genotype), and the finite formation of external appearances (phenotype). For the latter, the horse is a result of evolution, the accumulation of changes dictated by the environment and passed on across generations that have been sifted through natural selection so that the best survive so as to pass down better genes indefinitely. The myth of the birth (in complete form, without evolution) of the horse Sleipnir out of Loki's womb is for the modern scientist at best a cultural anachronism. Man in this view appears to be the product of many millennia of biological evolution from apelike *homo erectus*, Pithecanthropus, and Neanderthal man to *homo sapiens*, therefrom entering the stage of social evolution as described, for example, by Marx and Engels, who posited an evolution from a primitive communal system (primitive, unconscious communism) to capitalism and onward to (conscious) communism.[116] This idea of progress in the form of evolution was applied to the social sphere most colorfully in the American ideology of Social Darwinism.[117]

The most basic question of the origin of man should reveal within a pagan the depth and adequacy of himself to tradition. The combination of these two pictures is impossible. Claiming that the Gods created natural selection and gave impetus to evolution is equally irrelevant to both religion and science, and

---

116 See: Friedrich Engels, *The Origins of the Family, Private Property, and the State.*

117 A vivid representative of Social Darwinism was the Russian-emigrant-cum-American-philosopher of "objectivism", Ayn Rand (Alisa Zinovyevna Rosenbaum). See her *Atlas Shrugged* (1957).

comparing the idea of the evolution of species from ape to man to the myth of the creation of man out of the ash tree is impossible in principle. This position holds true for any other question of genesis, whether of man, animals, estates, or the cosmos. Let us emphasize in particular the declared universalism of the scientific language which stands in opposition to the plurality of myths on the origins of man across different traditions. Every tradition, every paganism and every people explains the origin of man and his folk with a special myth which traces the *rod* back to mythical heroes, Gods, or powerful beasts which are in turn revealed to be sacred animals of the Divine. Against this, the scientific picture of the world and the theory of biosocial evolution are asserted to be the one and only universal story of all of humanity, one which denies any religious worldview and myth.

The pagan chooses myth. Man is man and something else, another dimension which originates in God. Atman is Brahman. Modern man chooses evolution, for which man is only man, an individual.

Humanism

Humanism arose in the Renaissance as a worldview of "humanness" which put man at the center of the cosmos as the highest value. Humanism calls for understanding man democratically, ethically, and morally, which is to say that we are dealing with man as liberated from theology and hierarchy and generalized according to the lowest level of criteria. History has known attempts at creating a theistic humanism, such as that which successfully penetrated and decomposed the Catholic Church and would be inscribed in varying proportions into other denominations. The atheistic, theistic, classical, and all other forms of humanism are all united by their placing of the individual at the center of attention and their belief in his good intentions, capacity for self-perfection, and his fundamental value as the measure of all things.

We are interested in the basic question: What is a Human, and how does the Human correspond to the individual? The answer supplied to this question is what defines forms of humanism and lies in the field of taxonomy, the classification of living organisms among which man is considered. This posing of the question leads us to examine humanism and the taxonomies of man from anthropological positions, insofar as "anthropology wants to be a philosophical method, while humanism is a kind of variety of secular, autonomous morality which claims universalism. Speaking of the choice of anthropology as a starting point, we emphasize that we are interested in the philosophical aspects of humanism as a moral phenomenon."[118]

Alongside a number of extinct species, *Homo sapiens* forms the genus *Homo* (Man), with the ensuing species being the human races. If human is taken to be a species, then the genus would be animals or mammals. The possibility of such taxonomical operations suggests that the human is a universal taxonomic notion. The relevant and basic question thus becomes that of the relation between the individual and the human as a genus. In considering this question, it is imperative to take into account a very important yet subtle thing: the classification of man is an act of self-knowing and reflection. In other words, in classifying objects, man selects one or other characteristics and unites them into a group structured into a hierarchy. But in classifying himself, man engages in reflection, as he is both the subject that classifies and the object being classified. Therefore, the basic question of the relation between the individual and the species/genus is the act of self-knowledge and self-consciousness.

As a result, the question "Who is a human?" (or the question "Who am I?") has two answers, two paradigms: the individual human and the human-*eidos* (species). This picture can be illustrated by the metaphor of a circle with a point in the center, in which the center marks the unity and eidos (the species, higher taxon), and the circle is the multitude, the individuals. Proceeding on the basis of various philosophical doctrines, this model can

---

118 Dugin, *V poiskakh temnogo Logosa* [*In Search of the Dark Logos*], p. 79.

be imbued with different content, but it will still be effective. In the ensuing discussion we will rely on the doctrines of idealism, realism, and nominalism.

1. **Idealism:** In the philosophy of Plato and his followers, the anthropological center is ontologically primal. Only it Is. This center is the "Perfect Human" or "Idea of the Human." In this system, the Perfect Human is conceived as a reality, whereas the individual is close to an illusion without being, which it derives from the anthropological center. We have already seen this in the case of the estate, which traces back to the God-archetype and the body of God (*Brahma*) that stands higher than all society. With reference to language, such would correspond to the equipolent structure.

2. **Realism** is based on the philosophy of Aristotle, in which the individual is placed in the space between the circle and the center. Here the individual is primary, but is not self-sufficient and autonomous. His being consists of a mixture of form and material existing not before him (as in Platonism) but through him. The individual is composite, does not have his own content, but is a balance of matter and form (*eidos*) defined by the concentration and quality of the *eidos*. In the center is the pure *eidos*, which Aristotle called the "unmoved mover." The *eidos* and the individual are interdependent, as the *eidos* exists through the individual (without which it would be a pure abstraction), and the individual is dependent on the *eidos*. This corresponds to the gradual structure of language.

3. **Nominalism:** The nominalist approach is associated with such philosophers as Johannes Roscelin and William of Ockham. In the sphere of anthropology, nominalism affixes reality only to the individual. The *eidos* is seen as a conditional, conventional, generalized "name" created by a community of observers and scholars. In other words, only individuals exist, and their generic name "humans" is nothing more than a convention, an agreement. This is the principle of Ockham's razor and privativity in action.

On the basis of the above, we can distinguish three views on human essence and nature:

1. The human is universal and independent of the individual.
2. The human is an essence given in the individual, but is not equivalent to it.

3. "Human" is a name invented by an individual to denote the common traits of individuals.

In turn proceeding from these views, we can define three types of humanism. These three varieties can conditionally be termed the "higher taxa" of humanism within which there can be other types and sub-classifications of humanist thought, including the conditional "humanism" of ancient pagan societies.

The first type of humanism is "maximal" or Platonic humanism, which considers the human to be a living, active Idea, something divine and eternal. In Platonic humanism, the individual is an empty concept, a mere "glare" of the "Light" of the real, true Human. Here, human is that which one must become. The human is not born, and those born are not imparted with the abstract, formal taxon of "human" by default. This is the sphere of the Sacred anthropology of traditional societies, where the full title of "human" could be obtained only by passing through a series of initiations.

The second type of humanism is the realist, Aristotelian type, based on realist anthropology. Here, the human has form, contains the Idea (à la Plato) and possesses *entelekheia*. The end here is the conception of Aristotle. In other words, this humanism recognizes the significance of the individual but focuses attention on what it is that makes the individual, on what manifests itself through the individual. In this system, the Great Human is compiled out of many small people. This "collective" principle is characteristic of the traditional societies of the Christian Church, the Islamic Umma, and the Jewish community. This principle is also preserved in secular societies, as in Marx's "collectivization" of community around the individual based on their relation to the means of production, which Marx called "class." Attention to this aspect has also been paid by the sociologists Auguste Comte and Émile Durkheim, as well as the anthropologist Claude Lévi-Strauss. We can detect a form of realist humanism in nationalist and racist theories, in which, for instance, a secular collective is formed around the white human or the "Aryan" as in the National-Socialist myth. Special cases of this type of humanism can also be seen in esoteric and occult orders, sects, and unions, such as the Masonic, Rosicrucian or less organized alchemical associations from the Renaissance up to the final formation of Modernity.

The third type of humanism, liberal humanism, is based on nominalism and liberal anthropology, for which "the human" is a name invented by an individual to denote the common traits of individuals. The consequential, strictly conventional, secular approach to interpreting the notion of "human" allows for the content of such to be changed arbitrarily, thereby opening up the way to transhumanism and posthumanism. There is no doubt as to the fact that in the liberal optic the common denominator for all of humanity lies on the lower rung. From the point of view of Tradition, the equality prescribed by liberal humanism is oriented towards the last pariah, the lowest and poorest in spirit. Such equality, enshrined as equality of starting opportunities, as "humaneness", is rendered normative. The human of this humanism is he who is low, who meets the lowest criteria of bio-social identification, i.e., has a human appearance (regardless of race and gender), has reason (is functioning), and is educated at least minimally (regardless of culture and religion). Further lies only the freedom to survive. Liberal humanism is the established norm and maximal expression of Modernity. The result of the Cold War between the USSR and US, which expressed a confrontation between the ideologies of communism and liberalism, or of realist and liberal humanism respectively, was the victory of America in the late 20th century, as a consequence of which the latter's type of society, politics, culture, economy, and ideology became the most consistent and pure expression of Modernity.

The anthropology of the individual asserts that the human being is a bio-social creature endowed with a most important distinction from animals: reason. Sacred anthropology, on the contrary, is built around the Heart. The axis of the human passes through three points: the mind (consciousness), the Heart, and the base of the spine (the genitals). The Heart, the area in the middle of the human body, is the main point. In the Heart is consecrated the nature of a human as a God. When the titans dismembered Dionysus, Athena saved his Heart, i.e., his Divine nature. The world and man are (self-)recognized by the Heart; the light of the Heart is reflected by the mind; and its heat is expressed in the lower part of the body, by the animal and fertile element of man, the warmth and mobility of the human body's members. The path from the Heart can go up to the mind, ennobling it with the Divine light, as well as down to the animal abundance of life, the generation of the *rod*. As Heraclitus said: "The way up and down is one and the same." Indeed, if the path is begun from the Heart, then its light can ennoble any direction, all of which are embedded into one Sacred axis. But in the era of Modernity, the Heart as the center of the human is replaced by the Reason of the head. The rational human is the human of the Enlightenment who knows the world through reason alone. This is the human-automaton which operates with binary code. On the other hand, the disappearance of the Heart gives rise to animal-humans, the place of the Heart in whose constitution is replaced not by reason, by the mind, but by the genitalia. These are material people interested neither in the Gods nor the ways of science, but who respond most lively to the amusement and pleasures of the flesh and the belly.

It is on the relations of the rational, bodily, and animal elements of man, unbalanced by the power of the Sacred Heart, that modern psychology and psychoanalysis are built. The defining discovery of psychoanalysis was made by Sigmund Freud, who revealed two principles in the human structure: the conscious *ratio* and the unconscious which both affects and conflicts with the diurnal faculty of reason. As a true rationalist, Freud took the side of reason and proclaimed that the light of reason must be brought into the unconscious, that these two elements should be fitted under the primacy of rationality. Freud emphasized the individual history of patients, believed sexuality (the point of the human's genitalia), death, Eros, Thanatos and the traumas associated with them to be undertones of the effects of the unconscious, and devoted his works to the development of this approach. Freud's pupil, the great psychoanalyst Carl Gustav

Jung, in turn, took the side of the unconscious, the side of myth, in which he ordered the archetypes of the collective unconscious. Jung devoted special attention to the study of alchemy, Christian and Gnostic symbolism, interpreting the latter in terms of psychological phenomena and archetypes. Jung's archetypes of the Animus and Anima virtually expressed the Divine Male and Female elements in the language of psychoanalysis. Ultimately, the difference between the approaches of these two founding fathers of psychoanalysis led to the divergence of their paths.

Psychoanalysis would become very popular in the New World, where it was brought by Freud and Jung in the early 20th century. The rationalist psychology of Modernity found its apogee in America in the theories of behaviorism and social behaviorism. Behaviorism examines the individual as an automaton that reacts to external stimuli in definite ways. The internal processes of the psyche are not of interest to behaviorism, for which a human is a "black box" whose inner dimension is unknown. Whenever a stimulus is introduced, an individual shows a definite reaction, and the sum of reactions accumulated and learned through culture constitute the experience of the individual. An atypical stimulus, or when a person's responsive reaction does not meet the expected result, can be subject to doubt, requiring the development of a new reaction. In the periphery of behaviorism, one can find the opinion that there is a soul (psyche) within the "black box" of the individual, but its discovery and acquaintance is of no interest nor necessity if the human-"automaton" produces the right reactions. Social behaviorism extended this approach and method from psychology to sociology with a focus on positivism, i.e., the claim that only observable phenomena can be studied. Society, consisting of "black-box-automata", thus becomes an "automaton" itself. If something "works" in society, then it is "true"; if something "ceases to work", then it is subject to change and discarding (à la George Herbert Mead).

The dominance of behaviorism, which continues to be applied in psychology and pedagogy, was later replaced by the trend of cognitive psychology, which pays greater attention to the processes of consciousness, i.e., attention, memory, feelings, imagination, and logic. Today, cognitive psychology draws many parallels between human cognitive processes and computer calculative processes, thus converging with cybernetics, computer science, neurobiology, neurophysiology, and neuropsychology. Taken together, Freudianism, behaviorism, and cognitivism express the aspiration to subordinate human nature to reason, to the upper point. In fact, the very application of the terms "psyche" and "soul" to these vectors is an oxymoron. In the optic of these approaches, the soul becomes the totality of processes, effects, traumas, and diseases occurring in consciousness and their curing.

On the other hand, psychology also revealed the presence of holism in human consciousness, as in the theory of *Gestalt* of Christian von Ehrenfels and Max Wertheimer. Gestalt is the whole preceding the particular. Thanks to gestalt, the human perceives music as a complete work of art, not as merely a collection of notes, tones, and sounds, and a painting as a complete image, not a sum of smears. Gestalt theory is still successfully applied in rehabilitative and therapeutic practices. In the Jungian school and Gestalt we can see trends in psychology and psychoanalysis which are conservative, closer to, or in the very least, pay due homage to tradition and recognize just how unfounded is the pretension of reason to total domination.

As fruits of Modernity expressing a secular and progressivist approach, psychology and psychoanalysis accordingly see religion and "archaic remnants" as previous forms of the regulation of relations between the lower and higher points, between the body, desire, mind, and will. Religion in this perspective is a set of moral norms, counterbalances, and taboos (a most important term in Freud's philosophy) which ought to be abolished by the growing light of the human mind coming ever nearer to being able to resolve this duality without resorting to aged taboos and morals of faith, but through reason, analysis, development, healing, and harmonization alone. For psychology, insistences upon the presence of God, belief in magic, the practice of rituals, etc. are manifestations of various disharmonious processes occurring within the psyche. For instance, by practicing magic, a human is merely compensating for some personal failures. In modern society, there is no magic, and if one is a "magus" or references "extra-senses", then they might find good work and raise their social status using generally accepted procedures and methods, but faith in such is the last consolation that causes pity for the person who resorts to it. After all, for a "civilized" man, faith (in the Gods, in mysticism) means simply wasting time by trusting preposterous superstitions and biases. Rituals, from the point of view of psychology, can help harmonize a person by providing an outlet for stress, helping forget about (by displacing) failures. In this language, there is no place for the Gods even when they are mentioned. Accordingly, the question of the essence of a rite and the state of a person amidst a ritual is just as telling as the question of the origin of the person. During a rite, is the person in the circle in communication with their native Gods, participating in the cosmic cycles, and embodying metaphysical principles, or are they merely relieving stress, displacing social failures, and running away from problems into a "world of fairy tales" (escapism)? Is the rite - or pagan tradition itself - intended to awaken the sleeping Heart of man, or to somehow solve a problem of the emancipated mind and unrestrained genitalia?

In regards to Sacred anthropology, modern people, void of Heart, are not even people in full measure. They are not entirely people or are already no longer people. They are automata of rationality or poorly contained animals, non-harmonious personalities belonging to the horizontal plane. Evola openly considered the bourgeoisie and proletariat to be non-humans. Modern people are void of the fire of Zeus (the Heart), possessing only Prometheus' light of reason.

The Material View on Traditional Societies

For modern, "civilized" man, traditional societies are primitive and underdeveloped in structure. Viewing traditional, estate, tripartite society through the prism of material values, proletarian labor, or more broadly and simply, Marxism, the traditional pyramid of society is turned upside down. At the top of traditional societies stand the priests and warriors, the noblest and purest people closest of all to the Gods - the priests being more so than warriors, farmers, artisans, and slaves. From the material standpoint, the lowest estates come first as the foundation and basis of the pyramid. The emphasis of values is thus shifted from the top, from which emanates the light of Sacrality that permeates all levels, to the base, in the view of which it is as if the pyramid grows from the bottom up and the broad layers of common people are the guarantors of power and the stability of the system, whereas the priesthood and warrior-kings are usurpers and tyrants who, without broad support and the feeding and providing of the third estate, would quickly die due to an ability to work. We can see in this perspective a direct attack on the idea of Dharma and the due. Such a point of view absolutely corresponds to the lowest adharmic groups, such as outcasts, who seek to free themselves from the authority of the estate system.

As a result, we can see in the free society of Modernity the very same pyramid but erected along inverse criteria. Now the upper levels are occupied by the richest and famous, the oligarchy, and the business and cultural elites. Boundaries between estates are virtually absent, in place of which there is great opportunity for social mobility, status-changing, and moving from a lower class into a higher one given the right salary and television appearances.

If we look at the third estate in material or economic terms, then in antiquity it engaged in low-skilled, rough manual labor; in "classical" Modernity the same labor but in factories (the proletariat); and in today's realities it has passed into the sphere of services which similarly do not require any profound or fundamental knowledge - as is the case with science and technology - and forms a kind of "office proletariat." This economic view, while true for Modernity, upon projection onto antiquity misses the dimension of the Sacred that renders the third estate what it is. For the latter, it is not related to the means of production, qualifications, or the character of labor that makes shudras into shudras, but their ontological position within the sacred order, the hierarchy of Divine manifestation.

In Modernity, the martial estate is turned into an army of mercenary soldiers, on which point it is worth noting that the Latin word *soldus* meant coin. The priestly and philosophical estate, meanwhile, is regarded as a closed caste which has a monopoly on knowledge and rules through usurpation and the restriction of access. Thus arises the misconception that the priest/philosopher has absolute knowledge (consciousness) of all the spheres of life and the world, whereas the quantitative measure of knowledge, in fact, plays no role in the path of ascension to the Gods.

In conclusion, let us repeat that the merchant type was originally foreign to the Indo-European tripartite system, from which we can conclude that the self-producing structure of modern society is largely anti-Indo-European.

Reflection

One particularly unique trait of Modernity is its reflective representation of itself as being none other than that which is "modern", "contemporary", or "present." In other words, the man of Modernity understands that he is living in the Modern era. The man of Tradition did not know the "era of Tradition" and could not say "I am a traditional man" which, in principle, would be akin to saying "I am I", for the feeling of the permeation of Sacrality was always present. Yet in the modern era, man says "I am I, and only I am modern man."

Thus appears a fundamental reflection and localization of oneself in the span of history. It is out of this awareness of oneself in a concrete point in time, the era of Modernity, that the whole value-based attitude to the past and future is built. The past is disregarded as old, infantile, and underdeveloped, while the future is seen as the era of progress, development, and grace.

The totality of the language of Modernity, its privativity, possesses deep and subtle dimensions which penetrate consciousness, imperceptibly and firmly shifting consciousness in the direction of Modernism. We will now examine several fundamental, subtle constructs of Modernity which pagan philosophy has at times failed to reflectively see as titanic sabotage. Such are the concepts of reality and primitiveness.

Reality

One of the most fundamental and enduring ideas about the world asserted in Modernity is the notion of reality. The assertions of "the real", "objective reality", or "realism" are primarily evaluative, artificial constructs of the modern sciences, both the natural and social. Objectivity and reality are summoned to show the "real" character of a phenomenon or process that is independent of man (the subject) - in other words, that something is or is happening according to "objective" reasons that do not have a creator, actor, or interested party (a person, group, or state). "Reality" is summoned to distinguish that which is reliable, confirmed by experiments, calculations, observations, and formulas from the "subjective and "unreal" or "non-real." Such aims to claim the inviolability of the new view of the world, and asserts that the "unreal" does not influence measuring instruments, and therefore is to be discarded and disregarded.

Manifestations of miracles, the Divine, meeting a forest spirit in a forest, or traveling to another world are all treated as "unreal" and impossible insofar as they contradict the laws of physics, nature, and logic. In the best case, anything Sacred is attributed to the realm of subjective experiences, hallucinations, or effects. The "real" and "unreal" seem to divide the world into supporters of "objective" knowledge of the world and the supporters of myth and the Sacred. But this division introduces a subtlety. By defining ourselves as supporters of the "unreal", we thereby recognize the opposing side of the "real", which constitutes the second half of the word following the prefix "un-" or "not-". Expressions in the likes of "the reality of tradition" or "in the reality of tradition" thereby contain a subtlety. In Tradition, there is no notion of "reality" at all - it is directly absent since, relatively speaking, everything in Tradition was "real", even the "unreal." The statement "I am real" is impossible in a non-modern era, since "I am reality" excludes the holistic dimensions of Sacred anthropology, the point of the Heart and the backbone.

A similar situation can be seen with the term "natural" and its antithesis "supernatural." Natural is that of nature, real, and ordinary, that which is simply given as "reality." Magic, miracles, and hierophanies of the Gods are supernatural, i.e., they violate the laws of nature. The expression "it happened naturally" is analogous to speaking of processes as "objective reality." Pagan calls to turn to the natural mean that it is necessary to turn to nature and its laws, but in the modern case we encounter a substitution of these laws of Dharma and Sacred Nature with those of physics, ecology, geology, biology, etc. The supernatural is also understood as "the still unknown natural", and a "miracle" is treated as an "objective" physical process which is not yet understood but which, over the course of the development and perfection of instruments, man will be able to comprehend and reproduce.

Thus, the "reality" of Modernity, compared to Tradition, represents the altogether materially truncated level. Enormous dimensions of the cosmos do not fit into the devices and minds of scientists, and so are repressed and dismissed. Any measuring instruments and sensors, even the most complex, capture merely the thinnest, strictly material slice of the omnipresent Cosmos.

In the field of sociology, "reality" is understood to be that in which society believes and is therefore constituted as social reality (à la Emile Durkheim). If society believes in science, progress, and physical laws to which matter is subject, then such becomes a social fact at work. If, on the contrary, society believes in God, church institutions, and miracles, such can also become a social fact at work. In other words, both societies with different dispositions remain stable and functioning. Another example illustrating the social construction of "reality" is the very idea that a forest is a "forest." The very notion of a "forest" may seem to us to be so "natural" that we cannot even humor the thought that there would not be such a thing as a "forest" at all. "Forest" is a construct designed to give a name and set of characteristics, a definition to that which is not a "city", a "field", a "village", or a "desert." In other words, a "forest" is a space with dense vegetation of the arboreal variety mixed with shrubs and grass. Thus, a forest does not know that it is a "forest." In Tradition, a given grove could be the dwelling place of a God, such as the grove of Baldr or Apollo, or the dwelling place of mythical creatures akin to trees. They are not a forest, but a family or community of beings. In the same vein, many large stones do not know that they are merely "stones", but rather are quite sure that they are gnomes with their own rich gnomic lives, cares, and deeds.

This constructing of such concepts is transitory. We are now not surprised by parks of "artificial forest" consisting of fake trees. The latter are also "forests", simply "artificial" ones. Such is reality as a social construct derived from society. This approach's proposed freedom of choice for the trajectory of constructing reality - whether "scientific" or "religious" - directly refers us to the concept of the free and modern society that is alien to Tradition. In traditional society, the Gods are not the objects of "faith" of a given society or concrete individuals, but are themselves open manifestations and knowledge, which makes them omnipresent, and every person equal to them in nature.

Thus, it can once again be emphasized that there is no "objective reality." Here it is necessary to exercise tireless care in deciphering the terminology and use of language. That which is considered "real" in pagan traditions and that which is "real" in the modern world are very different "realities." Distinguishing between these two stratifications demands painstaking and intense work.

Primitiveness

The antithesis of the developed, enlightened society of Europe is represented by those primitive, underdeveloped societies retaining vestiges of archaic beliefs and customs. Christian and post-Christian Europe adopted a policy towards these societies based on graduality, by virtue of which these barbarian peoples could eventually convert to Christianity, enter the Church, the earthly community, and therefore become "one of them." Later, this came to mean accepting the view of the "New World", being "educated", and so on. This attitude was also directed against those other peoples of Europe and the Mediterranean which lagged behind the locomotives of modernization of Holland, England, France, and Germany.

In the space of the New World - future America - European colonists proclaimed the creation of a new society on a clean slate, de facto breaking ties with metropolitan Europe and its traditions. The construction of American identity proceeded in a strictly privative manner, which meant the categorical rejection of the local indigenous peoples. It is a historical fact that the human status of Native Americans was once a seriously debated question in Europe. The result was the total genocide of the underdeveloped, Christ-ignorant, Enlightenment-deprived American Indians, the only survivors of which were herded into concentration camps and reservations which exist to this day. Historically, the black slaves imported from Africa had greater rights and opportunities than the indigenous peoples, who flatly refused to be made slaves.

The biological approach to classifying living organisms from "simplest" to "highest", that is possessing more complex structures, was thus applied to humans. The more developed European, and later American, vanquished the less developed American Indians and enslaved less-developed Africans. In history, philosophy, and other sciences, this phenomenon acquired the name "chauvinism" - that with which, according to Nikolai Trubetzkoy, Oswald Spengler, and many other authors, all of Europe was sick. Chauvinism is an integral part of the progressivist system of values. It can even be found in the field of religious studies and the study of various traditions in constructed abstract histories of the evolution of religious ideas, which postulate a range of progress from primitive hunting customs and animism to the highly-developed philosophical systems and ritual ceremonies of Abrahamism.[119]

Today, belonging to a tradition is considered by modern man to be a declaration of primitiveness. If previously this was thought about the ancient pagan traditions, then in the consciousness of the man of Modernity such is embodied in images of African tribes, Polynesian Indians, and Papuans who, it is believed, will never be capable of achieving the modern level of development and consciousness.

But in the 20th century, the preeminent anthropologist Claude Lévi-Strauss rose against this progressivism directed against archaic societies and argued that "primitive" societies are in fact just as complex as developed civilizations or, in other terms, represent a complexity of a different kind. We have already encountered this complexity in our discussion of the span of public attention and how modern knowledge supersedes and takes the place of traditional knowledge. Claude Lévi-Strauss and the structural anthropology which he developed have proven that the difference between archaic tribal societies in the Amazon river basin and modern industrial societies lies only in the configuration of structure. The quantity of international connections, the complexity of language, interpretations of reality, culture, and logic are approximately equal in both cases. Thus, it was revealed that Modernity's declaration of its exceptionalism is based only on the grounds that Modernity is Modern, a point which we have repeatedly spoken to in terms of the fundamental parity of

---

119 This progressivist and biased approach to the study of religions was rejected by Mircea Eliade, who would go on to lay new foundations and principles, close to those of Traditionalism, for the scholarly study of religion in the 20th century.

the levels of the languages of Tradition and Modernity and their fundamental irreducibility to one progressivist theory of development. Modernity insists on the latter, but behind this mask lurks the titanic element.

Treating a tradition as "primitive" or "more civilized" is unacceptable, since this approach views tradition from the point of view of Modernity, and thereby automatically entails a value judgement. The very expression "good primitive tradition" is an oxymoron, since for the man of Modernity the primitive nowhere and never can be good. It is obvious that pagan philosophy's treatment of different traditions can in no way proceed from this logic. The sacred is not characterized by primitiveness or development in any way. Categories of "development" are relevant only to the quantitative, material principle of matter.

What happens to a "primitive" society if it does not develop as do the modern "civilized" states? The answer is very simple: society does not develop, it lives. Its life is rich, complex, pulsating, and in motion just as the circle of the year, and its life is absolutely not obliged to follow any strategies of development, quantitative growth, or expansion.

Gnoseological Racism

Knowledge in Tradition and knowledge in Modernity differ radically. Tradition is open, intense Life, in which different paths and metamorphoses are possible which determine the special means of knowing. The Heart is the organ of knowing in the traditional world. Since there was no "subject-object" dichotomy in antiquity, the knower ultimately became the knowable himself. If man in ancient society wished to know, for example, of the existence of the ocean, then when he came to know such, he himself became the ocean. To know means to become that which one knows. Life is a continuous revelation of truth on all levels. The world of Tradition is fundamentally, principally open and ever-transforming in the game of metamorphoses. Through meditation, observing austerity, ritual practices, ritual intoxication, or the reception of revelation and instructions from spirits and the Gods, man accomplishes a fundamental leap from the here to the there, from ignorance to insight here and now.

Traditionalists have called knowing and grasping the world with the Heart "intellectual intuition", which is only secondarily, on the mental level, clothed in logical, rational coverings and expressed in thought and word. It would be wrong to say that there were no sciences in antiquity; rather, they were built on a completely different method of knowing. They were Sacred, holistic sciences appealing to the Sacred and permeated with its rays. They were justly elitist, demanding special initiation, such as the science of craft, the science of the sword, and the science of carving runes. In his book *Pagan Imperialism*, Baron Evola distinguished between Wisdom and profane science in the following terms:

> The point to be borne in mind is that sacred and sapiential science, unlike secular science, is not a 'knowing' but a being, and cannot be taught by books or universities or transmitted by words: to gain it, it is necessary to be transformed, to transcend common life for a superior life. It measures exactly the quality and reality of individual life, of which it becomes an inviolable privilege and an organic part, rather than being a concept, or a notion, which can be put into one's head like something into a sack, without at the same time having to be transformed or to budge in the slightest in regard to what one is. Hence the natural aristocracy of Wisdom...[120]

In Modernity, knowledge is constructed along with the templates of progress and systematic doubt at each and every stage, from putting forth a hypothesis demanding verification, confirmation with facts and experiences, and testing correspondence to "reality", up to the construction of a theory on which the individual sciences, intra-scientific fields, specializations, and disciplinary intersections are

---

120 Evola, *Pagan Imperialism*, p. 100-101.

built.[121] But the truth here is relative. In the 1930s, the British philosopher and sociologist Karl Popper formulated a criteria for scientificity different from "verification", that of falsifiability. If verification is based on the search for facts which confirm a hypothesis, then falsifiability is constructed through the search for facts which refute a theory. According to Popper, a theory can never be irrefutable, as such would go beyond scientificity into the realm of pseudo-science and faith. If a hypothesis or theory is confirmed by one, some, or a number of experiments, this does not mean that it is true, as it is possible that facts or dimensions which may disprove a theory have simply not yet been discovered or established. Despite the fact that Ockham's razor calls for beings not to be produced, science repeatedly generates new theories, multiplies knowledge, facts, and thereby contributes to development. The nuance lies in the fact that Ockham's razor "shaves" vertically, not horizontally. If a theory is insufficient or does not work, then a new hypothesis is put forth to develop a new theory that is just as material as the previous. The introduction of new mathematical, physical, and empirical facts for the construction of new theories is not a "sin" of science, but it is absolutely unacceptable for the supernatural, the Sacred, the Gods and their messengers, and the vertical dimension of being to be incorporated into such a theory. The latter are "shaved off" by Ockham's razor, leaving only the horizontal, material development of science.

The man of traditional society knew the ocean by becoming one with it. The man of Modernity takes a photograph of the ocean, measures its depth, maps its floor, tests its water composition, the direction of its currents, and attempts (unsuccessfully) to create a mathematical formula to describe the movement of waves. In the end, he withdraws, believing that he has acquired sufficient knowledge about the ocean, only for another scholar from another science to describe the ocean with a different language, highlight different criteria, emphasize

---

121 The principle of verification, or the checking of correspondence to facts intended to distinguish between science and pseudo-science was put forth by the Vienna Circle of Positivists in the early 20th century.

different aspects, and so on, leaving us to count a number of definitions of one and the same ocean from different points of view. But is this knowing the ocean? From the point of view of Tradition, this is not knowledge. From the viewpoint of modern science, the sum of this knowledge will constitute the maximal contemporary approximation to knowledge of the ocean. The same could be said of the sky, the Earth, animals, war, peace, and so on and so forth.

Asserting itself to be exceptional and exclusive, Modernity creates its own version of the history of science and artificially dates the branches of knowledge that have emerged in the modern era back to the ancient philosophers and sacred sciences. For instance, the roots of mathematics and physics are traced back to Pythagoras and Archimedes, while the vertical dimension of Pythagoras and the Pythagoreans is left out, castrated. From the powerful and strict school of Pythagoras, maximally closed from the profane and where numbers were perceived as sacred and divine, only mathematical laws and multiplication tables remain. Archimedes is cut down only to his "eureka." Similarly, psychologists claim that their forefather was Aristotle with his treatise *On the Soul*. In the optics of modern sciences, their founding fathers are reduced to being objects of science itself. Mathematicians see only a mathematician in Pythagoras, whereas Pythagoras himself saw in mathematics the divine laws of the cosmos. Another dimension of this shift can be seen in the rediscovery and elevation of the ancient atomists and such critics of the sacred as Euhemerus, Xenophanes, and Democritus.

The dawn of Modernity saw the divorce of the esoteric and the natural-scientific along the path of regression from the religious picture of the world through theism and agnosticism down to apatheism and antitheism. The dissociation of the Royal Art of alchemy and strict chemistry took place in the 18th century. Over the course of his life, Isaac Newton compiled theological commentaries on the Bible which were close to the Arian heresy and permeated with rationalism, all the while as he was actively interested in Jewish Kabbalah and astrology.

Astrology too would later be castrated into astronomy. The stars would become clusters of gas in the sky and the galaxy. Thusly were killed the souls of the ancestors and spirits of the shamans looking down at their descendants and people from the sky. Piloting around a star kills the star which the ancestors used to look up to in the sky as to their folk on Earth. The crescent of the moon - the crescent of Mara or Shiva - disappeared when man reached the moon as a material satellite of Earth. The Sun is no longer Apollo or the eye of the God Ra, but merely the "yellow dwarf" among the classification of stars. We could once pose the question: What are the stars to modern pagans?

In light of the preceding, we can conclude that Modernity harbors, as an inherent, indelible trait, gnoseological racism. It denies the right to being, to meaning, and to otherness to all who have not become Modern. The path which Europe took from archaic to modern times is proclaimed to be the universal, singular true strategy and destiny of all of mankind. Other societies are only as valuable as they are modern. Other forms of rationality and other structures of being which, according to Lévi-Strauss, are in no way inferior in complexity to modern societies, are branded as "primitive."

Gnoseological racism manifests itself in strict privativity and the concentration of knowledge on the horizontal, material border. What is valued is that which corresponds to the logic of physics, that which is determined by rigid cause and effect of the physical "laws of nature." For Hinduism, such immersion into the rigidity of causal-effectuality is one of the signs of the Kali-Yuga, the worlds of hell and ignorance of the true Nature of the World.

Having located Modernity in the Time of the Iron Age, we can now turn to locate Modernity in space. The space of Modernity, its place of origin and development on the horizontal, geographical plane of linear history, is Europe. In particular, Holland, France, England, Spain, and Germany became the locomotives of Modernity, the vanguard of which was led by English and French philosophers. Extending itself geographically, its grip was loosened over the East, on the border with Eastern Europe and Russia. Yet with ease Modernity crossed the ocean with the colonists of the New World, the future America, where it met its special fate that has since come to define the whole face of the modern world. Europeans' particular view of themselves and the belief that Europe's path is the universal path of mankind is encapsulated in the maxim "The Destiny of Europe is the Destiny of the World." This particular type of European racism (gnoseological racism) has come to be called "Eurocentrism." In the Russian Empire, a remarkable example of this Enlightenment Eurocentrism was Dordzhi Banzarov's 1846 work *The Black Faith, or Shamanism among the Mongols*.[122] Banzarov's emergence, education, and success left an indelible impression on the scientific community by virtue of the fact that he himself was of "Asian physiognomy" - although we would say that such is the only trait which he inherited from his Asian tribe. In all other qualities, Banzarov belonged entirely to "European" society, being held up as an example of the hope for "educating" the savage tribes of Asia.

Gnoseological racism, which arranges all traditions, peoples, and societies into one universal linear series of historical development in line with the patterns of European Modernity, must be opposed with the principle of empathy in studying, describing, and entering into contact with different traditions, peoples, and societies. Empathy, which means putting oneself in the worldview of another tradition, is the bedrock of fundamental pluralism - cultural, linguistic, pagan, and in terms of values. Different traditions and societies ought not be dissected according to the templates of the European view; every tradition should be viewed through maximally absorbing its own structures, axes, values, and cumulative view of itself. Such an empathetic approach is capable of solving a number of inter-cultural problems and avoiding the many misconceptions

---

122 English translation published as: Dorji Banzarov, *The Black Faith, or Shamanism among the Mongols* (transl. by J. Nattier and J.R. Krueger), *Mongolian Studies* 7 (1981).

and "phantoms" in the picture of the world that are artificially "discovered" or inscribed onto a foreign society and tradition.

Technology

One special field of the application of scientific knowledge is technology. Mechanisms and technological devices were also known in ancient times, but their creation and use were ritual, sacred, and framed by the motto *non plus ultra*. Modernity is the time of unbound technology. It is the era of conveyor belt production, of diverse machines, smelters, and molds, the triumph of military and economic technologies, finding its apotheosis in electronic goods of mass consumption. Technology is the fate of the West and the man of Modernity.

Unlike the creative demiurgic act of the third estate, which creates household-economic, military, and ritual objects and therein realizes the manifestation of the divine demiurge through itself on its own level, machine and assembly-line production are void of this dimension and alienate the creator from everything unique to demiurgy. The artisan-creator falls to the level of the producing proletarian, the servant of the machine. The hunter and fisherman increase their catch plus ultra with guns, tracking systems, and all-terrain vehicles. The special ritual action of plowing the field and sowing it with songs, spells, offerings, and harvesting by means of sickle and scythe are lost. Instead of the harrow, the tractor plows in half a day, and another half is spent on harvesting in autumn. The driver only has to adjust the mechanisms of seeding, cutting, and collecting, all as modern synthetic fertilizers accelerate and multiply growth *plus ultra*. Scientists delegate calculations, analytics, forecasting, and accounting to machines and computers, the operating speed of which exceeds humans by orders of great magnitude.

Technology also introduces a particular dimension to war. Battle is no longer a clash of two armies on a field of battle, face to face. Glorious soldiers no longer see their enemy's face, feel the noises of hooves, the clang of metal, or the heat of blood mixed with earth. Artillery, firearms, and automatic weapons allow for fighting at a distance imperceptible to the naked eye. The warrior does not shoot an enemy, but in the direction of an enemy. Guns level the playing field and equalize people. Aristocratic dignity and skill with a sword fall before the shot of a commoner who himself is afraid of the sound of shooting. Once again, equality - now on the field of battle - sinks to the lowest level. With the increase of artillery and firearms, the appearance of troops changes from the sublime and emphatic hierarchy and aristocracy of colors into uniform camouflage designed to hide an army from the distant sight of an enemy. Tanks, submarines, heavy cruisers, and aircraft radically change the face of modern war. Now the direct clash of soldiers in close and melee combat becomes an exception. Combat between men is replaced by a showdown between guns. Man thus becomes an organic extension of the rifle or the howitzer, only serving the latter's might. The creation of nuclear weapons and rocketry opened a new page in the vision and conduct of war, now marked by the total destruction of an enemy with the striking power of an atom. Then sets in the prospect of a new field for warfare: space.

Space exploration was the culmination of all the power of theoretical science and its technological embodiment. Beginning almost immediately after the Second World War, the rocket science race developed into the space race between two countries embodying two elements of Modernity: the socialist USSR and the capitalist US. In the end, both powers realized the greatest rational and technological potential of mankind by taking man into outer space, landing him on the moon, and creating three orbital stations: the American SkyLab, the Soviet and Russian Mir, and the International Space Station. The breakthrough-leap into space in the late 20th century fascinated humanity, influencing culture, politics, and society. Fiction writers described space travel to distant worlds, the conquest of planets, heroic journeys through black, hostile space to its secrets and other civilizations. Society dreamed of space and contacting other worlds. Politics used this sphere of achievements for the purpose of propaganda, the justification of supremacy, and the deployment of space weaponry. In the 20th century, the great project of science, turned towards nature and space, thus found its maximal expression. Space exploration also found its application in the war against the sacred with the argument that "out there", in space, "there is everything but God."[123] The mastery of this new space was thus subordinate to the very logic of the de-sacralization of the world - there are no Gods, for astronauts did not see any.

The ability to understand, master, and produce technology also became a criterion of civilized society. If man understands science and takes the side of rationality, then he must understand and use technology, be open to it, and welcome technological innovations. "Primitive" societies, meanwhile, were left using rudimentary tools. The acquaintance of the archaic societies of North and South America, India, Africa, Oceania, and Polynesia with firearms and automatic weapons, automobiles and aircraft, and industrially-produced goods which were not present in their cultures, yielded a unique situation of contact between these still traditional, sacred-oriented societies and the no-longer traditional, uniformized society of Modernity. We would like to dwell on two illustrative examples of what happened amidst such contacts from the point of view of traditional societies and from the perspective of Modernity.

The first, well-known example is that of the cargo cults among the peoples of Melanesia, the islands located to the northeast of Australia. Cargo cults emerged en masse during the Second World War, when the Americans used these sparsely inhabited islands to construct air cargo terminals in the Pacific Ocean. During the construction of these airfields, they came into contact with the black aboriginal population of the islands and supplied them with modern food and various everyday items. After the war, the need for these airfields disappeared and

---

[123] These words are attributed to the first woman in space, Valentina Tereshkova.

the Americans vacated these lands. But the aboriginals, after the departure of these "white aliens", did not return to their former way of life. Instead, they began to build replicas of these airfields out of bamboo and leaves, to walk on them in imitation of the American army's marching, and to make stick models of rifles and mark them with US Air Force insignia. The cargo cults, named after the "cargo" inscriptions on the Americans' supplies, were cults of the supplies which the Americans shared with the local population. Other examples of cargo cults are known among the North American Indians, who believed incoming trains to be wagons into the spirit worlds. Some Indians in the Amazon basin would create imitations of cassette recorders and speak into them, believing that they were communicating with spirits. In Africa, cargo cults of household items, clothing, and entertainment of the white man are to be found ubiquitous.

From the point of view of modern anthropology, cargo cults are a manifestation of magical thinking of a society which does not understand the role of production, distribution, the origin and economy of goods, and treats such within the framework of their primitive culture. From the point of view of the aboriginals[124], the white people, whom they had never seen before, were spirits that had descended from heaven and bestowed gifts upon tribes, thus marking an era of grace and blessing. The disappearance of these "white spirits" thus marked the onset of a dark time, and so the repetition of the rituals of the "white spirits", such as marching and building airfield-temples, was intended to make them return. The indigenous peoples thus experienced contact with modern "civilized" man as a manifestation of sacred grace in the here and now. This was woven into and became part of the continuous fabric of myth.

Another example is that of contact between indigenous African populations, negroid tribes, with automatic weapons and Western clothing. Starting with the First World War and continuing throughout the 20th century, warring parties in

---

124 Without a doubt, here we can only claim to be attempting to explain the aboriginals' view in the language of our own thinking and logic.

Africa actively employed the indigenous population in their armies, thus arming them with weapons, the most popular of which would become the Kalashnikov. Europeans passed through the long historical path of the rational development of science and technology which allowed them to invent and produce automatic rifles, and so the European knows the history and origin of this weapon, knows that it is mechanics and the force of pressure of powder gases that shoot a bullet. But the African came to know the automatic rifle only in its finished, ready form. He did not follow the same historical path of development which the European pursued up to the invention of the machine gun. Thus, Africans proved capable of sacralizing the weapon, for them such is a "fire stick" and a "stinging fire cane." They use the gun in ecstatic rituals, consecrate it on altars, and use gunpowder along with other substances to acquire power and become closer to the weapon, to make it personal and uniquely connected with its wielder. Just as swords were consecrated with blood and forged for a particular aristocrat, so did the decoration of the rifle and the consumption of its bullets' gunpowder come to be practiced to connect its African owner. A similar situation with guns is to be found in India, where pistols and rifles are placed on altars to the Gods and are consecrated on par with blades and clubs. Recalling the metaphor of the obtaining of fire, here we can see the first manner, that of immersion into fire (tradition) of such force that it ignites any, even the rawest wood, from without.

The Russian poet Nikolai Klyuev (1884-1937) described the practice of purifying Western items in Russia in his *Song of the Great Mother*:

Шептали в ответ сапожки:	The boots whispered in response:
Тебя привезли рыбаки,	Fishermen brought you,
И звали аглицким сукном,	And called you English cloth,
Опосле ты стал зипуном!	And then you became a coat!
Сменяла сукно на икру,	You replaced cloth with caviar,
Придачей подложку-сестру,	Threw in the bargain the sister-lining
И тетушка Анна отрез	And Auntie Anna cut a bit

Снесла под куриный навес,	Laid it by the chicken coop
Чтоб петел обновку опел,	So that the rooster would crow on the new outfit
Где дух некрещеный сидел.	Where an unbaptized spirit lay
Потом завернули в тебя Ковчежец с мощами, любя,	Then they rolled you up into A chasse with relics, with love,
Крестом повязали тесьму Повывесть заморскую тьму,	They tied a braid with a cross To caste out that darkness from overseas
И семь безутешных недель Ларец был тебе колыбель,	And for seven inconsolable weeks The chasse was for you a cradle
Пока кипарис и тимьян На гостя, что за морем ткан,	In the meanwhile only cypress and thyme Per guest, so on that fabric from beyond the sea
Не пролили мирра ковши, Чтоб не был зипун без души!	They didn't spill buckets of myrrh So that the coat would not be without soul!

This poem describes the practice of the sacralization of the foreign in the spirit of the folk-Christian tradition.

The difference between cargo cults and the automatic weapons, clothing, and other objects which the aborigines and Africans encountered lies in that cargo cults exist in a state of "abandonment", whereas African tribes constantly receive weapons and things. All the while, their knowledge of the modern world is either fragmentary or altogether absent. They are capable of sacralizing artifacts coming from outside of their traditional life world. From the point of view of modern man, the African dressed in a uniform and holding a machine gun looks like him, which is to say looks modern. But the Africans themselves to this day still show their commitment to their native rituals and practices, including "barbaric" customs of waging war and eating a vanquished opponent.

This is a situation of contact between the archaic and the modern. The situation with paganism, which was to a certain extent preserved and then revived in Europe on the periphery of Modernity, is much more complex. As noted above, public attention can only hold on to a certain number of connections and things. The structure contains the constant. Archaic societies can integrate into their structure and sacralize incoming things in limited quantities, just as Athena and Zeus breathed soul and spirit into Prometheus' material creation. The rise of this quantity sees the beginning of the blurring of the traditional worldview and the modernization of society and consciousness. For pagans, the situation in Modernity is the opposite: there is no such force capable of spiritualizing the whole space of the West. Today's pagan communities are incapable of this. The important step to be taken is recognizing that Modernity did not appear in a vacuum, but that its mythological background, its hidden essence, is the titanic, chthonic element opposed to the world and Gods of myths. In this optic, man lacks the solar capacity to spiritualize the Promethean legacy. In other words, with the growth in the number of black gifts and titanic miracles, man descends into the lower states of being and regresses to the strictly rational or, in most cases, animalistic element. For the pagan who takes the side of the ancient Gods, the consistent rejection of such chthonic gifts is the ascetic path of ascent from the worlds of hell to solar Olympus, to the Gods. The European pagan, the pagan of Modernity, must give principled and firm answers to these dilemmas.

Freedom

Modernity's concentration on the horizontal level and its severing of things off from their higher and deeper meanings advances under the slogan of "emancipation." Liberalism comes from the Latin word *libertas*, or "freedom", which is understood in Modernity as "freedom from" - e.g., freedom from theology, freedom from hierarchy ("dictatorship"), freedom from traditional and estate traditions and customs, subordination, and obligations, emancipation from morality, and curtailing the authority of the state. Society and man are freed from everything archaic, from the deeper and higher dimensions of being. This negative freedom is localized on the horizontal level, and is paired with the positive "freedom" of "freedom for."[125] Friedrich Nietzsche put into Zarathustra's mouth the following, rather stinging question of liberal negative freedom as opposed to positive "freedom for":

"You call yourself free? Your dominating thought I want to hear, and not that you escaped from a yoke. Are you the kind of person who had the right to escape from a yoke? There are some who threw away their last value when they threw away their servitude. Free from what? What does Zarathustra care! But brightly your eyes should signal to me: for what?" [126]

Freedom "for" required a great idea, a higher dimension. Dharma is this great idea, the Divine law of order. Positive freedom implies will and responsibility and, if we are to speak of the Kshatriyan principle, the affirmation of one's own order and authority. Negative freedom emancipates from submission to one's nature and duty, thereby legalizing adharma. "Freedom from" maximally corresponds to the privativity of liberal humanism, the demand of science for liberation from the "dictatorship" of morality and ethics in its studies, the demand of artificial classes and degraded estates to be free from the oppressive pressure of the due and the sacred dimension of being. Liberalization only continued to rise from the era of the Enlightenment up to the middle of the 20th century, but over this course it did not transform the new worldview of the natural-scientific theory of progressive development of the world, matter, and society as a democratic contract of equals and man as indivisible (the individual).

Postmodernity

Following the Second World War, the paradigm of Modernity began to be replaced by a new picture of the world which neither creationism nor manifestationism had

---

125 The Modern concept of freedom was most succinctly expressed in the works of the English philosopher and theorist of liberalism, John Stuart Mill (1806-1873).

126 Nietzsche, *Thus Spoke Zarathustra*, p. 46.

encountered before. The development of this new paradigm, Postmodernity, began in the second half of the 20th century and is continuing to unfold at different paces in different societies today.

What is Postmodernity? The term itself suggests two constituent words: "post-" and "Modernity", i.e., "after Modernity," the paradigm following Modernity. Diachronically, this preliminary definition is valid, as the situation of Postmodernity began to unfold after the triumph of Modernity. Modernity had been constructed as the total denial of Tradition, in which everything that existed in antiquity was symmetrically mirrored or replaced with a double. Modernity represents the negative minus to the positive of Tradition. If traditional society is a statement, then modern society is the rejection of this statement. As for the next step, according to the laws of mathematical logic, as the negation of the negation of a statement, Postmodernity should take us back to the statement. In classical logic, this is represented as $A \to \neg A \to \neg\neg A = A$. Tradition (A) is negated by Modernity (-A), and therefore, logically, the negation of -A should close the circle and again equal A. But this is not the case in Postmodernity. The negation of Modernity does not return to Tradition. Instead, logic is disrupted altogether.

In order to more accurately analyze the nature of Postmodernity and its constructs in relation to Pagan Traditionalism, an important digression and reflection on Traditionalism itself is in order. Modernity began its active advance in the Renaissance era, and it is to this period that Mark Sedgwick has traced the roots of the philosophy of Traditionalism back to the Italian thinker Marsilio Ficino's translation of the *Corpus Hermeticum*, the authorship of which was attributed to Hermes Trismegistus.[127] Thus unfolded the notion of Philosophia Perennis, the Eternal Philosophy or Eternal Wisdom, which would later be developed with the rediscovery of the philosophy of Plato and the Neoplatonists. In

---

127 See: Sedgwick, *Against the Modern World: Traditionalism and the Secret Intellectual History of the Twentieth Century*.

the early 20th century, Traditionalism would be enriched by the discovery of the Indian *Vedanta* and the correlation of *Philosophia Perennis* with *Sanatana Dharma*, and would come to be expressed openly in the works of Matgioi, René Guénon, Julius Evola, Titus Burckhardt, and others. Thus, Traditionalism appeared simultaneously with Modernity, in the periphery of the latter, and came out into open opposition to Modernity in the 20th century. Yet if the Traditionalists' struggle had been crowned with success, then Modernity would have been displaced and we could speak of a Traditionalist "Postmodernity", a new edition of Tradition. But instead, after the Second World War the Modern world and the language of Modernity began to undergo radical changes of a non-traditional character which affected both the paradigm of Tradition (including both manifestationism and creationism) and the paradigm of Modernity itself, which would be transformed into something completely different.

We associate the main message of Postmodernity with the taking of the program of "emancipation from" to its maximum, with the message of the emancipation of Modernity from great projects, from structures, from itself. Insofar as Modernity was structured along the rejection of traditional structure, it itself harbored a reflection of this structure. Man did not simply overthrow the Gods, but took their place. Instead of rituals and rites, science was institutionalized, force was replaced by law, and religion by ideology. The Postmodernists, represented mostly by the French post-structuralists such as Gilles Deleuze, Felix Guattari, Michel Foucault, Jean Baudrillard, and Jean-François Lyotard, argued that the structures of Modernity are just as repressive and totalitarian as the structures of Tradition. Despite emancipation from theology and the Sacred, Modernists still erected hierarchical constructs, merely configured differently. The apparent homogeneity of the horizontal dimension of Modernity from the perspective of the Sacred turned out to possess its own compressed form of hierarchy and levels. Here we can recall Freud's revelation of two levels: the conscious and the unconscious in which the ratio of myth is localized.

Modernity adopted the dogmatism of traditional (Christian) society and clothed it in its own language of scientific facts, axioms, and natural and social laws. Postmodernism, in turn, proclaimed the deconstruction of the structures and constructs of Modernity, proposing a fundamentally different world-structure based on the rejection of any kind of hierarchy, even that of the modernist variety.

Of fundamental significance to Postmodernists is the rejection of any verticality, dictatorship, and authoritarianism as expressed in patriarchal society, science, consciousness, in the vertical Logos, in vertical orientation, and in phallism (patriarchy). Postmodernism constantly rejects any phallo-logo-centrism, i.e., any authoritarian structure regardless of the patterns (language) in which such is expressed, whether such be the science and secularism of Modernity or the Sacrality and theology of paganism. The emergence of the paradigm of Postmodernity following the Second World War de facto reflected a reaction to the horror seen in the faces of the totalitarianisms of the Third Reich and Soviet Union, and thereby designated the key motive of liberation from structures to be emancipation from "fascism" - "fascism" meaning any institution of any form of "norm."

The rejection of patriarchy, and as a consequence the final collapse of the horizontal into an absolute plane, excludes the establishment of any notion of "norm" in any form as a manifestation of dictatorship, as a violation of the horizontal homogeneity by the vertical axiomatically entailing the structuring of ideological, social, political, anthropological, and temporal space around itself. Here we are dealing with the chthonic element in its purest form. If the titans and titanic element, the offspring of the Great Mother hostile to the Gods and striving in their war to scale Olympus, which is to say to line up vertically like the Gods (but not being Gods), represented the underpinning of Modernity, then Postmodernity represents the chthonic and hypochthonic dimensions of the Great Mother. After all, the Mother of matter is below matter itself, in the subaquatic, slippery, unstable, sludgy silt.[128]

The world of Postmodernity is fundamentally new, and is even more subtle and dangerous of a challenge to pagan philosophy, communities, and societies today. At the same time, it is equally dangerous to both adherents of creationism and supporters of the classical worldview of Modernity. Nevertheless, Postmodernity is the logical extension of the program of Modernity, "freedom from" taken to the very end, its culmination. The divine withdraws, the titans triumph in battle and can now return to their Mother.

Now we will continue our journey through the conceptual space of this field of battle between Tradition, Modernity, and Postmodernity, focusing on the fundamentally new, extravagant proposals of the Postmodern post-view of the post-world.

Post-Ontology and Post-Gnoseology

The rejection of structure, of system, of hierarchy and, more broadly, any notion of the "due" and "norms" acting as orientations for life or the development of society and man, is the defining tendency of Postmodernity. The continuation of the program of "emancipation from", now applied to Modernity itself, deconstructs the world of Modernity as expressed in secular science. This impulse yields a certain emancipation from the grip of gnoseological racism towards traditional views - however, of principal importance, this does not lead to a return to traditional values or their affirmation. Postmodernity denies both the structures of Modernity and the structures of Tradition, carrying both of their fragments and forms down its stream. The repressive grip of Modernity is weakened, and renovated, humanistic Christianity in the face of Catholicism steps in the direction of Postmodernity in partially recognizing

---

128 On the Great Mother and the "Logos of Cybele", see the first volume of Alexander Dugin's *Noomakhia - The Three Logoi - Apollo, Dionysus, and Cybele* (Moscow: Academic Project, 2014), excerpted in English at *Eurasianist Internet Archive*.

the provisions of modern science, social changes, and repenting for its sins and policies of discrimination (*à la* John Paul II).

At the same time, the second half of the 20th century saw the beginning of that "dawn" of paganism in the modern era which we have mentioned. Although pushed into the periphery of public attention, culture, thinking, and language, paganism has nonetheless continued to exist up to our days, and its contemporary rise is taking place alongside the weakening of Modernity's clutch and amidst Postmodernity and its agenda. Yet it would be suicidal self-deception to believe that this loosening of Modernity's grip is any sign of recognition or acceptance of pagan Wisdom and an invitation to return and triumph.

Neither traditional truth nor scientific truth matter anymore, insofar as any notion of truth, of norm, is seen as dictatorship. Truth becomes fundamentally many. Every individual can wield their own truth on any question and know that another individual, even one with an opposing view, also has their own truth. Thus, the question of truth becomes a game in which truth as such is affirmed momentarily, only to just as rapidly dissipate. Gain, efficiency, and success become the criteria of truth: that which in the present moment is advantageous, convenient, and profitable is true. In other circumstances, any other point of view might be true. Referencing reality as "fact" becomes meaningless, for there is no longer any "in fact"; instead, there is only nothing in the flow of the game, random configurations, and the mixing of the immiscible. Everything appears to be a kaleidoscope of rapidly changing random configurations, among the most coincidental of which fall those which paganism holds to be the true view of the world, i.e., the Gods, Sacrality, hierarchy, and dharma, those held to as true by creationism, i.e., God, creation, the covenants and testaments, and service, as well as those considered truth in Modernity, i.e., empirical fact, progress, development, and science. In the whirling of the kaleidoscope, these "truths" are only differing coincidental configurations - none of which bear the character of absolute truth, while all of them are "true" for the moment that they appear in the eyepiece of the kaleidoscope. The randomness of kaleidoscopic configurations can mix fragments of different "truths" into one picture, and thus we might see in a given configuration certain elements of the pagan world mixed with space flights and fantastic inventions in the hands of satyrs or elves. Such a picture, needless to say again, has nothing to do with either paganism or science.

Knowing reality becomes impossible due to the absence of systematizing structures and orientations for cognition. In other words, a single language of interpretations, a single code of truth, is missing, whether Sacred knowing and identifying, verification or falsifiability. In the mid-20th century, the Austrian-American philosopher Paul Feyerabend proclaimed "epistemological anarchism", or the rejection of universal criteria for the truth of knowledge. According to Feyerabend, scientists are free to create or follow any theory whatsoever, even the most absurd and outdated. One of the results of this concept was putting scientific and religious knowledge on an equal level with other chimerical, absurd, and extravagant views.

In the field of fundamental theoretical physics, which seeks to explain space, time, and fundamental interactions, the shift away from Modernity began in the early 20th century and has, in our days, in all of its abstract, hypothetical and extravagant qualities, virtually "caught up" with esotericism in the profane sense as akin to something "mystical." Ernest Rutherford split the atom, proving that it is not "indivisible" but consists of smaller particles which, in turn, divide into subatomic particles and, on the basis of Albert Einstein's theory of relativity and Erwin Schrödinger's quantum mechanics, lead to the micro-level of contemporary string theory. Another prospective theory generalizing fundamental interactions is M-theory, the basic object of which is the membrane, i.e., a hypothetical multidimensional object constituting strings and objects of higher dimensionality. A specificity of these theories of quantum mechanics, membranes, and strings is their multidimensionality and the extreme difficulty of experimentally confirming them.

New theories are abandoning the three-dimensional (3D) understanding of the universe in favor of D-theory, for which time is merely one dimension. A number of opinions hold that it is a mathematical apparatus allowing to develop the means of experimental confirmation of these and a number of other theories that is missing today. The multidimensionality of strings allows for the existence of a multiverse or multiverses in which ours is merely one among many still unknown. A pluriversal interpretation is allowed by quantum theory, from which the cat experiment of Nobel laureate Erwin Schrödinger has entered mass pop culture. Another most "esoteric" example is the theoretical multidimensional space of Calabi–Yau[129], which has come to be known by laymen as something taken from the mythology of Mesoamerican Indians.

The extravagance and mergence of such non-classical theories of physics with mysticism and esotericism has generated borderline doctrines mixing fragments of religiosity, cosmic fiction, and quantum interpretations passed off as revelations from higher authorities. Many popular and academic works on quantum theory and strings are to be found in the esoteric sections of bookstores. But the "esotericism" of such quantum and string theories is illusory and has no relation to metaphysics and esotericism as Guénon understood such. Such non-classical theories plunge ever deeper into matter, multiplying versions, theories, fundamental objects and their dimensions all the while as they ignore traditional metaphysics. Despite the fact that membranes and strunes are more objects of faith than they are precise knowledge, their nature is human and material. Although these theories devote great attention to gravitation and cosmic objects (such as Black Holes), the exploration of space itself and dreams of the cosmic expansion of mankind came to nought just ahead of the 21st century. The American moon landing in 1969 and the deployment of reusable manned ships marked the peak of the space race embodying the full might of the science and technology achieved by man in the 20th century.

---

[129] Named in honor of the mathematicians Eugenio Calabi and Shing-Tung Yau.

The Apollo program ended with the last human moon landing in 1972, followed in 1988 by the first and only unmanned flight of the Soviet Buran shuttle two years after the crash of the American Challenger shuttle. The last shuttle, Atlantis, was decommissioned in 2011, eight years after the crash of the Columbia shuttle. The end of moon exploration and space shuttle programs marked a turn from large-scale, expansive projects towards the more mundane sphere of technologies and solutions for everyday life and comfort.

The peak of space exploration in the late 20th century thus occurred in parallel to the establishment in the West of a new type of society, the consumer society, and the cropping up of the heralding of Postmodernity. This societal shift was reflected in literature in the replacement of science fiction, which valued the criteria of scientific validity and which often bore prognostic prophecies of future technologies, by the genre of fantasy. The fantasy genre arose in the early 20th century in association with such names as Robert Howard, Edward Plunkett (Lord Dunsany), Clive Lewis, John Tolkien, Howard Lovecraft, Andrzej Sapkowski, and others, whose genre took as its forerunner Medieval epics, chivalric novels, and more ancient legends and tales. Such surviving ancient epics as *Beowulf* or the *Song of the Nibelungs*, although without a doubt affected over the course of editions by Christian trends and influences, nevertheless contain myths and chronicles of real value to traditions. Fantasy authors, basing themselves on such ancient myths as well as medieval, already Christian epics, created a number of myths which inherited the motifs of real chronicles and myths only in an external and stylistic sense, taking over the style (clan sagas, chronicles, and legends), structure, and mythological-cum-"fantastical" figures and characters. In such cases, the resultant works do not correspond to reality, nor to the values which such texts hold for tradition, even though they come maximally close to the images of such.[130] In the

---

[130] Here is had in mind so-called "high fantasy", the founding father of which is considered to be J.R.R. Tolkien, whose legendarium was founded on a mixing of numerous myths from different peoples and ages of Europe.

classics of fantasy, we meet elves, dwarves, trolls, gods, heroes, peoples, and myths, wars, and feats known to us from traditional myths, albeit translated into fictional races, spaces, lands, and the "mythology" of fictional peoples and gods. Vivid examples of such fantasy in Russian literature include the author of "Slavic fantasy", Maria Semenova, as well as, albeit with some reservations, Lev Prozorov.

Later, when science fiction (strictly concerned with validity) would be pushed into the periphery, the latter would be mixed into the fantasy genre, yielding worlds and narratives in which magical actions, deities, and miracles are explained from a scientific-technological point of view as akin to technologies superior to the ones available to modern humanity. Alternatively, there arose narratives in which scientific-technological means and the magico-fantastical coexisted and interacted, each according to their own laws without inciting a conflict of interpretations of reality from one position or another, whether scientific or conventionally magical (mythical). Accounts of this sort can describe worlds in which "mythical" creatures roam the galaxies in starships and "gods" actively use telecommunications and fantastical weapons, and heroes' battles against evil with the highest technological devices. The classic opponents of heroes, monsters, are represented as the results of genetic experiments, as robots, clowns, etc. Among the authors of such science-fantasy or techno-fantasy, we can point to some of the works of Herbert George Wells, the Strugatsky brothers, Roger Zelazny, Richard Halliwell, and Brian Ansel.[131] The maximal degeneration and dilution of this genre, and at once the maximal illustration of the point which we have suggested, is the world of comics which was created and reached its heyday in the United States.

We can recognize the formation of Postmodernity, with its rejection of normativity and its embrace of universal mixing,

---

[131] Richard Halliwell and Brian Ansel were the creators of the techno-fantasy-war game Warhammer whose motifs have been constantly, actively novelized.

in this case of the shifting tendency in literature from strict scienticity (the language of Modernity) to the imitation of traditional language and, finally, to the mixing, coexistence, and interpenetration of scientific and mythical/magical themes. In fantasy, we can find traces of traditional myths and epics, elements of science and technology, as well as elements of reality and history. But if we look away from these works to discover such in the real world, we will not find anything of the sort. Even if the development of technology has seen through the partial incarnation of elements of scientific fantasy in newly existing devices, technologies, and social changes (leaving that which has not found materialization to be only a matter of time and progress), and if traditional tales, epics, ballads, and legends already were (and always are) reality, then this leaves fantasy with no incarnation or basis in the real world. The worlds of fantasy, whether the high fantasy of Tolkien with detailed developed mythologies, geographies, peoples, and even artificial languages, or the techno-fantasy of Ansel and Stan Lee, are simulations and substitutes - in a word, simulacra.

Simulacrum, in the meaning of interest to us as employed by Jean Baudrillard and Gilles Deleuze, means a representation of something that does not exist, a copy without an original. Such an original-less copy or signifier lacks a counterpart of its signification in reality and can be conceptualized as a fake, an attempted reality that is not reality - for example, a digitally-created image processed into a picture and painted over onto a canvas. Another example of a simulacrum is the current of Ambient music, which represents a simulation, or fragmentary mixing of samples with real recordings, of sounds from surrounding reality, whether sounds of nature, cities, war, media, radio interference, etc. John R. Tolkien's legendarium is a prime example of a simulacrum in literature. An example of an artificial language outside of artistic production would be Esperanto.

With the development of three-dimensional printing, it has become possible to create not only semiotic simulacra in the field of culture, but also concrete, tangible things. In England, artificial raspberry juice, chemicals, and drop-dosing technologies have been used by engineers to "sculpt" berries seemingly identical in form to raspberries but consisting merely of drops of juice. The resultant berries look altogether similar to raspberries, but consist of absolutely nothing from a real raspberry. Such technologies are also used in Japan. In the field of medicine, three-dimensional printing has come close to creating exact copies of human organs for transplantation. The next logical step would be the printing of chimerical organic structures and genetically modified organisms.

Besides the field of culture and technology, simulacra can also come in the form of events "covered" as "tangible" by the media. Jean Baudrillard himself believed the Gulf War to be a simulacrum. Vivid illustration of the creation of simulacra of real events for political ends can be seen in the film "Wag the Dog", in which the US government hires a team of directors, screenwriters, and actors to shoot "chronicles" of a war in an Eastern European country which are relayed to the mainstream media as real events in order to divert from a scandal in the White House. In recent history, colorful examples of such simulacra include supposedly sudden outbreaks of acutely dangerous diseases, such as "avian flu", "Ebola," etc., which are meant to capture the attention of global media and shape the socio-political agenda for a short period of time. In such cases, epidemiological dangers fulfill the function of "wagging the dog", which is to say diverting attention from more important events to less significant ones overblown in the media. The simulation of reality, events, and their discussion is inextricably linked to means of modern virtual communication, mass media, and the attachment of the broad masses to these information channels and streams. Of relevance here is the thesis voiced by the main propagandist of the 20th century, Joseph Goebbels, that "a lie repeated a thousand times becomes truth." Of important note is that in the cases of fantasy literature, ambient music, and a number of other cultural trends, the simulacrum is the distortion of or disguising of reality. Let us recall the above-mentioned imitation by fantasy legendariums of medieval and more ancient epics or the production of imitation images and techniques of fine art. The next step in socio-political and media simulacra is the replacement of reality through the entanglement of traces of broadcasted images, opinions, and discussions of a supposed event in order to render such a reality. Often enough, upon trying to unravel a certain media trend by searching for its real grounds, one will find themselves in a closed ring, a Möbius loop, of links and quotes referencing one another, ultimately leading to no reality whatsoever. The broadcasted picture, people, and events are constituted by a set of decorations and actors in a "dream factory."

The final step is the abandonment of any concealment of the absence of real bases of an event, a pure simulation of sign flows not requiring any verification in reality which generates a flow of free interpretations and discussions. This is the endless recycling process of semiosis, or the generation of significations without references, the "factualization" of serious discussions over events which in fact have no reality whatsoever, but which are rather products of graphic editors, video editing, and text generators. None of this matters, of course, insofar as there is no "in fact" in Postmodernity, in which everything that "can be" already "is", and everything that "is", is an embodiment of what "can be." A most clear example of a pure simulacrum whose nature was not even hidden was the "outbreak" of Ebola in 2014, which came to be called "global problem number one."

Postmodernity allows for one to simultaneously operate with both the "truth" of Tradition and the "truth" of Modernity, or any other "truth" created by an individual, to mix them, to assert their simultaneous "truthfulness", and to bypass their fundamental irreducibility to one another by cutting off all higher and deeper dimensions and meanings. Postmodernity operates with forms and flat images which do not lead to anything serious, meaningful, or fundamental. Any attempt to derive a fundamental, real, root basis from Postmodernist discourse will end up with looped citations and references. Therefore, the ideal representation of reality under Postmodernity is the screen: an absolutely superficial surface projecting equally superficial images and texts which lead nowhere - in a word, signs without any signified.

The Post-Human

The very idea of the human is also subject to transformation under Postmodernity, which takes the message of liberal humanism to its climax with the concepts of transhumanism and posthumanism. The boundary between transhumanism and posthumanism today is not clearly defined, so these two concepts can be correlated as mutually complementary.

Transhumanism asserts as its aim the infinite improvement or "perfection" of the human body with the latest achievements of science from such fields as transplantology, cybernetics, biotechnology, nanotechnology, nootropic pharmacology, surgery, cryonics, computer science, and others. Immortality and the merging of the human with artificial intelligence are seen as the desired prospect, which would add a technological rung to the biological and social evolution of man. Man thus becomes an open project, a canvas for changes and perfections in the likes of supplanting organic muscle tissue in the hand with a steel prosthesis to lift larger loads, raising human memory with memory-module implants or a "brain-computer" interface, improving cognitive functions with medications - in a word, modifying the external form in accordance with any model. Such fundamental things which define human being and existence as racial, ethnic, or gender identity become variable. If so desired, today one can change their gender, eye shape, height, and skin color, and more than once. Or one can altogether reject gender and generic identities and transform their body in the direction of an imitation of animals or fully synthetic cybernetic entities. This is real today not only on the technological level, but is legally enshrined as the right of the individual and can be realized freely by many people.

Posthumanism, meanwhile, can be called the stage when the process of transhumanistic metamorphoses in the external and structural form of a person are changed to such an extent that the resulting entity cardinally differs from the normal human constitution. One of the programmatic aims of posthumanism is achieving the technological possibility of uploading consciousness into a computer, a network, and virtual reality. Insofar as liberal humanism establishes the definition of who is "human" as a matter of convention, a contract, nothing prevents the reconsideration of including in the definition of "human" new characteristics, including those which would render "human" an entity predominantly mechanical in its elements, printed organs, or even a "program" in virtual space loaded into the consciousness of a person and thereby embodied in a colorful "avatar" or "profile picture."

The significant development and popularization of the philosophy of transhumanism was the work of Fereidoun M. Esfandiary, more famously known by his transhumanist name FM-2030, who died from cancer in 2000 and is awaiting his resurrection by new technologies in a cryonic suspension space. In the socio-political sphere, transhumanists stand in solidarity with libertarians, post-gender movements, radical and ecological currents (which argue that the development of technology will lead to the improvement of the ecological situation), and actively defend the expansion of civil rights and freedoms. It is worth noting that some posthumanists have criticized transhumanism for fixating only on human evolution. Francis Fukuyama, meanwhile, has criticized transhumanism as an endless race for improvement lacking focus on relevantly arising social problems such as quality of life and potential social inequalities with regards to the high cost of biotechnological modifications for the general population.

Postmodernity thus entails the rejection of considering the human to be an individual, in the sense of being "indivisible", in favor of the concept of the "dividual" or "divisible" being. Man thus becomes divisible and dispersed between an infinite number of potential signs of corporeality and identification. Mutants, cyborgs, avatars, clones, and GMO-people become the familiar picture of the day. Traditional and Modernist approaches to the human, who is now free with the aid of bio-modifications (piercings, scarifications, tattoos, surgery, and implants[132]) to constantly alter their external appearance, combined with the variability of social identities (subcultures, groups, genders, professions, social statuses and niches) in which the incompatible can seemingly be made fit, are no longer in full force, but can be interpreted in a simulated manner. For instance, a person who undergoes multiple operations to change their appearance towards that of, say, an "elf" and indicates such as their "nationality" would seemingly be embodying the traditional idea of human metamorphoses and traditional accounts of such creatures as mermaids, centaurs, and fauns. On the other hand, such is done through purely scientific, technological, and legal advances. Thus, such modifications have nothing to do with tradition, nor with the scientific positivist paradigm, but are simulacra.

To this unfolding picture can be added yet another, no less important dimension of human "dividuation": representation in virtual space and networks. The Internet, as a platform of communication, especially in the form of social networks and services, offers a person an unlimited choice of possibilities for representing themselves to others. In virtual space, a dividual's account can be anything. They can change gender, present themselves as a centaur, an alien, a foreigner, an historical personality, an inanimate object, a stone, or a washing machine. Rapidly changing between these simulated guises is very possible. Today, virtual communication and social life are practically integral parts of modern man who, while at once a being living in the real world, is also constantly present online, thereby giving his virtual extension a form of life. In a dystopian perspective, a human would be conceived as a bio-offline appendage to their virtual (sub)personality, its servant.

---

132 One example is the Czech professor, composer, and teacher of theater art, Vladimir Franz, whose body is 90% covered with tattoos and piercings, and who ran for President of Czech Republic in 2013.

The postulate that everything that is "actual" is the embodiment of the "potential", and that the "potential" is "actual" is also at work on the human. Man should strive towards the maximal actualization of all of his potential, of everything that can be possibly embodied. A person should experiment with their corporeality, playfully changing roles and identifications and modifying their body. The whole range of potential possibilities to which one should strive has been termed in Postmodernist discourse the "body without organs", a notion attributed to the French philosopher and sociologist Georges Bataille. The human of Postmodernity is the rampant desire machine of Deleuze and Guattari, one who derives pleasure and satisfaction from the process of change itself, not from the result or goals, which are not intended at all. Under Postmodernity, the very biological constitution of man is declared a fascist dictatorship over the freedom of organs and joints to act as they will. The vertical posture of man and the tension of organ systems is seen as a dictatorship of consciousness over organs and corporeality. The internal parts of the human have the right to organize their own administration, their own parliament, and to make decisions. A remarkable example of this is illustrated in M. Khvorostov's *Telesnoe* ("Corporeal"), which narrates a complexity of contractual relationships between the legs, hands, eyes, liver, brain, and consciousness ("I") of a person in their everyday life. A conflict between the hands and legs erupts into a bloody drama, during which the human "I" forces down the hands with scissors, inciting shock and terror at such blatant dictatorship among the other organs, which collectively decide to shoot the "human."

Moreover, the search for extraterrestrial life on other planets has seen the putting forth of the rather revealing, strictly Postmodernist thesis that humanity, in trying to find signs of intelligent life or the conditions for its emergence in accordance with its own history and conditions needed for existence, is asserting "carbon racism", which references the defining role of carbon in life on Earth. In other words, the legal and political practice of tolerance and emancipation is automatically extrapolated to extraterrestrial life forms, the presence of which still has yet to be confirmed in any conclusive way (from the point of view of classical Modernity there is nothing of the sort to be found, just as there is no God).

The theses of Postmodernity should not be perceived as merely extravagant or sick, schizophrenic fantasies. For the US and countries in Europe, Postmodernity is a reality enshrined in law and practiced by numerous people. Russia as well has been subjected to these trends, although only partially, many cases of such being but avant-garde shock-value stunts and unhealthy behavior on the part of public freaks. For Pagan Traditionalists, the concepts of the dividual, the human without anthropomorphic features (cyborgs, computer-loaded consciousness, modificants), and the simulacra represent an arch-complex challenge at times further burdened by the fact that still far from all pagans have come around to reflecting on the concepts of Modernity.

What is Britain's artificially printed "raspberry" from the point of view of the agrarian mythology of the third estate and sacred demiurgy? How do electronic consciousness and the maximally robotized body relate to the sacred, initiated human? To these questions we can only give a definitively negative response. A being that does not come out of a mother's womb (and thereby is similar to kin and fellow tribesmen), who does not die and is not born over the course of initiation, and who does not go into the earth or the fire after death, is not a human being - perhaps similar, but below. Such are creatures of the lower worlds devoid of the Breath of the Gods. Robots and robotized bodies are like the golems of Jewish mythology whose lives and meaning are contained in a piece of paper placed in their mouths, in this case program codes of algorithms for actions and the interpretation of a controller's commands. We can detect a similar motif in the Russian tale "The Clay Boy",[133] in which a childless elderly man and his wife (a detail which

---

[133] Summarized here on the basis of Alexey Nikolaevich Tolstoy's rendition.

already reveals to us their inadequate vitality) mold a child out of clay. The boy first eats all the bread, the product of sacred tilling, then the "parents", the bull, the woodcutters, and all the men and women with rakes and scythes. In the end, the clay boy is tricked and shattered by a goat - the consecrated animal of the God Veles and one of the latter's most frequent disguises and personifications in winter koliadas - thus freeing those he had eaten. This motif of creation out of clay and the subjugation and captivity of life by the chthonic element directly refers us to Prometheus' demiurgic creation of the mankind of the Iron Age, which in turn is related to the motif of the golem in Mary Shelley's work *Frankenstein, or Modern Prometheus*. The Strugatsky brothers also directly deemed the golem created by Loew ben Bezalel, the chief rabbi of 16th century Prague, to have been the first cybernetic robot.

Post-Society

Having already partially presented some defining aspects of the post-society of Postmodernity in our examination of the masses and multitudes, we will continue our inquiry in this direction.

In striving to renounce the dictatorship of any notion of norm, Postmodernists such as Gilles Deleuze and Felix Guattari turned their attention to the family.[134] They conceived of the family as the basic cell of fascistic, totalitarian society, in which a child is forced to love someone who suppresses their freedom and dictates norms of behavior. These authors equate the psychological suppression of the personality in the family to social repression. Considering the family to be an Oedipal triangle, they conclude that the family is the source of dictatorship and complexes of the suppressed desires of the members of the family. According to myth, Oedipus' father Laius was foretold that if he married Jocasta, he would die by

---

134 See: Gilles Deleuze and Felix Guattari, *Anti-Oedipus: Capitalism and Schizophrenia* (Minneapolis: University of Minnesota Press, 1983).

the hand of his son. Disregarding this prophecy, Laius took Jocasta as his wife but, still fearing the possible outcome, pierced the legs of his newborn son Oedipus and ordered him to be thrown off Mount Cithaeron. The baby Oedipus was found by a shepherd and brought to the king of Corinth, Polybus. Upon maturing, Oedipus learned of the prophecy that he would kill his father, shunned Polybus, and set off for Delphi. Along the way of his travels, Oedipus encountered Laius, not knowing his identity, and killed him in an altercation. Subsequently arriving in Thebes, Oedipus freed the city from the Sphinx by solving its riddle, became king of Thebes, and married Laius' widow, Jocasta, who bore him children. For this crime, the Gods sent a pestilence upon Thebes to last until the murderer would be driven out of the city. Upon learning the truth, Jocasta hanged herself and Oedipus blinded himself. When his children ceased to treat him well, he cursed them as well. On the basis of this myth, Sigmund Freud introduced to psychoanalysis the concept of the "Oedipus complex", or the unconscious attraction to one's parent of the opposite sex accompanied with ambivalent (dual) feelings for the parent of the same sex. The female version of this complex was conceived by Carl Jung as the "Electra complex", the latter also being a reference to Greek myth in which Electra, the daughter of King Agamemnon of Mycenae murdered by his wife Clytemnestra, sought revenge with the help of her mother's brother and kills her.

Thus, the family with pronounced patriarchal (and, less often, matriarchal) domination is subordinated to its head, who "colonizes" the rest of the family members. Moving from family to society, we can see a similar picture to that of relations between the masses and authority, between society and the capitalist system. A lucid example of such relations is "Stockholm syndrome", or a defensive reaction expressed in sympathy on the part of hostages for their captors, whom they seek to understand and justify. The syndrome of a victim's sympathy for their aggressor can also arise in the case of terrorist attacks, detention in prison or concentration camp, in the family, in totalitarian sects, or in an indigenous population's attitude to its military conquerors. Deleuze and Guattari envisioned the abolition of the patriarchal component of the traditional family, as well as the preserved elements of patriarchal domination in the modern family, contrasting such to the ideal of the open society. In their view, insofar as the human is a machine of desires, then society is a society of desires which must be built on an open family of desire-machines. Thus, the removal of the father figure is seen as liberating the family and society from the vertical dimension, and as a result from dictatorship and fascism, rendering the family and society fundamentally open to the streams of desires emanating from within people.

In the realities of modern practice, we can turn our view to legislative initiatives in the social and family spheres in Europe and the US. Among such initiatives aimed at the realization of the concept of the open family and the defense of equal rights of all family members, we can see such programs as the "tolerant" sexual education of children from early school years, social programs for children to anonymously report domestic violence ("denunciations of parents"), the introduction into the social sciences of such families as "incoming parents", "same-sex families", the "Swedish family", and "civil union." In addition to the introduction into official documentation of such formulae and the replacement of the notions of "father" and "mother" with "Parent #1" and "Parent #2" in order to avoid discrimination of same-sex marriages and between people with arbitrary genders, we can also see the active integration of so-called "juvenile technologies" aimed at reforming traditional forms of child-raising in the direction of liberal concepts based on recognizing the child as a mature person with inalienable interests and rights.

Continuing their critique of Freudianism and psychoanalysis, Postmodernists have gone so far as to accuse psychoanalysis of being "fascist" and fulfilling the repressive function of a police-state. Reducing numerous scenarios to the "Oedipal family" and bringing the internal conflict of the personality to "normal" and healing, i.e., to being freed from the Oedipal complex, is seen as an act of totalitarian violence and the assertion of "norm." As is well known, totalitarian states have actively employed punitive psychiatry to eliminate and isolate opposition from society, and medical-pharmacological means have been used on the consciousness and behavior of people deemed by regimes undesirable. The use of medicine and psychiatry for political purposes has been known over recent centuries in the US, Germany, Eastern Europe, the USSR, China, and other countries. Such biased psychiatry has been used to justify oppression against black slaves in the US, opposition in the countries of the socialist camp, and dissident and religious actors in China. In democratic societies, psychiatry has also taken on a repressive political function, but the greater portion of responsibility for the "correction" of deviance and dissent has been placed on psychologists and psychoanalysts themselves. People with a sense of frustration or those who have been identified as deviating from norms have at times been sent to mandatory couch-sessions for specialized examinations. Through the "soft means" of therapy, pharmacology and processual extrapolation of a client's case, the state system returns a normalized unit to the bosom of the masses. Control and treatment are carried out by soft methods, cultivated by culture, literature, and cinema. In light of the fact that the social-humanitarian sciences and spheres of activity are always, without exception, ideologically dependent on the ideology and authority of the state, psychoanalysis has thereby also become an effective tool for the surveillance and correction of the masses.

Deleuze and Guattari opposed psychoanalysis with what they called "schizoanalysis", which, instead of psychoanalytical reduction to one model and theory of description and consciousness, proclaims variability, intersection, and the overlapping of different forms of knowledge of subjectivity. Further developing the notion of the human as a desire-machine, schizoanalysis deduces the desire for production using Marxist theory, i.e., liberates desire from reduction to family drama and opens up the way for the social investment of desire. Self-consciousness and awareness become but one of the machines of desire within the body. Hence dividuation, or the body without organs. The path to the body without organs runs through "deterritorialization", or the dispersion of the dividual, for which, among other things, the consumption of narcotics can be used to "untwist" and "shake" habitual, established consciousness. The latter is supposed to lead to a subsequent "reterritorialization", i.e., a new arrangement with new norms, views, desires, and behavior. Schizoanalysis and deterritorialization are the justifications for the above-described variance of identifications and representations of the (in)dividual in modern society and virtual reality.

Thus, the anti-humanistic masses prevailing over the individual become schizo-masses, or masses of deterritorialized desire-machines invested in society and withdrawn from the scenario of familial, Oedipal drama.

The Consumer Society

The Postmodern philosopher Jean Baudrillard described contemporary society as the consumer society, or a society in pursuit of a simulacrum of happiness. Baudrillard saw "happiness" as the cornerstone of the consumer and democratic society of universal equality, in which happiness is a set of signs before which all people are equal. By consuming things marked with signs of happiness and well-being, people reduce the social gap between classes and strata. This is how the democratic myth of equality is formed through the replacement of real participation in the life of the state and society with a chase after signs which allow one to count themselves among the category of successful people - a "myth" which masks real discrimination and inequality within society.

The consumer society dictates the pursuit of happiness as expressed in signs, which is to say that it produces consumption for the sake of consumption. Happiness becomes a goal that pushes away freedom and the texture of reality, replacing such with a semiotic texture of signs. The pursuit of happiness, whose sets of signs change ever rapidly, generates a certain wastefulness necessary for consumption. In such a system, free, rational choice is impossible, as it is entirely dictated by the sign system, formulated social values, and designated signs of happiness, success, and well-being. Man thus becomes a synthesis of the signs he consumes (dividuation/deterritorialization). The human being becomes what they consume, or rather the signs that they consume. In his analysis of the consumer society, Baudrillard evoked a comparison of the chase after signs with primitive cargo cults: "Without calling the anthropoid hunter-gatherers who today wander through our urban jungles primitives (though why not?), we might see this as a fable of the consumer society. The beneficiary of the consumer miracle also sets in place a whole array of sham objects, of characteristic signs of happiness, and then waits (waits desperately, a moralist would say) for happiness to alight."[135]

An enormous role in the consumer society is played by mass information culture and mainstream media. Fashion, as the ideology of the obsolescence of things, becomes the new religion of society, demanding that variability be constantly relevant and the engine that moves the change of signifiers of success and happiness. Fashion and the criteria of success based on such are embedded in such subcultures as those of hipsters and yuppies. Yuppie, being an abbreviation of "Young Urban Professional Person", refers to a class of pragmatists, businessmen, and secular-oriented young people of free mores. The heyday of this subculture was in the US in the 1980s. Hipsters and hippies, both of whose names go back to the slang "to be hip", meaning "to be in fashion", emerged as a subculture in the US in the 1940s. Both groups are products of the bourgeois consumer society and corresponding ideologies which differ only formally and stylistically.

---

[135] Jean Baudrillard, *The Consumer Society: Myths and Structures* (London: SAGE Publications, 1998), p. 31.

The art of the consumer society is mass-reproduced: pop art, digital copies, anti-elitism, contemporary art, and "events." A special place among broadcasted media images is taken by advertisements or "ads" which do not convince one of the usefulness or functionality of a product, but compel one to believe in its necessity and value as an advertising sign. Advertising itself comes to be seen as a field of art; advertisers become the new artists and directors. The strategy of marketers in advertising is not to justify the importance of a good, but to create an atmosphere of enveloping trust appealing to values of significance within a target group, and forming a trusting relation with the "product-consumer" for generations. On such media, Baudrillard remarked, "Media stupefies the masses, and the masses stupefy the media."

The consumer society packages and makes consumable absolutely everything: real things/goods, services, events, experiences, emotions, and consumption itself. Purchasing a gadget or service, a person is not actually acquiring the thing itself, but is obtaining a trademark that categorizes them as happy and successful. If we examine the technical, functional, and external characteristics of modern electronic devices, we find only minimal differences between them. Moreover, the components for different devices are often produced by one and the same or two monopolistic companies, or one company simply diversifies the consumption of its products by creating different logos and brands for what is essentially the same product. Buying a drink or coffee in the temple of consumption, the supermarket, a person in no way chooses between varieties and characteristics, but rather between brands and emblems to be demonstrated to others. Man consumes consumption, and this act momentarily makes him happy.

Even freedom of time disappears amidst the consumer society, dissolved between acts of consumption, the production of desires and the consumption of leisure. It becomes no longer possible to spend one's time freely, as every sphere of time is covered with signs and strategies of consumption. Time thus becomes a homogenous, monotonous act of consuming signs.

Amidst all the diversity of consumption, Baudrillard highlighted the most desired object of consumption to be the body and sex. The body, eroticism, and beauty are subjected to marketing calculations, exploited as advertising images, and themselves become objects of trade. Upon measuring, the body becomes an instrument for increasing sales, whether cars whose curves are meant to imitate a woman's waist, or bottles of alcohol similar to the hip of a woman with whom they can be enjoyed. All of this makes goods into sexually attractive items, and therefore more consumable. Baudrillard called such an economy based on the production and consumption of pure signs "semiurgy", which might also be called "post-economics."

As mentioned above, happiness is the cornerstone of the consumer society, in which happiness is a set of signs imbued to connote such. In other words, we are dealing with a simulacrum of happiness, not the real state, but a totality of signifiers consumed by a person. Thus, reality and man become mediated from one another by a layer of semantic texture. This mediation between reality, society, and social relations was theorized from a radical left-wing standpoint by the French philosopher Guy Debord, who introduced the concept of the "society of the spectacle" in his 1967 work of the same name. Debord examined the society of developed media and consumption to be a spectacle entailing the loss of direct, unmediated experience and participation. In the society of the spectacle, everything becomes mediated by signs, including relationships, social roles, and politics. Debord wrote:

> The images detached from every aspect of life merge into a common stream in which the unity of that life can no longer be recovered. Fragmented views of reality regroup themselves into a new unity as a separate pseudo-world that can only be looked at. The specialization of images of the world evolves into a world of autonomised images where even the deceivers are deceived. The spectacle is a concrete inversion of life, an autonomous movement of the nonliving.[136]

---
136 Guy Debord, *Society of the Spectacle* (London: Rebel/Aldgate Press, 1983), p. 7.

Toward the end of his life[137], Debord argued that a new type of the society of spectacle was imminent: the "integrated spectacle" in which, unlike the totalitarian USSR in which any freedom of speech was unacceptable, the democratic society of the spectacle would see the integration of the diktat of consumption (the fetishization of goods) and a strong repressive apparatus. Without a doubt, the United States of America is an example of such an integrated society of the spectacle today.

Revolt, Anomie, and Death in the Consumer Society

While the hippy trend emerged amidst the war in Vietnam (1957-1975) as an anti-war and pacifist movement, in the very same period of time and most climactically in 1968, on a wave of economic growth and amidst the rise of the consumer society, France saw a student revolution known as "Red May." The paradox of this event lies in the very reasons for this revolt by radical left youth, who experienced the main brunt of the rapid emergence of the consumer society and found themselves deprived of employment, access to education, and, as follows, the obtainment of signs of success. The youth uprising was subsequently joined by labor unions perturbed by the downscaling of wages and new legislation on social security. The heating up of youth led in May 1968 to the explosion of student unrest clothed in left-wing rhetoric which would subsequently come to be known as the "new left" movement. The student revolt was supported by famous teachers and intellectuals, such as the Postmodernist Michel Foucault and the ideologue of atheist existentialism Jean-Paul Sartre.

A ten-million-strong strike paralyzed France as youth spoke out against the government of Charles de Gaulle, which owned a monopoly on media and which student youth

---

137 Debord committed suicide by shooting himself in 1994.

held to be an obsolete, authoritarian reign. Calling for the emancipation of the media and speaking out against capitalist exploitation, the demonstrators became the locomotive of the Postmodern reform of society, a point which is eloquently spoken to by many of the May slogans.[138] The outcome of this revolt was the holding of early elections which saw de Gaulle's party garner more than 70% of public support. Yet this brief respite could not save France. The process had already been initiated.

Turning our attention to Guy Debord's concept, we can see the May 1968 events in France as the transition from a totalitarian society of the spectacle (expressed in Charles de Gaulle's authoritarianism and nationalism) to the integrated spectacle of soft, imperceptible, left-liberal Postmodernity. The hippy subculture and ideology, meanwhile, also cracked and collapsed, leaving some of its adepts to eventually put on suits and ties and return into the fold of society, while others abandoned radical ideas and found integration into society as a soft subcultural and historical element.

The consumer society embeds and integrates protest into its very structure and begins to produce a cult of violence on its periphery as a regulator of society. In the face of violence, cruelty, and pain encountered both in real society and in broadcasts from hot spots, consumers are propelled in search of the opposite, the pursuit of happiness. Violence becomes a tool, the barbed wire of the herds of consumers which keeps the latter on the road of the race. Violence itself is even to become consumable, framed in such a manner so as to not cause deep existential experiences and so as to lure true rebels. Colorful examples of the conceptualization of the role and consumption of violence in American society include Michael Moore's film "Bowling for Columbine" and Oliver Stone's "Natural Born Killers."

---

138 For example, "*Dans une société qui abolit toute aventure, la seule aventure possible c'est l'abolition de cette société!*" - "In a society which abolishes all adventure, the only possible adventure is the abolition of society!"

In 2013, modern society in its French face encountered real violence and loss when on 21 May the French historian, Pagan Traditionalist, and New Rightist Dominique Venner shot himself in the Notre Dame de Paris Cathedral in a sign of protest against the legalization of same-sex marriage. Venner intended his sacrificial suicide to cast off society's shackles of slumber and remind it of traditional values. The ensuing one-and-a-half-million-strong demonstration in support of the traditional family posed a thorn in the side of the consumer society. Venner's act proved impossible to be interpreted as an act of spectacle, a boundary from which to push off in a new rush for signs of happiness. The fact that the support for Venner's message, represented by a million-strong French demonstration, went virtually "unnoticed" by the "free" media only compounded the situation. The support for the traditional family marked by the blood of voluntary sacrifice could only be countered with shocking kitsch. This kitsch was embodied shortly after Venner's suicide in an action organized by French feminists, one of whom climbed on the altar of the Notre Dame, naked and painted with the slogan "Death to fascism!", and imitated committing suicide by putting a toy gun in her mouth. The Postmodern shock of naked feminism equating traditional families (mainly, the family itself) with fascism (reminiscent of Deleuze and Foucault) thus employed the sexualization of the body and kitsch to turn self-sacrifice itself into a consumable show.

In Postmodernity, it is as if the last refuge of meaning, existential charge, and the transcendence of the purely human level of being is the realm of Death and related themes and regions. In the external sphere relative to man and his spirit, any bloody and violent act will be turned to the benefit of consumption to be sold, replicated, and absorbed by the idle philistine eating dinner in front of the TV screen.

The Rhizome

Postmodernists' denunciation of any and all hierarchical structures, of the notion of norms and boundaries and, as follows, even atomicity, individuality, and the difference between subject and object leads everything to superficial flatness. Deleuze and Guattari introduced a new concept to denote postmodern realities: the "rhizome." The rhizome is a subterranean, horizontally spread network, a rootstock or mycelium, that contrasts a vertical structure, such as a tree. A rhizome has no center, beginning, or end, no centering axis or principle. A rhizome can be cut off and dismembered, but it will remain unchanged in structure and will continue to be able to reproduce. The rhizome is heterogenous, capable of generating random forms, intersections, and connections, constantly pulsating and reconfiguring or "reterritorializing." Absolutely everything can be included in a rhizome, whether a dividual and its parts, simulacra and signs, society and semiosis, cognition and languages of interpretation, all of which mix chaotically, unpredictably, and unsystematically. In light of the botanical analogy, it could be said that in the Postmodern point of view vertical growth is "fascism" and "dictatorship", whereas the rhizome can only spread and grow horizontally underground (and is therefore hypochthonic). Thus, the rhizome is anti-hierarchy, the antithesis of the tripartite, Indo-European sacred hierarchy embodied in the world of Tradition and still present in the world of Modernity in corroded forms. In the Postmodern rhizome, subject and object, essence and matter are mixed, and man no longer knows if he is a biological being of "divine origin" or a chair. Or he knows that he is everything at once and still on top - but only for a second, until the next turn of the kaleidoscope-game of configurations.

Post-Space

Virtual communication over a screen fundamentally differs from face-to-face communication and even from seeing oneself in a mirror. In meeting and communicating with someone in reality, we are in contact with an other, whom we really encounter as tangible without any doubts as to their "otherness", as to the fact that they are the other. Seeing oneself in the mirror also refers to the other, as we see a conditional "self" in view of which our deep mentality always doubts whether we are seeing our real self or if the mirror is reflecting another or another world. The motif of magical, dangerous, and guiding mirrors is widely known across ancient cultures and is even reproduced in some modern productions. But a monitor screen is not a mirror. When turned off, it has minimal reflective properties (pads, lenses, and protective layers of plastic and glass which do not relate to the structure of a mirror), and is an absolute plane that, reflecting nothing, projects a "whole world" onto itself.

The new "reality" of virtuality, expressed in billions of mazes of social networks, websites, services, networks, and their topologies, is striking in its apparent volume and its presentation of the possibility of contacting any point in the world from any other, of influencing the course of events in other countries and broadcasting images and signs across the world from one's own home. The Internet makes it possible to influence and be influenced by broadcasting, searching, and absorbing information on an unprecedented scale. The web appears as a limitless new world, partially duplicating the real world while also supplementing it with numerous new gaming, social, and professional worlds. A person can travel unprecedented distances and live a myriad of lives without leaving their desk. One can immerse themselves in a screen that broadcasts fantasy or stock exchange worlds, but as soon as they look at the other side of the monitor, there is only a plastic surface. The screen, as an absolute flat surface, creates the illusion of voluminous, endless spaces while remaining unchanged. Immersion into virtuality means bringing the world and oneself to the leveling, flattening superficial plane. The corresponding perception of the world is flat, meaningless, devoid of the depth of emotional and sensual experiences henceforth only depicted in the form of graphic and textual "smilies." Emotions and sensations become objects of simulation and consumption, superficial like ripples on water, which do not affect the deep chords of the human soul. Even the only, main fear of man - the fear of death - is appraised, sold, and broadcasted over the screen as a playful form of extreme entertainment.

There is no interlocutor or mirror reflection of the Other in the projection of the screen, since its dimension is simulative and void of the properties of reflection. The projection of one's own image onto the screen does not cause deep doubt as does looking into a mirror. The interlocutor is simple plain text, a stream of digital binary codes decrypted into sounds and images that can be easily simulated and replaced by others. One such phenomenon of the flattening of communication is the entertainment of communicating with virtual auto-answering machines and assistants programmed to maintain meaningful conversations (to the extent of the quality of their algorithms) with the user. The modern level of the development of three-dimensional modeling, which allows one to create a human face indistinguishable from photo images, opens up the possibility of generating fully-fledged virtual bot-personalities capable of holding conversations not only in text, but in audio-visual format. Thus, the real Other as an interlocutor (whether an enemy, partner, etc.) can be replaced by a picture, an algorithm, a simulacrum. In the latter's place, a chair might just as well be connected and equipped with sensors for interpreting vibrations into arbitrary text. The rhizomatic dividual will happily respond and communicate with its user picture.

In the US and Western Europe, in those countries in the vanguard of Postmodernization, the first decade of the 21st century witnessed the appearance of the spontaneous movement of "life-loggers", or young people who give up serious purchases (such as real estate and cars) in favor of renting and investing in mobile gadgets and technologies which are constantly connected to networks and stream logs (recordings) of their lives. Their gadgets record where they are, what they eat, where they have fun, what services and routes they use, as cameras record their entire days around the clock, uploading recordings or snapshots at regular intervals onto the web, network accounts, and blogs. Life-loggers are at once maximally detached from the real world and maximally immersed in the virtual world. Taking off or away their gadgets causes acute depressive reactions and loss of the meaning of life. A telling moment allowing one to see the blurring of a person in virtuality is when a gadget fails or errors, during which the online log of a person, available to all of their friends on networks, transmits a mistaken, absurd, or defective record of an event. In the situation of virtual Postmodernity, such a happening does not bear the character of a direct error, but itself comes to be perceived as something interesting, original, and unusual. What happened to someone and their device becomes a point of interest on its own. Then other users will imitate such, deliberately distorting photos in imitation of camera failures, and so on. In other words, technological failure distorting the transmission of data from a person to the virtual network will not be perceived as a "failure" at all, but as a form of novelty, entertainment, a valuable artifact and impression.

Post-Time

The time of Tradition, which affirms cycles and their logic, and the time of Modernity with its assertion of an arrow of development "from the bottom up" both collapse into the rhizome of Postmodernity. In his description of time in Postmodernism, Deleuze introduced two notions: *"chronos"* and *"aion."* Chronos is the eternal present, without a past and future and void of meaningful, qualitative content. It is the eternal present as a surface of corporeal folds that have rhizomatically merged in continuity but not mixed. Chronos is time devoid of any event, like a flat screen with all of its illusory superficiality translated into the *rhizomatic* time of spatial corporeality. The other pole of Postmodern time, *"aionic* temporality", has no present, only a past and future. If chronos is the hypochthonic rhizome, then the *aion* is the arbitrary sprouting of the stalk from the rhizome that constructs its "past" and "future." Like shoots growing out of a rhizome, time can be an infinite and diverse multitude. If the rhizome is the meaningless, infinitely-present *chronos*, and the stalk is the aion of the future-past, then the history constructed and interpreted by Deleuze is void of fundamentality, ontology, and meaning, bearing rather the character of a gnoseological game limited by the lifetime of the *aionic* stalk. Time differs, is multiple, and disintegrates and reassembles in variable forms. In *aionic* time there is no "present" which can be grasped in any way.

In this picture, the notion of time inherent to Tradition or Modernity becomes merely one among many variations of chronology. This means that other versions of history, other chronological models of the most delusional shades (e.g. the "new chronology" of Anatoly Fomenko) are possible, and allows for different perceptions of physical theories of time (e.g. Stephen Hawking's). A certain convergence of *chronos* and *aion* can be seen in Francis Fukuyama's proclamation of the "end of history", the "today prolonged into tomorrow" which is like a permanent now, but is not "now." At the same time, the past and future lose their differences and merge in homology. Let us recall that Fukuyama associated the end of history with the establishment of the global hegemony of the United States and liberal democracy.

In its depictions of the contours of post-time, Postmodernity once again references the languages of Tradition, such as in borrowing the ancient terms *"chronos"* and *"aion."* The temporality of the time of chronos/aion resembles the situation of sacred spaces and the temple, the change of sacred time within ritual. But in Tradition sacred space, the structure of a sanctuary, and ritual acting within space and time structurally recapitulate the paradigm of the Time of the Year, the Celtic Cross, and are manifestations of eternity, filled with being and sacred meaning. Postmodernity, however, produces random, chimerical, unobliging, meaningless stalks of histories and interpretations that are "forever without forever."

Post-War

The state of the post-world also impacts what Heraclitus deemed the very essence of things: war. The society of the spectacle and the consumer society displace war from their own territories out into the periphery, to countries of the so-called "second" and "third" worlds. The constant broadcasting of visual streams of the chronicles and course of wars and conflicts to the screens of citizens and society creates the effect of a barrier, a border from which a person rushes away to consume more signs of happiness. Moreover, as war increasingly becomes a media-show, it comes to be consumed just like any other entertainment of the industry of opinions, cinema, etc.

The enemy which the so-called "civilized man" of Western countries faces comes in the new faceless threat of terrorists and terror attacks. Terror began to be actively presented as a threat to the world community following the terrorist attacks of 11 September 2001 in the US, and its main preachers and actors have been declared to be radical Muslims in the likes of Wahhabis, Salafis, and international Islamic terrorist organizations. The second most active and significant actors of terrorism are various radical right-wing organizations.

Wishing to delay the end of history which he proclaimed with the establishment of liberal American hegemony in the late 20th century, Francis Fukuyama deemed the enemy of the West to be Islamofascism and terrorism. However, it is certainly well known that the intelligence services of the United Kingdom and United States (as well as a number of other countries) have been linked to as well as actively participated in the creation, support, and development of extremist ideologies and organizations related to Islam and ethno-nationalism in Eastern European countries, the post-Soviet space, and Asia. This fact reveals the simulative, manageable, and cinema-like "directability" of terrorist organizations and processes in the contemporary world. Terrorism as a global threat is thereby recognized to be a puppet, a simulacrum - a bloody one exploiting religion and national identities, but created or cultivated by external support. Terrorism is not the ideology of any concrete, established, sovereign state, and it itself does not wield statehood. The majority of attempts by Islamic terrorists to erect "Caliphates" or "emirates" have been of a virtual, declarative, and deterritorialized character. But there is no doubt that a number of countries can provide direct or indirect support to one or another terrorist cell or leader and, on this basis, form actors and processes of terrorism and accompanying state-companions which are conditionally managed by "ours" (e.g., of the US, the West, and its satellites) or "theirs" (e.g., of the "Axis of Evil"). The actions of "ours" can very much be passed off as the acts of "theirs", as is known as "False Flag Operations." In other words, once again we are faced with spectacle, manipulation, and simulation. At the same time, terrorists and states generally do not confront one another on fields of battle or face enemy saboteurs, as terror is committed in peacetime in countries that are not at war with anyone. Terrorism has a network, distributed structure which embodies the new understandings of the strategies of warfare in the post-industrial, Postmodern world - network-centric and network wars.

The concept of net-centric warfare and network wars was developed and instilled by the US Armed Forces in the 1990s. Here we will limit ourselves to a description of the basic principles of such. The concept of net-centric wars arose in the context of the rapid development of information and communication technologies and the advanced refinement of technological capacities and realities in the late 20th century, when the US remained the only superpower on the planet. The specificity of this phenomenon lies in the transition from hierarchical, central management of combat operations to the principle of network distribution which speeds up the exchange of information, automizes a number of command processes, and integrates into a single network different types of troops and structures, including diplomatic, economic, and media. Of key importance to this strategy is ensuring the universal operational informedness of all network nodes, increasing the speed of data exchange and self-synchronization and, as a result, lessening the participation of real fighters and losses while achieving supremacy in the information space. The Russian scholar of network warfare and international relations, Leonid Savin, summarizes:

> The aims of network-centric war consist in transforming a military structure into a configuration which makes troops more efficient: to work faster (and at a higher rate), consist of more dispersed forces, suffer a reduced death rate and at the same time reduce dependence on the use of weapons, and to have the capability of anticipating (as opposed to reacting to) and integrating new technologies into the network for the production of information and gaining speed-advantage over future opponents. Net-centric warfare sees the dividing-up of significantly growing access to information among all levels and the redefining of relations between mission participants as well as commanders and subordinates.[139]

The difference with the classical warfare of attrition thus lies in the transition to "war-as-control-over-all" - over direct enemies, neutral countries, their allies, and all the networks therein and in-between. Network elements in the media, economy, business, the social sphere, etc. become levers of influence and pressure on the domestic and foreign policy of a given country. Thus, a state loses real sovereignty and becomes the puppet of another state managing a network of agents of influence within it. In this arrangement, the need for large, powerful armies diminishes in favor of mobile, high-tech groups that engage in targeted, precision strikes using networks and extremist cells under their control in False Flag Operations and other acts designed to exert influence and pressure on all players in the world arena, without exception.

Another form of post-warfare is that of network war or netwar, the context of which lies in the profound change of society in

---

139 Leonid Savin, *Setetsentrichnaia i setevaia voina. Vvedenie v kontseptsiiu* [*Net-Centric and Network Warfare: An Introduction to the Concept*] (Moscow: Eurasian Movement, 2013).

connection with the development of information and social networks on the Internet and the advent of Postmodernity. A network structure can include television channels, Internet services, criminal gangs, ethnic enclaves and diasporas, banking and trade networks, political groups, etc., with the network structure itself remaining dynamic, amorphous, and open to innovation and the inclusion of new elements with similar codes of values and goals. Netwar is a conflict that takes place by way of Internet communications, signs, and representations. The actors of such a conflict exerting influence on politics and society can be ethnic, religious, political, environmentalist or, more broadly, practically any associations, cells, or organizations using the Internet, websites, blogs, and social networks to spread information, agitation, and calls to action. If net-centric warfare is a concept of military operations introduced from above by a government (at the forefront of which has been the US), then netwar is the concept of including actors in a conflict from below, through influencing and manipulating their self-organization and actions without direct or obligatory connection with the center and the issuing and receiving of commands, support, or instructions.

Netwars, such as cyberwars, are wars of signs and representations partially reminiscent of propaganda wars, in which each side creates its own picture corresponding to its code, and fights for the installation of such as dominant. The battlefield of cyberwar is network blogging and social networks and services. The presence of real combat operations and real acts is neither prime nor necessary. If necessary, a battlefield picture can be created by software and multiplied and distributed through network channels until it becomes a truth. It is not difficult to see in all of this wars of simulacra.

Thus, we can see how the remnants of war as a clash between the personal will of a warrior, king, and his army with another ruler and army, as a clash of warriors face-to-face with iron in hand, have disappeared and been replaced by the clash of signs, representations, depictions, caricatures, and propaganda videos. War for life, power, and the assertion of will has given way to war over the picture of the world presented to the minds of (in/)dividuals, transformed into conflict largely void of a "hot" dimension and clearly defined sides. Illustrations of such network wars can be discerned in the chain of riots in Arab countries in 2011 (the "Arab Spring") as well as the series of "Color Revolutions" (such as the "Orange Revolution") across the post-Soviet space in the 2000s.

One such manifestation of post-war with regards to Tradition is the creation of simulacra of "traditions" and "traditionalist", post-religious organizations, which Julius Evola addressed in his analysis of the strategies of "world subversive forces":

> Often the tactic of replacement develops efficaciously in the form of a tactic of counterfeits. It may happen that after the effects of the destructive work reach the material plane, they become so visible as to provoke a reaction, and thus ideas and symbols are employed for a defense and a reconstruction. In the best scenario they are values of the traditional past, which come back to life thanks to this existential reaction of a society or civilization threatened by dissolution. Then the occult war is not waged in a direct manner; often attention is paid to promoting only distortions and counterfeits of these ideas. In this way, the reaction is contained, deviated, or even led in the opposite direction.[140]

An Intermediate Summary

Without a doubt, many of the provisions of Postmodernity, especially in the military, virtual, and cultural spheres, have already been realized, albeit not uniformly across the geographical plane of states and among strata within states. There is no denying Postmodernity's presence, its influence on the paradigm of Modernity and, more subtly and dangerously, on Tradition. By loosening the grip of Modernity and creationist traditions, Postmodernity undoubtedly opens up a certain chance for paganism, but this chance can easily be

---
140 Julius Evola, *Men among the Ruins: Postwar Reflections of a Radical Traditionalist* (Vermont: Inner Traditions, 2002), p. 214.

turned into the enormous risk of losing any meaning amidst the preservation and production of mere signs and symbolic forms of pagan traditions. Moreover, the influence of Postmodern networks on pagan communities for the purpose of political manipulations, which represents a separate political risk for any pagan community of any state, cannot be ruled out.

Postmodernity actively borrows traditional images, language, and symbols. In many ways, Postmodernism thereby emits a semblance of Tradition, but only superficially. For pagans who do not rigorously, strictly guard themselves and their spiritual core or community, it is easy to be deceived and to be derailed off the path of the revival of Tradition into the meaningless stream of simulacra. Postmodernity is another decisive step deeper into the Kali-Yuga, an act of *Ragnarök* being played out.

Modernity's gnoseological racism towards traditional forms of life, the Sacred, the Divine, and myth finds expression in Postmodernism as gnoseological stupidity. Modernity knows that there is a different picture of the world which it denies and represses. Postmodernity is incapable of understanding that there is another worldview, that something is missing, that something is absent (depth and meaning). It is surprised at the questions it is posed and offers whatever is sought in any form, without understanding that it is concentrated merely on the superficial ripples of forms, on the plane of the screen, on rhizomatic randomness ever mixed with altogether non-traditional forms.

Therefore, the process of delineating pagan tradition from erosive Postmodern and Modern influences is an important, delicate endeavor demanding greater effort and tension than frontal confrontation with Modernity. Further along our journey, we will continue to address the hypochthonic element underlying this dilemma and attempt to further identify its signs and forms.

The Horizons of Counter-Initiation

Hitherto we have examined the fundamental concepts and terminologies of Modernity and Postmodernity in the most general terms. While a complete immersion into the context of these two anti-traditional paradigms would go far beyond the scope of one book, for our point of departure we took the quest to identify the counter-initiatic element leading man away from the path of self-knowledge and the self-realization of his sacrality and Divine nature as expressed in the traditions, customs, language, and culture of his folk. Behind the counter-initiatic element we have unmasked those figures and forces which, across the myths of different peoples, are held to be opposed to the divine element, to the sky, to Olympus, and which are associated with heavy Earth (the chthonic), the waters, titans, materiality, and the animal element, unleashed out of the sacred hierarchical pyramid of society in the masses of pariahs, chandala, outcasts, and the uninitiated.

Adherence to the due - to Wyrd, Dharma - appeals to the nature of the human soul and to the element which prevails within it, whether bronze, silver, or gold. The due is accomplished in accordance with nature and expressed in society in the form of estates, which in turn are functions of the Gods and the embodiments of their archetypes in the manifest world. Society itself is the embodiment of God (Brahma), a world ordered by the Gods out of the body of the first being (e.g., Purusa, Ymir). Thus, following the due means following the path of the Gods, to the Gods, by the Gods. Social outcasts and people void of rituals, nature, and order have nothing, are ignorant of the due and, as follows, the divine is inaccessible to them despite whatever formal awareness they may have.

We know that history unfolds in time according to the cycle, whose culmination is in universal decline and then Ragnarök, followed by a new beginning. We can see how the progression of time in the Kali-Yuga, with the corresponding emergence to the forefront and dominance of people without Dharma and folk, is at once the unique and logical manifestation of Sanatana Dharma itself. Things should happen this way, and that which has happened is the fulfillment of the due. This does not annul the rules and regulations of Tradition as given in differing epochs to different estates, but rather tightens their demands and raises the risk, danger, and difficult complexity of each path.

Postmodernity, in its playful, chaotic, and rhizomatic flux nullifying any and all deep meanings, not only plays with different forms and elements of Tradition, but actively simulates religious forms, generating chimerical cults and doctrines which constitute the peculiar sphere of post-religion.

Post-Religion

The transformation of the notion of what religion is and should be in correspondence with the new paradigm of Postmodernity has structured into its axes various trends of syncretism, generalization, and universalization.[141] The general term of religiosity in Postmodernity is the determination of such to be the religion of a New Era or New Age. New Age is founded on an appeal to the advent of a new era or aeon, the Age of Aquarius, and the call to rethink and create new forms of spirituality corresponding to the criteria of human life in the modern world. New Age religiosity emerged and took shape in the second half of the 20th century, but its roots lie in the 19th century movements of spiritualism, Theosophy, Hermeticism, and various superficial understandings of magic, occultism, and healing.

René Guénon devoted two works to critiquing spiritualism and Theosophy, *The Spiritist Fallacy* and *Theosophy: History of a Pseudo-Religion*. Guénon began his critique of Theosophy with a distinction on the very term "theosophy", which

---

[141] René Guénon argued for a strict delineation between the notions of "synthesis" and "syncretism", in which the first is integrative, qualitative transubstantiation and the second is only superficial, fragmentary mixing.

he associated with such occultists and mystics as Jakob Böhme and Louis-Claude de Saint-Martin, who claimed an esotericism of a peculiar Christian shade. Guénon called the "Theosophy" in the likes of that founded by Helena Petrovna Blavatsky "Theosophism", thus emphasizing the lack of any relation to Theosophy proper and highlighting the peculiarly profane, syncretic, and anti-Christian (contrary to real, historical theosophical) character of Theosophist doctrine. The pillars of the latter doctrine, set forth in Blavatsky's works *Isis Unveiled* and *The Secret Doctrine*, consisted of an evolutionary view of spirituality, superficially understood Eastern doctrines, in particular those belonging to the Buddhist and Hindu traditions, and the original fabrication of the Mahatmas, the alleged "great teachers of mankind." In the very beginning of his critical analysis of Theosophist doctrine, Guénon emphasized the incompatibility of the concept of "evolution" as such arose in the West in Modernity with Eastern and Western spirituality, and dwelled in detail on the perversion of the Hindu doctrine of cycles, superficial astrological derivations, and the myth of the Mahatmas. The Mahatmas were mystified (at best) to be the highest initiated adepts guiding humanity in its evolution, entrusted with purely supernatural abilities achieved by virtue of their unprecedented development and union with the divine. Theosophism's imagination and characterization of the Mahatmas were significantly influenced by the concepts of humanism and the technological development contemporary to the founding Theosophists. For instance, the Theosophist Gottfried de Purucker (1874-1942) described the Mahatmas thusly: "There is nothing supernatural in these great men. They are the most healthy-thinking people on the planet, the most keen, the most good, the most compassionate, the most empathetic, the most peaceful and wise striving more than anyone else for brotherhood."[142] The effects of the rationalism and humanism of Modernity on Theosophy are most obvious.

---

142 Quoted in Andrey Ignatyev, "*Mif o makhatmakh v teosofizme Blavatskoi*" [*The Myth of the Mahatmas in Blavatsky's Theosophism*] (2012). Translated from the Russian.

As Guénon wrote: "The Theosophists regard the 'Adepts' as living men, but men who have developed faculties and powers that may seem superhuman. Such for example is the possibility of knowing the thoughts of others and of communicating directly and instantly through 'psychic telegraphy" - on which point translator and commentator on Guénon's work, Andrey Ignatyev, remarks: "Such was a term of the 19th century, when the telegraph seemed to be the height of progress; now they would likely claim 'psychic internet.'"[143] Overall, the Theosophism of Blavatsky was in many ways the matrix for the vast majority of New Age religious forgeries.

The notion of "secret teachers of humanity", of higher initiated humans, deeply pervades all New Age religions and is one of their distinct hallmarks. On this point, we can take important note of the universalism of the Mahatmas, who are not teachers or gurus within a particular tradition, school, or doctrinal current as would be the case in pagan traditions, but are universal, global teachers of all mankind. According to this view, all the great men of history are Mahatmas or sacred teachers bestowing their doctrine to mankind. Theosophist and New Age lists of such teachers include Moses, Jesus Christ, Muhammad, the Buddha, Zoroaster, Solomon, and other ancient wisemen and saints alongside modern ones, such as Mother Teresa and the Dalai Lama. The very fact of mixing into one line such numerous traditional figures from different, not infrequently antagonistic traditions with their own views of the world, spirituality, social prescriptions, etc., is very telling and revealing of the postmodern rhizome of flat mixing. In the 20th century, it was not uncommon for scientists like Newton and Einstein as well as completely fictional characters from literary fiction or openly destructive, sectarian teachings to be added to this pantheon of great universal teachers.

---

[143] René Guénon, *Theosophy: History of a Pseudo-Religion* (Hillsdale: Sophia Perennis, 2004), p. 43; Andrey Ignatyev, "*Mif o makhatmakh v teosofizme Blavatskoi*" [*The Myth of the Mahatmas in Blavatsky's Theosophism*], appendix to the Russian translation of Guénon's work (Kaliningrad: 2012).

Following the above is the notion of the universality of spiritual path and the "evolution" of humanity. The roots of this notion of a universal spirituality for all peoples are to be found in Christianity and Judeo-Christian mysticism, the original breeding ground of post-religiosity. Progress and evolution are obvious elements of Modernity. One of the manifestations of this idea in New Age post-religiosity is the conviction that the supreme Absolute (or Teacher of Humanity) adapts its teaching for different peoples for the sake of accessibility. We can detect in this a certain rift between the world, peoples, and the higher Absolute, in which the supreme Absolute for some reason submits to the qualitative diversity of relatively lower peoples, humanity, and reduces itself to different forms, adapting itself to the needs of the lower levels instead of elevating peoples and humanity to its level.

It is well known that initiatic ascent reveals Unity, the One, the ultimate point at which the paths of different traditions converge. But New Age draws the opposite conclusion, namely, that the ultimate One of the Center also means the universality of forms on the periphery, which is to say that, in speaking of the One, traditions are saying the same thing in the same way, and therefore their mixing is not to be seen as something abnormal or painful. Thus, instead of following the path of one's own tradition, the adept begins to follow a random set of different practices. In the end, the path to the center turns into a path around the circle.

The further fate of New Age religiosity unfolded in the 20th century, featuring active appeals to the East in connection with the first translations of traditional Hindu, Chinese, and Japanese sacred texts, but the assimilation of these doctrines proceeded just as superficially and in the spirit of interpretation through the prism of humanism. Following the Second World War, New Age trends emerged which actively mixed scientific discoveries and achievements with spiritual evolution and the psychological development of man. Such currents came to include a whole number of elements taken from traditional doctrines, such as reincarnation, the notion of the Absolute, holistic approaches to health, household magic, and psychedelic practices mimicking the use of sacred intoxicants in the mysteries.

One of the most extravagant currents to emerge out of the matrix of New Age post-religiosity was UFOlogy, or the belief in humanity's contact with extraterrestrial races from outer space, not uncommonly referred to as Mahatmas. A less grotesque yield of these currents was the aspiration to justify the development of spirituality through the biological and anthropological sciences, including the desire to modify the quantity and quality of human chromosomes and activate untapped potential in the genome. The spread of New Age was facilitated by the beatnik and hippy movements with their mixing of the new spirituality with narcotic experiences, radical pacifism, and libertarianism.

The association of New Age with the coming Age of Aquarius destined to replace the Age of Pisces (identified with Christianity) can be traced back to Alice Bailey (1880-1949), who used these terms as synonyms. In turn, Marilyn Ferguson's 1980 book, *The Aquarian Conspiracy: Personal and Social Transformation in the 1980s*, became a sort of manifesto of New Age. Although not all New Age currents focus on this shift of the astrological era, the concept of the onset of "new times" should be examined in detail in light of rhizomatic post-religiosity and the temporality of aion and chronos. Traditions and Traditionalism unambiguously and unequivocally speak of the End Times, of an even deeper immersion in time in which time itself will begin to recede into the background and be reflected less and less as a dimension of duration, thereafter generating various chaotic interpretations, versions, theories, and ideas of a "new time", "new era", and "new history." When humanity is so immersed in time that it no longer understands the depth of its immersion and does not know Eternity above Time, it begins to rave and hallucinate, which in turn is legitimated as the "norm" of the paradigm of Postmodernity.

The New Age idea of the spiritual transformation of humanity is based on individualism and the individual quest, allowing for the mixture and sampling of different practices, doctrines, and teachings from different traditions and teachers, as well as the addition of scientific and technological advances. New Age ideology is emphatically soft ("soft theology" and "soft ideology") and devotes considerable attention to the smoothing out of contradictions between mixed traditions and giving the adept the right to interpret teachings, mix them, and share the results of their own accord.

The "softness" of New Age is also evident in how many of its doctrines and organizations try to escape religious definitions and instead mimic humanitarian, social, and anthropological sciences, non-traditional medicinal centers, and cultural-leisure and sporting organizations and centers. The tendency towards mimicking a cultural movement was most successfully pursued by the followers of the Russian artist and mystic Nicholas Roerich (1874-1947) and his wife Helena Roerich (1879-1955) who, initially being followers of Theosophism, reworked its main provisions in their works Living Ethics and Agni-Yoga. The Roerichs claimed to have received their knowledge from the Mahatmas themselves, and thereby attempted to usurp the legacy of Blavatsky and assert their sole legitimacy in the development of Theosophism. Roerich's followers built a cult of personality around this family of mystics and pursued their activities into the cultural sphere on the basis of the Roerich Pact[144] and the establishment of a network of museums and centers devoted to Roerich's paintings and works.[145]

The historical emergence of New Age in the 20th century temporally coincided with the new dawn of pagan traditions

---

[144] The "Roerich Pact" or Treaty on the Protection of Artistic and Scientific Institutions and Historic Monuments, signed in 1935, was the first international agreement on the protection of cultural valuables in history.

[145] For further details on the Roerichs, see: Andrey Ignatyev, *Mir Rerikhov* (*The World of the Roerichs*), 2 volumes (Kaliningrad: 2013).

and the revival of the pagan worldview with which we began our work. New Age's claiming of traditional forms and the infiltration of resurgent paganism by Modernist and Postmodernist ideas pose a great problem. The scholarly community has construed all manifestations of the revival of pagan traditions to be part of this neo-paganism and New Age. Here we can confidently parry such with the fact that paganism, existing in full force thousands of years ago and having passed through history in different forms of transmission, cannot be related to quasi-spiritual teachings invented within the last century or less. Otherwise, paganism is held hostage by this scholarly approach. In Russia, the complexity of classifications of religious movements and distinguishing between traditional and ancient and the fictional and modern is frustrated by the strong position of the Russian Orthodox Church, which de facto dictates the scientific apparatus in this field and has been actively involved in the operations of state religious studies commissions under the Ministry of Justice.[146]

It is not difficult to separate New Age forgeries from pagan traditions insofar as the former openly appeal to humanism, planetary and historical universalism, "Mahatmas", technology and plain fantasy. But in a number of borderline cases, penetrations, mimicry or the strength of conviction are such that New Age teachings have embedded themselves under the ancient pagan heritage to such an extent that this question will demand more detailed consideration in a section below.

Overall, to summarize, New Age currents represent the direct continuation of Postmodern strategies applied to the sphere of spirituality, with all the accompanying and resulting Dharmic relations.

---

146 Since 2009, the chairman of the Council for the Conducting of State Religious-Studies Expert Analysis under the Ministry of Justice of the Russian Federation has been the Orthodox theologian Alexander Dvorkin, an active theoretician of the Russian anti-sect movement.

The Fate of Europe - the Destiny of the World?

In considering the decline of Tradition in historical and paradigmatic perspectives, we have frequently referred to the Greek, Germano-Scandinavian, and Slavic-Russian pagan traditions and to the Indo-European estate social structure (*à la* Dumézil) inherent to and embodying the spirit of these European traditions. At the same time, it has been shown and illustrated that it is Europe that became the driving force of modernization and the renunciation of Tradition in favor of scientific anti-theism and, eventually, rhizomatic disorder.

European history and European man have achieved unimaginable depths of reflection and detail in the narration of history and spread their worldview on an unprecedented scale in the era of colonialism and post-colonialism. The institution of educational programs along the templates of the European Enlightenment in the colonies, with no consideration whatsoever for local traditions, which were disdained as "archaic barbaric remnants", undoubtedly dealt a severe blow to indigenous peoples and their pagan (and other) traditions. But, at the same time, colonial subjects who were educated in this system of coordinates and learned the language of Modernity came to be included in the context of European history and its unfolding fall. Thus, not through direct territorial and colonial rule but through education, culture, and language, Europe influenced enormous spaces and strengthened the Eurocentric world-perception, in which Europe is conceived to be the center and driving force of human development, a role model to be imitated and aspired to. The fate of Europe thus came to be believed to be the destiny of the world.

But what is modern Europe from the point of view of Pagan Traditionalism? The Europe here and now, and more broadly the West, is in its moment of death and decay. Traditional

Europe in its ancient climax was replaced by Christian, feudal, fragmented Europe only to then renounce its sacred structure and identity. Europe chose the path of rejecting the Divine, eradicating, vulgarizing, mixing, and ridiculing any religiosity. Agreeing with Baron Evola, who titled the first part of his work *Pagan Imperialism* "We, anti-Europeans", we can say that for us, pagans and Traditionalists, modern Europe is not needed and modern, "civilized" European society is of no value. We could go even further and state that by virtue of its rejection of primordial European traditions and structures, Europe has become an anti-Europe, leaving Julius Evola and Pagan Traditionalists as the true Europeans.

The forerunners of this denial of Euro-optimism were Oswald Spengler and Friedrich Nietzsche. Spengler described the decline of Europe, and before him Nietzsche revealed the abyss of European nihilism. The meaning of Nietzsche's cry "God is dead!" lay not so much in this philosopher's anti-Christianity as in the death of Europe and the onset of the nihilistic post-Europe, or anti-Europe. In turn, the appropriate radical revision of values was declared by the 20th century Traditionalists, who declared a firm "no" to Modernity and anti-Europe and sought to return to the ideals of Tradition. The struggle for true Europe is a struggle against the contemporary anti-Europe, whose Eurocentrism has turned into a funnel with a hole in the center which sucks out the peoples and states embedded in the European context. Therefore, the fight for tradition is a struggle against contemporary Europe with its Modernity, Postmodernity, and its language, constructs, and strategies. If the fate of Europe is the destiny of the world, then this destiny is to die in the ignominious filth of decomposition. Therefore, the return to primordial traditional identity is of special importance, just as is untying ourselves from Europe and ceasing to see it as a model. This holds true for the real Europe as well, as Dominique Venner, Alain de Benoist, and Russian Traditionalists have said.

In the East, the white man of the times of colonization who sought to join one or another spiritual school was almost always rejected, seen as merely a "white ape" incapable of perceiving higher spheres. The striving to assimilate the riches of the East without the proper instructions of a guru only generated whirlwinds of spiritual disintegration. The East and Asia have turned out to be more immune to Western expansion and have preserved their traditions to a greater extent, hence why Traditionalism's respectful and deep interest in Hindu doctrines is all the more telling, as the salvation of Europe was then thought to come from the East.

Julius Evola also expressed the rather optimistic thought that if Europe was the first to enter the stage of decline, the Kali-Yuga, then it is destined to be the first to emerge out of such renewed. Looking at the contemporary Europe of the 21st century, the Baron's hope seems to be too utopian and demanding of a shock, altogether difficult to imagine, capable of turning Europe and Europeans back onto the path of the rebirth of their glorious, genuine being.

The Place and Time of Postmodernity

The historical and geographical localization of Postmodernity requires particular elaboration, insofar as such allows us to understand some of the nuances and peculiarities of this paradigm. From the point of view of sacred time and history, Postmodernity, like Modernity, is to be located in the lower left quarter of the Celtic Cross as corresponding to Ragnarök or the Kali-Yuga. Postmodernity represents an even deeper plunge into the metaphysical Night of the World, in which even memory of the light of the Sun is called into doubt.

Despite the fact that the theoreticians of Postmodernity have predominantly been European, particularly French philosophers and sociologists, Europe's relationship to Modernity and Postmodernity is one towards historical projects which still have to be realized in the future. Europe has thousands of years of history encapsulated in a material and mental heritage that greatly affects the tempo of its development and its forms. In the Renaissance and the Enlightenment, when Modernity was framed as the project for the European (or, we would say, anti-European) future, a series of great geographical discoveries were made and new lands were colonized, a key place among which, North America, was occupied by a number of colonies which would lay the foundations for the future state of the United States of America.

The colonial history of America before the Declaration of Independence was distinguished by its predominant constitution by English colonists belonging to various Christian sects and denominations which in turn shaped these settlers' perceptions of their new life in the New World as a certain divine predestination, and this view would be inlaid at the heart of messianic notions of the special fate and role of America in history. The 18th century saw the emergence of the United States of America as an independent state, an immediate, distinctive feature of which was the view of Modernity not as a project which should be realized, as was the case in Europe, but as the starting point. The founding fathers of the US thought of Modernity as a given state with which a new society could start with a blank slate. America does not boast thousands of years of such historical context and, as follows, the effects. Europe proclaimed an aspiration for equality of opportunities and democracy, whereas America began as a democracy proclaiming equal starting opportunities for all. This tabula rasa attitude extended to all territories of the continent, inciting the systematic and unconditional genocide of the entire indigenous population. For the enlightened American society of Modernity, the "Indian savages" were worse than animals or slaves and were void of any being.

Starting off with the "free democratic society" of Modernity as the foundation for the construction of a new state, the US rapidly emerged as a leader in the world arena and became the first to fully realize the program of Postmodernity. What European postmodernists proposed as a new program for the postwar future of Europe blossomed in America - free from historical ties, memory, and preceding stages of fate. Americans do not think of their history as the history of Europe spanning across the Atlantic Ocean to new lands. They see their history as that of a young, free country, autonomous from the Old World of decrepit Europe. Meanwhile, in Europe new initiatives representing the imperatives of Postmodernity were faced with millions of outraged conservative citizens, suicide-attacks, and existential terror.[147]

The US became the driving force of Postmodernity, the first to realize new technologies and corresponding political and social changes, such as the introduction of television, mass media and mass production, pop-culture, virtual networks and the Internet, widespread emancipation, the consumer society, religious syncretism, and post-war technologies and techniques, with which the aggravation and escalation of inter-religious and inter-ethnic relations is ongoing in the present. It is no coincidence that Deleuze and Baudrillard frequently referred to the American experience in their writings.

The theoretico-philosophical conceptualization of Modernity and Postmodernity was accomplished in Europe as the latter's project, but the practical incarnation of Modernity and Postmodernity has happened in the US, which has become the vanguard of such. Taken together, we can consider anti-Europe and the US to be the generalized West, the periphery of the diffused multitudes, the embodiment of anti-traditional forms, universalism, and globalization along the lines of the American model - cultural, ideological, and economic.

The Potential of Russia

Speaking of Russia in the context of our account, we can identify a definite potential for Russian paganism and the

---

147 The "Years of Lead" in Italy in the 1960s-'80s were marked by de facto civil war between ultra-right and ultra-left groups. Julius Evola has been alleged to have been one of the inspirations of the ultra-right groups. A number of the acts of terror committed in those years were more manifestations of existential protests against Modernity than demands for political reforms.

paganism of Russia's indigenous peoples in comparison to the situation of anti-Europe. The historical context of Russia-Europe relations is too incredibly multifaceted and complex to outline in full in the context of one section, so we will limit ourselves to the principal lines of interest to our journey.

The long history of conflictual confrontation between Russia and Europe, and more broadly the West, intersects with the discourse of Pagan Traditionalism very little, and not directly at that. It was the opposition between the Western Catholic and Eastern Orthodox branches of Christianity that marked the beginning conceptualization of the peculiarities of the two special paths of these two unique civilizations, the European and Russian. European Catholicism, with its Machiavellian spirit of intrigue and aspiration for worldly power yielded the Protestant denominations which represented the direct, broad bridge to Modernity, to secular, civil, conventional society. Russian modernization, on the other hand, was largely a reaction to the challenges posed by the West, and the period of the Russian Empire (1721-1917) saw Russia come to constitute a fairly tolerant, multiethnic and multi-traditional ensemble. But in this very same period, the Empire's elite was predominantly made up of Germans who actively engaged in the process of modernization, the first, clear impulse to which was imparted by Peter I. Among the people, meanwhile, the official dominance of Orthodoxy left a broad space of freedom for local beliefs and customs, for the observance of which frequently only a tax was required. Indigenous peoples were not recruited into service and the army until the 20th century.

The second historical stage demanding attention is that of the confrontation between the USSR and the US. Earlier we indicated that the deep structure of both the Soviet and American ideologies was spawned by Modernity and was anti-traditional in letter and spirit. The modernization of Russia in the pan-European context was of a defensive, reactionary character with regard to Europe itself, and was designed to defend through competitive emulation its own civilizational uniqueness as some kind of "non-Europe" and "non-Asia." But alongside Europe, Russia's modernization bore the character of a project aiming for the basic installation of the triumphing Modernity with which the United States started in the very beginning. In European eyes, Russia has always been seen as a backward, barbarian neighbor with kindred traits that sometimes peak through. This view reflects a Eurocentric approach and, with Europe's eversion into anti-Europe, can be interpreted in the contrary direction: "backwards Russia" has remained more European than rapidly Postmodernizing anti-Europe. For America, Europe is the decrepit Old World whose time has passed, and as follows Russia occupies a level slightly higher than that of Native Americans in the US' eyes. Following the Revolution of 1917 and the victory of the USSR in the Second World War, the confrontation between Red Russia and the United States came to determine the nerve of planetary history and politics for half a century. This opposition can be seen as a battle between two titanic elements, between the figure of Prometheus the Proletarian in the East and shrugging Atlas (*à la* Ayn Rand) in the West. The nuance lies in that Russia in its Soviet incarnation, even with all of its machines, detonated churches, and dialectical materialism, was insufficiently anti-traditional and still "dormant" in this regard. All of such was indeed part and parcel of the program of Modernity, but in this case such turned out to be inferior in its depths of degradation (or "progress" from the point of view of Western optimists) to that of America. America, being the country of successfully established Modernity and the rapid transition to incarnated Postmodernity, thus turned its forces on still modern, insufficiently chthonic Soviet Russia.

If we compare the atmosphere of democratic Europe and the US to that of the totalitarian Soviet Union in terms of the rebirth of pagan traditions and the emergence of pagan organizations, then the freedom for dissemination of information, the creation of associations, communities, and practicing paganism was a positive fact on the side of Europe. However, this positive side was nullified by outright Modern and Postmodern infiltrations on the one hand, and on the other, the meaninglessness and degraded importance of confessional identity amidst pluralistic society. Europe's pagans had freer hands, but who has taken their teachings - and namely teachings, not private political, criminal, and terrorist practices - seriously? In Europe, pagans have become "one of many" with the right to remain such under the distribution of basic "universal human values." As Julius Evola wrote in his "Orientations": "The distinctive character of Americanism is that the attack against quality and personality is not put into effect by the brute force of a Marxist dictator and the mind of the State, but it happens almost spontaneously, by the ways of a civilization ignorant of ideals higher than wealth, consumption, productivity, production without brakes."[148]

In the Soviet case, the atmosphere of a totalitarian dictatorship of a materialist bent exerted great pressure on spiritual seekers, insofar as the most terrible crime in a totalitarian society, according to George Orwell, is thoughtcrime. The persecution of dissent, even if not aggravating any oppositional political protest or activism, was a common practice. Under such conditions, the pursuit of the High became a kind of initiatic ordeal, a feat, the punishment of which could be exile to labor camps and criminal prosecution, as was the case with Dobroslav under and after Soviet power. In addition, such dissidents could be pressured with social ostracization and displacement to the marginal periphery of society, as we can see in the fate of the Silver Age poet who heralded pagan Gods, Sergey Yesenin, and the situation of the participants of the Yuzhinsky Circle, for instance Evgeny Golovin, in 1960s Moscow. Voluntary yet compelled deportation from the country was one possible fate, such as that of the founder of the Yuzhinsky Circle, the famous writer, philosopher, and expert on Hinduism, Yuri Mamleev. Or criminal prosecution and emigration could befall a guru and his disciples, as was the case with Bhairavananda (Adinath Jayadhar) in Belarus in the 1990s.

---

148 Julius Evola, "Orientations", *Gornahoor* (29/7/2012).

In the end, pagans on both sides found themselves in a situation of pressure, whether the pressure of democratic freedom and the degradation of the meaning of pagan beginnings which rendered pagans "just others", or under the pressure of a repressive apparatus that persecuted any dissent. Which of these two unfavorable conditions posed the greatest test: preserving and realizing the aspiration for Tradition under open pressure, or under soft pressure wrapped in freedom and flushing the sparks of *Dharma* out of any constructions and acts? This question is perhaps a rhetorical one.

Following the collapse of the USSR, Russia embarked on a course towards democratization and liberalization, once again playing "catch up" with the West. Starting in the 1980s, paganism in Russia thereby had the chance to rise, multiply, and strengthen itself - which has indeed happened. At the same time, looking to the West, i.e., to Postmodernity as a model has set in motion a whole range of quasi- and pseudo-pagan New Age movements which, already a reality in Europe, in Russia became a logical consequence of Westward looking. In recent time, in parallel to the writing of this book, Russia has seen the institutionalization of a political-technological (or "political spin doctor") ideological simulacrum based on appeals to Orthodox spirituality and the active lobbying of the Russian Orthodox Church of the Moscow Patriarchate. The simulative nature of this ideology has no strict relation to "ideology" itself, which requires serious political subjects and important decision-making. If this truly were the case, then Russia would declare a return from being a secular state to a religious one, declare Orthodoxy to be the state religion, and grant permission to various confessions to operate. At the same time, this simulacrum is not strictly identical to Orthodoxy in its adoption of the methods of the spectacle, situationism, actionism, performance, and other practices of Postmodernism in recruiting activities, and in its appeal to intra-Church semi-sectarian extremist trends such as uranopolitism and flirtation with Protestant sects. Thus, the restoration of Russia's spiritual dimension through appealing to Orthodoxy is not recreating the situation of the Russian Empire, in which the formal dominance of the Church coexisted alongside the preservation of the broad pagan heritage among the people and the profession of native faiths by indigenous and small peoples. At present, there is a glaring tendency, arising from the simulative and manipulative nature of this quasi-ideology, towards religious intolerance, pogroms[149], and the aggressive clericalization of society. This is happening in tandem with the heating up of nerves in relations between the West and Russia, but this time such bears (or will bear?) a special, peculiar character, insofar as Russia is turning neither to the Soviet model nor to the Russian-Orthodox imperial model directly, but is instead creating something new and simulative out of their various fragments.

Thus, we can see that on the contemporary world map there is not a single state that has chosen the values of Tradition as its orientation. Neither Europe nor Russia are exceptions, and Russia itself, especially in its megalopolises, is increasingly resembling a "civilized" European country. In view of these prospects, there is no point in seeking potential for paganism in the dimension of the state. Nevertheless, as a people predominantly of the third estate, Russians and their state, finding themselves behind "progress" and thereby more European than contemporary anti-Europe, have turned out to be a depository and conduit of traditional structures and forms from antiquity to the present.

The degradation and destructive influence of creationism has mainly affected the elites, while the common people, scattered across the vast space of Russian nature, have always been in the periphery of this influence's attention. The potential of paganism in Russia thus lies in the deep layers and archetypes of the Russian people which have, in a unique, peculiar way, been conserved by Orthodoxy as the most conservative form of Christianity which the common folk have reinterpreted and

---

149 The vandalism and desecration of pagan shrines as well as holy places of shamanism and Buddhism has become common practice.

enriched with pagan relics so profoundly that Christianity as a whole and Orthodoxy in particular are frequently seen as different traditions. Orthodoxy was followed by an insufficiently titanic form of materialism, expressed in Sovietism, which was also influenced by the popular masses so that the workers' and peasants' system and mindset resonated with the agrarian archetypes of Russians.

Today, as the grip of Christianity and materialism has loosened, paganism in Russia, Ukraine, Belarus, and among the small peoples and former Soviet republics is faced with a real chance to claim subjectivity, to root itself in a true understanding of the pagan worldview, in *Lad*, *Dharma*, and *Wyrd*, and to draw conclusions which suit historic challenges. Postmodernity, with its simulacral and "emancipating" strategies is a not always obvious but quite dangerous challenge - a challenge which must be accepted and overcome.

***

IV
THE CONTEMPORARY PAGAN EXPERIENCE

In this chapter, we will embark upon a more detailed examination of the infiltrations of the pagan worldview and experience by Modernity and Postmodern post-religiosity, which have frequently become objects of criticism for opponents of paganism as well as points of inter-pagan disputes. In his article, "Basic Problems with Pagan Traditionalism", Martin Haggkvist formulates one of the most important problems:

> Modern pagans striving to find tradition and reconstruction are more vulnerable than anyone else to modernist "infiltration" of their ideas. Any "true Christian" would most likely feel like they are committing a mistake by interpreting the Bible in a spirit that would suit their highly atheistic, liberal, socialist, or contemporary so-called 'conservative' rulers. For self-proclaimed 'pagans', this is not a problem. Hence why we can see the majority of neo-pagan organizations focusing attention on their commitment to individualism, democracy, progress, 'tolerance', pacifism (or, sometimes, war for war's sake), feminism, and whatever else should come up in a propaganda war, in order to gain more converts and to fight against Christianity, a fight which many believe much more important than fighting modernism, materialism, and consumerism.[150]

Here it is important to take into account paganism's principal position towards time and ends, a position which rescinds any romanticism towards tradition and plans for social reform, instead placing emphasis on the inner, spiritual, and due essence of the quest for the Divine in our days. Alain de Benoist formulated this position in the following manner:

> In fact, it is not a question of "returning" to the past, but of connecting with it - and also, by that very fact, in a spherical conception of history, to connect to the eternal and cause it to surge back, to have consonance in life, and to disentangle itself from the tyranny of the logos, the terrible tyranny of the Law, so as to reestablish the school of the mythos and life. In ancient Greece,

---
150 M. Haggkvist, "*Grunnleggende problemer med hedensk tradisjonalisme*", KulturOrgan Skadinaujo 2 (2003).

Jean-Pierre Vernant observes, "the effort to remember the primary purpose of everything is not the construction of the individual past of a man who remembers, the construction of his individual time, but conversely it is what allows him to escape time." In the same way it is a question of referring to the "memory" of paganism not in a chronological way, so as to return to an "earlier time", but in a mythological way, to seek for that which, through time, surpasses time and still speaks to us today. It is a question of connecting to something that cannot be surpassed rather than to something that has been "surpassed."[151]

A similar position is taken by practically all leaders of pagan communities and organizations today. The aim of paganism today is not to push society back into the past, but to find a connection with the eternal to find being and meaning in the present. An opposite pole also exists, one which insists on a literal return to forms and orders of being from the past (with some nuances, we might count Dobroslav among this category), for which a comparison could be drawn with the hard Traditionalists. These two poles constitute two mutually-enriching perspectives in the pagan milieu.

Connecting with the eternal means connecting with the Sacred, the Divine, and this is accomplished through initiation. The meaning and being acquired therein are due and dutiful to one's nature and surrounding reality - *semper fidelis* and *polemos*. The struggle for purity of one's worldview is a struggle waged not only against an external aggressor, the world of the Iron Age, but is also one turned inward, for the sake of purification, and is the key to successfully fulfilling the due. To this end, it is necessary to discriminate between one's own and the foreign, sometimes following to the letter the famous expression "by blood."

The Authentic and the Foreign

The question of authenticity was posed in all of its severity to paganism beginning with the Renaissance and the Enlightenment. European thinkers' appeals to Antiquity

---
151 De Benoist, *On Being a Pagan*.

in culture, philosophy, and poetry proceeded under the condition of reinterpreting such in Christian, humanist, and Enlightenment keys. Authentic paganism - which has no need for such an adjective whatsoever - existed in the time and space of Tradition, and in a small fraction still coexists today in remote regions. Paganism was primordial and dominant but then, with the rise of creationism, went into the periphery, continuing to live on in the deep layers of peoples, their cultures, beliefs, and interpretations under the Christianity that came down from above, from the elites

The paganism of Modernity, arising simultaneously with the latter, found itself under the influence of a new picture of the world, a new language for describing reality. This raised the question of establishing a connection with the eternal and the embodiment of forms adequate and authentic to the spirit of tradition in new conditions. No small role in this matter has been played by the estate nature of those pagans themselves who have resolved to turn to pre-Christian traditions amidst Modernity. We can discern an overwhelming presence of representatives of the third, agricultural estate and its patterns of perceiving the Gods, the due, strategies of behavior, as well as its corresponding weaknesses before the influences of the new force of the Enlightenment. The manifestation of the true warrior and priestly estates becomes extremely problematic and rare, but at times can affect whole ensuing generations and directions of pagan movements. People of a warrior nature inspire and point the right way forward - the path of struggle and heroism, which Friedrich Nietzsche believed to be the most non-Christian and the most opposite to that of the humble martyr who accepts a lesser fate. If the third estate has in secret, in re-formulation, and as "contraband" smuggled pagan culture and striving towards the Gods into Modernity, then Modernity confronts the priest with a problem demanding colossal intensity: the establishment of a connection with the Gods. The priestly path is largely a personal one, a quest for the discovery, systematization, cleansing, restoration, and due shaping and inspiriting of the surviving pagan heritage, a path of inspiring pagans to follow the paths of the Gods in the Koshchny Age. The Icelandic writer, founder, and first high goði of the first modern Icelandic Asatru community, the Ásatrúarfélagið, Sveinbjörn Beinteinsson, said of the role of the priest: "The Godi shall lead the way in the development of the religion, but he does not have the sole responsibility for such development."[152]

The paganism of Postmodernity is a post-religious pseudo-paganism of people lacking any estate nature. We will examine this matter in greater detail below. The *leitmotif* of authenticity in Postmodernity is inherited from Modernity, but with even stricter requirements and heightened attention paid to the tangled, looped, self-centered, and self-referencing threads of the rhizome.

The authenticity of a pagan renaissance lies in careful, delicate, and at once rigorous, strict recourse to the known surviving and preserved heritage. In the Middle Ages and the Renaissance, paganism was described from the point of view of the church, its apologists, missionaries, and theologians who attached to paganism grotesque and emphatically abnormal traits and characteristics frequently being the pure fiction of these authors. As Julius Evola noted, any attempts at reviving paganism based on Christian texts are knowingly doomed to failure, due to both the incompetence of these texts' authors as well as, resultantly, the inadequacy of the constructions derived from them. Any paganism based on interpretations of Christian, deliberately biased texts would be a caricature, the blind worship of the material forces of nature without the higher dimension of the Spirit.[153]

The emergence and ensuing development of the academic study of religion also excluded objectivity in its examination of the traditions of different peoples, at first imposing Christian

---

[152] Irv Slauson, *The Religion of Odin* (Red Wing: Asatru Free Church Committee/ Viking House, 1978), p. 20.

[153] See: Julius Evola, "Against the Neo-Pagans: The Misunderstandings of the New 'Paganism'", *Counter-Currents* (4/11/2011).

evaluative criteria and later Eurocentric gnoseological racism. A substantial change in this situation occurred in the 20th century with the works of Mircea Eliade, who reformed the approach to studying different traditions in a Traditionalist key. Before, the most productive scholarship was that which turned to the least judgmental sciences of folklore studies, archaeology, ethnography (with certain qualifications), linguistics, etc. In the experience of contemporary Russian paganism, meriting special respect is the late Boris Alexandrovich Rybakov, the author of numerous works on Slavic mythology who, despite not identifying with pagan tradition, was posthumously honored with a commemorative pamphlet entitled "A *Trizna* for Boris Alexandrovich Rybakov" (*"trizna"* being the traditional Slavic funeral feast).[154]

Reliance on adequate sources, the study of history and the preserved heritage compose the foundations for rising up to establish the necessary connection with the Sacred. Tradition, as has been pointed out many times, is not the preservation of ashes, but the transmission of fire. Therefore, a new flame must be lit on the basis of the ancient heritage, one which connects the past with the present not in forms, but in principle. Indicative in this regard in the case of Russian paganism is the emergence of new forms that have organically corresponded to deep principles and archetypes as well as met the requirements of the present, such as Dobroslav's introduction of the *Kolovrat* symbol and Veleslav's coining of *Rodnoverie*, i.e., *Rodnaia Vera*, "Native Faith", to be the self-designation of Russian paganism.

Many complex sets of sacred and magical views, held by the Slavs as well as other peoples, pertaining to the agrarian, hunting, dwelling, and communal sphere of life are no longer relevant to today's forms and life conditions. This demands the organic reinterpretation of old traditions or the manifestation of organic new ones which meet the relevant issues of the surrounding world. The key to organicity lies in reliance upon

---

[154] M.V. Tresviatsky (ed.), *Trizna po Borisu Alexandrovichu Rybakovu* (Moscow: Institute of Humanities, 2002).

credible, adequate knowledge, authenticity with respect to such and, simultaneously, resonance with the deep structures of a person, their people, and their tradition. One example of this is the term for the due in Russian paganism. The term *Darna* proposed by Velimir has ultimately not taken root to become an organic component of Native Faith, whereas the terms *Lad* and *Prav'* have. For the restoration of the lacunae in the fabric of the heritage of tradition, it is also possible to turn to the heritages and experiences of neighboring, fraternal peoples, or even more geographically removed but structurally similar peoples. The tripartite division of the cosmos into *Prav'*, *Yav'*, and *Nav'*, or the Higher, Middle, and Lower worlds, respectively, stably entered Russian paganism from the infamous forgery *The Book of Veles* (*Velesovaia kniga*), which was evidently created by Yuri Petrovich Miroliubov to attract the Russian-speaking public's attention to the sacred texts of India, as is suggested by such obvious traces as *Kryshen'* for Krishna, *Vyshen'* for Vishnu, and numerous other borrowings. Despite his mystifying goals, Miroliubov touched upon certain layers of the Russian depths which have been met with interest not so much in the fraudulent book itself (and this evaluation is indeed the dominant, normative position among contemporary Russian paganism) as in the proposed tripartite scheme of the cosmos, a motif which is partially confirmed by known folkloric and philological data.

Turning to the experience of neighboring peoples is justified by the fact that modern state-territorial borders do not reflect the arrangements of ancient times, when some presently divided peoples were one ethos with sub-ethnic variations differentiated by dialect, emphases on venerating one or another deity within the pantheon, unique embroidery styles, carving traditions, etc. The mutual enrichment of cultures, traditions and supporting and appealing to the common roots of tradition is known by the Scandinavian-Germanic paganism of modern Iceland, Norway, Denmark, and Germany, by Slavic-Russian paganism in Russia, Belarus, Ukraine (which were previously one people only altogether recently divided), Poland, Czechia, Bulgaria,

Lithuania, and others, as well as by Romano-Hellenic paganism in Greece and Italy.

A well known but simultaneously most controversial and risky practice is that of translating the elements of one tradition into the language of another with the aim of restoring or covering gaps. The experience of translation requires sensitive, attentive, contextual immersion both in the tradition out of which the translation is being made as well as the tradition into whose language the translation is being introduced. In this process, it is important to convey the structure and meaning, sometimes at the expense of external forms but to the benefit of organic embedding and restoration. On this matter, Nigel Pennick has quoted the words of Antonio Gaudi which reflect our own comments: "Those who look for the laws of Nature as support for their new works collaborate with the creator. Those who blindly copy do not."

Such recourse is also justified by the larger framework of Indo-European commonality which is most often localized between the three large regions of Europe, Russia, and the East/Asia. The most intensive exchanges have been in the following directions: Scandinavian-Germanic communities have turned to Hindu traditions, while Slavic-Russian pagans have turned to Germanic-Scandinavian and Hindu ones. Many scholars believe that the Vanir farmers of Scandinavian mythology were historically Slavs who fell under the rule of the viking Aesir, a hypothesis that fits into the allogeneic theory of the origins of the state. This hypothesis holds great potential for finding connections and kinship between these two traditions and cultures. A special position is also occupied by the philosophy of ancient Hellas, in which a number of the structures of pagan Sacrality are described maximally succinctly and precisely. The Hindu tradition, meanwhile, has over the course of its whole history remained extremely indifferent to near and distant traditions and ideas, paying attention to them only in exceptional cases.

A Typology of Pagans

In the absence of a natural and precise definition of the inner nature of a person through birth into a corresponding caste and estate, Modernity entails the construction of an alternative typology of pagans. Since the inner nature of a person is a determining force that manifests itself even without awareness, even in taking on deformations the resultant types largely align with estate characteristics and can correlate with them up to the point of coincidence. In designating these main types, we partially follow the typologies which have been adopted in the academic field of religious studies.[155] However, due to the complete profaneness and incompetence of a number of scholars, we will restrict ourselves only to partial convergence in approaches to classification. The primary types which can be distinguished are: the mystical, the political, the naturist, and the reconstructionist/reenactor types.

The mystic's approach to tradition rests in immersion into its depths, kindling its fire within himself and sharing the fruits of his experience with fellow believers. For the mystical approach, of importance are Spirit, Blood, and the inner dimension of tradition, at times to the detriment of literal interpretations, external forms, and social activity. Personal spiritual experience and the interpretation of such, as well as the deep hermeneutical analysis of texts and heritage are, for the mystical type, in the first place.

The political approach to pagan tradition presents paganism as an instrument for social and political changes in society. This type is in many ways associated with warrior archetypes, demanding a certain depth of immersion into tradition, but less so than the mystical and reconstructionist/reenactment approaches. In this perspective, the pagan heritage is interpreted in line with political necessity and for the creation

---

155 See: Shizhensky, *Pochvennik ot iazychestva: mirovozzrechenskie diskursy volkhva Velimira (N.N. Speranskogo)* [*A Pochvennik from Paganism: The Ideological Discourses of Volkhv Velimir (N.N. Speransky)*].

of an ideological platform, which constitutes the driving force of all activities for these pagan types.

The naturist approach, meanwhile, is the most simplified and easy perception of the doctrines of paganism, and consists of honoring nature and its forces, spirits, and laws as foundational principles. For the naturist, large complexes of myths and traditions are left in the periphery (but not rejected), whereas the harmonization of soul and spirit in correspondence with the spirit of nature comes to the forefront. To some extent, this approach's appeal to the most basic experience of merging with the divine body represents a response to the problem of the transmission of tradition over long intermittent periods of the dominance of foreign religions and secular ideologies. At the same time, this type preserves the calendar structures of holidays, the life- and year-cycle, simple forms of cultural manifestation such as carving, embroidery, praises, songs, music, and rituals, as well as a small pantheon of gods, usually including the most important ones.

This typologization is concluded with the type that is furthest removed from the spirit of tradition while being fully immersed in its forms. This is the reenactor or reconstructionist type, the meaning of whose approach lies in the maximal, one-hundred-percent identification with reproduced traditional forms, especially external ones, such as weaponry, clothing, household items, fabrics, patterns, architecture, forms and means of housekeeping, building, speech, and so on. The essence of this approach is achieving the most authentic correspondence to the word and letter, with authenticity being the end in itself. Any discrepancies are to be eliminated, and any alternative interpretations or innovations are discarded as not satisfying historicity and authenticity. Reenactors can be skilled masters of craft, experts in history, language, and archaeology, as well as knowledgeable of many of the nuances of folklore and the material culture of tradition, but rarely come into contact with its spirit and blood.[156]

---

156 A glaring example of submergence in the most ordinary nuances can be seen in the discussions over the authenticity of the 10th century Russian custom of rolling up one's sleeves and wiping them on the hem of the tunic which surrounded the reenactment project launched in 2013 "Alone in the Past" (*Odin v proshlom*).

These types are ideal, whereas in real life and practice one can meet two or even more typological elements that might complement or balance one another in one person. The mystical approach in its essence coincides with the higher estate and can be enriched by the strictness of the reenactor/reconstructionist type when it comes to the principles of authenticity and organicity. Without a doubt, the warrior spirit can be expressed in a political approach aspiring to assert and realize power, it can manifest its strictly martial element in struggle. At the same time, this type can manifest a limited perception of tradition compared to that of the higher estate and a degree of disregard for material-craft forms. The naturist type corresponds to the agricultural nature of the third estate, which reflects dependence on the land and the natural elements affecting harvest and catch. In their striving to highlight the most common, basic features of traditions, naturists can come close to the mystical approach in striving towards the center and the comprehension of the structure and essence of tradition. Reenactor and reconstructionist types relate most of all to the castes of artisans and servants (shudras), and without a doubt often have no equals when it comes to questions of restoring the material heritage and artifacts of tradition. Their communion with the spirit of tradition - with the fire, not its ashes - is possible through appealing to other types, often the political, or by virtue of curbing their desire for external authenticity in favor of comprehending deeper meaning, including on the level of material demiurgy. On this point, let us recall that the study of the Vedas in India was available to all three upper estates, and shudras were prescribed service and the fulfillment of instructions for more favorable rebirth.

Subcultural Infiltrations

The phenomenon of "subculture" appears in Modernity, starting in the late 19th century and reaching its height in the 20th. Like the adepts of the pagan worldview, subcultures first appeared and existed in the periphery of society as marginals. Starting in the mid-20th century, the place and influence of subcultures within society as a whole began to rise, some of them becoming dominant or affecting social consciousness on a large scale - predominantly in the West. Subcultures as phenomena are tightly linked to fashion, the consumer society, and mass culture.

A number of modern sociologists are inclined to see any sub-identity, whether professional, social, role-based, ethnic, age-related, etc. as subcultures within the greater common culture of a society. In other words, any sphere of activity, thought, or variations of cultural forms and the communities formed around such shape their own micro-values and subcultural patterns of behavior, type, and other characteristics. At the same time, one person can simultaneously belong to several subcultures and change their modes of identity over the course of work, life, and time, whether professional, cultural/ethnic or age-related. On the basis of the multitude of subcultures and by way of complex interrelations, the culture of society comes to be formed as including both dominant and marginal types. We can recognize in this the modern approach to the construction of the common through the conventional sum of individuals, i.e., atomism. In relation to the dominant (sub)culture, there arises a hierarchy of all other subcultures: those which, although not dominant, do not oppose but are parallel or alternative to the main cultural group, and those counter-cultural and lumpen-groups in the extreme periphery which are rejected and condemned by both the dominant culture and many subcultures.

Following the logic of this approach, religious identity appears as merely one among many existing social subcultures. In the societal context of Modernity and Postmodernity, the traditional pagan subculture finds itself in the periphery. Given the mainly anti-Modernist message of Traditionalism and pagan Dharma, traditional identity ends up in the position of a counter-culture, is subjected to surveillance, ridicule, and repression by the dominant secular culture and those subcultures neutrally embedded into the mainstream. Likewise, Pagan Traditionalism rejects Modernity, its values, culture, and its subcultural classifications.

However, the localization of paganism in one corner of the marginal periphery alongside other, non-traditional subcultures, as well as paganism's initial disorientation and lack of strictness towards the contemporary world, have together rendered paganism in practice susceptible to a number of influences which bring it closer to being a subcultural phenomenon cast into the margins rather than a fundamental worldview and language for describing the world. The vast majority of these influences fit into the structure of the consumer society, i.e., are based on sign-representations whose importance comes to the fore while the meaningful spiritual element is suppressed.

The main conduit for the "subculturalization" of paganism has been youth, while the main conductive spheres have been politics, commerce, and culture in the forms of leisure and music. Subcultural infiltration by the political sphere proceeds in correspondence with the political type of pagan, in the face of the deformation of paganism more in the direction of the political away from paganism as a traditional identity. In other words, tradition ultimately becomes an instrument of political and ideological constructs, and political-subcultural identity comes to the fore. A glaring example of this is the evolution of nationalist subcultures towards their respective traditions as foundations of identity. This appeal to paganism is characteristic of the vast majority of various nationalist ideologies in various countries. In contrast to a real political party, fully-fledged ideology, or a cultural or civilizational paradigm based on the traditional heritage, subculture is always secondary, fragmented, and located on the lower levels of the societal structure. Belonging to a pagan (or Abrahamic) tradition is reduced to the representation of a certain set of signs, e.g., clothing, symbols, accessories, music, etc., employed often without knowledge of their history, significance, or any understanding of their meanings, and is reduced to the performance of actions believed to be traditional, or the inclusion of values and ideas which have never been attested in tradition, being instead the fruits of the Enlightenment and modernization.

The same could be said with regards to subcultures based on the role-playing of plots and themes from fantasy - but not only - literature. Fantasy itself has no relation to traditions, and the correspondingly arising subculture founded on such will be one step further from tradition, secondary to secondary. The borrowing of plots from (traditional) sagas, epics, and tales for the creation of works of fantasy generates an inverted interest in these prototypes and primary sources which turns into a superficial interest in mythology and folklore on the part of the role-playing subculture. The playful, superficial character of such can only render meaningless and erode the body of tradition. The opposite case, when rigor and strictness towards authenticity and sources are observed by reenactment subcultures, comes close to and is almost identical to the type of pagan reenactor discussed above. If the pagan reenactor is maximally focused precisely on tradition, then the subcultural reenactor can participate in the play-like reenactment of different periods, epochs, and countries. Subculture also manifests itself in the game itself's division of time and space between authentic reconstruction/reenactment sessions and everyday life. In other words, the subcultural reenactor is always at a distance from the reenacted situation and era. At the same time, authenticity is the end-goal of the game itself. Thus, we can see that these two subcultures are products of the consumer society and are forms of leisure and entertainment, and nothing more. The fragments of the pagan heritage become signs, elements of decor, a game for entertainment. These subcultures are positive, not antagonistic towards the society of subculture in its purest form.

In the cultural sphere of influences, let us consider two more currents that have claimed elements of paganism for their narrow needs: sports and music. Obsession with sports, especially mass forms and championships, is a painful psychosis of mankind. Fascination with watching senseless competitions does not even draw pity for this type of final man. Julius Evola called sport one of the most senseless forms of labor and deemed the elevation of popular sportsmen to the role of idols and elites pure anomie and degradation. The Olympic Games revived in modern times are but a parody of the ancient cult activities dedicated to the Gods of Olympus which consisted of more than mere physical competitions. Today's sportsman is an extremely anti-intellectual type claiming elite nature and popularity. Sport itself is a great selling show, an entertainment program of the mass media. Such sports' evocation of the warrior spirit and will in the spirit of antiquity can only be met with laughter, aimed as they are not at transcendence and battle, war, or heroic feats, but towards the entertainment of ever stupider and rootless masses. The sphere of physical competition was originally related to military training, volitional transcendence, and forging the essence of the masculine, which we can relate to the warrior, political type. Today, sports appeal to the feminine demonstrativeness of forms, addiction to cameras and tabloids, the desire to sell oneself, and the fear of falling from the "Olympus" of ratings. The slavery of defeated warriors left to entertain patricians in the arenas of Rome and the slavery of modern athletes' dependence on spectators and symbols of success, such as ratings, tables, and tests providing for better sales for the next round or championships, differ only in form. The non-complementariness of sports and the pagan sphere is obvious, not to mention the absolutely feminine and modern hedonistic cult of the sensual body that is just as far in essence from sport as it is from Tradition.

Another classic approach to classifying and describing the formation of subcultures is the reference of musical styles which form around themselves unique scenes of music coupled with styles of appearance and aligning values. In the 20th and early 21st centuries, paganism has been influenced most of all by two musical movements which we can, without a stretch, correlate with the mystical and political types. These are black metal and hardcore.

Black metal originated in England and Sweden in the late 1980s, its heyday and the true embodiment of its spirit taking place in Norway in the 1990s, where it came to be called "true Norwegian black metal." Without dwelling on questions of genealogy and tune, we can note that the axis of this style was constituted by an orientation towards occultism, Satanism, anti-Christianity, fantasy themes, politics, philosophy, and nature-related and pagan motifs and lyrics. We can also include in this list the dominance of lyrics of an externally informal type, asociality, and the delineating of opposition to the everyday society in musical terms. The main point in black metal was conveying an ideological message located in the extreme periphery of society and contrasting commonly accepted values. Even change in sound towards more melodic tunes and diversity of instruments was perceived as weakening, as a retreat from the idealism of this style in favor of greater popularity and commercialization. Heightened ideological conviction, anti-Christian orientations, sympathy for paganism and its anti-Modernist challenge were, without a doubt, the factors that led to a convergence between the metal scene and paganism and a certain mutual influence. A manifestation of this "mutual movement" was the appearance of "pagan black metal", "folk metal", and "viking metal" devoted to pagan themes, merging the metal style with folk instruments, lyrics, and vocals, and narrowly specializing in the viking and Nordic themes. Of these, the closest of all to "true black metal" is pagan metal, while folk and viking metal have migrated in the direction of more melody, the philosophical component yielding to folkloric and musical elements.

One figure who would become iconic to the mutual influence of paganism and Norwegian black metal in the 1990s was the founder and sole member of the group Burzum, Varg Vikernes. Varg achieved widespread fame in 1993 when, following trial for the murder of the leader of the Norwegian "Black Metal Inner Circle" occult-music association, Øystein Aarseth, Varg was sentenced to 21 years in prison. Prior to this, Varg had been accused of being implicated in a series of arsons against

Christian churches in the early 1990s. Vikernes thus became one of the most famous, dangerous, asocial representatives of the black metal scene. During his imprisonment, Varg wrote and published two books of articles, essays, and short stories, *Vargsmål* ("Varg's Sayings") and *Vargsmål II*, in which he discussed the fate of Norway, the state of society, and actively propagated his own version of Norwegian neo-paganism. Varg's references to Theosophy, the scientific worldview (such as his equating of the Gods to planets in the scientific understanding), and his bias in favor of primitive racism rule out any traditional quality of his neo-paganism. Varg's popularity and prolificness in music and writing have made him one of the most famous right-wing pagan authors, at times even overshadowing other, more authentic and Traditionalist forms of the Scandinavian tradition.[157] Varg has since admitted that his first works were written by his young and expressive self which he has outgrown, and he has since withdrawn from the metal scene, which he has begun to despise in favor of its Ambient sub-genre.

The origin of the hardcore scene dates back to the late 1970s and early 1980s in the US and the United Kingdom, where such emerged as the result of punk's divergence with its previous asocial, rebellious, "freedom-from" spirit and agenda. External shock-value was replaced with greater restraint and lyrics referring to social problems, freedom, politics, violence, and the rejection of the unhealthy lifestyles, anarchy and hedonism which punk had elevated to a cultic degree. Like punk and black metal, the hardcore scene also originated in the periphery of culture and society and was originally of a self-contained character. Hardcore intersected with and penetrated paganism through the political right wing of the scene, through the political type and the traditional motifs of honor, valor, spirit, and will woven into hardcore lyrics and themes. Hand in hand with the hardcore subculture emerged the "straight edge" or "sXe" subculture, which is sometimes considered to be

---

[157] For example, in his work on Dobrovolsky the religious studies scholar Roman Shizhensky repeatedly compares the fates and narratives of Dobroslav and Varg Vikernes. Varg himself has never positively spoken of Slavic paganism.

its own subculture, "sXe-hardcore." Straight-edge subculture was an ideological response first and foremost to the worldview of punk and the surrounding reality of social decomposition. Straight edge opposed social decomposition with the renunciation of drugs, tobacco, alcohol, and sexual promiscuity. This subculture's harder form, "hardline", rejected meat, animal products (veganism), coffee, and synthetic medicines in the "drug-free" spirit, and professed anti-consumerist, environmentalist, and animal rights principles. The messages of individualism and personal freedom were continued. The "X" sign originated as the stamp or paint on the wrists of underage club visitors designating that they should not be sold alcohol. Three x's together, "XXX", came to represent the sXe subculture's three basic provisions of no drugs, no alcohol, and no promiscuous sexual relations.

Many aspects of the sxe-hardcore/hardline subcultures are similar to some of the provisions of pagan traditions. Heightened attention to ecology and the protection of animals is similar to the sacred perception of the animal as a totem or beast dedicated to a God, and veganism is similar to the practice of refusing animal meat in Hinduism, which is also substantiated in sacred terms as non-violence. Its anti-social and anti-consumerist messages partially make sXe kin to conservative positions, which is further deepened by right-wing nationalist-oriented lyrics and appeals to warrior archetypes and war. However, here we can also note a substitution of aristocratic force with plebeian violence, primitive violence (*à la* "hatecore"/"peoplehate"), and teenage misanthropy. The difference between these subcultural likenesses and traditional forms and prototypes is enormous and obvious: sXe subculture, in all of its diversity, is a product of Modernity, and its substantiations of itself are predominantly Modernist. This substitution of numerous pagan attitudes with subcultural patterns gives rise to absurd claims on the identical qualities of pagan values and sXe ideals.

If hardcore was a reaction to the decomposition of the punk subculture, then it is still not oriented to the higher forms of spirit, but instead to forms of Modernity taken from another end, those of sobriety, social criticism, violence, veganism, etc., as if such are meant to temper the spirit. Behind the pathos of these declared ideas, there shines through the openly superficial hedonism that is characteristic of any subculture that insists on its alternative otherness to the mainstream. In this sense, socially/personally-responsible hardcore is no different from asocial punk. Their proclaimed values, intended to temper will and spirit, have nothing to do with the Will and Spirit embodied in the traditional aristocracy. Rather, they reflect a plebeian understanding of the same mere signs whose representation, according to the rules of the consumer society, creates the illusion of happiness, replacing meaning. To be "straight edge" but not exhibit the signs of belonging to this idea, i.e., to strictly observe its internal message but without externally showing such, means in the logic of this subculture that one is not straight edge at all. Belonging to a subculture is always supposed to be represented with its signs, otherwise, any such affiliation is absent. Thus, form is placed above content, which is hedonism.

The commercialization of subcultures is inseparable from their very nature and the logic of subculturality, which is the aspiration to distinguish and personalize a circle or scene. According to the law of the market, demand creates supply: if part of society does not want to consume generally accepted, standard goods and signs, then goods and signs will be created and sold which this anomic sector will wish to show off and consume. Thus, all of the tension between the marginal periphery and the commonly accepted center is annulled by the field of economics, is equalized and linked by producers and sellers. Only the moral, ethical, and political spheres remain. We can recognize in this the emergence of the playful nature of conflict, the blurring of sharp boundaries and antagonisms between subcultures, and between subculture itself and the general culture. The music industry, standing on the pillars of fashion and commerce, is a pure spawn of Modernity that skillfully ensnares both the center and the periphery, mixing them, supporting their development, and reselling them to consumers. Subcultures founded largely on music are therefore of an ephemeral nature. They are doomed to naught.

For paganism, the commercialization of the subcultures connected to it poses the threat of the very same blurring of values and emasculation of the meanings of symbols and forms. Striving to sell the relevant clothing and attributes as signs, the market opts for the creation of quasi-pagan brands with swastikas and runic ornaments, mantras and mandalas, the concoction of new symbols, and the outright falsification of the meaning of known symbols becomes common place in the drive to interest the consumer, to sell and profit more. In Russia, the sale of goods with the Scandinavian rune Odal has been endowed with numerous advertised "true Russian" meanings ranging from *Rod* to the falcon, wolf, and other equally absurd associations unconfirmed by any sources. A similar picture can be observed with the Slavic symbol of roots presented in one of Boris Rybakov's works, which for commercial aims has become the "star of Rus" and the "square of Svarog." The mixing of traditional ornaments, pattern elements, and the fine arts of different traditions with the signs and symbols of subcultures has become ubiquitous over the past half-century. Runes woven with the hardcore subculture's "X" are advertised as reflecting unity of values and goals, which is in fact an absurd claim. Commercialization generates simulacra readily consumed by the unassuming subcultural public and then retranslated outwards, replacing the body of authentic tradition itself. Subculture is anti-intellectual, since referencing strict sources and real work on oneself in Will and Spirit is too difficult and contradicts the signs broadcasted by scenes and their simple, mostly false axioms and interpretations of the pagan heritage.

With the emergence of Postmodernity, the dichotomy between marginal subcultures and the commonly accepted cultural center is annulled in favor of a kaleidoscope-puzzle of different blurred and blended subcultures in the absence of any one culture, all amidst universal consumption. Even the most "marginal" and anti-society groups become merely "one among many" using the same Internet services and stores in their representation of different shades of the homogenous, flat space of the screen.

Wherever subcultural identity, the identity of signs (clothing, accessories, emblems, and logos), and the elevation of individual elements into a cult are dominant over traditional identity, we will always be dealing with chimeras and deviations from traditional ideals, from authenticity, in favor of fashion and lies. Unraveling the tangle of subcultural stratifications and infiltration is important as an intellectual practice of self-cleansing, of growth over and despite one's environment or milieu. In its ultimate, ideal dimension, the phenomenon of subculture itself should be overcome as a manifestation of degradation void of any meaning to Pagan Traditionalism.

The Contemporary Experience

The history of the contemporary experience ought to be traced starting from the 19th century and, more attentively, the 20th. The first pagan communities to emerge had their roots in the occultist circles of Europe. In 1978, according to the records of the Asatru Free Church Committee, the US and Europe counted no less than 11 pagan organizations.[158] At this time, Evgeny Golovin and Alexey Dobrovolsky were active in Russia. At the time of this book's writing, there are hundreds of pagan communities of different traditions across the world, as well as the World Congress of Ethnic Religions, since 2010 known as the Europe Congress of Ethnic Religions.

The contemporary status of paganism is largely dependent on a given country's conditions and the activities of pagans themselves. In Iceland, for instance, Asatru is a most powerful competitor to the official Lutheran church, and in India Hinduism has been preserved as dominant uninterruptedly

---

158 Slauson, *Religion of Odin*.

to the present day. In Germany, the practice of paganism has been complicated by the historical legacy of the Third Reich, which has cast a shadow on any appeals to ethnic roots and culture. The late 20th century also saw the appearance of the first communities aiming to revive the pagan tradition of Egypt, Kemeticism - however, the latter movement is based in the US, the most famous organization of which is the House of Netjer, and the founder of American Kemeticism Tamara Logan Siuda's ties to Wicca and this vast territorial rift with Egypt rule out any authenticity and initiatic quality of this initiative. In the late 20th and early 21st centuries, the restoration of pagan traditions has also begun on the territories conquered by Islam: voluntary attempts at returning to paganism have been undertaken among the Ossetians, Chechens, Kabardians, Georgians, Armenians, Yazidis, Arabs, and Iranians.

Paganism in Russia has been of nature close to that of a diaspora, a network of officially unregistered communities and organizations which are geographically scattered across the whole post-Soviet space without any formal centralization. This is in part due to the modest historical experience of contemporary pagan practice - which, in the opinion of Nikolai Speransky, dates back no further than the past 30 years - as well as to the strong influence of Orthodoxy. Although pagans in Europe had freer hands, they have become hostages to the harsh frameworks of political correctness and humanism and have been compelled to reduce their ritual practices, sacrifices, and relations with the rest of the world and within communities themselves to the patterns of tolerance, artificial pacifism, and such humanistic norms of Modernity as individualism, democracy, and civil law.

Another notable feature of contemporary paganism is the fact that it has primarily spread and developed in urban environments. Scholars of religion who have researched the phenomena of neo-paganism have noted that such mainly concerns urban intellectuals. This is only partially true, as far from all of the prominent personalities of contemporary Russian and worldwide paganism fit this vague definition, not to mention ordinary community members. "On the ground", paganism is present itself more in villages close to cities, where urban-residing pagans go in search of *Lad* with nature and for a healthier society and lifestyle. Paganism also appears in places of so-called "esoteric tourism", such as the Altai Mountains, Arkaim, Khakassia, and Buryatia. One prominent example of urban paganism departing from civilization was Dobroslav's move to the village of Vasenevo in the rural Kirov region, where he lived, hosted guests, and organized annual holidays until his death.

The predominantly "diasporic" status of pagan communities in both Russia and elsewhere in the world reflects the structural peculiarities of paganism as consisting of traditions which have not been formed into institutions in the likes of Christian churches. In other words, paganism is composed of more than one pole of attraction within a given tradition. Paganism is polycentric. The figure of a chief patriarch, pontifex, or head hierarch who establishes and interprets dogma is absent in paganism. We can see confirmation of this in the structure of the Greek *poleis* which, while being independent units not uncommonly at war with one another, still preserved a unity of culture and tradition. We can observe the same trend in the history of India, where the domination of Vishnu/Krishna or Shiva has varied across regions and historical stages. In Russian history, one village could especially venerate one God, while another *volost'* (a medieval Slavic principality or administrative district) could primarily worship another.

The question of the establishment of a single, centralized pagan "church" has more than once been raised in Russian paganism, primarily for the purpose of establishing Slavic-Russian paganism as a cultural heritage of Russia and defending religious rights and sanctuaries, i.e., for more utilitarian and practical ends than for the development of strict dogma and forms. In the opinion of Nikolai Speransky, a pagan church is needed in Russia so as to, among other things, test and confirm the spiritual explorations and constructions of more authoritative priests across Russia. We can see in this the traces of a universalist approach which treats a church as an institution asserting a dogma/norm against which other opinions are verified and, if not passing tests for "heresy", are rejected.

The question of a pagan church in Europe has equally not been of great relevance. Local legislations are fairly open to the registration of pagan organizations, which has contributed to preserving diasporic status. The experience of Iceland, where the *Ásatrúarfélagið* (Asatru Fellowship) in existence since 1973 has lobbied broad privileges for Asatru, including for the construction of the first official temple in several centuries, not far from Reykjavik, is an interesting exception. The dominance of this community can be a good example, especially insofar as it has not become an institutionalized church along the Christian model despite the fact that it is attended by more than 2,000 people amidst a total population of 322,000. Russian followers of Asatru have also been in the vanguard, having successfully registered two communities in central Russia in 2013-2014.

In Italy, the contemporary pagan religious organization Nova Roma has under UNESCO actively participated in the restoration of a temple complex on Palatine Hill and conducted active educational and proselytizing work, modeling itself along the principle of being an ancient state within the modern state, which is a rather extravagant example of pagan practice.

Opposite to the idea of a pagan church is the format of pagan autonomy. The essence of the latter lies in abandoning even community forms of organization and hierarchy in favor of micro-groups of believers, whether individuals, families or small groups of friends. Such pagan autonomies are independent units which maintain indifference to the problems raised within the pagan milieu at large, living instead in their own closed circles and frequently practicing strictly reconstructionist/ reenactionist and naturist approaches to tradition. Meanwhile, the majority of pagans pursue practice within the framework of numerous pagan communities, together forming an ensemble of diversity against unifying dogmatism. The extreme minus of the communal, and to an even greater extent the autonomous forms we would highlight to be the particularism of their approaches to life, manifest in a kind of secularism that separates tradition and its values from everyday life or other social and professional spheres. In other words, the problem lies in the entrenchment of the opinion that traditional configurations are not complementary to professional, social, and everyday situations, or that religious views are merely personal matters or, in the best case, matters whose place, time, value, and role is heightened on holidays or during other rituals. Along this line, it is argued that tradition, rites, folklore, and culture are on one side, while everyday life, work, and politics are on the other, and neither should affect or influence the other. In the best case, it is recognized that tradition can but should not exert influence on all spheres. In the worst case, thinking of such influence does not even arise. Such a state of affairs reflects the Modernist infiltration of secularism and the division of spheres of life in which religion is not primary and generally marginal. In our point of view, this is an instance of insufficient rigor with regard to traditional identity. The particularist approach revives tradition only into a subculture, making it one of many identities and spheres of activity, leisure amidst the consumer society.

To counteract this form of secularism which, although not of the greatest urgency, does not deserve the place to be a fact, we affirm the need for the rigorous subordination of all spheres of life to the values and forms of tradition as much as possible. Tradition is a comprehensive language for describing the world, a worldview which includes all spheres of human activity and links them through estate, caste, and other levels and forms of manifestations. Nothing in Tradition exists in autonomy and disconnect. Here it would be appropriate to once again quote the words of the Australian Pagan Traditionalist Wulf Grimsson, the relevance of whose truth extends far beyond this place: "I would call on fellow pagans and Traditionalists to consider the true Radical nature of our path. It is not enough to be weekend pagans', we must transform our whole lives, every minute detail. We need to limit our exposure to the pernicious influence of fundamentalism, monotheism and materialism and reprogram ourselves to be true pagans."

Personalities

In studying the contemporary experience of pagan communities and emphasizing the potential of the Russian space, we agree with the scholar of religion Roman Shizhensky's thesis on the importance of the role of personalities in the formation of communities and the development of paganism in Russia. An outstanding personality is capable of mobilizing and attracting followers, organizing stable communities, revealing the depths of tradition and imparting such with new contributions. Shizhensky himself has devoted two monographs to such iconic figures as Alexey Dobrovolsky (Dobroslav) and Nikolai Speransky (Velimir). We have chosen the following list of personages for their significant, although not uncontroversial impacts on the formation of paganism in Russia, and by virtue of the fact that in some cases they came close to embodying Pagan Traditionalism in Russia (and in Europe). These figures shaped the main contours, trends, and axes of the contemporary pagan experience, while also at times posing evident examples for our consideration of the question of infiltrations and problems of authenticity.

Dobroslav was at once one of the first modern Russian pagans and one of the most original and colorful representatives of pagan mysticism flowing through the prism of nativism and naturalism. It could be said that Dobroslav was a mystic of nature who turned to the essence of Slavic paganism while leaving forms a secondary matter. Despite his critical attitude towards other outstanding pagan thinkers and his frequent divergence with them on a number of questions, many such pagans hold Dobroslav to have been a true volkhv worthy of respect.

Dobroslav founded the Moscow Pagan Community, counting several dozen members, in 1989. In its first two years, the community actively engaged in proselytizing and propagandistic work, although already in 1990 Dobroslav broke with civilization and moved with a group of like-minded associates to the abandoned village of Vasenevo in the Shabalinsk area of Russia's Kirov region. Subsequently, although only Dobroslav and his family permanently remained out of the first wave of settlers, the village itself became one of the centers of Russian paganism, drawing to its summer Kupala festival pagans from across Russia, many of whom would acquire their initiatic names from Dobroslav.

Vasenevo continued to be the center of Dobroslav's activities, and around him the Arrows of Yarila community was formed and dedicated to local history and educational operations. Dobroslav was subsequently proclaimed the elder of the non-centralized Russian Liberation Movement, in the arena of which he continued educational-proselytizing activities. Indeed, one of the red threads running through Dobroslav's life was his political struggle with government authorities. In 1958, Dobroslav suffered repression and served a short, three-year sentence in the Mordovian camps, where he met Stanislav Rudolfovich Arseniev-Hoffman who, in turn, introduced Dobroslav to an ideological circle associated with German National Socialism, Germanic youth societies, and völkisch mysticism. Dobroslav subsequently grew closer with other dissidents and actively participated in the National Labor Union, also known as the National Alliance of Russian Solidarists, which ended with a two-year sentence in the sensational "case of four." Following the collapse of the USSR, Dobroslav continued to be persecuted under political articles, accused of nationalism and anti-Semitism, as a result of which all of his works and even some of his small articles remain banned in Russia to this day.

Dobroslav's philosophy and worldview, especially on the level of external forms, might be critiqued from the standpoint of Julius Evola's criticism of neopaganism, particularly in terms of materialist naturalism and "closure" on the immanent level of nature-worship. However, if we delve deeper into Dobroslav's philosophy and attempt to evaluate his intellectual, mystical field and space, as well as the sheer weight of his influence even on pagans who otherwise disagreed with his fundamental positions, then we can discern that Dobroslav's nature-mysticism was merely the external shell of an inner path to Tradition. The "classical" Traditionalism of Guénon or Evola and Dobrovolsky's "philosophy of good force" are separated by a respectful distance, although more bridges might be found between Dobroslav's works and those of Alain de Benoist or Dominique Venner. [159]

With his passing on 19 May 2013, Dobroslav left behind an immense legacy contained both in books and in minds and souls, inspiring numerous pagans across Russia. Dobroslav set his children (two sons) on the path of Native Faith, and they have continued his work. The colorful final chord of Dobroslav's earthly incarnation was the traditional rite of cremating his body on logs, which became a landmark event in the practice of Russian paganism. Before the latter, according to various sources, ritual cremation had only been carried out one or two times in recent history. Dobroslav's ascension in flame was attended by representatives of virtually every pagan association and numerous independent pagans. Thus, even in his death, Dobroslav and his rod contributed to the formation of Native Faith (which Dobroslav called "young paganism") in their native land.

An incarnation of a competent pagan of the reconstructionist/ reenactor type - with the influence of the political element - is Vadim Kazakov (b. 1965), who founded in 1997 and resigned as head from in 2011 what would become one of the first and largest pagan organizations in Russia, the Union of Slavic Communities of the Slavic Native Faith. Kazakov set as his

---

[159] For a more detailed examination and comparison of the pillars of Traditionalism and Dobroslav's own worldview, see our article *"Dobroslav: vzgliad traditsionalista"* [Dobroslav: A Traditionalist View] (*Svarte Aske*, 2014), appended to the Russian edition of *Polemos* and available online.

task the reconstruction of the pagan traditions of the Slavs as a fully-fledged religious confession in modern Russia. This path was embarked upon in 1993, when Kazakov founded the Kaluga Slavic Community which, in 1997, would alongside a number of communities in Moscow, Obninsk, Ryazan, Rybinsk, Smolensk, Orel, and Tambov join in the establishment of the Union of Slavic Communities of the Slavic Native Faith. This organization, founded by Kazakov, was distinguished by its striving to be as authentic as possible in its reconstruction of ancient Slavic beliefs, extensively relying on ethnographic, archaeological, historical, and folkloric accounts. The USCSNF has organized ethnographic activities and expeditions and has collaborated with the Russian Academy of Sciences.

The political component of Kazakov and his organization's activities consists not in participating in the political process as one party, but in the aspiration to establish Native Faith as a fully-fledged religious confession in Russia. This approach has allowed for extensive contact with academic institutions, the establishment in 2008 of the School of Slavic Native Faith, and the publication of the periodical journal *Rodnoverie* ("Native Faith"). In 2014, the USCSNF would be officially registered as an "Inter-Regional Social Organization" with the mandate of "officially cooperating with government agencies and other social organizations on the development and preservation of the culture and customs of the Slavic people." This political striving, without a doubt, has left a particular mark on the tradition itself in the form of a definite unification (although not dogmatization) with a particularly elaborate, well-developed, branching bureaucratic structure for the Union of Slavic Communities.[160] The priestly ladder adopted by the USCSNF provides for different *volkhv* functions and magical capabilities for the higher estate by virtue of their activities and nature, with divided and designated titles and hierarchical "ranks" for individual figures. In this structure, we can discern a timid step towards the format of a pagan church - with all of the risks

---

[160] See the USCSNF's 2013 handbook *Slavianskaia Rodnaia Vera* [*Slavic Native Faith*].

entailed, especially for the mystical path of knowledge within tradition. Since 2011, the administration of the USCSNF has been led by Maksim Ionov, and in the same year the pagan temple and cultural center of the USCSNF, Krasotynka, was founded near Kaluga. Presently, the geographical extent of the USCSNF encompasses ten communities in different cities across Russia and is one of the largest, most centralized associations of Russian Native Faith in the post-Soviet space.

Despite Dobroslav's political radicalism, these two figures of Russian paganism and the schools established by them can be seen as soft, cautious traditionalists who, although not directly referencing the philosophy of Traditionalism or the Primordial Tradition, insisted on the priority of the values and ideas of Slavic paganism and the necessity of returning to them amidst modern conditions of the degradation of society. Both pursued authenticity but combined different types in their activities, which refers us to their estate natures. However, the path of reviving ancient tradition can never be completely smooth, and in the modern experience of Russian paganism, we can find an example of failure to restore tradition. Volkhv Velimir (N. Speransky) is one such example.

Velimir emerged as the head of the Koliada of Vyatichi community formed out of the unification of the two groups Koliada and Vyatichi in 1997, which in 2003 would join (and then later depart from) the Circle of Pagan Tradition. Velimir's works compose a complex entanglement of both competent and authentic notions of paganism, proposals for the contemporary experience, as well as numerous, extensively depreciating relics and conceptual infiltrations from Christianity, Modernity, and Soviet socialism. In Velimir's worldview and activism, even in his negative theses, we can discern a certain element which, naturally flowing from the structure of the historically agrarian Russian people, gravitates towards the third estate which has preserved the pagan heritage on the folk level over the course of history. This is the phenomenon of the volkhv generated by the third estate, who turns his thought and rhetoric towards precisely this third estate. This discernment is suggested by the vivid domination in Velimir's discourse of the topics of pagan morality, e.g., the Moral Law of the Rod, and the continuation of the rod, which has always been accented on the everyday level of the estate of farmers, artisans, etc. Velimir himself practiced the craft of carving and painting and believed the cult of labor and work therapy to be necessary for pagan practice, in which the sub-estate proletarian cult of labor is clearly visible. Another Soviet relic of Velimir's legacy was his claim to a socialist nature of pagan community, encapsulated in the slogan "paganism is socialism" and, vice versa, the claim to pagan relics in the practice of the USSR, such as the restoration of the cult of the eternal flame, the unknown soldier, kurgan (barrow) burials, and other instances which, in Velimir's view, helped achieve victory in the Great Patriotic War.

Despite his correct claim that the origins of the volkhv estate fall under the patronage of the God Veles (or, alternatively, Chernobog) and his pointing out that, before the reform of Vladimir I, the Gods Perun and Veles were not held to be in opposition like the forces of Good and Evil in the Christian optic, Velimir's rhetoric nevertheless inherited a considerable deal of Christian language and attitudes, for instance towards the peculiar but absolutely traditional forms of extreme practices of Hindu Tantra (Shaiva and Shakti-Tantrism). Velimir also directly called "Satanism" the analogous practice of the Shuynyi put', or "Left-Hand Path" (from the old Russian word for the left hand, shuitsa), developed by Volkhv Veleslav in the context of Russian paganism. Such a statement, from the point of view of language, takes the person expressing such out of the field of paganism and puts him in the field of Christian terminology, values, and worldview. Another example of this is the "Formula of Faith" under which Koliada Vyatichi was registered in 1998, which contains the following statement directly traceable back to Christianity: "We find that a man who follows the destroyer-gods is satisfying his vices and is not happy. After death, his soul will burn in the inferno of

Chernobog." Indirectly related to this case, we might add that numerous authors have drawn parallels between communism, socialism, and Christian ideals, which closes these two trends in N. Speransky's worldview "behind the curtains."

On political and civilizational questions, Velimir drew the correct conclusion that the West is the source of the proliferating degradation of society and traditions, and therefore took a stance against globalization, as in his book of a similar title, *Volkhvs against Globalism*. But in other fields, Velimir negates these theses by introducing strictly Modernist, positivist methods into paganism. Despite his declared particularism of spiritual and professional activity, this layer was the deep effect of Speransky's education and professional research engagement at the Faculty of Physics of Moscow State University. Velimir's call for building a special pagan church-temple in which the theories of contemporary pagan authors would find confirmation is a direct embodiment of the principle of verification applied to the scientifically unverifiable sphere of the Spirit. Other examples of such include attempts at scientifically-technologically explaining Slavic mythology as well as blatant gnoseological racism towards what he deemed the "primitive" and "immoral" traditions of Hinduism, Tantra, and Zen Buddhism which, in Speransky's opinion, preach the primacy of personal pleasure. The absurdity of such a perception of Zen Buddhism should be left to Velimir's own conscience. As for Hinduism, as founded on the Vedas and Upanishads, Velimir argued that this tradition is "immoral" for its caste structure and "specialization" of Indian society. In another place, Velimir emphasized the fundamentally anti-democratic character of the Russian people and Russian paganism.[161] The result was a contradictory rejection of both the "unnatural" equality of democracy and the sacred hierarchy of estates. Thus, while speaking against the degraded West (the US), globalism, democracy, and capitalism,

---

161 See: N. Speransky, *Volkhvy protiv globalizma* [*Volkhvs against Globalism*] (Samoteka, 2014), and Shizhensky's study, *Pochvennik ot iazychestva: mirovozzrechenskie diskursy volkhva Velimira (N.N. Speranskogo* [*A Pochvennik from Paganism: The Ideological Discourses of Volkhv Velimir (N.N. Speransky)*].

Velimir simultaneously asserted the very same values of Western Modernity: a positivist approach to the spiritual quest, gnoseological racism, socialism (Promethean Titanism), and Christian moralistic principles.

In the preceding examination of Velimir's worldview, we have touched upon the most striking contradictions, although many more are to be found woven more subtly and elude superficial and unprepared glances. If one cuts off those areas in which Velimir was the most contradictory, which would be the fields of politics and metaphysics[162], then we are left with a fairly authentic and earnest teacher of *Lad*[163] who upheld the continuation of the rod, moral character and craft, and whose sermons and teachings are of use to the third estate and should be localized within such, on this one level.

Against the backdrop of other pagan communities and personalities in Russia, it seems to us that Velimir's community and worldview were quite naturally in line with the many unresolved contradictions to be found in the periphery of paganism in Russia. The figure of Velimir thus becomes quite problematic insofar as, by virtue of his combination of a reconstructionist approach with a whole host of anti-traditional positions, he cannot be directly referred to as a representative of post-religious pseudo-paganism; at the same time, his current absolutely cannot be seen as adequate Pagan Traditionalism. Rather, the case of Velimir is a glaring example of the need for a rigorous approach to reconstructing traditions and avoiding chimeras.

In the circle of the most prominent pagan figures and authors, the one who is closest of all to the concept of Pagan Traditionalism which we put forth is Volkhv Veleslav (Ilya Cherkasov, b. 1973), who has arrived at such in open form. Being a native of Moscow and a representative of so-called "urban paganism", Veleslav's life embodies the principle of lighting the Fire of Tradition under the most anti-traditional

---

162 Velimir categorically denied Traditionalist philosophy any value.

163 To recall, Velimir's proposed term Darna has been rejected by Russian pagans.

conditions. After several years of non-public practice and ethnographic research represented in Veleslav's first books dating back to the early 1990s, in 1998 Veleslav organized the Russian-Slavic Native Faith Community "*Rodoliubie*" ("Love for *Rod*"), therein coining the very term *Rodnoverie* ("Native Faith"). Slightly later, in 1999, Veleslav and his community became co-initiators of the Circle of Veles community, which is today the second most significant pagan association in Russia, equal in size and influence to Kazakov's Union of Slavic Communities of the Slavic Native Faith. Since 2013, both associations have periodically held joint celebrations of the Summer Solstice which have gathered thousands of participants.

The formulation of the goals and tasks of the Veles Circle allows one to clearly attribute its current to the mystical, priestly type, as is suggested in the very charter of the community: "The aims of the Veles Circle fellowship of communities are: (1) the rebirth, preservation, and multiplication of the Spiritual Heritage of our Ancestors; (2) the practical mastery and realization in life of the Volkhv Knowledge of our Ancestors." This line of the association's activities, with a minimum of bureaucratism, formalities, and political pretensions, is a direct embodiment and reflection of the mystical type and the higher natures of its founders who, besides Veleslav, include Stavr, Drevleslav Novoseltsev, and Bogumil Gasanov[164], to the latter of whose pen belongs an exemplary, competent reconstruction and adaptation of Slavic traditions to contemporary practice in the form of the book *The Foundations of Modern Koliada*, which analyzes the customs of caroling on the Winter Solstice, Koliada, through the prism of contemporary urban and rural conditions and the personal experiences of the author and his community members.

Veleslav's contributions to the emergence and propagation of Native Faith in Russia will be rightfully appreciated perhaps only in the future, insofar as his legacy is so great and at times

---

[164] The leader of the Triglav Native Faith Community of Obninsk, founded in 1993 and subsequently joining the Veles Circle.

seems so natural that it is rarely reflected upon for what it is - an altogether recent effort in the systematization, (re)discovery, revelation, and restoration of the pagan heritage. To restore the gaps in available ethnography and folklore, Veleslav has accomplished the great and delicate work of translating a number of ideas from Hinduism, Odinism, and Mediterranean traditions into the language of Slavic-Russian paganism. His formula underlying this approach is "Study the wisdom of other Rods, but follow the wisdom of your own *Rod*", in which "*Rod*" is understood as the *narod*, the people or folk, the *ethnos* and tradition. Not all of the latter have been met with lively responses in the pagan community, but many practical and theoretical developments, textbooks, and excerpts of Veleslav's have become axiomatic lines in pagan practice in contemporary Russia. Some of them have represented genuine revelations and manifestations of hidden, previously unreached depths of the wisdom of the Russian tradition, expressible in one of Veleslav's maxims which succinctly describes all three estate levels of the sacred hierarchy: "What is *Rodnoverie* (Native Faith)? What does it mean to be a *Rodnover*? I answer: 'Sacredly venerate Native Gods and ancestors, live in accordance with conscience and in harmony [*Lad*] with Nature, and if you seek Higher Knowledge, know thyself." The first part of this maxim - "sacredly venerate Native Gods and ancestors" - concerns the agricultural estate, patriarchal family cults, and relating to the Gods as to the demiurges of the cosmos. The second - "live in accordance with conscience and in *Lad* with Nature" - is addressed to the warrior and ruling estate, being a guideline as to how a good leader should be and how they should follow their own nature. As for the higher, priestly estate, "and if you seek Higher Knowledge, know thyself" speaks of knowing the self as Divine, of the return of consciousness as a divine manifestation to the source. Thus, the ending of this maxim integrates both the middle and the beginning as not contradicting the divine embodiment itself in different faces and on different estate levels.

Veleslav Cherkasov is also one of those few Russian pagans rather widely known at once within Native Faith and among pagans in Europe, where his work has influenced pagan practices, including to a lesser degree Odinism in Eastern Europe and England. This is despite the fact that out of Veleslav's numerous works, only one has been translated into English.[165]

As a Traditionalist, Veleslav meets the requirements of authenticity, distinguishing between known and source-confirmed experience and his own spiritual quest, and actively appeals to Traditionalist philosophy, although at the first stages of his work without expressing such openly, instead clothing such in forms accessible to the language of Russian paganism while accurately noting the problems of the formation of Native Faith in its present stage and its relation to modern influences. Veleslav's opinion on a "pagan church" is well known:

> The most terrible thing for paganism in contemporary Russia would be its official recognition, which would inevitably lead to an internal struggle for power and to disputes over who is a "true" pagan and who is not, as well as, ultimately, to the monetization and the routinization of living faith. For now, as long as we gather in forests and aren't paid money but, on the contrary, are required to make investments, paganism is attracting people who are genuinely "burning" and living by tradition.

Veleslav would later openly realize his Traditionalist potential, publishing under the name "Satyavan" multiple books on Tantrism, the extreme tantric practices of Vamachara, alchemy, and integral Traditionalism, with direct references to the constellation of classical and contemporary Traditionalists. We can absolutely accurately correlate Veleslav with the mystical type of pagan, being a representative of true priestly nature, an author and activist who is maximally close to Pagan Traditionalism, and one who stands literally on the border between soft Traditionalism within Native Faith and open Traditionalist philosophy.

---

165 Volhv Veleslav, *The Great Perfection Doctrine* (Fall of Man, 2016).

Without any doubt, the founding father of the Russian school of Traditionalism in both a historical and pagan perspective - and, as so often happens, virtually unnoticed by contemporary Russia's pagan community itself - was Evgeny Vsevolodovich Golovin (1938-2010). The figure of Evgeny Golovin is so multifaceted and multidimensional that it would be impossible to fit him exclusively within the framework of Pagan Traditionalism, and a detailed description of his life and philosophy would demand a volume comparable in scope to the present book. Golovin was a mystic, a poet, an alchemist, a translator, a Traditionalist, a composer of songs, a writer, a pagan of wine and, as those who knew him personally have said, an incarnation of Dionysus and Dionysianism.

Evgeny Golovin was the center and driving force of a unique mystical underground that existed in the mid-20th century in the very heart of Soviet Moscow. This was the Yuzhinsky Circle of dissidents, who differed from the "mainstream" gray mass of liberal-human rights dissidents by their absolute indifference to this problem, devoting themselves instead to mysticism, magic, and tradition. In the words of Alexander Dugin, the Yuzhinsky Circle in the Soviet Union was something which, in the USSR with its materialism and totalitarianism, could not have existed in principle, but did. Igor Dudinsky wrote of the emergence of the Yuzhinsky Circle: "The circle was formed in the reading room of the Lenin Library, or rather originated in the smoking room there, with books on philosophy, mysticism, and esotericism (the KGB did not yet realize the extent of their influence, and all of this wealth was still available to the public, which people read and discussed). Gradually, everyone got acquainted with one another and [Yuri] Mamleev started inviting people to his place, as he lived closest of all."[166] "Closest of all" meant on Yuzhinsky

---

166 Krizhevsky, Alexey."*Interv'iu 'Barkhatnoe podpol'e: Igor' Dudinsky o zhizni sovetskoi bogemy*" [Interview: "The Velvet Underground: Igor Dudinsky on the Life of a Soviet Bohemian"]. *Russkaia zhizn'* [*Russian Life*], 1/2/2008. For an English-language introduction to the Yuzhinsky Circle, see: Jafe Arnold, "Mysteries of Eurasia: The Esoteric Sources of Alexander Dugin and the Yuzhinsky Circle" (University of Amsterdam, 2019).

Alleyway, in a now demolished house that then belonged to Yuri Mamleev, who would become a famous writer, Indologist, and philosopher. Virtually the whole constellation of Russian Traditionalists came out of Mamleev-cum-Golovin's circle: the Muslim thinker Geydar Dzhemal, the Orthodox Old Believer/Co-Believer[167] Alexander Dugin, the poet and singer Alexander F. Skliar, Sergey Zhigalkin, and others. The confessional affiliations of this Russian school of Traditionalists cover virtually all the main lines of creationism, manifestationism, as well as currents of occultism, alchemy, mysticism, dark poetry, and the literary prose of "restless presence." The Yuzhinsky Circle introduced Russian readers to the works of René Guénon, Julius Evola, Titus Burckhardt, medieval alchemists, European mystics, and the modern Traditionalists Jean Parvulesco, Alain de Benoist, and many others. The circle produced the writing and publication of a number of the most important works and books which laid the foundations of Traditionalism in Russia. The heart and teacher of this school was Evgeny Golovin, who bore the title "Admiral."

Golovin was not a pagan in the likes of the image evoked by widespread cliches and which first comes to the mind of philistine consciousness. He did not participate in any pagan community, rites, nor did he wear ceremonial clothing or exhibit other stereotypical attributes. Instead, Golovin was an incarnation of ancient Platonism and Neoplatonism, and his Gods were the Greek Gods, Apollo, Aphrodite, and especially Dionysus, to whom the anthology *Madness and its God* edited by Golovin and two of his public lectures would be dedicated. Golovin was a pagan friend of satyrs, fauns, the Muses, wine, and poetry bestowed upon him by the Charites. Golovin's detachment from the pagan communities of modern Russia, his Traditionalist strictness, and his wide breadth of interests and activities conditioned the fact that he remains practically unknown and unnoticed by contemporary pagans. In the book

---

167 "Co-Believer" refers to *Edinoverie*, the current within the Old Believers Rite which cooperates with the Russian Orthodox Church.

In Search of the Dark Logos, Dugin wrote of Golovin: "He did not create his own tradition, but concentrated within himself the lines of numerous traditions bearing some kind of approach to the present extreme situation of the End Times, the apogee of the 'crisis of the modern world' (*à la* René Guénon)."[168] Thus, Golovin embodied the purest principle, beyond forms. A pagan reading of his works and person is only one possible approach, but one that is a genuinely necessary condition for attaining a new intellectual level and expanding the notion of paganism beyond simple pantheism and the worship of nature. Evgeny Golovin passed away in 2010 at the age of 73. As he predicted, it snowed on the day of his funeral. Twos years later, an obelisk was erected on his grave in Moscow's Volkovsky Cemetery, the very same that was once built on the kurgan burial mounds of Scythian and Hyperborean warriors.

As can be seen, Russia boasts a powerful school of Traditionalism and a wide constellation of pagan actors, authors, and organizations representing the whole spectrum of pagan types, albeit predominantly gravitating between the reconstructionist and warrior types. The breeding ground of this spectrum has largely been the third estate which has historically dominated Russian agrarian society. The heights of self-initiation and self-knowing have been attained by personages who have come maximally close to Traditionalism, some of whom even became Traditionalists, embodying the kindling of Fire amidst the totally anti-traditional ice of the capital of socialist Russia, Moscow, in the form of Evgeny Golovin and Veleslav and the schools they created. On the other hand, as a negative example we have described the contradictory views of Velimir, the head of the Koliada of Vyatichi, whose rhetoric mixed pagan reconstructions with relics and infiltrations from Christianity, socialism, and Modernity and thereby generated an entanglement of contradictions that nullify this third-estate discourse.

---

168 Dugin, *V poiskakh temnogo Logosa* [*In Search of the Dark Logos*], p. 443.

Compared to the situation in Europe, Russian paganism and Russian Odinists are young, which gives them age potential which needs to be fully realized by turning not to the level of the state, but towards popular potential, towards structures that are more European than those represented by the contemporary Anti-Europe, and by turning towards the Russian schools of paganism and Traditionalism. Russian pagans are generally stricter, more careful and cautious with their pagan heritage, trying to minimize its perversion into a "weekend paganism" as has become so characteristic of many superficial pagans in Europe and America - a consequence of the liberal decomposition of traditions.

The defense of Europe's traditional, pre-Christian values from attacks of monotheism, Modernism, and liberalism has been the life-long endeavor of the outstanding French thinker and Traditionalist, Alain de Benoist (b. 1943). De Benoist is the author and editor of numerous books and journals, some of which have become for all intents and purposes iconic, such as the magazine *Éléments*. In 1968, de Benoist founded the Group for the Research and Study of European Civilization (or GRECE, from the French: Groupement de recherche et d'études pour la civilisation européenne), of which *Éléments* became the main press organ. GRECE's activities centered around Traditionalism, conservatism, the defense of paganism and the environment, and critiquing Modernity, liberalism, communism, and creationism. Alain de Benoist and GRECE would become the foundation for the emergence of the French "New Right" (*Nouvelle Droite*) movement, which opposed both multiculturalism in the West and communism in the East while standing against the biological and ethnic racism and Nazism typical of the ultra-right, instead shifting attention to cultural differences and the plurality of traditions and cultures. In other words, the ideology of the New Right sought to overcome gnoseological racism. De Benoist himself has described the legacy of the New Right thusly:

> We are a theoretical and cultural movement...While I cannot say that, after these many years, the [European] New Right is

accepted everywhere - that is obvious - I can say that, in ever wider circles, it is accepted in France as a part of the cultural-political landscape. Moreover, it is because the New Right has taken up particular themes that particular debates have taken place at all. I refer, for example, to discussions about the Indo-European legacy in Europe, the Conservative Revolution in Germany, about polytheism and monotheism, or about I.Q., heredity or environment (which is partly a rather false dichotomy), participatory democracy, federalism and communitarian ideas, criticism of the market ideology, and so forth. We were involved in all these issues. As a result, I think, the situation in France today is a bit different.[169]

Another notable figure of the New Right movement was the above-mentioned Dominique Venner.

In Russia, most of Alain de Benoist's works have not seen the light of day of publication, with the exception of various articles and his major work *On Being a Pagan* (whose Russian title is "How to Be a Pagan"), which sharply polemicized against monotheism, insists on upholding the viewpoints of antiquity, and comes altogether close to the positions of Pagan Traditionalism. De Benoist has actively collaborated with the Traditionalists of Alexander Dugin's school, but remains little known as a thinker and Traditionalist among pagans.

In the context of European and American Odinism, we can distinguish two significant figures who have shaped Odinism and Asatru in modern conditions. The first is the former head (*allsherjargoði*) of the Icelandic Asatru Fellowship (*Ásatrúarfélagið*), Sveinbjörn Beinteinsson, (1924-1993), who established the fellowship in 1972 and, in 1993, half a year before his death, achieved official registration for Asatru in Iceland as an autonomous church possessing all the corresponding legal rights, such as for recognized weddings, burials, and property.

Sveinbjörn, in his own words, was a natural-born farmer. Here we once again encounter the role of the third function as exerting a decisive influence on pagan practice and, correspondingly, another refutation of the claim that

---

[169] "The 'European New Right' Defining and Defending Europe's Heritage: An Interview with Alain de Benoist by Ian B. Warren", *New European Conservative* (2014).

contemporary paganism is mainly urban. To some extent, Sveinbjörn's case is similar to the experience of Dobroslav's reclusion. Sveinbjörn was also a talented poet who collaborated with counter-cultural music circles, in which we can find a trace of subcultural proximity to marginals on the periphery. Among the Gods whom he venerated the most, Beinteinsson singled out Thor, the Guardian-God, whose motif is the main one to be found in modern Asatru and also corresponds to the values of the third estate.[170] The Icelandic pagan also drew attention to the negative impact of rapid technological development as detaching people from nature and the natural way of life. Today, despite all the difficulties which Iceland has experienced, the Asatru Fellowship is under the leadership of its fourth supreme goði, Hilmar Örn Hilmarsson. We regret to be compelled to remark that if Beinteinsson was the fellowship's mystic and "patriarch", then Hilmarsson has been trying on the image of a pop figure, acting in movies and staging a rock opera based on Nordic mythology.

Another contemporary figure worth mentioning is the American Asatru activist Stephen McNallen (b. 1948), who in 1971 began publishing the journal *Runestone*, around which the Viking Brotherhood was formed in 1972. The Viking Brotherhood would gain registration as a religious organization and, in 1976, was renamed the Asatru Free Assembly. In 1986, due to disagreements over whether Asatru should be conceived as a universalist or ethnically-conscious movement, the Assembly splintered into the *völkisch* Asatru Alliance, upheld by McNallen, and the Ring of Troth, which rejected an ethnic binding for Odinism and thereby opposed the very structure of pagan traditions. After several years of absence, in 1994 McNallen revived his organization under the name Asatru Folk Assembly, which exists to this day. As an activist, McNallen has been known for his advocacy of environmental conservation and the liberation of Tibet from Chinese occupation. As for

---

170 See the interview with Beinteinsson in Gisela Graichen, *Die neuen Hexen. Gespräche mit Hexen* [*The New Witches: Conversations with Witches*] (Munich: Goldmann, 1999), various English translations of which can be found online.

minuses and infiltrations, the following points from the AFA's Declaration of Purpose can be singled out: "V. The promotion of true diversity among the peoples and cultures of the Earth... VII. The use of science and technology for the well-being of our people, while protecting and working in harmony with the natural environment in which we live."[171] In the latter, we can see a certain contradiction similar to that of Velimir's mutually exclusive opinions, which calls into question the authenticity and initiatic competence of the organization reconstructed by McNallen. It is worth noting that in his fundamental work *Asatru: A Native European Spirituality*, McNallen, being an outstanding American Odinist activist, calls his confession "European spirituality."[172]

Critical Remarks on Practice

In this section, we will dwell on some critical remarks on the contemporary state of pagan traditions, not in relation to specific personalities or organizations. Our remarks, first of all, concern only the most recent period of history, the 20th-21st centuries, and, as follows and secondly, are concerned with manifestations related to the shift in societies - in global society - and the influence of such on various traditions.

The first matter which immediately comes into view is the problem of conceptualizing rapid scientific-technological development, its influence on and its incorporation into the pagan view of the world. In the above, we offered our principal Traditionalist response to this question by identifying technological development, as the embodiment of the idea of progress, with the anti-sacral pole, with the titanic element, and with the correspondingly arising Dharmic relations of war. The myths of traditions undoubtedly know the Titans, the Asuras, the Thursar, and the demons, but they know them

---

[171] https://www.runestone.org/declaration-of-purpose/

[172] Stephen A. McNallen, *Asatru: A Native European Spirituality* (Nevada City: Runestone Press, 2015).

as defeated, subordinated, and cast into the periphery of the Divine Cosmos, to the borders of Chaos. But in contemporary paganism, both in its reborn forms and in the preserved beliefs of small peoples, this approach is not ubiquitous. Instead, to a greater degree, a neutral particularism is widespread, which is to say that the pernicious influences of Modernist infiltrations are not subject to reflection, or are treated as resolved by dividing spheres of activity - for example, during ritual practices and rites any technological devices and means which are not authentic to tradition are excluded as much as possible. Thus, two worlds are created: the everyday world and the communal-confessional world, between which there arises a substantial and irremovable difference of forms: immersion into the modern world on the one hand, and fencing off from the modern world on the other. Adding to this the even more subtle level of difference between the languages of Tradition and Modernity, we can state that the external removal of objects of technological progress is often precisely of an external, superficial nature lacking reflection on the level of language. But turning to Tradition and initiation into and within tradition demands adoption of the totality of its language and values, not merely that temples and altars be fenced off from the profane signs of modernity on holidays and during festivals, but that the Fire of Tradition be brought into the present and illuminate amidst everyday life the due order of things. Initiation demands turning escapism into tradition in the opposite direction, into a powerful wave that can wash away the modern picture of the world in favor of Divine Sacrality.

The most disastrous and marginal resolution of the problem of the interrelations between Tradition and Modernity is represented by those attempts at conceptualizing the technological achievements of Modernity and Postmodernity, as well as their corresponding social and global changes, in a positive spirit of development and reconciliation with the Gods. In this practice, mobile phones, computers, and virtual networks are declared to be blessings of the Gods bestowed upon humanity, spirits and Gods are introduced as the patrons of social networks, technology, and the IT-sphere, and technological devices are actively used in ritual practice. The priest reads praises not from the Heart, but from the screen of a mobile phone, the forest is consecrated not by fire, but by electrical illumination, and all sorts of technology are employed to create a theatrical effect for participants. Thus, the rite is leveled down to a spectacular quasi-ethnic setting of special-effects. Hand in hand with this practice proceeds the syncretism of traditions, or the assertion that there is no need to belong to one tradition alone, that anyone can praise any Gods. In this can be seen, distinctly and without a doubt, the Postmodernist, post-religious syncretism which excludes any initiative dimension and authenticity. Here once again we can recall the possibility, still preserved among some remote, small peoples living in hard-to-reach localities, of sacralizing objects from without in relation to their life circle in the world, thus giving expression to the first means of raising fire - the placing of things into the still strong flame of Tradition.

One tradition that has traversed a long, difficult path through time and history is shamanism, a unique, ancient phenomenon which has embraced the peoples of Asia and Siberia and elements of which have been identified in Scandinavian mythology in the magic of the Vanir. The principal bearers of shamanism are the Turkic peoples, the Tuvans, the Buryats, the Khakas people, and the Mongols. Dordzhi Banzarov traced the word "shaman" back to the Manchu *saman*, from the root *sam* related to a number of Manchurian and Mongolian words meaning "to interfere", "to splash", "to disturb", and "to dance." *Saman* means the frenzied, outraged, restless state into which the shaman falls during trance. The Russian pronunciation - "shaman" - was likely borrowed from the Tunguz. Other Siberian peoples have their own words for shamans, e.g., the Tatar *kam* and Buryat *böö* or *böge*.

We can highlight three waves of decisive influence on shamanism: the adoption of Buddhism in Mongolia and Russia's Siberian regions, the Christianization of Russia's Far East in the period of the Russian Empire, and the influence of the Soviet anti-theistic propaganda of materialism. Mongolia's adoption of Buddhism as the official religion in 1578 left shamanism in the position of the lower faith, that of the lower strata of the population "unenlightened" by Buddhism. Hence the origin of one of the names of shamanism: the "Black Faith", the faith of the dark commoners contrasting the "Yellow Faith" of Buddhism. Buddhism pushed shamanism into the periphery of Mongolian society and significantly suppressed the shamanism of the Siberian and Far Eastern regions of Russia. In response, shamanism adopted a number of Buddhist elements, resulting in a dual-faith synthesis: on the one hand, Buddhism adopted a number of shamanistic notions, and on the other shamans began to use Buddhist mantras and images of the Gods in their practice. But this did not proceed without repression: the adoption of Buddhism in Buryatia in the 16th-17th centuries and the Russian Tsar's approval of Buddhism as the new religion of the Buryats saw mass persecutions of resistant shamans and the burning of ongons and shamanic instruments with the support of the Tsarist police. Simultaneous with the establishment of Buddhism, the small peoples - Evenks, Buryats, Nenets, Mansi, and Khanty - were Christianized. Christianity affected shamanism to a significantly lesser degree than the doctrine of Gautama Buddha, giving rise to a surface-level dual-faith and an even more obvious reverse influence on local Christian parishes, which not uncommonly came to perform shamanic functions. Shamanism, in turn, reinterpreted Christian saints as cosmic spirits and God and Satan as two equal upholders of the cosmic structure. Mircea Eliade cited the following cosmogonic myth reflecting such dual-faith:

> Thus, for example, one Russian myth says that neither God nor the Devil were created, but that they coexisted since the beginning of time. According to myths attested among the Southern Altaic peoples, the Abakanian Kachins, and the Mordvins, the Devil was created by God. But the way in which he was created is telling: God created the Devil in form out of his own substance. Here is how the Mordvins tell it: God stood alone on a cliff and said "If I had a brother, I would

create the World!", after which he spit into the Waters. Out of his spit was born the Mountain. God pierced it with his sword, and out of the mountain came the Devil (Satan). As soon as he appeared, the Devil invited God to fraternize and create the World together. "Brothers we will not be", God responded, "but we will be companions." And together they engaged in creating the World. [173]

At the same time, the Russian Empire's legal norms for shamans who violated Christian or state laws regulating the religious spheres were milder than those for Muslims who committed similar offenses. For instance, the punishment for "seducing the faith of an Orthodox", e.g., conducting a ritual for a baptized child or other believer, was punished by confiscation of the drum, robe, and instruments. A Muslim who "seduced" Christians to Islam was punished by death, according to the Synodal Code of 1649. A reversal from adopted Orthodoxy back to Shamanism was punished by epitemia and confiscation of property.

Christianization and the establishment of Buddhism were followed by the period of Soviet anti-theism, which took aim at both Christianity and shamanism. However, it proved much more difficult to persecute and uproot shamanism since, unlike Christianity, shamanism was neither centralized nor unified, did not have a single leader, center, or holy book, and instead was passed down through the family-tribe orally from relative to relative. Instead, greater damage to the traditional culture of the small peoples was dealt not by direct attacks on shamanism and traditions but through the widespread inculcation of the Russian language and secular, Europeanized education, which cut a rift between generations, between the elders educated in and knowledgeable of the language, customs, and tradition and youth who, first, received both educations simultaneously and later only secular education. This was a manifestation of the pure, unreflective repression of traditional knowledge by Eurocentrism and Modernity as expressed by the Soviet-Bolshevik enlighteners. The contemporary state of shamanism, despite the still preserved continuity of this tradition's transmission in remote regions, is

---

173 Mircea Eliade, *Mephistopholes and the Androgyne: Studies in Religious Myth and Symbol* (New York: Sheed and Ward, 1965). Translation from the author's Russian.

still in decline in the wake of Soviet influence and three decades of the contemporary Russian socio-economic system, in which traditional crafts and lifestyles can no longer provide for large families and are partially restricted by law. In other words, the coming of "great enlightened civilization" has undermined the traditional way of life of small peoples and has had a negative influence on their faith.

Shamanism today, the pressure on which has somewhat weakened since the collapse of the USSR, has undergone a number of changes which might be characterized as responses to the challenges of the times and as partial infiltrations by Modernism. The unification and centralization of the tradition around several official centers is one such development that meets the eye. From a tribal-family tradition, shamanism has come to be institutionalized in some lines as a religion and, more narrowly, in centers of folk medicine where the personal problems of patients are more important than the affirmation of doctrinal dogma.

Since 2008, the Council of Shamanic Communities of the Baikal Region has been operating in Irkutsk as an advisory and coordinative body. The council conducts educational work among the population in the field of knowledge and observance of ancient Buryat customs. In Tuva, the official Dungur and Adyg-Eeren centers are active alongside numerous unofficial associations. Among the most well-known shamans we might highlight Ai Churek Oiun, Mongush Borakhovich Kenin-Lopsan, the first Tuvian scholar, and Kara-ool Tiuliushevich Dopchun-ool. The most problematic regions are Altai and Yakutia. Altai has become one of the focal points of "esoteric tourism" in contemporary Russia, attracting numerous New Age adepts and propagandists who have spoken out on and affected the customs represented there, degenerating them for touristic entertainment and mixing in white Europeans who come for new experiences on quasi-spiritual quests. Among the Khakas people, the Northern Yakuts, and the Nganasans, shamanism can be encountered only in remote sites, and not even everywhere in these places due to the closed nature of the tradition and the small number of its preserved lines of transmission. Sergey Filatov writes on the position of the authorities of the Republic of Sakha (Yakutia) towards the religion:

> The official ideology of the current Yakutian authorities is so-called "cultivation", or the acceleration of the education, science, and culture of the Yakut people, which should lead to turning the Yakuts into one of the most civilized nations in the world. There are few places in Russia where so much attention is devoted to the education system and cultural construction. Here everything is done so that every young person can by all means receive a full secondary education, enormous efforts are expended on grants for Yakut students to study abroad, and new museums and cultural centers are always being created. In this cultivation project of the Yakutian authorities, great attention is attached to "spirituality" and religion. The strategic position of President Nikolaev [of Yakutia] is (quite, it must be said, in the tradition of Yakut dual-faith) regenerating the national tradition, culture, folklore, and self-consciousness of Yakuts and, at the same time, completing the process of converting them to Orthodoxy that was interrupted by the revolution. Amidst this, national "spirituality" is conceived as being a secular component of national ideology while Orthodoxy is thought to be its proper religious expression. In accordance with this cultivation project, the government of the republic has established public observance of national holidays, first and foremost the pagan Ysakh New Year, and the national mythology, calendar, and "folk traditions" are studied in educational institutions. At the same time, the government sincerely seeks to lend this operation a secular, exclusively "cultural" character.[174]

As can be seen from this account, the government is pursuing a mutually-exclusive policy of enlightenment and education of youth simultaneous to the cultivation of folk customs. As a quite natural result, tradition is perishing, leaving only external ashes in the form of folk festivals, holidays, and

---

174 Sergey Filatov, "*Iakutiia pered religioznym vyborom: shamanizm ili khristianstvo*" [Yakutia before a Religious Choice: Shamanism or Christianity], in Sergey Filatov (ed.), *Religiia i obshchestvo: Ocherki religioznoi zhizni sovermennoi Rossii* [*Religion and Society: Outlines of the Religious Life of Contemporary Russia*] (Saint Petersburg: Letniy Sad, 2002).

theatrical productions, while the significance and elements of tradition are understood by few, even among organizers, but are presented as "rich cultural heritage." This situation is part of a pattern that holds true for all the small peoples of Russia from the Volga (the Mari and Chuvash) to the Far East. The genuine revival of the real cultures of these small people is possible only when enlightened man - the (anti-)European - will leave these peoples in peace to their own self-sufficiency and not encroach upon their identity with the "light of reason." Of course, this scenario is utopian in modern conditions.

In the early 20th century, a new religion began to spread in Altai, at the core of which lies a rejection of shamanism and blood sacrifice, and non-violent struggle for an independent Altaic state: Burkhanism, also known as the "White Faith" (*Sut dang*). The dualistic influence of Christianity is lucidly evident in Burkhanism. At the same time, with the support of Yakut authorities the neo-pagan, monotheistic cult of Aiy has developed, an extensive description of which is offered by Filatov:

> Back in the mid-1980s, the current leaders of Yakut pagans, Lazar Afanasyev, Ivan Ukhkhan (Nikolaev), and Anatoly Pavlov endeavored to create their own ideology and social movement totally opposed not only to the current republican and Russian government, but also the ongoing modernization of Yakut society as a whole. At the dawn of Perestroika the leading ideologist of the neopagan movement, Afanasyev (a philologist by education), came to the conclusion that the plight of the Yakut people is the result of the violation of the deep connections between man and nature and Yakuts' loss of their spiritual identity. The degradation of the nation, in his opinion, can only be overcome by reviving the traditional Yakut way of life, worldview, and religious - pagan - system of values. Afanasyev thus engaged in "researching" (which in fact meant creative reconstruction) of the religious views of his people. The results of his work found reflection in the book Aiy *uorete* (*The Divine Teaching*). In the first few years this work, which has not been translated from Yakut into any other of the world's languages, spread among the nationalist-oriented Yakut intelligentsia in typewritten copies. This work de facto became the doctrinal book of Yakut neopaganism. Afanasyev sought to isolate in numerous pagan myths and beliefs a coherent monotheistic system and declared the most venerated and powerful

gods of the Yakut pagan pantheon to be hypostases of one Creator-God (Aiy or *Tangra*). The *Aiy* doctrine is thus a modernized, Yakut version of the pan-Turkic pagan religion of Tengrianism. According to Aiy doctrine, the world is a system consisting of ten heavenly tiers. Each sky has its own pantheon of gods and spirits, and at the very top, in the ninth sky the pantheon is headed by the supreme creator-god *Aiy (Tangra)*. Man is located at the very bottom of this system, on Earth, above which stretches the first sky. Thus, between man and Aiy, who is frequently depicted as the Sun (or fire), are nine celestial tiers. The life force called *Sur* emanates from *Aiy* through these heavenly tiers. Sur is the energy that animates, inspirits a person and makes them human. Man himself is threefold, and after death splits into three souls. The earth-soul (the body) disappears, the air-soul (the psychic level) resides in one of the nine heavens depending on the virtue of the deceased, and the mother-soul returns to *Aiy*. The mother-soul is otherwise called *Kut*, the core of man ignited by the divine *Sur*. This is at once the "life force" in man and his "divine image." Man can lose his kut and it can be kidnapped by spirits or evil shamans. Throughout his life, a Yakut fears losing his kut, which is needed both in earthly and posthumous life. His main spiritual task thus boils down to preserving his kut. Afanasyev leaves the state of a living person's soul, their prosperity, and their posthumous state dependent on the moral state in which a person maintains their kut. Thus, he draws the attention of his people to enduring traditional values and proposes a way for achieving them in the formulation of the nine commandments of *Aiy*:

1. Do not commit adultery.
2. Honor nature.
3. Increase your household.
4. Do not destroy (do not kill).
5. Find your talent.
6. Be truthful.
7. Learn the truth (study).
8. Guard your *kut*.
9. Honor the commandments of *Aiy*.

Afanasyev and his associates not only seek to affirm monotheism, but to break it out of the circle of shamanic ideas that have been preserved from all of the paganism in the consciousness of the Yakut people. They thus assert what is actually a new religion constructed by them as "spiritually and morally elevating Yakuts" and forbid each other from practicing shamanism. They believe themselves to be fulfilling the role of "white shamans", i.e., priests of *Aiy*. At their gatherings these neopagans perform common prayer and offer bloodless sacrifices.

As can be seen, the cult of Aiy expresses a just aspiration for cultural autarky and returning to roots, but the syncretic doctrine erected on this basis harbors imprints of Christianity and overall goes against the traditional shamanism of Yakutia, outright rejecting it. In sum, this crosses out the authenticity and initiatic quality of the enterprise of the Aiy cult and renders it a glaring example of post-religiosity among small peoples. Postmodernist influence has thus affected most of all those "white" pupils of shamans who represent European culture and have decided to go down this path.

Another front, one directed not towards syncretism but synthesis, is the mutual appeal of Russian Native Faith to shamanism and of shamans to the Slavic heritage. Banzarov argued that in antiquity shamanism was spread across Russia from the Volga to Siberia, which would mean that it was in contact with the Slavic tribes and - if one were to accept the hypothesis of identifying the Slavs with the Vanir - would have also reached contact with such European tribes as the ancestors of the Germans, Scandinavians, and Finns. Slavic shamanism was also the subject of N. Speransky (Velimir's) book *The Gift of Shamanism: The Gift of Volkhving [/Magic]*. It is predominantly Russian *Rodnovery* who turn to shamanism, while indigenous shamans generally treat the reborn Russian tradition with great skepticism. This issue is more simply resolved in cases when a shaman has two bloodlines - Russian and an indigenous line - which determines predisposition toward synthesis on a deep level.

Concluding this topic, let us taken note of the fact that shamanism has not avoided the post-religious simulations of neo-shamanism and universal shamanism, which assert an openness and universality of shamanic practices for all peoples and moderns with an emphasis on psycho-therapeutic functions. The emergence of neo-shamanism is owed to the American anthropologist Michael Harner, who put forward the main syncretic provisions for "basic" shamanism. Other well-known authors propagating New Age shamanism, with emphasis on the customs of the American Indians, include Olard Dixon, Dmitry Ilyin, and Carlos Castaneda.

The first and foremost problem facing Odinist pagans in both North and South America is, besides authenticity, the issue of pagan legitimacy and, inextricably tied to this, their identity. The genesis of the American nation was its irrevocable break with Europe, with the Old World, entailing the assertion of its own destiny and self-conceptualization as the "New World." America's European colonizers themselves were bearers of the ideas of the Enlightenment, and the construction of American society was based on Modernity as a given, not a project like it still remained in Europe. Americans, predominantly being English immigrants, did not conceive of themselves as being Europeans or harbingers of Europe on the other side of the Atlantic Ocean. By breaking with Europe, they divorced the thousands of years of development of European civilization, including the enormous pagan heritage of the Celts, Greeks, Romans, and Germanic peoples as well as the influence of the Christian religion. The subsequent history of the formation of the American nation is encapsulated by the capacious term "melting pot", in which representatives of numerous peoples and cultures are to be mixed and fused into a unified American identity.

An American's declaration of belonging to a European pagan tradition, or to any other tradition of the Mediterranean, Europe, or Asia, thus comes into contradiction with the very identity of being American, as belonging to a tradition must be legitimately grounded. The claim which we can encounter in the documents of the Odinist Movement that Odinism is the genuine religion of Western Civilization uniting higher Indo-European ethics and ideals with the best ideas of Western society, thereby presenting a Western religion for Western man, is to a great extent disputable and unjustified. For the legitimization of European paganism, whether Odinism or any other on the territory of North and South America, there are three fundamental criteria: spatial ties, blood ties, and initiation into language.

The aspect of spatial ties was already mentioned above, where we emphasized the break between European and American identity in the emergence of the US and Canada in North America. These new continents, unlike Europe, were not the natural area of settlement of the Germanic, Scandinavian, and Gothic tribes. The history of inter-ethnic interactions in Europe is not relevant to America. As follows, it becomes impossible for American pagans to fully claim that they are reviving the ancient faith of these places. On the other hand, Americans and Canadians have for this question a well-known possible response. namely, the widely-recognized fact that the first to discover the American continent were vikings, who founded a number of settlements there. In the late 10th century, the ruler and baptizer of Greenland, Leif Erikson visited territories now belonging to North-Eastern Canada (the Newfoundland and Labrador provinces) and northern parts of the East coast of the modern US, where camps were set up and the visited areas were given the names Vinland, Helluland, and Markland. The name Vinland is used today by some American and European pagans for North America. Having colonized Greenland and Iceland, these settlers treated America as one of many new lands on which they would attempt several times to establish settlements. However, facing resistance from Native Americans, they abandoned these lands. This is how a small space of the North-Eastern coast of America came to be included in the geographical and cultural circle of European colonizers, as presented in the *Saga of Erik the Red* and the *Saga of the Greenlanders*.

The documents of the Asatru Free Church Committee thus named the three sacred Asatru towns to be New Ulm in the United States, Uppsala in Sweden, and ancient Troy. New Ulm, in the state of Minnesota, is the site of a monument to Arminius, whose victory over the legions of Quinctilius Varus in the Battle of Teutoburg Forest has become symbolic of pan-Germanic patriotism. Swedish Uppsala is the site of a complex of ancient kurgan burials of kings of cult significance. The inclusion of ancient Troy in this list is due to the works of Snorri Sturluson, particularly his *Younger (Prose) Edda*, in which Sturluson offered an euhemeristic Christian interpretation of the origins of the Scandinavian Gods as being the warriors who retreated from fallen Troy and were accepted in Northern Europe as kings and Gods.

The citing of the presence of Icelandic settlements and the corresponding aspiration to lay down a unique bridge between America and Europe through the linking of cultic towns reflects the correct striving of American Odinists to legitimize their belonging to this tradition beyond its native ecumene. Regarding the Icelandic settlements, we can conclude that the most favorable place for pagan practice in the US and Canada would be the North-Eastern coast of the continent, especially the small area where the remnants of viking settlements have been found. But the situation is complicated by the fact that Leif Erikson was a baptizer, a bearer of the Christian faith. Knowing the peculiar aspects of the instatement of this new religion and its historical era we can presume that the character of the worldview of these immigrants was that of a dual-faith.

The principle of direct spatial ties as foundations of legitimization can be examined in the case of the history of Rus' as well, where the Varangian vikings played a significant role starting from neighboring and trade relations along the "path from the Varangians to the Greeks" and culminating in the invaluable role of the Varangian warrior-band of Rurik in the formation of Russian statehood, a case which fully conforms to the allogeneic theory of the origins of the elite and the state. This is confirmed by historical chronicles, archaeological findings in the form of Mjölnir pendants, and the prevalence of Norman names among Russians. Russia's inclusion in the Scandinavian context, and the Scandinavians' involvement in the Russian, is an indisputable fact which, in terms of spatial criteria, substantiates the legitimacy of Odinism within the borders visited by the Varangians on the territory of the contemporary European part of Russia.

The second significant criterion of legitimacy, one which directly follows from the very nature and name of paganism, is blood, genealogy. Blood ties even more so than spatial relations connect man to his ancient roots, to his folk which bore one or another pagan tradition in antiquity. We have spoken of the unity of the nature of God, man, and the folk, using the comparison of the elders and youth of the *rod* (but without descending to the level of a materialistic euhemerism), and on this basis blood is imbued with a special meaning. Blood connects the chain of generations in this world with both tradition and the Gods.

On this point we can once again recall that the greater part of the colonists of America was composed of English Protestants, and the future policy of the construction of the American nation would be the principle of the "melting pot." The blood criterion could also encompass the spatial factor, insofar as the chain of kin in one way or another and in a greater or lesser historical perspective takes genealogy back to an authentic space, that place where a people historically embodied their tradition, i.e., to a geographical space that is embedded in blood, in archetypes, and in physical appearance. For American Odinists, the question of identity in terms of blood is key. Hence the disagreement between the American Odinists of the Asatru Assembly and the Troth, the latter of which disregarded belonging to the Scandinavian tradition by blood and ethnos. Religious openness to all peoples is a distinctive trait of the creationist religions. However, the shadow of the "tolerance" of political correctness still hangs like Damocles's sword over pagans in the US, Canada, and Europe.

Metaphorically speaking, we could call language the blood in which a tradition is expressed. The English language belongs to the Indo-European language family, in particular to the West Germanic group and, more specifically, to the Anglo-Frisian subgroup. The ancient formation of the English language was tied to the tribes of the Angles and Saxons who migrated to the British Isles. In the subsequent era, the English language was influenced by Latin by way of Christianity, and at the same time a set of Normanisms was inlaid in the language by viking raids. The new period of the English language began in the 15th century and continues to this day. The modern language of Americans differs significantly from British English as well as the historical "high English" of Shakespeare. In the above we localized the space that is the "heart" of Postmodernity in the West, with the US in its vanguard; accordingly, the modern, privative American English language is the "blood" of the modern world. Therefore, we once again emphasize the necessity of initiation into language, into the continental Germanic languages or into Icelandic, for American Odinists.

From the consideration of these three criteria of legitimacy we can draw the following conclusion: for an American, being a pagan means not being an American. Genuine, strict, Traditionalist adherence to the tradition of Odin demands that an American establishes connection with traditional space (the North of America in the very least), identifies their bloodlines and the presence in them of sufficient Germanic blood, and seeks initiation into language and purifies their everyday language of privativity. A pagan in America is a European who has found themself outside of their home - Europe - and, moreover, has found themself in the territory of a state pursuing a consistently anti-traditional policy. Therefore, any pagan who claims to be initiated into a European tradition must legitimize their claims based on these three factors and, in the end, become an anti-American.

The widespread expression "honor your roots" should be taken not as a superficial tribute to the custom of honoring ancestors in paganism, but as a call and challenge to raise awareness of deep identity. For an American, "honoring roots" is not about praising the founding-fathers of America, but of turning against such for the sake of Tradition. This radical break and choice in favor of Tradition is for the ordinary person a forceful, existential experience demanding profound reconsideration of identity and values. American pagans tend to avoid this problem as such, resulting in a lack of due reflection, a substitutive particularism, and in special cases finds reflection in reverse form: in excessive patriotism on the part of Odinists for the United States and the absolutely voluntaristic claim of a unity between the cultures and values of American democracy and those of Northern paganism. It is impossible to consider this approach to be initiatic.

The principle of legitimacy which we have examined in the case of American Odinists holds true for any geographical region and any tradition as a starting point. If a region was absolutely not part of the North-European context, then two criteria remain: blood and language. South America was colonized by the Spanish and Portuguese, and thus for Odinists of this region the spatial criterion works against them. Here we can agree with Bhairawananda Djaidhar's recommendation that Russian Tantrists at the very least commit pilgrimages to the sacred places of India to advance in *sādhanā*, and thus conclude on the necessity of visiting the original lands of the Scandinavian tradition. Italian Odinists, meanwhile, have solved the problem of legitimacy by referring to the legend of the origin of the Longobards, the ancient Germanic tribe considered to be one of the ancestors of modern Italians. The short length of this legend allows us to quote it in its entirety in the version of the Longobardian historian, Paul the Deacon:

> The Winnili then, having departed from Scandinavia with their leaders Ibor and Aio, and coming into the region which is called Scoringa, settled there for some years. At that time Ambri and Assi, leaders of the Wandals, were coercing all the neighboring provinces by war. Already elated by many victories they sent messengers to the Winnili to tell them that they should either pay tribute to the Wandals or make ready for the struggles of war. Then Ibor and Aio, with the approval of their mother Gambara, determine that it is

better to maintain liberty by arms than to stain it by the payment of tribute. They send word to the Wandals by messengers that they will rather fight than be slaves. The Winnili were then all in the flower of their youth, but were very few in number since they had been only the third part of one island of no great size. At this point, the men of old tell a silly story that the Wandals coming to Godan (Wotan) besought him for victory over the Winnili and that he answered that he would give the victory to those whom he saw first at sunrise ; that then Gambara went to Frea (Freja) wife of Godan and asked for victory for the Winnili, and that Frea gave her counsel that the women of the Winnili should take down their hair and arrange it upon the face like a beard, and that in the early morning they should be present with their husbands and in like manner station themselves to be seen by Godan from the quarter in which he had been wont to look through his window toward the east. And so it was done. And when Godan saw them at sunrise he said: "Who are these long-beards?" And then Frea induced him to give the victory to those to whom he had given the name.' And thus Godan gave the victory to the Winnili.[175]

Another, rather extravagant means of legitimizing faith in the Aesir on the Apennine Peninsula was reported to the author by an Italian Odinist, who claimed that when the vikings visited these lands (meaning the viking state in Sicily), they allowed slaves to adopt their faith. This is indeed a worthy argument and would be an accurate account of the placement of a foreign new-believer at the very bottom of the social hierarchy.

As we can see, the question of legitimacy in one way or another affects virtually all organizations and people who wish to count themselves as belonging to the Scandinavian-Germanic tradition. The solutions to this issue have been diverse, ranging from denying the presence of any problem at all to attempts at laying down a bridge towards the European context, but the most authentic and radical (from the Latin *radix*, meaning root, fundamental) way out of this problem lies in completely redefining one's identity in favor of Tradition.

---

175 Paul the Deacon, *History of the Langobards* (Philadelphia: University of Pennsylvania, 1907).

Modernity and globalization have also impacted *Sanatana Dharma* in India, resulting in the emergence of so-called "neo-Hinduism", whose distinct forms and examples can be traced back to the early 20th century. Many of the sources of changes in Hinduism are to be sought in India itself under the influence of the English colonizers. Having partaken in European education and the European view of themselves as backward archaic barbarians, some educated Hindus have taken the side of the modernization of Indian society in the spirit of the Enlightenment, democratization, and the liberalization of varna-society. The most famous figures in the field of liberal, pacifist nationalism in India were Mahatma Gandhi and Jawaharlal Nehru, who accepted the main provisions of Modernity - progress, an open social system, the need for modernization - and softened the religious element in favor of these aims (Gandhi) or insisted on secularism and universalization (Nehru). The emergent situation, seeing, on the one hand, a positive attitude towards their native culture and country, the desire for liberation from colonial oppression for the winning of independence, and on the other, the restructuring of society according to the patterns of the colonizers themselves, including their views of progress and the development of society, gave birth to an inner conflict by virtue of this fundamental contradiction. India is *Sanatana Dharma*, *Vedanta*, and the caste system. Such is its structure, nature, and essence. To wish prosperity and independence for India while at the same time rejecting its identity and thousands-year-old structure is a glaring example of the Modernist infiltration of India's political elites affecting not only the socio-political, but also the spiritual sphere.

Neo-Hinduism, sometimes referred to as "universal Hinduism", is a reinterpretation of the provisions of the Vedanta in the direction of adaptation to Western European thinking, the values of humanism, and liberal democracy. The key provisions of Dharma which represent the very structure and nature of

Hinduism are thereby treated as allegorical, and entry into the tradition is liberalized for non-Hindus, thus universalizing Hinduism. *Varṇāśrama dharma*, the sacred hierarchy of India, was reinterpreted by Swami Vivekananda to be degrees of spiritual initiation, allowing for anyone, despite their type of activities, to achieve the level of Brahmin. Aurobindo Ghose in turn strove to present *varna* as a set of social institutions akin to professional guilds, not as pertaining to the deep nature of man and the corresponding divine functional dimension.

The principle of non-violence, *ahiṃsā*, was interpreted in the spirit of humanism, thus leading to rapprochement with Christianity and other religions deformed by humanism. Neo-Vedantists came to treat Jesus Christ as an avatar of Vishnu who revealed himself to the third estate. The pop-guru Sathya Sai Baba thus called himself, among many other things, the Christ of Christians. The founder of Sahaja Yoga, Shri Mataji Nirmala Devi, took a step further in calling herself the Christ of Christians, the Messiah of the Jews, and the Mahdi of Muslims all at once. All of this contributed to the adaptation and popularization of superficial Hinduism among hippies and pacifist counter-cultures. The founder of the International Society for Krishna Consciousness, Bhaktivedanta Swami Prabhupada, and Sri Chinmoy were supported by the Beatles and rock musician John McLaughlin while riding a wave of popularity. At the same time, secular *ahiṃsā* was introduced into international politics as a peacemaking ideology. Boris Knoppe chronicles:

> Thus, it was precisely within UNESCO that the decision was made in 1966 to build the city of Auroville in honor of Aurobindo Ghose for his peacemaking efforts (despite his previous terrorist activities) and to hold large-scale events under his name. Since 1970, Ghose's follower Sri Chinmoy has organized regular "Peace Meditations" at the UN headquarters, and later the Sri Chinmoy Association would be admitted to the UN as a non-governmental organization. Peacemaking races under the title "Peace Run" have been regularly held once or twice a year, involving several dozen countries around the world. In 1980, the Brahma Kumaris

organization (whose official name is the Brahma Kumaris World Spiritual University) became a non-governmental organization-member of the UN.[176]

Moreover, Neo-Hinduism completely excludes any metaphysical component from yogic practices, which become a set of exotic gymnastics supposed to lead to spiritual harmonization merely by virtue of unique body postures (*asanas*). This goes against the very philosophy of yoga as a practice aimed at calming the mind and achieving liberation (*moksha*) for the adept from the shackles of *samsara*. The immense popularity of yogic gymnastics across the world excludes the true metaphysical meaning of this doctrine, leaving only a part of the practice extolled as whole and self-sufficient and thereby generating absurd currents in the likes of "food yoga", "home interior yoga", etc., which speak to the subordination of yoga in the West to the discourses of the consumer society. A similar fate has befallen popularized Tantra, which has been reduced to a set of exotic means of intercourse completely ignoring the metaphysical context and meaning of such teachings.

Active syncretism can also be traced in the teachings of Babaji, Nirmala Devi, Sathya Sai Baba, Osho Rajneesh, and other pop-gurus who gained media popularity and wealth in Europe and the United States. The basis of their activities was commerce and enrichment, which goes against the principles of training with a guru in India and the free giving of teaching and *dakshina* (gratitude) from a guru's pupils upon completion of training. The foundation for these pop-gurus and their Westward-facing ideas within Hinduism was Vaishnavism or Bhaktism, which represents one of the inner poles within the Indian tradition (in the broad sense) and a part of intense intra-Indian dialogue. The approach of Vaishnavism lies in truncating the basis and apex of Hindu metaphysics' non-duality (*Advaita*) and worship of the supreme God Brahma as a formless absolute, Brahma Nigurna, instead adhering to a doctrine of duality

---

176 Knoppe, "*Induizm: ot globalistskoi adaptatsii k al'ternativnomu globalistskomy proektu*" [Hinduism: From Globalist Adaptation to an Alternative Globalist Project].

(*Dvaita*) and devotional worship of the Gods, especially Vishnu and Krishna, to whom are attributed qualities and personal anthropomorphic forms and manifestations which correspond to the second manifestation of Brahma as Brahma Saguna - the God with qualities. For *Advaita*, the principal standpoint is the non-duality and non-conflictual perception of Brahma Nigurna as the highest apophatic instance and Brahma Saguna as the cataphatic, phenomenal instance of God-as-the-world. For the *Bhakti* and *Dvaita* schools, the first place is occupied by the personal, devotional veneration of the Gods, which we can identify with the nature of the third estate, as is also suggested by reference to the creationist religions' emphasis on the devotional perception of the prophets. However, within Hinduism this does not give rise to contradiction, as the Bhakti have their own recognized great Brahmins, philosophers, and gurus who polemicize with Advaitists. This constitutes the intra-traditional dialogue of India expressed in the Vedanta, the Upanishads, Tantra, Agama, and the many darśanas (philosophical schools).

But compared to the latter, modernized Bhaktism/Dvaita appears even more secular and materialist, especially as coupled with Modernist readings - secondary even to the authentic Bhakti/Dvaita thought of India's medieval philosophers, such as Ramajuna, the author of the Vishishta-Vedanta, and Madhva, the author of Dvaita-Vedanta - of the Vedas from the position of rejecting the Advaita philosophy of Adi Shankara, the author of the Brahmasutra that crowns Indian metaphysics. If the polemics of the great Indian thinkers constitute the inner -*machia* or *polemos* of Hinduism, then globalized Bhaktism and the diverse neo-Tantric and neo-yogic profanizations are in the marginal periphery of Hinduism altogether. As would be logical, they have found popularity in none other than the West where, having abandoned the realm of the Indian ecumene, they become mere deviations.

The dualistic worship of Vishnu expresses itself in a gap between man and God. If Advaita-Vedanta asserts the possibility, as natural and primordial, of a living being (*jiva*) comprehending the nature of Brahma Nigurna and identifying with him, then the Bhakti path stops at the levels of Vishnu or Krishna, before whom the faithful adept can only bow. It is worth noting that the adepts of Bhaktism call themselves *das/dasa*, meaning "servant", which dates back to the name for the tribes conquered by the Raja in the ancient era of Indian history, in which context *dasa* also meant "slave", "enemy", "demon", or "barbarian." Here we can once again see a parallel with creationism where, as in Christianity, believers refer to themselves as "servants of God", while the name Islam itself means "submission." In Dvaita, a difference arises between the creator (Vishnu, Ishvara) and the *jiva*. From this position to monotheism there remains but one step, which we can recognize in the strict veneration of one divine figure from the trinity. From the Trimurti of Brahma-Vishnu-Shiva, the middle God Vishnu is singled out, leaving the other Gods treated as his faces and manifestations. The bringing of Vishnu to the fore, let us note, overshadows both the supreme God, Brahma (Nigurna), and the destructive God Shiva, who is the most revered Divinity of *Advaita* (*à la* Adi Shankara, Abhinavagupta, and others). Both of the latter find themselves in the periphery, secondary to Vishnu.

One extreme form of distorted Bhaktism is none other than one of the most widespread and powerful sects, that of guru Bhaktivedanta Swami Prabhupada, the International Society for Krishna Consciousness, founded in New York in 1966. Prabhupada is known for his commentaries on one of the most fundamental and canonical Indian texts, the Bhagavad-Gita, in which the doctrines of Dharma and Yoga are expounded in the context of a dialogue between Prince Arjuna and his charioteer, Krishna. Prabhupada's commentary is a paradigmatic example of a Modernist interpretation, and, moreover, was used to benefit the creation of his own cult which has enjoyed unprecedented commercial success in the West while being actively stigmatized by Vaishnavites in India itself. In Prabhupada's sect, instead of sacred texts, Hindu culture and the *varṇāśrama* (the very embodiment of Brahma in Indian society), the guru's utterances, interpretations, and democratic, anti-caste approach take first place. This secular approach rules out any principled legitimacy of belonging to tradition, and although the Krishna-dasas of ISKCON make pilgrimages to India, other criteria are ignored and the very ideological underpinning of such pilgrimages casts a shadow over any of the benefits of visiting Indian shrines and ashrams.

In conclusion to this section, we will briefly examine the perspectives and prospects of the restoration of ancient traditions in Ciscaucasia and the Caucasus. Ciscaucasia, or the North Caucasus, covers the following regions that are part of the Russian Federation: Karachay-Cherkessia, Kabardino-Balkaria, North Ossetia, Ingushetia, Chechnya, and Dagestan; while the Caucasus includes Georgia, South Ossetia, Abkhazia, Armenia, and Azerbaijan.

The main, most accomplished legacy of the peoples of the Caucasus is the *Nart Epic* or Sagas, consisting of cycles of legends of heroes (the Narts) expressed in both poetic and prosaic forms. The roots of the *Nart Epic* or saga date back to the Alan epic cycle and the culture of the North-Iranian Sarmatians and Scythians, the epic itself presumably having taken shape in the 8th-7th centuries B.C.E. The Nart sagas can be found among the Abkhaz-Adyghe peoples, the Karachays, the Balkars, the Chechens (Vainakhs), the Ingush, and the Ossetians. In the version of the epic held by the Ossetians, the only Indo-European people of the Caucasus, Georges Dumézil saw the purest expression of the trifunctional system: among the Narts, the Akhsartagkata represent the warriors, the Borata the agriculturalists, and the Alagata the priests. Each people has its own versions of this epic with respectively dominating cycles and characters, but overall they constitute the space of one ancient legend and plot.

In the structure of Ciscaucasian traditions, elements of totemism are also present, expressed in the special veneration of animals, such as the snake, wolves, dogs, horses, deer, and sheep. Virtually every animal is accompanied with tales and superstitions which exist to this day. In the legends and tales of the Ingush and Chechens which also reflect the motifs of the Nart cycles, we encounter elements of shamanism, such as the consumption of intoxicating substances, descent into lower worlds, ascension to the sky, ritual death and dismemberment followed by reconstruction of the parts of the body and rebirth (initiation), as well as the role of animals as guides to other worlds. Besides shrines and temples, the status of sacred places is also borne by gorges and mountains in which Gods and spirits live, mountain passes and water springs.

A most significant event in the history of the Alans and Ossetians was the invasion of the Mongols, whose campaigns through Rus and the Caucasus came under the leadership of Batu, followed by Tamerlane. As a result of the Mongol conquests, the Alans moved up into the mountains and returned to their pagan traditions, many of which have been preserved to this day. Under the influence of Christianity by the 11th century, the pagan heritage of the Caucasus peoples was reinterpreted and its structures subordinated to the motifs of Christian mythology and mysticism, giving rise to a stable dual-faith in which form Caucasian traditions have existed over the course of recent centuries. For instance, to the figures of the Gods Uastyrdzhi and Uatsilla, the Gods of thunder, were appended the figures of St. George and St. Elijah respectively. The God Uatsilla in turn was close to other thunderers, such as Shible (Ele), the Abkhazian Afy, the Vainakh Seli, who was also the patron of fertility. According to legends, it was by the will of Uastyrdzhi that the temple of Rekom was erected, which is one of the most revered places in all the Caucasus. Rekom's construction is dated to approximately the 14th century. Overall, the situation in the Caucasus is in many ways identical to that of Russian dual-faith, but the peoples of these mountains were not willing to adopt Christianity, and instead chose Islam.

Scholar Vitaly Tmenov writes:

> Originally Islamization touched primarily the social top of North Ossetia, especially the Digorian and Tagaurian feudal lords (whose lands directly bordered Kabardia), and then the peasants dependent on them. In the first half of the 18th century, there existed a number of settlements (Koban, Kora-Usdon, Karadzhaeva-Khaznidon, Donifars, etc.) whose inhabitants were overwhelmingly adherents of Islam. This is evidenced by Muslim epigraphic artifacts (albeit not numerous) identified in Khaznidon and dated by L.I. Lavrov to 1741-1742. It was quite characteristic of the greater mass of Islamized mountainous villages of North Ossetia to not have their own mosques, insofar as after annexation by Russia the Tsarist administration attempted by all means to limit the influence of Islam on Ossetians.[177]

Thus, the native traditions of the Alans, Ossetians, Vainakhs, and other peoples were caught between the hammer of Christianity and the anvil of Islam. Yet the folk genius responded with strengthening the dual-faith strategy of retelling Christian and Islamic myths in a traditional spirit, which was also facilitated by the fragmentation and territorial remoteness of mountain villages.

At the present stage, these regions, which it has long since been "traditional" to consider Muslim, are seeing active movements setting before themselves the task of reviving the ancient traditions and returning to their native faith. The main vector of these movements is focused on "cleansing" the Christian or Islamic layers in the structure of their dual-faith. This approach is fraught with distortion, as pointed out by Julius Evola in his critique of restoring tradition by relying on the distorted accounts of church adherents. In other words, approaching restoration from the position of starting with the dominating tradition imposes certain limits and distortions on the very *corpus* of traditional texts, their interpretation, and ritual practice. Tradition thus loses its essence and becomes

---

[177] V.Kh. Tmenov, "*Osetinskoe iazychestvo v sisteme srednevekovykh religioznykh verovanii narodov Severnogo Kavkaza*" [Ossetian Paganism in the System of the Medieval Religious Beliefs of the Peoples of the North Caucasus], in *Problemy etnografii Osetin: Sbornik nauchnykh trudov tom 2* [*Problems of Ossetian Ethnography: A Compilation of Scholarly Works, Vol. 2*]. Vladikavkaz: SO NII, 1992.

merely an instrument of anti-Islamism. Another danger is the intolerance of any forms of polytheism that is most punctuated in Islam. This compels many pagans in Ossetia, Chechnya, and Dagestan to operate virtually underground.

Perhaps the greatest interest in Transcaucasia is presented by Armenia, which boasts thousands of years of history and tradition. The ancient Armenian tradition is of a markedly solar character. The Sun, Arev, is the manifestation of the Higher Force of Ar, from which is derived Armenian pagans' self-appellation, Arevordi, or "Children of the Sun." Solar symbolism is abundant in Armenian temple carvings, murals, and embroidery, and is similar in appearance to Slavic solar symbols. Animal cults are also present in the structure of Armenian tradition, such as the eagle and lion, as are ancestor worship and hero cults. The Armenian tradition reflects many Indo-European motifs and was influenced by Zoroastrianism, which saw the appearance and elevation of the God Aramazd and the Goddess Anahit, as well as Hellenism. A comparison of Armenian and Greek Gods looks as follows: Aramazd = Zeus, Anahit = Artemis, the hero Vahagn = Hercules (possibly also comparable to Thor), Nana = Athena, and Tir = Apollo. Descriptions of the ancient Armenian tradition can be found in the commentaries of Herodotus, Plato, Strabo, and medieval Armenian writers. Among modern scholars, the poet, philologist, historian, and author of the work The Old Beliefs, or Pagan Religion of the Armenians, Ghevont Alishan (1820-1901), contributed greatly to the exposition of the Armenian faith.

After the official adoption of Christianity in 301 under King Trdat (Tiridates) III, paganism in Armenia was subject to persecution. On the lower level of society, stable layers of dual-faith took shape. For example, the function of the serpent-slayer Vahagn was divided between Archangel Gabriel and John the Baptist. In recent history, we cannot ignore the Armenian military strategist Garegin Nzhdeh (1886-1955), the founder of the Armenian national ideology of Tseghakronism, in which significant space is devoted to the cults of the folk, family, homeland, honor (*fides*), and language. The Armenian Native Faith reconstruction/reenactment movement, Hetanism, which has engaged in the revival of Armenian paganism, owes its origins to Tseghakronism. Following the collapse of the USSR in 1991, Hetanism gained official status as *Arordineri Ukht*, or "Order of the Children of Ari." Adherents of Hetanism include the ex-Prime Minister of Armenia, Andranik Margaryan, which speaks to a certain popularity and demand for the ancient tradition.

Overall, the societies of the Caucasus are in many ways more conservative than their neighbors, a factor which has conditioned the long lifespan of folk traditions and customs despite changes of official religion. The latter, in turn, have had limited effect on customs and lifestyles, ensuring the maintenance of a dual-faith that is so closely interwoven with the Abrahamic traditions that at times it is impossible to divide them bloodlessly.

For the pagan traditions of the Greater Caucasus to experience a flourishing dawn, the societies inhabiting these territories face two yokes: the yoke of Modernity and the yoke of creationism (Islam and Christianity). Therefore, existing trends of returning to the ancient pagan traditions (where this is possible) require the particular carefulness, attentiveness, and strict rigor of the Traditionalist method.

Simulacra and Sects

In this section, we will focus on examining those plain simulacra and destructive sects which, being unrepresentative of paganism, actively employ pagan motifs and forms in their activities or strive to pass themselves off as pagans. Whereas our preceding examples and critical remarks were concerned primarily with the practices of traditions, communities, organizations, and personalities, i.e., people striving for tradition, in this section we will look in greater detail at those simulacra and sects which are oriented in the opposite direction, away from Tradition, even if they claim otherwise. Here we will be encountering instances of post-religiosity on the attack against pagan traditions.

As we described above, New Age simulacra reference virtually all traditions, mixing them both with one another and with classical and post-scientific theories, thus giving birth to chimeras. The problem of such frauds and forgeries is relevant to all traditions that have preserved even a minimum of transmission and are practiced today. Hindus are fighting off neo-Hinduisms in all forms, shamans are criticizing neo-shamanism, Asatru and Odinists are striving to cleanse themselves of profane, speculative, superficial interpretations of their tradition, and Russian Native Faith pagans are actively propagating a competent approach to the revival of tradition and denouncing fakes and sects.

At the same time, we should be cognizant of the fact that on this question the approach of scientific religious studies expresses its profane essence, even going against the principles of scientific objectivity and the need for immersion into the context of the studied subject by consciously ignoring the obvious and proclaimed difference between pagans and such simulacra. For example, authentic Hinduism is examined by some scholars as on equal footing with neo-Hindu sects, and the success of the International Society for Krishna Consciousness (ISKCON) has even been interpreted in terms of the provisions of the Advaita school.[178] Russian scholars of religion have also examined *Rodnoverie* and pseudo-pagans as equal manifestations of neo-paganism, ignoring the difference in their approaches and the extensive arguments advanced by adherents of Native Faith against quasi-pagans.[179]

---

[178] See: Boris Knoppe, *"Induizm: ot globalistskoi adaptatsii k al'ternativnomu globalistskomy proektu"* [Hinduism: From Globalist Adaptation to an Alternative Globalist Project] in A. Malashenko and S. Filatov, *Religiia i globalizatsiia na prostorakh Evrazii* [*Religion and Globalization on the Expanses of Eurasia*] (Moscow: Neostrom/Carnegie Moscow Center, 2005).

[179] The scholar of religion Roman Shizhensky openly admits this in his works. Shizhensky's above-mentioned comparison of the worldviews of Dobroslav and Varg Vikernes in search of commonalities between Scandinavian and Russian ideologues can be called one such error, given that such completely ignores the fact that Odinist milieux see Varg as an extravagant upstart-extremist.

We employ the term "sect" on the grounds that many simulacral ideas and organizations posing as representatives of pagan or ancient traditions often turn out to be commercial structures whose aim is to gain money and power or to satisfy the egotistical, sexual, pathological needs of their leaders - for example, when pseudo-teachers begin to perform on evening television shows, entertaining audiences to satisfy their own vanity and pride and thereby become elements of the consumer society and spectacle. We recognize the originally neutral meaning of the term "sect" from the Latin *secta*, or "school", and *sequor* "I follow", which is close to the Indian *darśana*. In the academic study of religion and sects, the term is not unambiguous and does not have a generally accepted interpretation, and consequently has become an ideological, manipulative tool.[180] This situation gives rise to confusion and creates problems for proper paganism and communities when they are compared to simulacra. Therefore, we designate the number of quasi-pagan ideologies and organizations which we examine here as destructive sects (to borrow a technical term from the sciences) whose activities contradict spirituality and are strictly counter-initiatic.

In examining pseudo-pagan simulacra, we should not lose sight of the fact that the concepts of post-war - e.g., net-centric and network warfare - provide for the integration of religious communities and ideas into netwar operations as instruments of communication, intelligence gathering, and levers of influence. Keeping the strategic-military aspect of the question of sects in mind can help us identify the truly artificial nature of various organizations which merely masquerade behind confessional, traditional identities while pursuing altogether different goals. We do not endeavor to examine inter-state relations as part of our analysis, but in one way or another geopolitical and ideological confrontations by all means exert influence on the sphere of traditions, potentially turning them into instruments for the

---

180 For example, in Russia the study of sects has on the efforts of Alexander Dvorkin been turned into an ideological tool for lobbying the interests of the Russian Orthodox Church.

propagandization of different values and identities. Simulacra of paganism can be seen as attacks by Postmodernity on Tradition, which in worldly terms might be embodied in conflict between countries, cultures, and their value-systems. In the preceding sections, we localized two, confronting poles: on the one hand, the generalized West of Modernity and Postmodernity, represented by the United States and anti-Europe as well as various countries' elites which have declared commitment to the language of Modernity and its values; on the other, the Indo-European traditions and, more broadly, Tradition itself, the real, deep Europe, as well as the marginalized, broad ensemble of the indigenous peoples of Indo-Europe who remain under the pressure of the anti-traditional paradigm. Over the course of post-war, the creation or subordination of different religious groups and ideologies to one pole's interests is absolutely natural, as is the use of the tactic of false flag operations. From the point of view of Tradition, this is the purest manifestation of counter-initiation, of artificial constructions which lead man away from the Sacred into the plane of the meaningless rhizome and the titanic masses of matter. Thus, the military-tactical and rhizomatic-random geneses of pseudo-pagan sects are in principle no different, insofar as both represent cases of counter-initiation.

We have also described in the preceding some of the key provisions concerning authenticity in contemporary practices, the infiltrations of Modernity, Postmodernity, and various subcultures, as well as the principles of legitimacy. All of this can be seen as the continuation of the study of the problem of initiation and counter-initiation and their qualitative criteria. The prepared reader and practitioner should, on the basis of the principles, examples, and currents of thought which we have outlined, find it of no particular difficulty to independently engage in the deconstruction of ideas pretending to be pagan and claiming the heritage of the ancient Gods. Now we will turn to review some of the most historically iconic pseudo-pagan ideas and the organizations which have emerged therewith.

The West

As the definite "homeland" of pseudo-paganism and pseudo-traditions, we shall begin with the West, from late 19th-century Europe up to contemporary America. This geographical and temporal localization coincides with the space and time of Modernity and Postmodernity, and also emphasizes one of the most important characteristics of pseudo-traditional simulacra, namely, their universalism (anti-ethnicity) and globalism. However, various esoteric societies and teachings claiming traditionality have not emerged in the West alone - degenerate sects from the East and Asia have also found their place and flourished in the West. We have already considered the misconceptions of the Theosophists and Roerichs and mentioned "neo-Hinduism" in the likes of neo-Tantrism, yoga gymnastics, Osho sects, ISKCON, Prabhupada, and many others which have found their flocks far from the homeland of those traditions whose distortions they have taught to Europeans thirsty for spiritual exotica.

One doctrine that has claimed for itself the whole Germanic pagan heritage and at a certain time even exercised strong influence on the rebirth of Germanic and Scandinavian paganism is Armanism (from the *Armanenschaft*), the founder of which was the Austrian poet and occultist Guido von List (1848-1919), whose followers included the monk Jörg Lanz von Liebenfels (1874-1954), Karl Maria Willigut (1866-1946), and other figures. Guido von List sought to grant substance and justification to the idea of the greatness and superiority of the German people in line with the prevailing nationalistic mood and search for German identity of his era. List's works compiled and synthesized well-known historical data about the Germanic peoples (such as from Tacitus), tropes from Theosophy, scientific theories (such as theories of atoms and evolution), elements of Christianity, medieval chivalric epics (particularly the *Song of the Nibelungs*), the Scandinavian *Edda*, as well as elements of

Freemasonry, the result of which was presented as the genuine history and heritage of the Germanic peoples.

List claimed that ancient Germanic society was divided into three castes: the intelligentsia (*Lehrstand*), warriors (*Wehrstand*) and the peasantry (*Nahrstand*), which he compared to Tacitus' description of the division of Germanic society into the *Hermionen* ("*Armanen*"), *Ist-fo-onen*, and *Ing-fo-onen*. From the name of the higher caste, the Armanen, List derived his name for the special, elite doctrine and gnosis, "Armanism." The exoteric, outer manifestation of this gnosis was "Wotanism", the philosophy of which in pre-Christian times List called "theosophy." The guardians of the esoteric, inner doctrine of the *Armanen* were the kings, priests, scholars, and magi, charged with guarding the *Rita*, or the law, order, and practical application of the metaphysical knowledge of the folk.[181] The term "*Rita*" was directly borrowed from the Vedas, where in Sanskrit it literally means "the order of things", and merged in Armanist doctrine with the notions of Dharma or Wyrd. Here we can see a certain similarity between the traditional trifunctional system of Indo-European societies and Guido von List's ideas, as well as the borrowing of the term for the "due order of things" and the construction of a two-level topography and degree of dichotomy between "Wotanism" and "Armanism", in which the first is the more pagan, more "folkish", external, and "profane" and the second is the true gnosis of secret groups of initiates.

In his quest for the ancient Germanic high culture, Guido von List and his followers rarely and only selectively referred to ancient times, instead actively taking medieval tales and forms to be representative manifestations of ancient Germanic valor and order. In a broad-handed stroke, myths of the Grail were explained to be Germanic, and the Knights Templar, Teutonic Knights, and the Knights Hospitaller of St. John were identified as secret orders of aristocrats of the spirit (Rita). Fundamentally syncretic Masonic doctrine was seen as deserving of positive

---

181 See: Guido von List, *The Religion of the Aryo-Germanic Folk: Esoteric and Exoteric* (Bastrop, Texas: Lodestar, 2017).

appraisal for coming close to the medieval expression of the ancient peasant estate of the Ing-fo-onen supported and patronized by crusader-aristocrats.

The blending of Germanic themes with Judeo-Christianity was manifested not only in the attempt to impose on the crusaders the image of secret orders of initiated Armanen, but also in the direct reinterpretation of Biblical myths through the lens of Germanic mythology. List treated Christianity as a degenerate form of Wotanism transformed by the Franks. On this point, List cited his ideological associate Lanz von Liebenfels, who prioritized the substantiation of the Germanic roots of the Bible. Karl Maria Willigut, meanwhile, who became the "court magician" and priest of the Ahnenerbe, believed that the Bible described the history of "Baldr Krist", hence the name "Christians", Baldr being in Germanic-Scandinavian myth the son of Odin and the young God who dies and is resurrected, identified with spring and the sun.[182] In his work Armanism and Kabbalah, Guido von List claimed that the knowledge of the Armanists and Wotanists had been preserved in synagogues and is today known as the doctrine of Kabbalah. After the Second World War, Rolan Dionys Josse would publish the book *Runic-Astrological Kabbalah* based on List's works. In turn, Friedrich Bernhard Marby would create the syncretic doctrine of "runic yoga."[183]

The voluntaristic mixing of the Bible, Kabbalah, and the Germanic pagan heritage spawned the idea of "Ario-Christianity", which preached the "Aryan" heritage and legacy of Christ and located the events of the New Testament in Europe.

---

182 Willigut is associated with an alternative name for Armanism, "Irminism", named after the Irminen whose settlement he sought in the Black Forest and whose rituals he introduced to the SS. Willigut was removed from his post by Heinrich Himmler in 1939, when it was revealed that Willigut had previously been diagnosed with schizophrenia. Another "reviewer" of Willigut was Julius Evola, who evaluated the former's works' relevance and correspondence with the ideas of the SS, which in turn deemed Baron Evola's ideals to be contradictory to those of the Nazis.

183 See also: Karl Spiesberger, *Runenmagie: Handbuch der Runenkunde* [*Rune Magic: A Handbook of Runecraft*] (Burstadt: Paul Hartmann Verlag, 2009).

To this day, the ideas of Armanism and Ario-Christianity have modest popularity among European and even Russian followers. Despite their obviously Theosophist, syncretic approach which completely ignores the difference between the doctrines of creationism and manifestationism, the latter constituting the very essence of paganism, the ideas of this trinity of Armanists have affected folkish European pagans, especially those embodying the mystical and political types. Overall, Guido von List's narrative was scattered, poorly substantiated, and a falsification of the "great history of the Germanic peoples" that only casts a shadow on their genuinely deep and beautiful tradition and Gods.

In connection with the esoteric dimension of the Third Reich associated with such "Ariosophy", we cannot avoid the post-war phenomenon of "esoteric Hitlerism", the main figures and ideologues of which (although not associated with one another) were the former Chilean diplomat Miguel Serrano (1917-2009)[184] and the author of English, French, and Greek heritage, Maximiani Julia Portas, better known as Savitri Devi (1905-1982).[185] Miguel Serrano's main ideas were set out in his books *Adolf Hitler: The Last Avatar* and *The Golden Chain*, in which he presented a vision of the true history of mankind as a confrontation between the ancient spiritual Hyperboreans and the demiurge and his creations (the Neanderthals). The motif of opposition to the demiurge and his creation expresses the gnostic foundations of the ideas of Serrano which he, being a member of an occult society that worshipped Hitler as a Bodhisattva whose mission was to overcome the Kali-Yuga, adjoined with mysticism and research into the Third Reich. Serrano believed that Hitler was not dead, but had disappeared into an inner cavity of the Earth, from which he should reappear in due time to claim victory.

---

184 Miguel Serrano was a close friend of Carl Gustav Jung and Hermann Hesse, and also knew Julius Evola.

185 Portas adopted the name Savitri in honor of the Indian Goddess of the sun, Savitri, as part of her marriage to the brahmin Asit Krishna Mukherji, the editor of a newspaper which supported Nazi Germany.

The main body of Serrano's ideas was composed of a mixture of Hindu, Buddhist, and Scandinavian myths with legends of the Grail, secret Nazi experiments in the techno-magical field, and hypotheses on the goals of the SS's Tibetan expeditions. A Theosophist thread can be detected in the theme of the Hyperborean Bodhisattvas, one of whose avatars was Adolf Hitler, understood as saints of humanity, as well as in the eclectic mixing of different traditions.

No less eccentric were the ideas of Savitri Devi, set forth in her books *Gold in the Furnace* and *The Lightning and the Sun*. Savitri saw the German Führer as the avatar of Kalki, a manifestation of Vishnu, the avenger destined to appear in the Kali-Yuga. Savitri posited Hitler to be the crowning figure of a chain including the Egyptian Pharaoh Akhenaten and Genghis Khan. Once again, here we are faced with Theosophist eclecticism and a variation of the Mahatma idea.

The esoteric Hitlerism of Serrano and Devi has been in the periphery of contact with European paganism and Traditionalism. While sharing with the latter a common view of the modern world as the Kali-Yuga, such is to a greater extent an example of the extravagant eclecticism that pervaded Theosophy. Simultaneous referencing of the Traditionalism of Guénon and Evola, Wotanism, and the esotericism of Serrano are present in the works of Wulf Ingessunu, the head of the contemporary English organization Woden's Folk, in which we can find the whole complex of esoteric Hitlerism still alive in our days.[186] A common feature of both Armanism and esoteric Hitlerism is the syncretism and assertion of ideas which are supported neither by traditional doctrines nor the scientific data of anthropology, archaeology, ethnography, history, and even physics' description of the Earth, nor even the modern level of technological development, which refutes the technologies described by Serrano. Their ideas have no relation to the true European, especially Germanic pagan heritage.

---

186 See: Wulf, *Collected Writings of an English Wodenist* (Black Front Press, 2014).

The second half of the 20th century also saw the emergence in England and popularization of the neo-pagan religion of Wicca. The founding father and popularizer of Wicca was the English writer Gerald Gardner (1884-1964), who simply called his religion "witchcraft." The name "Wicca", which became attached to the religion later, is derived from the Old English *wicca* and *wicce*, meaning "wizard" and "witch", which are in turn derivative from the Proto-Germanic *wikko*, "to conjure." From Gerald Gardner and his followers' official history and description of Wicca we can highlight the following. Wicca began to gain popularity following Gardner's publication of two books, *Witchcraft Today* and *The Meaning of Witchcraft*, published in 1954 and 1959 respectively. These works laid the foundation for the ensuing development of the new religion. According to Gardner himself, these books were composed out of reworked materials from a witches' coven into which he had been inducted in New Forest, Hampshire, England. The coven insisted on upholding the continuity of an ancient magical religion of England, dating back to pre-Christian times, which had been transmitted and taught in secret. In the 1960s, Wicca spread to America, where it developed into several currents (those of Gardner, Doreen Valiente, and others), covens were established, and individual Wiccans emerged. Despite Wicca's claim to initiatic quality, the principle of initiation and the transmission of authority for the creation of a coven are ubiquitously ignored to this day. While recognizing the authority of Gardner's works, many Wiccans have taken such as the foundations for their own fantasies and organizations, or have simply practiced witchcraft on their own.

The core of the Wiccan religion consists of a pair of deities: the Celtic horned God, Cernunnos (sometimes identified with Pan) and the Triple Goddess, whose archetypal age hypostases are the Maiden, the Mother, and the Crone. The Goddess is the most venerated, and Wicca itself is commonly considered to be a feminine religion. On the periphery of the pantheon there is the unnamed High God, who is not uncommonly interpreted through the image of the Goddess to be the Supreme Mother of all. Magic, witchcraft, and sorcery are the foundation of the religious practice and the essence of Wicca. Through witchcraft, the Wiccan adept is to know the world of nature and influence it, to communicate with the spirits of the forest, rocks, and things, and to be in contact with the spirits of dead ancestors. Following Gardner, Wiccan practice also came to include the spiritualism popular at the time along with the use of Ouija boards.[187] From classical Western occultism, Wiccans have borrowed the notion of five elements: Spirit, Air, Fire, Water, and Earth, symbolized in one of the main emblems of Wicca, the pentagram, frequently depicted with the central symbolic circle (the Moon) of the Triple Goddess. Another popular, but not original symbol of Wicca is the triquetra.

Wiccans do not have any sacred books besides the works of Gardner and other authoritative mystics and occultists, which lends additional grounds for syncretism and numerous variations of the so-called "Book of Shadows", a compilation of magical practices, spells, and diary entries to be kept both by solitary practitioners and stored in covens. The ritual side of Wicca consists of the observance of eight annual holiday-sabbaths: Samhain (the day of the dead, 31 October - 1 November, Yule (winter solstice), Imbolc (the coming of spring, 1/2 February), Ostara (spring equinox), Beltane or May Eve (the symbolic beginning of summer, 1 May), Midsummer or Litha (summer solstice), Lughnasad or Lammas (harvest day, 1 August), and Mabon (the autumnal equinox). As we can see, the wheel of Wiccan holidays reproduces those of the Year-Wheel, while adding to them intermediate dates. This calendar is a syncretic mixing of Celtic (Samhain, Imbolc, Beltane, Lammas) and Germanic (Yule and Ostara) pagan holidays. As for rites of initiation into the religion, as we pointed out above, such are declared by adherents of Gardnerian Wicca, but are ubiquitously violated or ignored. "Traditional" British Wiccans trace a chain of initiations up to Gardner.

---

187 The Ouija board was devised by the 19th century American inventor Elijah Bond as an entertainment game.

Of some interest are the Wiccan wedding ceremonies and practices of "baptizing" children, known as "handfasting" and "Wiccaning" respectively. A common feature of Wiccan rituals is their liberalism towards adepts: those who marry through handfasting conclude, as it were, a preliminary test-marriage lasting one year which can be dissolved without any obligations. Wiccan "baptism", or "Wiccaning", is also aimed not at induction into tradition, but merely at presenting the newborn to their God and Goddess. Wiccaning is not of any binding or initiatic nature, and the child is left with free will to accept or reject the religion upon reaching adulthood. Wiccan religion manifests strictly Modernist humanism, a secular approach, and liberal morals, as expressed in the Wiccan maxim "An Ye Harm None, Do What Ye Will." Wicca also explicitly borrows or imitates the Eastern principles of ahimsa and karma, as expressed in their Law of Threefold Return which states that any action (especially an evil one) will return to a person threefold. Gardner's 161 laws, or "Ardanes", have been met with criticism for being overly patriarchal, today representing more of an artifact than acting precepts in force for Wiccans.

In the end, Wicca represents a brilliant example of a pagan simulacrum in terms of its imitation of pagan communities in the form of covens and the simultaneous recognition of solitary Wiccans, its claims to initiatic quality and yet its ubiquitous violation of this provision, and its imitation of the Year-Wheel and traditional doctrines of behavior and morality, all distorted by concepts of Modernity. The disunity of opinions among Wiccans themselves is similar to the pluralism of pagan traditions, but concerns not so much folkloric, cultural, and esoteric differences as it reflects the absence of a unified opinion on the very essence of the religion, its theology, cosmogony, ritual practices, ultimate aims, and behavior. Wicca as a term can in fact take under its roof the whole spectrum of modern neo-witchcraft, sorcery, and magic, and this is facilitated by the democratic aspirations of Wiccans and the rhizomatic, network structure of their organizations and covens, numerous of which emerged in the absence of lines of transmission and initiation, amidst sub-traditions which only partially reference the basis laid by Gerald Gardner.

The very origins of Gardner's version of Wicca have been the subject of profound doubt.[188] The existence of a coven in New Forest has never been proven and besides Gardner himself has no known external manifestations. The thread of the concept of the Triple Goddess leads back to the works of another English fiction writer, Robert Graves (1895-1985), who authored the mythological treatise *The White Goddess* in 1948. In the latter work, Graves examined the representations of Goddesses across different cultures as manifestations of archetypes of a White Goddess, the Virgin, Mother, and Crone and the related three phases of the moon. Graves devoted great attention to poetry born out of the worshipping of the Goddess and myth, which relates his work to the poetic and fictional fields of literature. Academic scholars largely ignored Graves' treatise, while others criticized it for being inconsistent with facts and arbitrary in its interpretations. Female figures associated with birth, maturation, and death can be encountered in the face of the Greek Moira and the Scandinavian Norns, where they are the Goddesses of Fate, but are not supreme Goddess-mothers or protectors of the cosmos and its cycles. Also far from the image of the Triple Goddess are the Greek Charites, Aglaea, Euphrosyne, and Thaila, the three Goddesses of grace and beauty that inspire artisans corresponding to the Roman three Graces. Visible here is the connection between Graves' poetic strivings and the Charites' functions pertaining to inspiration, beauty, abundance, the patronage of poets, artists, etc. But the Charites and Graces are the daughters of Dionysus and Aphrodite or Zeus and Eurynome (*à la* Hesiod), which is to say that they are a subsequent generation of the Gods, neither supreme nor primordial Divinities and, moreover, not faces of a single Goddess. Traditional figures of Triune Goddesses, or ones close to such in name, can be found in the Roman and Scandinavian

---

188 See: Aidan A. Kelly, *Inventing Witchcraft: A Case Study in the Creation of a New Religion* (Loughborough: Thoth Publications, 2008).

traditions, in the Roman Juno and the Scandinavian Freya, but these Goddesses embody not the three phases of life and the moon, but the three functions of the Indo-European structure. Juno is the Goddess of fertility whose Capitoline name was Regina, a name which associated her with sacred authority and warrior strength. Freya, a Goddess from the race of the Vanir, the sister of the God of fertility Freyr, and the supreme Valkyrie and masteress of seiðr, manifests the magical-priestly, pedagogical function. We can see that these traditional "Triune Goddesses" do not coincide with Graves' version.

Another source-base of Gardner and his followers was the space of Western occultism, ideas and texts from which have been reworked and incorporated into the corpus of Wiccan literature. Francis King has pointed to Gardner's plagiarism of the works and ideas of Aleister Crowley, and scholars have in more than a few cases pointed out similarities between Wicca and Crowley's Thelema. The influence of spiritualist ideas practiced by Gardner, which unequivocally cannot be attributed to traditional practices, is also well known.

The emergence and formation of Wicca in the late 20th century and its active spread in the post-1960s United States coincided with the shift of the paradigm of Modernity to Postmodernity, the imperatives of which include the rejection of patriarchal vertical structures and norms in favor of the pursuit of syncretism, collages, and kaleidoscopic configurations. On the ideological level, Wicca's imperatives of worshipping the Triple Goddess (matriarchy), eclecticism as the standard of practice, and the rhizomaticness and liberal-democratic character of Wiccan organizations and covens are completely identical to Postmodern post-religiosity.

At the present stage, Wicca is a globally widespread neo-pagan religion with representative centers in the United States, where it has official recognition, as well as in Europe and Russia. Wherever it travels, Wicca absorbs the local ethnic-cultural background and folklore while retaining its own positions. The circle of Wiccan annual holidays is not uncommonly taken as a substitute for the authentic year-circles of Odinism and Celtic paganism, and is frequently passed off as the universal wheel of pagan sacred days, which is facilitated by its inclusion of Celtic, Irish, and Germanic holidays covering nearly all of the dates of the solar and agricultural calendar. Wicca can be seen as an example of the syncretic universalization of notions of magic and witchcraft as an independent, global "tradition" with a place in all cultures. Thusly occurs the degradation of the integral body of tradition through the extraction of one part - magic and witchcraft - to become an independent, self-sufficient element embedded into the network of Wiccan interpretations and values which, in turn, are but Postmodern simulacra and chimeras of quasi-paganism.

It is noteworthy that among European pagans, predominantly Odinists, as well as Russian Native Faith, relations towards Wicca are often taken to be an unspoken marker of the adequacy of a given organization. A positive appraisal of Wiccanism is a discrediting factor. One example of such discrediting is that of the Pagan Federation International, founded in 1971, which has actively cooperated with and spread through Wiccans, including in Russia. The PFI is a liberal human rights organization which seeks to establish tolerance towards paganism in society in the spirit of recognizing the authority of the secular approach to religion enshrined in article 18 of the UN International Declaration of Human Rights. Pagan Federation International is de facto a virtual structure with paid membership which claims to accept "followers of all pagan spiritual traditions and currents without restrictions." In Russia, the PFI is represented by the Circle of Pagan Tradition. We could also mention the Spanish Platforma Pagana, an organization uniting various pagan groups to lobby for pagan interests in the legal field. Wiccans have also figured in the initiative of the "revival" of Kemeticism in the United States, which also seems to us to be dubious to the highest degree. Anything more than Wicca with Egyptian decorations is hardly to be expected from such. A similar situation of Wiccan "decorating" can be encountered in the case of the Scandinavian tradition in the works of the contemporary writer Freya Aswynn.

Taken together, Theosophism, Armanism/Ariosophy/Ario-Christianity, Serrano and Devi's esoteric Hitlerism, and Wicca constitute the main lines of the pseudo-pagan fallacies of the modern West that have found representation in other regions of the world. On their repeatedly fragmented and arbitrarily mixed bases, numerous small, uninteresting local sects, groupings, quasi-teachings, and "revelations" have emerged. Underneath them are those open simulacra of the New Age, the absurdity and ridiculousness of which is so obvious to any pagan that no further detailed explanation is needed here.

Russia and the Post-Soviet Space

Now we shall turn to examine those pagan simulacra which have spread primarily in the space of the states of Russia, Belarus, and Ukraine, as well as the neighboring Baltic countries which have large Russian-speaking communities. This zone also indirectly concerns the space of Eastern Europe inhabited by Slavs who, aspiring to return to the ancient Slavic traditions which existed before the Slavic peoples' division into their modern state formations, have turned their eyes and interest towards Russian sources and the contemporary Russian pagan experience. The situation of pseudo-paganism in the post-Soviet space might, by analogy with Wiccanism as a household name for the whole sum of similar New Age religions, be considered an integral phenomenon within which there exist different trends imitating traditional structures and forms with their own centers of gravity, confrontations, trajectories of mixing, etc. Taken together, these currents constitute the broad phenomenon of Russian pseudo-paganism whose main center and platform of spread is in Russia.

Beyond Russia's borders, pagan simulacra have been further compounded by the peculiarities of recent artificially constructed nationalities, such as the Ukrainian and Belarusian, which previously formed the unified Russian people and for more than a millennium were joined within one state. The modern artificial forging of such national-geneses has been based on contrasting these newfound identities to previously existing ones expressed in Russian Imperial and Soviet statehood, a process which has given rise to alternative histories of Ukrainian and Belarusian nationalities whose pursuit of confirmation of historical uniqueness goes against historical, linguistic, and cultural reliability and authenticity. Thus suffers the authentic side of returning to ancient customs, as the real heritage is distorted to the benefit of modern political interests by each according to their own views and new political aims. At the present stage, we can distinguish a strong tilt of the new Ukrainian identity towards Polish-Ukrainian syncretism, and of the new Belarusian identity towards Lithuanian-Polish-Belarusian syncretism. For pseudo-paganism in the post-Soviet space, this entails linguistic syncretism, new arbitrary historials (Postmodern aions) for neo-pagan religions, and heightened political engagement and bias to the detriment of authenticity and validity. We will keep this particularity in mind while only minimally touching on the political interests of contemporary profane state entities. In our earlier discussion of the potential of Russia for paganism, we noted that this potential lies in the people itself, not in state structures. The same is true for Ukrainians and Belarusians as peoples who are Russian in their history and structure, but which have their own external cultural peculiarities. Political peripeteia might neutralize this potential by way of false aionic-historical, cultural and linguistic simulacra, but might also preserve such in some cases. However, at the time of this book's writing these processes are still far from their foreseeable conclusion and do not lend towards stable forecasting, so we can only conclude that what is presently underway is the centrifugal rupture of the ancient community which yielded the Russian people and the Ukrainian and Belarusian sub-ethnoi belonging within its composition and intrinsic to the very antiquity of its tradition. This discrepancy, together with the main body of pseudo-pagan ideas, is also misinforming and creating false pictures among those representatives of other Slavic peoples of Eastern Europe who have manifested interest in Russian Native Faith and reviving the Slavic tradition as a whole.

The spectrum of simulacra in Russian pseudo-paganism encompasses practically all spheres of tradition. For every phenomenon, form, and affirmation there is a syncretic, perverse double. Despite its wide range of doctrines, organizations, and individual personalities, Russian pseudo-paganism nonetheless aspires to ideological integrity, i.e., many of its provisions are in one way or another shared, transmitted, and produced throughout the environment of the adepts of these pagan simulacra despite their individual differences. Russian pseudo-paganism emerged later than its counterpart in Europe due to the already-mentioned specific circumstances of Soviet authoritarianism, and only began to gain strength in the late 1980s. The ideological forerunners and partly fertile soil in the late Soviet period for future pseudo-pagans were the circles of followers of the Roerichs and Blavatsky, i.e., once again Theosophism in its various editions. The late 1980s in Russia also saw the influx of missionaries of global sects, a surge of interest in extrasensory perception (ESP) and spiritualism, and an overall search for at least some kind of spirituality following decades of prohibition. In these years, the volume and accessibility of esoteric literature also increased manyfold, thus opening up previously forbidden philosophical currents and schools, including not only Traditionalism, but also the diverse quasi-esoteric forgeries that had been taking shape outside of the USSR and Russia.

The substantive ideological core of Russian pseudo-paganism was thus in many ways identical to that of its Western counterparts: Theosophism and its derivatives, the syncretic approaches of Wiccanism and Armanism, the infiltration of

Modernist and Postmodernist conceptions, and the influence of neo-Hindu ideas. Original innovations began with applying these methods and concepts to Russian history, culture, and tradition, thus generating phantasmagoric narratives which were presented as the truth. As is to be expected, it is impossible to find full confirmation and the roots of such simulations of "true knowledge." A simulacrum closes the path to the source onto itself, on the one hand rendering it scientifically unverifiable, which at once excludes some elements of the scientific and technological paradigm of Modernity while mixing others with the fragments of traditional doctrines, while, on the other hand, integrating quasi-traditional claims which are not supported by the known preserved heritage and the data of archaeology, folklore, history, and linguistics. In other cases, arbitrary superstructural interpretations are built over reliable accounts which, once again, cannot be confirmed or verified in terms of scientific-technological ideas. At the same time, various authors and ideologists of pseudo-pagan doctrines not uncommonly refer to "secret" sources, among which one can often find analogues of the Theosophist Mahatmas in the form of higher beings, aliens, "ancestral memory" or sets of secret writings such as, for instance, the gold plates of runes which the adepts of Ynglism claim harbor inscriptions of the foundations of the Slavic worldview, secret "ancestral" books, or historical forgeries and fakes which are thereby completely, uncritically accepted as faith, such as the *Book of Veles*, etc. Confirming the real existence of such hidden sources, "golden plates", "ancestral books and memory", and "gospels from above" is impossible by virtue of their very "occultation." Thus, simulacra once again close onto themselves. In these cases, the only source of a doctrine is the author or group of authors who found a given pseudo-pagan sect, to whom alone are accessible by virtue of "supernatural reasons" such hidden sources, the voices of higher entities, and the right to interpret these and everything else. This situation is a classic one, and in the study of sects is seen as one of the hallmarks of a totalitarian sect or destructive cult in which knowledge is usurped or access to knowledge is limited to one person or group, a practice which stands in contrast to the aspirations of traditional religions for harmonious existence and the revelation of the Sacred in man and the world. This usurpation is suggestive of the head ideologue's desire to satisfy their own needs and realize their own personal aims. As we have done with contemporary adequate, competent paganism, our examination of pseudo-pagan simulacra is boiled down to an overview of key personalities, organizations, and their proposed "true" doctrines.

The main current competing to be the fully-fledged matrix of the whole pseudo-pagan simulacrum in Russia and the post-Soviet space is the doctrine of Ynglism, the author of which is Alexandr Khinevich (b. 1961). During the esoteric boom in the late 1980s-early 1990s, Khinevich, a native of Omsk, engaged in healing seances, ESP, and sought contact with UFOs in the "anomalous zone" near the village of Okunevo in the Omsk region, famous among Russia's New Age esotericists. The doctrine of Ynglism was created and formed into an organization between 1992 and 1998, with its main center in the city of Omsk, called by Ynglists none other than Asgard, and with an extensive network of supporters throughout Russia and neighboring states.

The doctrine of Ynglism, whose full title is the "Ancient Russian Ynglist Church of Orthodox Old Believer Ynglings", was named after the Yngling dynasty of Scandinavian kings that once ruled in Sweden and Norway whose semi-mythical history was told in Snorri Sturluson's *Ynglinga Saga*. Sturluson's desire to present the Norse Gods as immigrants from Near Asia (Troy and the Caucasus are mentioned in the Saga) gave impetus to interpreting the saga itself and the Yngling dynasty to be Slavs, and to revising the geographical localization of the mythical worlds, such as Asgard, to be in the space of modern Russia. The Ynglists hold that "Ynglia" was the primordial fire of the cosmos. The other titles included in the name of the Ynglist religion include "Prav-worship" (*pravoslavie*) and

"Old Believers" (*starovery*), which refer us to the linguistic fallacy of interpreting the term *pravoslavie* as meaning "to glorify Prav'" (*slavit' Prav'*), i.e., to glorify the higher realm. The term "Old Believers" is in turn taken from the name of the Old Believers Rite (*staroobriadchestvo*), the Russian Orthodox Christian movement that emerged out of schism with the Church following the reforms of Patriarch Nikon in the 17th century. Here we can see a play on words and terms intended to emphasize an ancient continuity stretching from the noble Yngling clan, which is dated back to Freyr, to Russian *"prav'-slavie"* ("*Prav*-glorifying"), punctuated by emphatic opposition to the Russian Orthodox Church.

Ynglist doctrine is essentially a mixture of a broad array of the traditional doctrines of different peoples - the Slavic, Germanic, Hindu, Greek, Jewish, etc. - with legends of various epochs and science fiction fantasy. A large part of Ynglist teachings consists of open borrowings and plagiarism of other authors and works, such as the famous Russian Germanist Mikhail Steblin-Kamensky, Veleslav Cherkasov, the "Legends of the Knights Templar", and even the Book of Mormon. The insertion of elements of science fantasy fiction into religious doctrine has its roots in the works of the American ideologist of the sect of Scientology, the science fiction author Ron Hubbard. Ynglist doctrine is built around an original historial (aion), configures around itself fantastical and real historical events, personages, and artifacts, and is set out in five books under the title *The Slavo-Aryan Vedas*, which imitate both the Jewish Torah of Moses and the four Indian Vedas.

In Sanskrit, the word *veda* means "knowledge" or "teaching" and is cognate to the Russian *vedat'* ("to know"), *svedushchii* ("knowledgeable", "competent", "adept"), *vedun* ("sage", "wizard") and *ved'ma* ("witch", "sorceress"). But this is the only fact that unites the whole set of pseudo-Slavic "Vedas" authored by Khinevich, Alexander Barashkov (Asov, the author of the "Russian Vedas"), Igor Gologanov (the forger of the "Veda Slovena"), Oleg Torsunov, and others of their ilk with the traditional heritage of India. For Russian pseudo-paganism the adjective and characterization *"vedic"* is virtually "sacred" in and of itself, referring as such does to *vedat'* as opposed to *verit'* ("to believe") and to the Indian Vedas, which is taken to support the antiquity and global prevalence of their writings many centuries ago. Those neo-pagans who actively borrow Indian terms, words, the names of Gods and Asuras ("Asur" is one of the fantastical Slavic warlords of Khinevich's "Vedas"), and imitate Sanskrit in their alphabets, mandalas, yantras, and iconography, are not uncommonly called "Indo-Slavs", an appellation intended to emphasize that they primarily glorify a foreign culture while belittling their own native Slavic and Russian tradition. Within pseudo-paganism, such linguistic affinities are taken as grounds for identifying the ancient Indo-Aryans with the Slavs and for justifying the mixing of these traditions as if they were one and the same.

The Traditionalist notion that in his initiatic ascent to the Center man comprehends the One embodied in different traditions-*iazyki* on the periphery is thus replaced by a view positing a uniformity of meaning of all the different forms on the periphery, excluding the notion of the Center. It is not the One that is revealed with the diminution of external forms expressing differences, but the mixing of external differences in forms into a homogenous conglomeration that is thereby passed off as the "unity" of all traditions. This is one of the characteristic features of pseudo-pagan simulacra which is most distinctly embodied in Ynglism.

Alexander Khinevich and his followers claim that Ynglism is the most ancient and only faith of the Slavs, in comparison to which all other world religions, sacred books, myths, and legends are either confirmations of Ynglism or are secondary, simplified derivations of it. Ynglings respect the figures of Christ, Muhammad, the Buddha, and many other ancient saints, as well as modern scholars and thinkers whose wisdom they attribute to the ancient "vedic" knowledge of Ynglism. The contradictions that arise between individual traditions and in the paradigmatic rift between Tradition and Modernity are not taken into consideration at all. The diverse aggregation of saints and teachers of mankind, as well as Ynglism's pretension towards universality and its usurpation of all possible knowledge in its favor, with all the corresponding contradictions, is recognizably reminiscent of the New Age approach whose roots trace back to Theosophism.

In his narrative of the creation of the cosmos by the God of Energy Ra-M-Khat, Khinevich presents an alternative view of the origins of the stars, galaxies, planets, and evolution which at times opposes the theories of academic science and at others actively cites their data whenever such seems to support his own theories. The mixing of mythological fragments with scientific tropes results in an identification of the world of Prav with our galaxy and the naming of planet Earth "Midgard-Earth", home to the city of Omsk-Asgard-Iriy. We can see in this a mixing of the names of the Scandinavian worlds of people and the Aesir with the modern names of planets and cities, and the identification of one of the worlds of light beyond with the mythical Slavic land of Iriy (also known as Vyray or Vyriy). According to Ynglists, Iriy is the Irtysh River which flows through China, Kazakhstan and Russia, in particular through the Omsk region. The ancient ancestors of the Slavs and the Gods are held to have been highly technologically and spiritually advanced beings who could travel between worlds and galaxies on special "Vaitmana" chariots. The latter word is borrowed from the myths of India, where vimāna referred to the chariots of the Gods. In the Ynglist interpretation, the "vaitmanas" are the spaceships of the Gods, a theme which we can clearly trace to the New Age UFO religion and related ideas of the influence of extraterrestrials on the evolution of humanity, as well as the ideas of Ron Hubbard. The ancestors who inhabited the Ursa Major constellation are said to have traveled to Midgard-Earth on their vaitmanas to the now sunken continent of Daaria, whose prototype would be the Greek Hyperborea, the land of the Far North. From Hyperborea-Daria the ancient Slavo-Aryans, consisting of four races - the kh'Aryan, the Da'Aryan, the Rassens, and the Svyatorusy ("sacred Rus") migrated between the many mythical and cult countries and places found across the world's mythologies. In Russia, they settled in the mythical land of the Russian Old Believers Rite, Belovodye, which is also to be found in the Omsk region.

In their exaltations of the Slavo-Aryans, Ynglists attribute them victory in various intergalactic wars with other races, such as the "gray" hermaphroditic ancestors of the Jews and over the Chinese Empire, which is alleged to be depicted in the icon of St. George the Victorious striking the dragon (i.e., China). All the events of the great history of the Slavo-Russo-Aryans are placed in deep antiquity, which voids any question of the possibility of their real, objective confirmation in scientific terms, or any mentions of these fantastic events in the mythical and historical chronicles of the Slavs, the Chinese, and neighboring states.

A more detailed analysis of the cosmogonic and historical fantasies of Ynglism would demand a volume much greater than our work, but the examples which we have already examined are more than telling for the characterization of Khinevich and his sect's ideas as fantastical, counter-initiatic New Age teachings. Now we will turn to briefly focus on some characteristics and works of Ynglism which, posing as authentic elements of tradition, have aggressively penetrated pagan and Native Faith milieux.

Revealing testimony as to the quality of the theology of Ynglism is offered by Khinevich's syncretic pantheon. Among the many Gods claimed by Ynglism, we encounter authentic Slavic Gods and figures from other traditions alongside absolutely fictional ones. Khinevich's inventions include:

- Ra-M-Kha (or RAMKHA), the One High God;
- Yngl - the Eternal Guardian of the Cosmic Fire;
- RAMKHAT (Brama, Rama) - the God of Judgement, a spin-off of both Hinduism's Brahma and Ra-M-Kha;
- Chislobog - the God of Time and the motion of cycles and history, the God of the Calendar;

- Baba Yoga (Yogi-Mother) - the everlasting lover and patroness of orphans. (Here we see a free-handed interpretation of the Slavic evil spirit Baba-Yaga, who is depicted as a deformed or crippled old woman, blended with the Hindu current of yoga);
- Bog Pater Dii (Diy/Dyi) - the God of celestial space, the inexhaustible force of the Earth of *Dei*, and the guardian of the Ancient Truth.

The name "*Pater Dii*" is a direct spin-off of the academic study of religion's reconstruction of the Indo-European celestial Father-God, Supreme God, and Creator-God of the Cosmos, *Dyeus Pater*, which is one of the epithets of the God Zeus (whose name is related to Deus, Dei) as well as other leading Gods, such as Indra in Hinduism and Odin in the Germanic-Scandinavian tradition. In Ynglism, *Pater Dii* also refers to the rank and status held by Khinevich himself. It is worth noting that in the third volume of the *Slavo-Aryan Vedas*' presentation of the symbol of Ynglist faith, the iconographic portrait of Pater Dii is clearly reminiscent of Khinevich. Other Gods borrowed from the Scandinavian and Hindu traditions include Thor, Odin/Wotan, the Valkyries, Varuna, and Indra. Vyshen and Kryshen, Miroliubov's spin-offs of Vishnu and Krishna in the *Book of Veles*, also find mention in Ynglist doctrine, along with the God Agni from the Roerichs' teachings. Ynglism's representation of the Slavic Chernobog is also imparted with the functions of Satan. The trifunctional triads (and triple-heads) of the Gods are absent in Ynglism, and the functions and interpretations attributed to each of the Gods either bear only distant resemblance to their original roles in native traditions or are altogether fictitious.

No less curious is the Ynglists' version of the ancient and primordial Slavic language and writing, in which is manifested at once the subtlety and comprehensiveness of this pseudo-pagan simulacrum's aspiration to substitute itself for all aspects of tradition. The *Slavo-Aryan Vedas* themselves are written in three languages: in pre-1918-reform Russian, the commentaries are in modern Russian, and the books also feature texts written in a peculiar Ynglist runic, the "kh'Aryan runes", which, according to Ynglist adepts, are neither runes nor hieroglyphs, but rather mysterious, secret "thought-images" which immediately convey ancient knowledge. The Ynglist runes are a modern form of writing created especially for the needs of Khinevich's teachings which externally appear to be a blend of Scandinavian rune-symbols, the "runes" of the Ainu people of the Japanese islands, Old Slavic and Sanskrit letters, as well as various arbitrary figures. The Ynglist runic text is presented under one unifying sense and meaning, that of immersion into Sanskrit writing.

The relevance of the problem of the Slavic alphabet lies in continuing debates on the emergence of writing among the Slavs. The dominant theory states that the Old Slavonic language and its script, Glagolithic, was established by the missionaries Cyril and Methodius, and that the Cyrillic alphabet developed out of such later. The need for this new script and language was for the translation of sacred Christian texts from Greek into the Slavic languages. The translation was synthesized on the bases of the Greek and Bulgarian languages, which thus gave birth to a new Slavic language of the gradual system with corresponding changes in thinking. At the same time, of particular interest are the birchwood (Novgorodian) writings of the 11th-15th centuries, which, used primarily for private correspondences, preserved traces of the everyday alphabet of early Cyrillic and linguistic artifacts predating the reform alongside several forms of Scandinavian runic. The latter has allowed for the hypothesis to be put forth of a pre-Christian Rus' runic writing. The treatise *On Letters* attributed to Chernorizets Hrabar also sheds light on the existence of runic writing among the Western Slavs in the Middle Ages. In particular, this document contains the following line:

| Прѣжде оубо словѣне не имѣхѫ писменъ • нѫ чрътами и рѣзами чьтѣхѫ и гатаахѫ погани сѫще | Being still pagans, the Slavs did not have their own letters, but they read and divined with figures and cuts. |

In other words, before their baptism the pagan Slavs (here called *pogani*) practiced divination "with figures and cuts," i.e., a symbolic system similar to the Scandinavian (Varangian/Viking) runic later applied to writing. Also of cultic and magical significance were the robushy, or "notches", sticks with straight and oblique cuts and points which collectively presented many different combinations. A number of runic and runic-like artifacts have been preserved in Poland, Czechia, Slovakia, and Bulgaria. The most widespread version of Slavic runes is that of the Wendish runes. "Wends" or "Weneds" was the German collective name for the Slavs later assigned to the Polabians. Records of the Wendish runic system date back to the works of Trogillus Arnkiel (1691) and Hans Heinrich Klüver (1728), who are supposed to have adapted Danish runic writing to Slavic. On the basis of the Wendish runes, Anton Platov has proposed a more modern variant closer to the modern Russian language with significant influence from the Scandinavian futhark. The Wendish runes in the versions of Arnkiel, Klüver, and Platov are today perhaps the most reliable, but not indisputable variations of runic writing which have been adapted in Native Faith milieux.

As we can see, various authors have attempted to fill the gaps in the pagan heritage. Among these figure different variations of pseudo-pagan simulacra, such as the kh'Aryan runes of Ynglism, the script of the *Book of Veles* created with the modern Russian alphabet, Shubin's *VseIaSvetnaia* system, and the "glyphs" of Valery Chudinov, to whom also belongs the fictional Slavic Deity *Yar*. In order to fully understand the problem of language and writing in Russian pseudo-paganism, it is necessary to go beyond examining Yngilism alone and to cover the problem in its wider scope, especially as many authors have in one way or another reproduced the historial and matrix of Ynglism even while rejecting and denying its doctrine.

We have already considered the important, fundamental role of language in thinking, understanding, preserving and transmitting the pagan worldview. In the pseudo-pagan world, language is also devoted considerably attention in a peculiarly post-religious, syncretic key. Approaches to Russian or other languages differ from author to author, but we can highlight several principal positions which form the nodes between which the rhizomatic network of such diverse theories, interpretations, and alphabetic and runic variations have been formed. This is the matter of pseudo-etymologies and the interpretations of words, the decryption of alphabets, and the decryption and interpretation of ancient inscriptions and artifacts of writing.

The traditional, holistic perception of the world beholds language as more than just sound, speech, and writing whose function is to convey and exchange information. In Tradition, language is Sacred and its function of transmitting information is far from being in the first place. In Tradition, language creates, destroys, enchants, liberates, and shows the fundamental laws of the Divine cosmos, and in many ways the knowledge of language, knowledge of the names of the Gods, and of incantations and formula is initiatic knowledge, knowledge of the Divine itself. There are sacred sounds, such as the Hindu mantras, a special place among which is distinguished for the primordial mantra "Om" or "Aum", which contains literally everything. According to the not undisputed theory of Herman Wirth, the whole cosmos from its manifestation to destruction is contained in the symbol of the Year-Wheel and expressed in the vowels A-I-U, which are consonant with Aum.[189]

The attaining and understanding of the runes is associated with the mystery of Odin's self-sacrifice on Yggdrasil, as a result of which the runes were revealed to him as secret magical symbols. The use of the runes as an alphabet for writing was a much later phenomenon, for which multiple sets of runes, the futharks, are designated. Thus, magical symbols originally converge with language and writing, thereby constituting the broad space of sacred language. Language itself and the word-as-sound are powerful instruments of creation or destruction, as well as for knowing and revealing the Divine. The Pythagoreans,

---

189 See: Askr Svarte, "A-I-U and Stillness: A Commentary on Herman Wirth's Study of the Year-Wheel", *Warha Europe* 2 (2018-2019), p. 18-30

for instance, practiced vows of long silence and imposed such on neophytes wishing to join their association. Another initiatic element was the transmission to the initiate of the name of a God or secret word and its functions and sacrifices.

Pseudo-pagan simulations mimic the holistic principle of language and writing as something greater than self-identical privative givens, and also strive to impart such with their own additional "higher" meanings and interpretations of "hidden meanings." As in other cases, the Ynglists and similar authors' versions contradict both the data and methods of the academic sciences of linguistics and etymology as well as the views of various traditions on the Sacred content of their own languages. In other words, their treatments of language once again constitute mixtures of modern and traditional forms appended with their own arbitrary inventions. The simulacra of sacred language in pseudo-paganism completely ignore the history of the development of languages, their tree classifications and the historical-comparative method of discerning degrees of kinship, only occasionally involving disparate data and facts to reinforce their truths and gains. One of the most common claims put forth by such pseudo-paganisms is that the modern Russian language is the most ancient on the planet, from which all other languages and writing systems developed, often by way of degradation, in antiquity. Modern Russian words are taken as bases for comparison with ancient words from the languages of other peoples, for the decryption of consonant words and the explanation of their meanings by way of assigning free-handed interpretations based on their consonance alone. Kinships between words and languages are established in terms of the external, superficial, flat similarity of their sounds regardless of whether they may in fact have any kinship at all or possess different etymologies and meanings in their respective languages. One such example is the pseudo-linguistic interpretation of the Brahmin priest as being "he who murmurs/mutters" due to the similarity of sound between the *br-* and *bor/br-* in the Russian words *bormotat'* ("to mutter, to murmur") and *breshit'* (in the sense of "to speak" and "to cast a spell") which, according to the theories of some pseudo-pagans, makes the Brahmin "he who mutters spells" or "the mutterer." Another example is the treatment of the English word "nation" as a distortion of the Russian word *nash* ("ours") by virtue of similar connotations and the fact that in English the *-tio-* makes the sound "*sh*." In the process of such interpretations, the structure of a language and its morphology is completely ignored. While special attention is devoted to the roots of words as the most stable parts, any part of a word can be taken as a starting point for interpretation, even in violation of the rules of a language. An exhaustive example of such extrapolations of the similarity of words and their meanings by way of turning to the root is the case with the root-word *rod* as related to the Slavic God Rod. To Rod's name are attributed all words with the same root, e.g. *priRODa* ("nature", taken to mean "standing in front of Rod"), *RODina* ("homeland"), *RODnik* ("water source", taken to be a short form of *RODa NIKakogo*, i.e., "of no *rod*", "rootless"), *ROZHenitsa* ("a woman in labor"), *vodoROD* ("hydrogen"), *ugleROD* ("carbon"), etc., thus mixing both scientific terms and folkloric and mythological ones. All of these words are explained as manifestations of the creative, generative force of *Rod*. Of course, the deity Rod has nothing to do with these elements of the periodic table or with such arbitrary treatments of the notions of "nature" and "water spring."

In the process of splitting apart words into components to be decrypted in search of their secret meanings, the integrity of roots, suffixes, prefixes, and endings is violated. Instead of holistic integrity, a word de facto becomes a mosaic, a rebus of different parts and letters, each of which harbors a "secret." Hence the heightened interest of pseudo-pagan pseudo-linguistics in breaking words down into syllables and highlighting special "sacred" syllables in writing. The Ynglist *RA-M-KHA* is one example, in which "RA" is taken to be a sacred syllable meaning light and sun and "M" is taken to refer to "Om"/"Aum." In another case, the word *radost'* ("joy") is written as *RA-dost'*, i.e., "achieving RA, communion with the sacred light of the Sun God RA." We also encounter widespread practices of reading words backwards as a means of supposedly revealing their additional meanings. One of the most famous followers and perpetuators of Khinevich's work, A. Trekhlebov, interprets the Russian writing of the Japanese word haberu, which means "to serve" and samurai, thusly: "The Samurai is the knight who directs his 'I' [Ia] to Paradise [Rai] (Sam- is 'himself' [Russian sam], -ur- is the light of Jīvātmā, and -rai is the Heavenly Kingdom). To preserve his honor he can commit harakiri (hara- = the umbilical energy center, k = [Russian] k, meaning 'to/ toward something', and -iri is Iriy, the Heavenly Kingdom)." As can be seen in this example, the written form of a word takes priority over its vocal speech and sound, since such is alleged to distort a word and its meaning, consequently giving rise to different dialects. The absurdity and arbitrariness of such interpretations is obvious, and there are more than enough examples to be found in the literature of Ynglism and similar pseudo-paganisms.

Thus, hidden meanings in words and syllables lead to the decryption of secret knowledge in alphabets, partially in similarity to the synthesis of magical and writing functions in the Scandinavian runes, but predominated by the above-described arbitrary and fantastical constructions. Close to this are the various "deep readings of secret meanings" of ancient inscriptions in different languages. For example, artifacts which pose great difficulty to scholars of archeology and linguistics, such as the Rongorongo tablets from Easter Island and the Phaistos Disc from Crete, in the pseudo-pagan milieu have more than one version claiming reliable decryption and reading. Moreover, the belonging of such artifacts to their indigenous cultures and traditions is ignored, and they are instead attributed to the ancient Slavic heritage. There are no few illustrations of such "decryptions." The most well-known popularizers of pseudo-Slavic pseudo-linguistics include Alexander Khinevich, A. Trekhlebov, V. Chudinov, Anatoly Fomenko, A. Dragunkin,

K. Lipskikh, N. Vashkevich, M. Zadornov, G. Grinevich, Sergey Alexeev, G. Sidorov, and others.

In close connection with such treatments of alphabetic symbols and pseudo-runes is the problem of pseudo-Slavic symbolism popularized by the adepts of Ynglism. A full list of swastika-like symbols with varying color semantics and interpretations is presented in the third volume of the *Slavo-Aryan Vedas*. These symbols consist of mixings, reworkings, and new inventions upon historically attested swastika-symbols across the various Indo-European cultures. These include swastika patterns from Hindustan and China, Russian traditions of embroidery, ceramics, and architecture, as well as artifacts from the Germanic heritage. Each symbol is given its own name - names which frequently consist of borrowings from different words and are often unrelated to the symbols from the Hindu, Slavic, and Germanic traditions altogether. Almost all of the decryptions of these symbols' meanings in one way or another double one another, repeating the same pattern in different variations. One of the principal "innovations" of Ynglism is the borrowing of the nine-pointed star from Western occultism[190], renamed the "Star of Ynglia." The creation of a wide array of pseudo-Slavic symbols has been one of the endeavors of Khinevich and his former associate, Vladimir Yanvarsky. Starting with genuine symbols found in Russian embroidery on sashes, *rushnyk* cloths, and bedspreads, etc., they have created an alternative code of names and interpretations which easily confuse the untrained and inexperienced. Thus, authentic heritage is once again substituted by the simulacrum which adapts such. This substitution of notions is close in character to the subcultural commerciality which we discussed above. Outlandish narratives and promises of achieving success and blessing by "native" symbols become well-selling signs marking belonging to the relevant subculture. Pseudo-Slavic symbolism does not conflict with the consumer society and subcultures.

---

190 The symbolism of interwoven stars can be found in Hermeticism and Aleister Crowley's Thelema, and finds similarity in Gurdjieff's enneagram. In the Slavic tradition, the depiction of stars in this manner is rare.

Concluding our brief overview of linguistic and semiotic simulacra in Russian pseudo-paganism, let us take note of the imitation of archaic forms and the quasi-sacred interpretations of words, syllables, and letters of the alphabet. Structurally, these forms are absolutely modern and privative. This imitation of ancient pagan equipolence - although we presume to doubt that such pseudo-linguists are acquainted with or understand Kolesov's concepts - remains on the level of superficial, flat, simulating phantasmagory. In fact, the pseudo-pagan approach to language fully fits into the Postmodern drive to reject any norms, rules, structures, and order. Pseudo-pagan pseudo-linguistics commit upon language, including the language of symbols, the operations which pop into their head without any pursuit of checking authenticity and competence.

One extension of the practice of "alternative linguistics" is the Ynglist calendar, presented in the second volume of the *Slavo-Aryan Vedas*, which is called the *Krugolet* ("Circle-Year") or the Calendar of the Koliada of Offerings. The Krugolet is under the patronage of the invented Ynglist God Chislobog, who holds a shield in his right hand on which is depicted the "Da'Aryan" calendric circle. This calendar-circle has the Star of Ynglia in the center, around which circle the first nine "houses" with kh'Aryan runes and names, surrounded by the external wheel removed a few degrees relative to the inner one consisting of 16 "houses" and their names. Taken together, the Krugolet is similar to the Chinese Ganzhi calendar system, which combines decimal and duodecimal numerations. The Ynglist calendar system is based on 16 "greater houses/years" as the sum of nine (the number of points of the Star of Ynglia and "lesser houses/months") and seven - one of the sacred numbers of Judaism referring to the seven days of creation. Also adjoined to the Krugolet are Yao trigrams (in "four-line" form) borrowed from Chinese philosophy. The Ynglist calendar is based on the Gregorian, modified by the 16-system. Instead of a leap year of 366 days, however, Ynglists introduce a "Sacred Summer" of 369 days once every sixteen years. The accumulated difference plus one day for each four years is summated and reset once every 16 years in the amount of four additional days to the year. In this system, the number of days in a month is increased.

Despite the anti-Judaism embedded in Khinevich's theory of the origins of peoples, Ynglism nevertheless borrows much from the tradition of the Jews and Kabbalah. For instance, the names of several "Slavo-Aryan" months are directly taken from the letters of the Jewish alphabet used in Hebrew and Yiddish. While January is bestowed the name of the supreme RA-M-Khat, at least five other months are named after Hebrew letters with slightly modified endings for the sake of word formation: *"Ailet'"* from *Alef* (א), *"Beilet'"* from *Bet* (ב), *"Dailet'"* from *Dalet* (ד), *"Tailet"* from *Tav* (ת), and *"Kheilet'"* from *He* (ה). The ninth day of the week in Ynglism is called *nedelia* ("doing nothing"), copied from the Jewish Sabbath on which many activities are forbidden. In Ynglist ritual practice, priority is given to the dates of holidays that arose during the era of dual-faith. The Summer Solstice (Kupala) is thus celebrated not on the astronomical solstice of 21-22 June, but on the day of John the Baptist, 7 July. The Ynglist calendar includes other dual-faith dates of the veneration of Orthodox saints who partially took over the functions of the pagan Gods of the Slavs, and Ynglists observe a number of periods of fasting close to those of Orthodoxy. Compared to Wicca, Ynglism's calendric representations are even further removed from the paradigm of the Celtic Cross. Thus, we can see in Ynglism an ever greater mixing of an increasingly large number of traditions with a dominant bias for the calendric customs of China, to which the Gregorian calendar and dating of dual-faith-era holidays are adjusted and blended with the influence of Jewish Kabbalah.

To summarize this brief overview of the pseudo-Slavic simulacrum of Ynglism, it can be concluded that Ynglism presents a fairly developed and convincing system, which has ensured it a lengthy existence and large number of followers. Ynglism is, in its own right, the matrix and canon of errors and delusions besetting Russian paganism. Moreover, a broad circle of pseudo-pagan authors and independent communities are oriented towards Ynglism and its ideas even without recognizing the hierarchical authority of Khinevich. This is a glaring manifestation of the rhizomatic principle which we have already encountered in the network of Wiccan covens and solitary Wiccans. In the case of Ynglism, the "solitary" role is also occupied by individuals and local communities.

Ynglism's comprehensive coverage of topics, wordplay, and its aggressive PR campaigns in virtual space have attracted the attention of seekers of the Spiritual Path within the Slavic tradition as well as Russian adepts of the Hindu traditions (Vaishnavas, Shaivites, Vedantists), thus forging the illusion of uniformity and oneness between the Hindu tradition and pseudo-Slavic paganism. By playing with the words "Vedas", "Vedic", and "Russian Vedic culture", along with other terms borrowed from Hinduism, pseudo-pagans generate an image of confidence reinforcing the authenticity of both their own simulacrum and those adepts of other traditions' persuasion as to the correctness of their own ephemeral constructions and borrowed phrases. The most active convergence is that between Russian pseudo-pagans and Russian neo-Hinduists, a mergence which is conditioned by their liberal and syncretic approach to post-religions and ritual practice. The significance of the term *Indoslavie* (a play on words meaning "Indo-glorifying" and connoting "Indo-Slavic") sometimes applied to Russian pseudo-paganism is thus revealed in new light. It is also important to note the feature, characteristic of Ynglism and other simulacra, of considering all other traditions as degenerate derivatives of the ancient faith of Ynglia and seeing any transition from Ynglism to other traditions as betrayal of the Slavo-Aryan race and faith. In this lies the essence of the sectarian dimension of Khinevich and his coauthors' doctrine. People aspiring to revive ancient traditions in an initiatic spirit do not need or demand totalitarian subordination to a person nor the establishment of dogmatism. One of the functions of the priest is to connect man and society (the community) with the Sacred and, if needed, to help students and those suffering with this. In sects, the place of the Sacred and the Gods is taken by the personality of the founding guru, in Ynglism by Khinevich in the image of Pater Dii. Demanding devotion not to one's own Divine Nature and to the Due (to *Lad* and Wyrd), but to the leader of a sect is a manifestation of modern privative thinking. At the present stage in Russia, both the church and doctrine of Ynglism are recognized as extremist, and Khinevich, Trekhlebov, and a number of their followers have been facing legal prosecution. The details of their criminal prosecution under political articles points to the pronounced political component of this doctrine and its functional dimension's likeness to the perception of tradition of the political type of pagan. We will find a similar vector in a number of other pseudo-pagan doctrines and organizations introduced below.

For its part, the Native Faith community has been actively working to dispel such pseudo-pagan "myths." In 2009, the Circle of Pagan Tradition and the Union of Slavic Communities of the Slavic Native Faith published an official statement, "On the Substitution of Notions in the Language and History of the Slavs and Pseudo-Paganism", which condemned the provocative and subversive activities of Ynglists. In 2010, this statement was supported by the Ukrainian Great Fire movement as well as by members of the Veles Circle and numerous independent communities across Russia. Such pseudo-paganism was also criticized by Dobroslav.

Unfortunately, however, in soft form Ynglist ideas continue to infiltrate the people. Academic scholars of religion and sociologists have also failed to distinguish between restored ancient traditions and such pseudo-pagan simulacra despite the numerous appeals of the former against the latter and this approach. This once again confirms the profane character of science on questions of tradition, as well as the incompetence and inconsistency of scholars with regards to their own criteria of objectivity.

Insofar as a comprehensive examination of all the aspects and manifestations of pseudo-paganism would claim an independent, voluminous work of its own, in conclusion we present only a short list of some of the most colorful personalities who further illustrate the neo-pagan simulacrum:

- Sergey Strizhak - the author of the series of films, "Games of the Gods", dedicated to Ynglist teachings;
- Nikolai Levashov (1961-2012) - psychic, healer, and writer who speculated on Russian tradition and history with the mythologies of Ron Hubbard and Khinevich;
- Vladimir Goliakov, a.k.a. Bogomil II Goliak - leader of the pseudo-pagan sect Skhoron ezh Slaven ("Togetherness of all Slavs") in Saint Petersburg. According to Goliakov's own claims, which have never been confirmed, he is the hereditary (second) high priest of all Slavs. Goliak's works fall in the line of Ynglism.
- Konstantin Petrov (1945-2009) - ideologue and head of the "Course of Truth and Unity" political party whose ideological doctrine is that of conspiracy theory based on New Age teachings adjoined with popular esoteric tropes. Shortly before his death, Petrov began to preach his own version of neo-paganism structurally similar to Ynglism.
- Lev Silenko, who founded the Native Ukrainian National Faith (RUN-Vera) in the United States in 1966. Silenko's ideas are largely similar to Ynglism, in particular his inflation of the antiquity of Ukrainian history and presentation of Ukrainians as the Aryan fathers of global spirituality. In line with the artificial construction of religion as the basis of a new national identity, RUN-Vera is emphatically Russophobic, and its headquarters' location in the United States speaks to the political nature of this simulacrum. Silenko himself has the status of "prophet" in RUN-Vera.

- Vladimir Megre - former businessman turned author of the book series "The Ringing Cedars of Russia" and ideologist of the movement of the same name, which sets forth an alternative history of the Slavs as the "Ved-Rus" ancestors of Asians, Europeans, Russians, and Americans. The ancestors of the Russians are said to have wielded supernatural abilities and to have been highly developed in deep antiquity. Overall, the structure of Megre's doctrine repeats the general patterns of New Age. Megre has named the source of his ideas to be Anastasia, a female nature spirit whom he met in the Siberian Taiga. There are no historical, authentic mentions of such a spirit or deity among the Slavs or the indigenous peoples of the region, nor are there any other confirmations of her existence by other encounters. The principal novelty of Megre's teaching lies in its emphasis on universal spirituality and peace as achievable through the creation of a highly-developed (but not high-technological) society of ecological family-clan estates. Such family-clan estates would be plots of land no less than one hectare, passed down by inheritance, on which life could be structured according to the moral commandments of Anastasia and Megre's views on the right form of economic activities. The idea of family-clan estates is in many ways resonant with widespread neo-pagan ideas of building "sacred" cities of the Sun or communal ecovillages. The idea of such settlements was negatively remarked upon by Dobroslav, who pointed to the possibility of easy manipulation and subjection of such villages to governmental authorities aiming to enclose and level the protest potential of paganism. In Dobroslav's opinion, such settlements would be reservations akin to those in which the descendants of the American Indians live. The structure of Megre's movement, known as the "Anastasians", is predominantly of a network character and lacks any hierarchical system. Megre's own doctrine takes a fundamentally anti-priestly position. Across Russia, the Anastasians count several independent associations and settlements, and Megre himself holds several non-commercial foundations, "Anastasia" and "Vladimir", as well as the commercial organization "Megre" which produces merchandise with the symbols of the Anastasian movement. In this case we once again encounter the consumerist and commercial elements, which allow for Megre's doctrine to be characterized as a marketing strategy for the circulation of goods and the shaping of a circle of consumers of its signs.

The classification of sect studies today identifies a sect as combining the principles of network marketing, direct commerce, and a quasi-spiritual ideological mission for a company to generate a situation of sustainable consumption. This approach itself is another expression of the post-religiosity of Postmodernity.

The East and Asia

The space of the East and Asia poses complex difficulty to the isolation and classification of pseudo-traditional doctrines, sects, and organizations for a number of reasons. For one, in Hinduism there is a distinct absence of any negative understanding of the phenomenon of sects, insofar as any separate group of people headed by a guru can represent its own branch of philosophy (darśana) within a tradition and have the right to its views and practice. Hindus are distinguished by a flexibility towards other traditions, a non-conflictual character, and by their unilateral integration (inclusion) of elements of other religions. For Hindus, it is quite normal to see Jesus as an avatar of Krishna, to perform puja in a temple of Shiva or namaz in a mosque, insofar as such fits into the inclusive Logos of Hinduism. For Hindus, other Gods are simply other Gods to whom one can turn among others. This is the realization of the manifestationist view of traditions.

Naturally, this is not observed by creationism and the Abrahamic traditions, which are emphatically exclusive and insist on their exclusivity and intolerance of other cults.

Therefore, the identification of pseudo-pagan currents in Hinduism, and more broadly in Asia, is partly a matter of external analysis, a view from without, whereas the view from within Hinduism will differ. Nevertheless, we can take note of the coincidences between the above-mentioned neo-Hinduism and its manifestations in the West and within India itself, as well as in neighboring countries. The extremely reductionist practices of yoga-gymnastics, emasculated of metaphysics and the Sacred, the Ayurveda medicine so exotic to the West, the reduction of the wisdom of Tantra to "unique" approaches to sexuality, etc., all profanize the diverse and profound doctrines of India. Thus, traveling beyond their historical borders, fragments of traditions can become objects of consumption, signs of happiness and "healthy" lifestyles so important to modern Western society. The fragmentation and conversion of traditional doctrines into simulative signs is a common feature whose thread runs through all negative infiltrations and post-religious constructs.

Above we already mentioned the totalitarian neo-Hindu sect of Swami Prabhupada, the International Society for Krishna Consciousness, which has actively spread throughout the West. As well, there is the populist sect of the neo-Hindu Sathya Sai Baba (1926-2011), whose teachings were maximally simplified, syncretized, and mixed with Abrahamic traditions for assimilation in the West. Sai Baba asserted a unity of all religions and deemed himself to be sacred "for all peoples." Another liberal and reductive version of Hinduism was propagated by Bhagwan Shri Rajneesh, also known as Osho (1931-1990), who achieved formidable commercial and pop-cultural success around the world despite the ban on his organization in many countries and resistance against his teachings in his native India. These figures all became elements of Western pop-culture as merchandise of the sphere of spiritual consumption.

Of further particular interest is the new syncretic religion claiming the status of a global monotheistic religion which emerged in Iran, with its present-day center in Haifa, Israel: Baha'i. Baha'i, from the Arabic *baha*, "light", emerged in the 19th century as a sect within Islam based on Shiism. This current was indebted to the figure of Sayyid Ali Muhammad Shirazi (a.k.a "Báb", 1819-1950), who rejected the laws of the Quran and Sharia in favor of equality and democracy, and to Husayn Ali Nuri (a.k.a Bahá'u'lláh, 1817-1892), the founder of Baha'ism, in which he is believed to be the last incarnation of God following Abraham, Moses, Jesus Christ, Muhammad, Sai Baba and Krishna, Zoroaster, and the Buddha. Baha'ism preaches the unity of all religions and rejects fundamental identities (*ethnos*, nation, class, religion) in favor of pacifism and individual spiritual quest within Baha'i practice. This new religion emphasizes its recognition of scientific knowledge and the necessity of cultivating such through general education. Throughout its history, Baha'ism has been subject to persecution by the traditional Islam of Iran, but has actively spread across the world, currently numbering more than five million followers as well as boasting UN recognition and cooperation. In the case of Baha'ism, we can see the formation of a simulacrum bearing all the signs of post-religiosity, but one founded not on the pagan heritage, but primarily out of a creationist religion (Islam), resulting in a concept of the progressive spiritual development of humanity through a chain of saints and prophets belonging to different peoples, eras, and metaphysics. It can be seen that the Baha'i neo-religion, like other post-religious doctrines and pseudo-pagan simulacra, reproduces the main features of the paradigm of Postmodernity, not sparing play on the pagan heritage and pagan forms.

Post-religions are global. The fragments of various doctrines, cells, and communities can be found even in the most remote corners of the world. In the heart of the modern metropolis, one can find popular yoga centers and courses on Tantric sex just as one can find pilgrim-supporters of the "Slavic-Aryan Vedas" in India, followers of the "Aryan heritage of the North" (à la Serrano) in Indonesia or Brazil, and countless "stray" European Bhaktivedantist-preachers of Vaishnavism, Krishnaism, and various neo-Hinduisms. All of them are merely wandering, straying in the dark of their own and others' illusions.

Compromises

We have defined *polemos* as the nerve of being, as that which according to the myths and teachings of traditions creates and orders the world. War was the beginning of the world (as the *kosmos*), war is its history, and war is its resolution. For Pagan Traditionalism today, war means not simply the confrontation of one army against another for glory or power, but war for itself, war for the sake of the fulfillment of the due, for the affirmation of one's Divine nature, for the Gods, Tradition, and initiation.

Today, the titanic, material element is dominant, is on the attack, and is dissolving the Divine dimension of man and the world into the rhizome. The direct confrontation of Modernity is being replaced by the creeping strategy of Postmodern poisoning. We have given a brief overview of the concepts and strategies of these two paradigms in the preceding chapters.

War cannot be ended simply by refusing to consider it the father of all things and the nerve of history. In war one can win, fall in battle, become a hero, a saint, a traitor, a renegade, or a fugitive. War will end only with the end of the world itself. The end of war will be the Mahapralaya, the Great Dissolution, the incineration of the world by Surtr in Ragnarök. It is this attitude, relation, and approach towards the modern world that constitutes the defining marker of a Traditionalist, a pagan, and of doctrines and communities.

Every tradition configures the borders and forms of war in its own way. In Iranian Zoroastrianism, the two elements expressed in the figure of the God of Light, Ahura Mazda (Ormuzd) and the personification of evil, Ahriman (Angra

Mainyu), are equipolent. Their battle constitutes the foundation of existence for the Zoroastrian, who embodies such in their righteous life. Out of the pair of Ormuzd and Ahriman, neither can possibly nor should be removed, for such would destroy the whole structure of Zoroastrianism and its cosmos. The order of Ormuzd is defined by its opposition to that of Ahriman, and Ahriman is always on the attack against Ahura Mazda. This is an eternal battle between two equal elements which define themselves against one another. He who wreaks evil, excess, and outrage embodies the element of Angra Mainyu; he who purifies himself and observes the established order comes near to Ahura Mazda.

In the Indian Vedanta we can see a different configuration from that of Zoroastrianism. Here the heights are occupied by the numerous Devas who govern the world and its aspects. Against the Devas stand the Asuras, with their armies of Rakshasas and demons. Everyone - people, the Asuras, and the Devas - is subordinate to the singular laws of the cosmos and employs their own spiritual and ritual practices. Sometimes, through long periods (which, in human standards, would be eternal) of ascesis, *sādhanā*, and yoga, the Asuras gain blessings and *siddhi* from Brahma, only to channel their acquired capabilities, power, and authority towards violence, enslaving people and even the Gods, as a result of which the Gods not uncommonly find themselves in a stalemate, the way out of which is found in the aid of the heroes of the wrathful hypostases of the Goddess Kali-Durga, Shiva, and Krishna. Such is the nature of the Asuras and Rakshasas - they do not follow the precepts of the Vedanta, the path of liberation from samsara, fully formulated in the conversation between Krishna and Prince Arjuna in the Bhagavad-Gita as renouncing (converting all actions into sacrifices) the fruits of their efforts (*sādhanā*) and acquiring the highest fruit of all - liberation. The Asuras obtain the fruits of their ascesis only for their consciousness to be carried away by them, by their new capabilities, authority, power, and invulnerability. That which for the ascetic and yogi is merely an instrument and at once a temptation of the Gods to stray from the Path, is for the Asuras the desired end-goal which captures them and leads them off the Path of Liberation. We encounter this story in the Chandogya Upanishad, in Virocana's delusion as to the nature of Atman, as well as in the wide cycle of myths of the Goddesses Kali and Durga. Thus, we can see the complicated pattern of the battles between the Asuras and the Devas in Hinduism. The doctrine of Liberation is available to the demons, but they are incapable of following it without being deceived by *siddhi* and material blessings, which spells disaster for people and the Gods.

We also encounter complex conflictual relations between the titans and Gods in Odinism, in which the Aesir and the Vanir oppose the Thursar, the army of *draugar/aptrgangar* and the monstrous spawn of Loki. To the Thursar the Aesir owe the walls of Asgard and the horse Sleipnir (with Loki's participation), and in the quest for wisdom Odin visits the giant Vafþrúðnir. Yet the conflict between the Aesir and the jotuns, between the Aesir and Loki, whose figure is just as complex and contradictory as that of Prometheus, leads to the eschatological battle of Iðavöll.

We have also spoken of the Hellenic Titanomachy, the central topic of many ancient poets. In the 20th century, attention was drawn to Titanism by Ernst and Friedrich Jünger, the latter of whom saw that the titans rule wherever there are no Gods, that the noise of machines and hammers is pleasant to the titanic element, and that the primal element of technology should be sought in the nature of the titans.

As in antiquity, so now are there metaphysical powers and people who have chosen their sides in this conflict, thereby fulfilling Dharma or *adharma*. Those who have chosen the side of the Divine and the Sacred are those Traditionalists and Pagans to whom has been revealed the whole existential terror of the field of battle in whose very heart they find themselves. This terror reveals the value and essence of the Sacred, the Sacred Terror of the first awakening.

In such a situation, opposing the surrounding degradation, striving towards purification, and aspiring towards the ancient and Eternal Gods is the truest and inevitable conclusion. Adequate pagan communities are all, in one way or another, dissatisfied with the world, with globalization, and are waging their struggle in different forms. We can liken the majority of them to soft Traditionalism, to soft power which effects change in people and their immediate surrounding environment. Such paganism finds itself surrounded by the enemy and compelled to partial compromises with the enveloping reality and its laws, forms, and order. Here might occur the partial re-coding, reinterpretation, and re-enchantment of the world of Modernity in favor of Tradition. As we have said in the preceding, Tradition is the transmission of Fire, not the preservation of ashes. Modernity itself did not appear in a vacuum out of nowhere. Therefore, by cleansing intellectual infiltrations, some of the achievements of the modern era can be accurately, carefully adopted, or rather can be temporarily, begrudgingly used. Here we can recall Klyuev's poem on the procedure for expelling the English spirit from the cloth by saturating it with the native Russian spirit. Such procedures, relations, and approaches towards all of the surrounding reality should become the norm for paganism.

For Pagan Traditionalism in such a situation, the purification and preservation of tradition and the transmission of initiation are important tasks. Such means maintaining the heat of *polemos* even in the absence of the possibility of real actions, maintaining faithfulness to the Gods in any situation. The brightest example of this existential intensity and uncompromising *fides* is that of Baron Julius Evola.

Those pagans who choose the side of the Titans, Asuras, and Jotuns are actively and willingly compromising with the surrounding world. They pointedly like the material world of consumption, such does not cause them sufficient discomfort and conflict in consciousness with regard to the line of fidelity to the Gods and the falsity of the material path of the Asuras.

Alongside materiality, the universalist provisions of Modernity in the scientific, social, and political spheres, and following them the rhizomatic positions of Postmodernity, are acceptable, as is lucidly expressed in the phenomenon of "tolerance", the infiltration of which comes through "subculturality", individualism, individual syncretism in theory and practice in religion (e.g., Wicca, Ynglism), and material and scientific-technological orientations. This titanic paganism generates numerous chimeras expressed in patron Gods of the Internet and technology and in the mixing of scientific and traditional doctrines which we encounter in severe infiltrations of adequate paganism (e.g. Velimir, Varg) as well as in the ubiquitous features of the post-religious simulacrum.

We can consider pseudo-pagans to be simply pagans who have chosen the Titans and the chthonic element instead of the Gods and the Sacred, secular modern society instead of Sacred order. We can encounter a very interesting remark on this choice in the Indian *darśanas* of Advaita (e.g., Kashmiri Shivaism, Tantra, and others), which argue that man's ignorance (*avidya*) of his Divine Nature plunges him into the wheel of samsara and karma, and that the ignorant man is completely bound by the laws of cause and effect. In other words, he who steps onto the initiatic path towards the Sacred gradually liberates himself from the shackles of materiality, samsara, and karma, i.e., from the ties of cause and effect. Meanwhile, the law of causal determinism as maximally formulated in the language of mathematics and logic is the basis and blood of the scientific approach of Modernity built on the denial of the Sacred (*adharma*).

For example, in Tradition flight is no unattainable problem for man. Man can take off and fly just as he might simply walk or steal the feathers of birds and angels. The ease and lightness of this "impossibility" is substantiated by the fact that all of the cosmos and Nature is permeated with the rays of the Sacred, which makes the world "lighter" or "easier" for metamorphosis, in which man is "light." For the man of Modernity, flight is the result of a long process of development, of the progressive chain of discoveries of the laws of physics, technological solutions, the combination of trials and errors, new studies, discovered materials and, finally, man can take off in an aircraft which exists within the strict framework of the laws of physics. Man's flight in Modernity is determined by scientific achievements, without which he never tears himself off the surface of the Earth, but even with which he is enclosed in a material apparatus subject to material laws. The flight of Modernity and the flight of Tradition are, in the end, completely different flights - one purely physical, the other magical. A vivid example of the difference between these approaches is the legend of Icarus and the artificial wings he created. The latter allowed Icarus and his father to fly, that is, to fulfill the task for which they were created. But Icarus wanted to ascend on them to the Sun (to the Sacred and the Gods). He died, scorched by its rays. Ascent to the High is impossible by material, technological means. Icarus' wings were artificial, and he fell from his daring takeoff. But he who spreads the wings of the Spirit can fly freely with the Gods. In this lies the difference between the myths of the Gods and the myths of the Titans, between the Sacred and material languages and pictures of the world.

Today, the most consistent adepts of the "tradition" of the Titans are those typical, everyday inhabitants of the world of matter and consumption, those most ordinary, godless people mired in the flows of signs, semiurgy, consumption, and representations, the Promethean humanity of broken shards of clay. Their "priesthood" is that of idols on TV screens, the "stars" of virtuality, and genius marketers and scientists granting ever newer gadgets, brands, fashion trends, and signs. The semiurgy of Postmodernity is the black magic of the Titans. It is black and absolutely flat.

In the spatial-state dimension, Titanism is maximally concentrated in the West, in the US and Europe, where it has attained its peak and triumph, spreading thereout to the whole world. But geographical criteria should not be used alone as orientations and a frontline. Modernity, while concentrated within and on the attack in the face of Western countries, is not limited to them. The West is always the present Modernity, but the present Modernity is broader than the West. Wherever state, political, cultural, and media elites are of a Eurocentric upbringing and education, the substance of Modernity is to be found hidden under external, cultural, national forms. The modern West's attacks on Russia and the countries of the East and Asia can be seen as the continuation of the principle underlying the confrontation between the US and the USSR: the already fully Postmodern West is attacking the still Modern, in some places still traditional East and Asia. The more titanic, material, and hypochthonic is attacking and smashing up against the less titanic and insufficiently chthonic.

Thus, it can be said that in its maxim the modern world is not located in the West, in shopping and business centers, in the White Houses or on the squares which everyone so badly wants to seize and destroy. The modern world is not located on the Internet or on stock exchanges, nor is it to be found in the offices of the UN. The heart of the modern world is in only one place - in the Mind, in Man's Thinking. Such is his anthropology, in which there is equal possibility and opportunity for turning to the Gods as well as turning to the Titans. The latter turn has created the familiar, everyday world which we know, the "real and natural" world in which Modernity and Postmodernity are everywhere - the heartless world.

Therefore, the first and most important task which we must fulfill is to change our thinking. We must not simply declare commitment to Tradition, but make Tradition our Heart and Mind. This is the most fundamental change, without which no external acts will live up to be fully authentic and effective.

Heraclitus bequeathed to us: "War is the father of all." The nerve and main struggle of this war is in our Hearts and Minds.

***

EPILOGUE

In the first volume of our work, *Polemos: The Dawn of Pagan Traditionalism*, we have examined the main structures of the pagan worldview of manifestationism. In the second volume, *Polemos: Pagan Perspectives*, we continue our account by turning to a more detailed consideration of the interrelations and interpenetrations between paganism and Abrahamism, and manifestationism and creationism in general, analyzing the dichotomies of paganism and Judaism, paganism and Christianity, and paganism and Islam.

Also taken under examination in the second volume is the question of the place and role of sexuality and Eros in paganism, ranging from antiquity to contemporary paganism. Phenomena of sexual deviations in Modernity, the degree of their infiltration of paganism, as well as the extent of the influence of Abrahamic morality on the emergence of various taboos in contemporary paganism are subject to analysis.

Further, a large section of the second volume is dedicated to the political dimensions of paganism, from ancient paradigms to the modern, profane political ideologies of liberalism, communism/socialism, and the spectrum of right-wing ideas. The strategies of political non-participation, apoliteia, and questions of ethnocentrism in pagan philosophy will be duly inspected.

In the concluding part of the second volume, we examine in detail two paths for contemporary paganism: the fatal Dharma of the Hero, known as the Right-Hand Path, and the transgressive Dharma of non-conformism within Tradition, also known as the Left-Hand Path.

Taken together, the two volumes of *Polemos* constitute a single, whole account unifying the common semantic chain and vector of the study of contemporary paganism, its perspectives and prospects in the Postmodern era.

***

BIBLIOGRAPHY

Andrén, Anders, Kristina Jennbert, and Catharina Raudvere (eds.). *Old Norse Religions in Long-Term Perspectives: Origins, Changes, and Interactions*. Lund: Nordic Academic Press, 2006.

Anonymous. *Doktrina Radikaln'nogo Primitivizma* [*The Doctrine of Radical Primitivism*]. 2014.

Arnold, Jafe. "Mysteries of Eurasia: The Esoteric Sources of Alexander Dugin and the Yuzhinsky Circle." University of Amsterdam/Centre for History of Hermetic Philosophy and Related Currents, 2019.

Asatru Folk Assembly. "Declaration of Purpose." Runestone, 1994/2018.

Balushok, V.G. "*Initsiatsii drevnerusskikh druzhinnikov*" [The Initiations of Old Russian Warriors]. *Etnograficheskoe obozrenie* [*Ethnographic Review*] 1, 1993.

_____ "*Initsiatsii drevnikh slavian*" [The Initiations of the Ancient Slavs]. *Etnograficheskoe obozrenie* [*Ethnographic Review*] 4, 1995.

Banzarov, Dorji. "The Black Faith, or Shamanism among the Mongols". Translated by J. Nattier and J.R. Krueger. *Mongolian Studies* 7, 1981.

Bataille, Georges. *Literature and Evil*. Translated by Alastair Hamilton. New York: Penguin: 2012.

Baudrillard, Jean. *America*. London: Verso, 2010.

_____*The Consumer Society: Myths and Structures*. London: SAGE Publications, 1998.

_____*The System of Objects*. Translated by James Benedict. London: Verso, 2006.

_____*The Transparency of Evil: Essays on Extreme Phenomena*. Translated by James Benedict. London: Verso, 2009.

Benoist, Alain de. *On Being a Pagan*. Translated by Jon Graham. North Augusta: Arcana Europa, 2018.

——————— *Vpered, k prekrashcheniu rosta! Ekologo-filosofskii traktat* [*Forward, to the End of Growth! An Ecologico-Philosophical Treatise*]. Moscow: Institute of Humanities, 2012.

Beskov, Andrey. *Vostochnoslavianskoe iazychestvo: religiovedcheskii analiz* [*East-Slavic Paganism: A Religious-Studies Analysis*]. Lambert Academic Publishing, 2010.

Burnakov, V.A. "Erlik-khan v traditsionnom mirovozzrenii khakasov" [Erlik Khan in the Traditional Worldview of the Khakas People]. *The Archeology, Ethnography, and Anthropology of Eurasia* 1:45, 2011.

Chudinov, Sergey. *Traditsiia i istoricheskoe mirovospriiatie v fenomenologicheskom mire neoiazychestva* [*Tradition and Historical World-Perception in the Phenomenological World of Neopaganism*]. Novosibirsk: Novosibirsk State Architectural University, 2014.

Cleary, Collin. *Summoning the Gods: Essays on Paganism in a God-Forsaken World*. San Francisco: Counter Currents, 2011.

——————— "What is Odinism?". *Tyr: Myth, Culture, Tradition* 4. Ultra, 2014-2015.

Cleary, Thomas (ed.). *Zen Antics: 100 Stories of Enlightenment*. Boston: Shambhala, 2014.

——————— *Zen Essence: The Science of Freedom*. Boston: Shambhala, 2000.

Coburn, Thomas B. *Encountering the Goddess: A Translation of the Devi-Mahatmya and a Study of its Interpretation*. New York: State University of New York Press, 1991.

Cologne, Daniel. *Julius Evola, René Guénon y el Cristianismo*. Titania: 2008.

Coughlin, John J. *Out of the Shadows: An Exploration of Dark Paganism and Magick*. Cold Spring: Waning Moon, 2016.

Danielou, Alain. *Gods of Love and Ecstasy: The Traditions of Shiva and Dionysus*. Rochester: Inner Traditions, 1992.

_____*Shiva and the Primordial Tradition: From the Tantras to the Science of Dreams*. Translated by Jean-Louis Gabin. Rochester: Inner Traditions, 2007.

Debord, Guy. *Society of the Spectacle*. Translated by Ken Knabb. London: Rebel/Aldgate Press, 1983.

Deleuze, Gilles and Felix Guattari, *Anti-Oedipus: Capitalism and Schizophrenia*. Translated by Mark Lester. Minneapolis: University of Minnesota Press, 1983.

Deleuze, Gilles. *The Logic of Sense*. Translated by Mark Lester and Charles Stivale. New York: Columbia University Press, 1990.

Dmitrieva, Viktoria. (ed.). *Kashmirskii shivaizm. Naslazhdenie i osvobozhdenie* [Kashmiri Shivaism: Pleasure and Liberation]. Moscow: Ganga, 2010.

Dowden, Ken. *European Paganism: The Realities of Cult from Antiquity to the Middle Ages*. New York: Routledge, 2000.

Dugin, Alexander. *Absoliutnaia Rodina: Puti Absoliuta, Metafizika Blagoi Vesti, Misterii Evrazii* [Absolute Homeland: The Ways of the Absolute, The Metaphysics of the Gospel, Mysteries of Eurasia]. Moscow: Arktogeia, 1999.

_____"Counter-Initiation: Critical Remarks on Some Aspects of the Doctrine of René Guénon (1998)". Translated by Jafe Arnold. *Eurasianist Internet Archive*, 11 June 2019.

_____(ed.). *Elementy* [Elements] Nos. 1-9, 1992-1998.

_____*Ethnos and Society*. London: Arktos, 2018.

_____*Etnosotsiologiia* [Ethnosociology]. Moscow: Academic Project, 2011.

_____*Ethnosociology: The Foundations*. London: Arktos, 2019.

_____*Filosofiia politiki* [*The Philosophy of Politics*]. Moscow: Arktogeia, 2004.

_____*Konspirologiia* [*Conspirology*]. Moscow: Eurasia, 2005.

_____(ed.). *Milyi Angel* [*Sweet Angel*] Nos. 1-3, 1991-1998.

_____*Noomakhia: Voyny uma. Angliia ili Britaniia? Morskaia missiia i pozitivny sub'ekt* [*Noomakhia – Wars of the Mind: England or Britain? The Maritime Mission and the Positive Subject*]. Moscow: Academic Project, 2015. [English-language previews and excerpts of all the Noomakhia volumes can be found at Eurasianist Internet Archive].

_____ *Noomakhia: Voyny uma. Germanskii Logos. Chelovek apofaticheskii* [*Noomakhia - The Germanic Logos: Apophatic Man*]. Moscow: Academic Project, 2015.

_____ *Noomakhia: Voyny uma. Latinskii Logos. Solntse i Krest* [*Noomakhia - The Latin Logos*]. Moscow: Academic Project, 2016.

_____ *Noomakhia: Voyny uma. Logos Evropy: sredizemnomorskaia tsivilizatsiia vo vremeni i prostranstve* [*Noomakhia - The Logos of Europe: Mediterranean Civilization in Time and Space*]. Moscow: Academic Project, 2014.

_____ *Noomakhia: Voyny uma. Po tu storonu Zapada: Kitay, Iaponiia, Afrika, Okeaniia* [*Noomakhia - Beyond the West: China, Japan, Africa, and Oceania*]. Moscow: Academic Project, 2014.

_____ *Noomakhia: Voyny uma. Po tu storonu Zapada: Indoevropeiskie tzivilizatsii - Iran, Indiia* [*Noomakhia: Beyond the West: The Indo-European Civilizations - Iran and India*]. Moscow: Academic Project, 2014.

_____ *Noomakhia: Voyny uma. Tri logosa: Apollon, Dionis, Kibela* [*Noomakhia - The Three Logoi: Apollo, Dionysus, and Cybele*]. Moscow: Academic Project, 2014.

_____Noomakhia: Voyny uma. Frantsuskii Logos: Orfei i Meliuzina [Noomakhia - The French Logos: Orpheus and Melusine]. Moscow: Academic Project, 2015.

_____Noomakhia: Voyny uma. Tsivilizatsii granits: Rossiia, amerikanskaia tsivilizatsiia, semity i Sikh tsivilizatsii, arabskii Logos, turanskii Logos [Noomakhia - Border Civilizations: Russia, American Civilization, the Semites and their Civilization, the Arab Logos, and the Turanian Logos]. Moscow: Academic Project, 2014.

_____ Postfilosofiia. Tri paradigmy v istorii mysli [Post-Philosophy: Three Paradigms in the History of Thought]. Moscow: Eurasian Movement, 2009.

_____ Radikalnyi Sub'ekt i ego Dubl' [The Radical Subject and its Double]. Moscow: Eurasian Movement, 2009.

_____ Sotsiologiia russkogo obshchestva. Rossiia mezhdu Khaosom i Logosom [The Sociology of Russian Society: Between Chaos and Logos]. Moscow: Academic Project, 2011.

_____ V poiskakh temnogo Logosa (filososko-bogoslovskie ocherki) [In Search of the Dark Logos: Philosophico-Theological Outlines]. Moscow: Academic Project, 2013.

_____ Znaki Velikogo Norda. Giperboreiskaia teoriia [Signs of the Great North: The Hyperborean Theory]. Moscow: Veche, 2005.

Dumézil, Georges. Verkhovnye bogi indoevropeitsev [The High Gods of the Indo-Europeans]. Moscow: Nauka, 1986.

_____Gods of the Ancient Northmen. Los Angeles: University of California Press/Center for the Study of Comparative Folklore and Mythology, 1973.

Dvorkin, A.K. Sektovedenie: Totalitarian Sects. Opyt sistematicheskogo issledovaniia [The Study of Sects: Totalitarian Sects, the Experience of Systematic Study]. Moscow: Christian Library, 2007.

Dzermant, Alexey. "Traditsionnaia etnicheskaia religiia v Belarusi" [Traditional Ethnic Religion in Belarus]. *Against the Post-Modern World*, 2011.

Dzhemal, Geydar. *Orientatsiia-Sever* [Orientation: North]. Novosibirsk: Svarte Aske, 2013 (1979).

_____*Revoliutsiia prorokov* [*The Revolution of the Prophets*]. 2003. Moscow: Ultra Kultura, 2003.

Eliade, Mircea. *A History of Religious Ideas, Volume I: From the Stone Age to the Eleusinian Mysteries*. Translated by Williard Trask. Chicago: University of Chicago Press, 1978.

_____*A History of Religious Ideas, Volume II: From Gautama Buddha to the Triumph of Christianity*. Translated by Williard Trask. Chicago: University of Chicago Press, 1982.

_____*A History of Religious Ideas, Volume III: From Muhammad to the Age of Reforms*. Translated by Williard Trask. Chicago: University of Chicago Press, 1985.

_____*Mephistopheles and the Androgyne: Studies in Religious Myth and Symbol*. Translated by J.M. Cohen. New York: Sheed and Ward, 1965.

_____ *Myth and Reality*. Translated by Willard Trask. Long Grove: Waveland, 1998).

_____*The Sacred and the Profane: The Nature of Religion*. Translated by Williard Trask. New York: Harvest, 1959.

Ellis, Hilda Roderick. *The Road to Hel. A Study of the Conception of the Dead in Old Norse Literature*. New York: Greenwood, 1968.

Engels, Friedrich. *The Origins of the Family, Private Property, and the State*. Marxists Internet Archive,1884/2000.

Evola, Julius. "Against the Neo-Pagans: The Misunderstandings of the New 'Paganism'". *Counter-Currents*, 4/11/2011.

_____"Dionysus and the Left-Hand Path." Translated by G.A. Malvicini. *Counter-Currents*, 23/3/2016.

_____*Eros and the Mysteries of Love: The Metaphysics of Sex*. Rochester: Inner Traditions, 1991.

_____*Fascism Viewed from the Right*. Translated by E. Christian Kopff. London: Arktos, 2013.

_____*The Hermetic Tradition: Symbols and Teachings of the Royal Art*. Translated by E.E. Rehmus. Rochester: Inner Traditions International, 1995.

_____"The Limits of Initiatory Regularity." *Hercolano* 2 English Library, 2005/2010.

_____*Men Among the Ruins: Postwar Reflections of a Radical Traditionalist*. Translated by Guido Stucco. Vermont: Inner Traditions, 2002.

_____"Orientations." Translated by Cologero Salvo. *Gornahoor*, 29/7/2012. [https://www.gornahoor.net/?p=4541].

_____*Pagan Imperialism*. Translated by Cologero Salvo. Gornahoor Press, 2017.

_____*Revolt Against the Modern World*. Translated by Guido Stucco. Vermont: Inner Traditions International, 1995.

_____*Ride the Tiger: A Survival Manual for Aristocrats of the Soul*. Translated by Joscelyn Godwin and Constance Fontana. Rochester: Inner Traditions, 2003.

_____"On the Secret of Degeneration". *Deutsches Volkstum* 11, 1938.

_____*Rabochii v tvorchestve Ernsta Jüngera* [*The Worker in the Thought of Ernst Jünger*]. Saint Petersburg: Nauka, 2005.

Evola, Julius, Frithjof Schuon, and René Guénon. *Kasty i rasy* [*Castes and Races*]. Tambov: Ex Nord Lux, 2010.

Filatov, Sergey (ed.). *Religiia i obshchestvo: Ocherki religioznoi zhizni sovermennoi Rossii* [*Religion and Society: Outlines of the Religious Life of Contemporary Russia*]. Saint Petersburg: Letniy Sad, 2002.

Findell, Martin. *Runes*. The British Museum, 2014.

Flowers, Stephen. *Black Rûna - Being the Shorter Works of Stephen Edred Flowers: Produced for the Order of the Trapezoid of the Temple of Set* (1985-1989). Rûna-Raven Press, 1995.

_____*Blue Rûna: Edred's Shorter Works* Vol. III (1988-1994), Rûna-Raven Press/Lodestar, 2001/2017.

_____*Green Rûna - The Runemaster's Notebook: Shorter Works of Edred Thorsson*, Volume I (1978-1985). Rûna-Raven Press, 1993.

_____*Red Rûna: Shorter Works* Vol. IV (1987-2001). Rûna-Raven Press, 2001.

Fukuyama, Francis. *The End of History and the Last Man*. New York: Penguin, 1992.

_____*Our Posthuman Future: Consequences of the Biotechnology Revolution*. London: Profile Books, 2002.

Gabarev, Murat. "Iazycheskie prazdniki osetin" [The Pagan Holidays of the Ossetians]. *Vestnik Kavkaza*, 28/6/2009.

Gal'kovsky, N.M. *Bor'ba khristianstva s ostatkami iazychestva v drevnei Rusi* [*Christianity's Struggle with the Remnants of Paganism in Old Rus*], 2 volumes. Moscow/Kharkov: Printer of A.I. Snegirevaia/Eparchy Typograph, 1913/1916.

Gasanov, B.A (Volkhv Bogumil). *Osnovy sovremennogo koliadovaniia* [*The Foundations of Modern Koliada*]. Moscow: Veligor, 2013.

Gavrilov, D.A. and A.E. *Nagovitsyn. Bogi slavian. Iazychestvo. Traditsia* [*The Gods of the Slavs, Paganism, and Tradition*]. Moscow: Refl-Buk, 2002.

Gavrilov, D.A. Trikster. *Litsedei v evroaziatskom fol'klore* [*Trickster: The Pretender in Eurasian Folklore*]. Moscow: Socio-Political Thought, 2006.

Gaydukov, Alexey. *Ideologiia i praktika slavianskogo neoiazychestva* [*The Ideology and Practice of Slavic Neopaganism*]. Saint Petersburg: Herzen State Pedagogical University of Russia, 2000.

Girard, René. *Violence and the Sacred*. Translated by Patrick Gregory. Baltimore: John Hopkins University Press, 1977.

Glinka, G.A. "Drevniaia religiia slavian" [*The Ancient Religion of the Slavs*]. 1804.

Golovin, Evgeny (ed). *Bezumie i ego bog* [*Madness and its God*]. Moscow: Enneagon, 2007.

_____"Dionis-2" ["Dionysus 2"]. Moscow: New University, 2005.

_____"Era ginekokratii" [The Era of Gynecocracy]. *Elementy* 6, 1996.

Graichen, Gisela. *Die neuen Hexen. Gespräche mit Hexen* [*The New Witches: Conversations with Witches*]. Munich: Goldmann, 1999.

Grimsson, Wulf. *Loki and Odin: Rites of Initiation and Sorcery*. Australia: Loki's Mannerbund, 2011.

_____*Loki's Way: Essays and Musings*. Australia: Loki's Mannerbund, 2011.

_____*Male Mysteries and the Secret of the Mannerbund*. Australia: Loki's Mannerbund, 2011.

_____*The Mind of a Sorcerer*. Australia: Loki's Mannerbund, 2012.

Gromov, D.V. and A.A. Bychkov. *Slavianskaia runicheskaia pis'mennost': fakty i domysly* [*Slavic Runic Writing: Facts and Speculations*]. Moscow: Sofia Publishing House, 2005.

Guénon, René. *The Crisis of the Modern World*. Translated by Marco Pallis, Arthur Osborne, and Richard C. Nicholson. Hillsdale, NY: Sophia Perennis, 2004.

_____*Perspectives on Initiation*. Translated by Henry D. Fohr. Ghent: Sophia Perennis, 2004.

_____*The Spiritist Fallacy*. Translated by Alvin Moore, Jr. and Rama. P. Coomaraswamy. Hillsdale: Sophia Perennis, 2004.

_____*The Symbolism of the Cross*. Translated by Angus Macnab. Ghent: Sophia Perennis, 1996.

_____*Theosophy: History of a Pseudo-Religion*. Translated by Alvin Moore Jr., Cecil Bethell, Hubert and Rohini Schiff. Hillsdale: Sophia Perennis, 2004.

Guerrero, Fernando. "Stranded in Miðgarðr: Draugar Folklore in Old Norse Sources." Oslo: University of Oslo/ Centre for Viking and Medieval Studies, 2003.

Gundarsson, Kveldulf (Stephan Scott Grundy). "Loki's Role in the Northern Religions." Idunna 93-96, 2012.

Gurevich, A.Y. *Izbrannye trudy: Drevnie germantsy. Vikingi* [*Selected Works: The Ancient Germanics and the Vikings*]. Saint Petersburg: Saint Petersburg University, 2007.

Haggkvist, M. "Grunnleggende problemer med hedensk tradisjonalisme" [Basic Problems with Pagan Traditionalism]. *KulturOrgan Skadinaujo* 2, 2003.

Hansen, H.T. "Julius Evola's Political Endeavors." In: Evola, Julius. *Men Among the Ruins: Postwar Reflections of a Radical Traditionalist*. Rochester: Inner Traditions, 2002: 1-104.

Heidegger, Martin. *Being and Time*. Translated by Joan Stambaugh. New York: State University of New York Press, 2010.

_____"Letter on Humanism". In: *Martin Heidegger, Basic Writings: From Being and Time to The Task of Thinking*. London: Harper, 2008.

_____*On the Way to Language*. Translated by Peter D. Hertz. New York: Harper, 1982.

Hesiod. *Theogony and Works and Days*. Translated by Catherine Schlegel and Henry Weinfield. Ann Arbor: University of Michigan Press, 2007.

Hobsbawm, Eric. *Nations and Nationalism since 1780: Programme, Myth, Reality*. Cambridge: Cambridge University Press, 1990.

Ignatyev, Andrey. *Mir Rerikhov (The World of the Roerichs)*, 2 volumes. Kaliningrad: 2013.

Ivanov, Alexander. "Khristiane do Khrista" [Christians before Christ]. *Traditsia* [*Tradition*] 3. Moscow: Eurasian Movement, 2012.

John-Stucke, Kirsten and Daniela Siepe. *Mythos Wewelsburg: Fakten und Legenden*. Paderborn: Schoeningh Ferdinand, 2015.

Jones, Prudance and Nigel Pennick. *A History of Pagan Europe*. London: Routledge, 1995.

Julian the Apostate. *The Arguments of the Emperor Julian Against the Christians*. Translated by Thomas Taylor. 1809.

Jung, Carl Gustav. *Dictionary of Analytical Psychology*. Ark, 1987.

Jünger, Ernst. *The Forest Passage*. Translated by Thomas Friese. Candor: Telos, 2013.

_____*A German Officer in Occupied Paris: The War Journals, 1941-1945*. Translated by Thomas Hansen. New York: Columbia University Press, 2019.

Jünger, Friedrich Georg. *Griechische Mythen* [*Greek Myths*]. 1947.

_____*Die Titanen* [*The Titans*]. 1944.

Kaldera, Raven. *The Jotunbok: Working with the Giants of the Northern Tradition*. Hubbardston: Asphodel, 2006.

Kareev, Nikolai. "Glavnye antropomorficheskie bogi slavianskogo iazychestva" [The Main Anthropomorphic Gods of Slavic Paganism]. *Slavianskii vestnik* [*Slavic Bulletin*], 2014 (1872).

Kelly, Aidan A. *Inventing Witchcraft: A Case Study in the Creation of a New Religion*. Loughborough: Thoth Publications, 2008.

Knoppe, Boris. "Induizm: ot globalistskoi adaptatsii k al'ternativnomu globalistskomy proektu" [Hinduism: From Globalist Adaptation to an Alternative Globalist Project]. In: *Malashenko, A. and S. Filatov, Religiia i globalizatsiia na prostorakh Evrazii* [*Religion and Globalization on the Expanses of Eurasia*]. Moscow: Neostrom/Carnegie Moscow Center, 2005.

Kolesov, V.V. *Drevniaia Rus': nasledie v slove, 4 toma - Mir cheloveka; Dobro i zlo; Bytie i byt; Mudrost' slova* [*Ancient Rus: The Legacy in the Word, 4 Volumes: The World of Man; Good and Evil; Being and Life; The Wisdom of the Word*]. Saint Petersburg: Faculty of Philosophy of Saint Petersburg State University: 2000, 2001, 2004, 2011.

Korablev, Leonid. *Jón Knizhnik-Charodey* [*Jón's Book of Sorcery*]. Ignis, 2009.

Krause, Arnulf (ed.). *Die Götterlieder der Älteren Edda* [*Songs of the Gods of the Elder Edda*]. Stuttgart: Philipp Reclam jun. GmbH Verlag, 2006.

Krizhevsky, Alexey. "Interv'iu 'Barkhatnoe podpol'e: Igor' Dudinsky o zhizni sovetskoi bogemy" [Interview: "The Velvet Underground: Igor Dudinsky on the Life of a Soviet Bohemian"]. *Russkaia zhizn'* [*Russian Life*], 1/2/2008.

Kvilhaug, Maria. *The Maiden with the Mead: A Goddess of Initiation Rituals in Norse Mythology?*. VDM Verlag, 2009.

Ledeneva, Lada. "Otgoloski iazychestva u karachaevtsev i balkartsev" [Echoes of Paganism among the Karachays and Balkars"]. *Vestnik Kavkaza*, 3/5/2011.

List, Guido von. *The Religion of the Aryo-Germanic Folk: Esoteric and Exoteric*. Bastrop, Texas: Lodestar, 2017.

Markova, L.A. *Filosofiia iz khaosa: G. Deleuze i postmodernizm v filosofii, nauke, religii* [*Philosophy out of Chaos: Gilles Deleuze and Postmodernism in Philosophy, Science, and Religion*]. Moscow: Kanon+, 2004.

Matgioi (Georges-Albert de Pourvourville). *Metafizicheskii put'* [*The Metaphysical Path*]. Saint Petersburg: Vladimir Dal', 2014.

McNallen, Stephen A. *Asatru: A Native European Spirituality*. Nevada City: Runestone Press, 2015.

_____ "The Method of Transcendence in Germanic Tradition", 2015.

_____ "Tribes vs. Empires".

Miloradovich, V. "Ocherki o malorusskoi demonologii" [Outlines of Little-Russian Demonology]. Novosibirsk: Svarte Aske, 2013.

Misiureva, L. *Predaniia i skazy Zapadnoi Sibiri* [*Legends and Tales of Western Siberia*]. Novosibirsk: Novosibirsk Book Publishers: 1954.

National-Anarchist Movement. "Why We Are Pagans". 26/1/2014.

Neapolitansky, S.M. and S.A. Matveev. *Entsiklopediia tantry* [*Encyclopedia of Tantra*]. Saint Petersburg: Institute of Metaphysics, 2010.

Nietzsche, Friedrich. *The Antichrist*. Translated by H.L. Mencken. New York: Alfred A. Knopf, 1924.

_____ *Thus Spoke Zarathustra*. Translated by Adrian del Caro. Cambridge: Cambridge University Press, 2006.

Nikolaev, A.P. "Pravoslavnaia tserkov' i shamany v Iakutii (XVIII-XIV vv.)" [The Orthodox Church and Shamans in Yakutia (17th-19th centuries)]. *Sibirskaia Zaimka*, 30/9/2002.

Nosova, G. *Iazychestvo v pravoslavii* [*Paganism in Orthodoxy*]. Moscow: Science, 1975.

Paul the Deacon. *History of the Langobards*. Translated by William Dudley Foulke. Philadelphia: University of Pennsylvania, 1907.

Pennick, Nigel. *Practical Magic in the Northern Tradition.* Loughborough: Thoth Publications, 2005.

Plato. *Complete Works.* Indianapolis/Cambridge: Hackett Publishing, 1997.

Platov, Anton. "Put' nad Bezdnoi: Traditsia v epokhu Ragnareka" [The Path Above the Abyss: Tradition in the Era of Ragnarok]. *LiveJournal*, 21/5/2013.

Pribylovsky, V. (ed.). *Russkii natsionalizm mezhdu vlast'iu I oppozitsiei* [*Russian Nationalism between Power and Opposition*]. Moscow: Panorama Center, 2010.

Raido Group. *A Handbook of Traditional Living.* London: Arktos, 2010.

Rekwaz, Rowo. *Hwitaz Hrabnaz.* Novosibirsk: Svarte Aske, 2015.

Russov, Stepan. *Variazhskie zakony s Rossiiskim perevodom i kratkimi zamechaniiami* [*The Varangian Laws with Russian Translation and Brief Remarks*]. Saint Petersburg, 1824/2014.

Rybakov, Boris. *Iazychestvo drevnikh slavian* [*The Paganism of the Ancient Slavs*]. Moscow: Science, 1981.

Saussure, Ferdinand de. *Course in General Linguistics.* Translated by Roy Harris. Chicago: Open Court, 1986.

Savin, Leonid. *Setetsentrichnaia i setevaia voina. Vvedenie v kontseptisiiu* [*Net-Centric and Network Warfare: An Introduction to the Concept*]. Moscow: Eurasian Movement, 2013.

Schuon, Frithjof. "A Note on René Guénon". *Studies in Comparative Religion* 17:1-2, 1985.

Sedgwick, Mark. *Against the Modern World: Traditionalism and the Secret Intellectual History of the Twentieth Century.* Oxford: Oxford University Press, 2004.

Shirokova, N.S. *Mify kel'tskikh narodov* [*Myths of the Celtic Peoples*]. Moscow: Astrel / Tranzitkniga, 2005.

Shizhensky, Roman (ed.). *Colloquium Heptaplomeres: Nauchnyi almanakh* [*Colloquium Heptaplomeres: A Scholarly Almanac*]. Nizhnii Novgorod: Minin University, 2015.

_____ *Filosofiia dobroi sily. Zhizn' i tvorchestvo Dobroslava (A.A. Dobrovol'skogo)* [*The Philosophy of Good Force: The Life and Works of Dobroslav (A.A. Dobrovolsky)*]. Moscow: Orbita, 2013.

_____ "*K voprosu o terminologii slavianskikh variatsii 'indigenous religions' (na primere termina 'neoiazychestvo')* [On the Question of the Terminology of Slavic Variations of 'Indigenous Religions' (The Example of the Term 'Neopaganism')]. In: *Etnichna istoriia narodiv Evropi: Zbirnik naukovikh prats'* [*The Ethnic History of the Peoples of Europe: A Compilation of Scholarly Works*]. Kiev: UNISERV, 2010.

_____ "*Nekotorye aspekty kodifikatsii fenomena sovremennogo slavianskogo iazychestva po dannym polevykh issledovanii*" [Some Aspects of the Codification of the Phenomenon of Contemporary Slavic Paganism According to the Data of Field Studies]. In: *Vera i religiia v sovremennoi Rossii: Vserossiiskii konkurs molodykh uchenykh - 25 luchshikh issledovanii* [*Faith and Religion in Contemporary Russia: All-Russian Young Scholars' Competition - The 25 Best Studies*]. Moscow: August Borg, 2014.

_____ "*Neoiazycheskii mif o Vladimire I*" [The Neopagan Myth of Vladimir I].

_____ "*Opyt sravnitel'nogo analiza tekstov A.A. Dobrovol'skogo i G.F. Wirth'a (k voprosu ob istochnikovoi baze rossiiskikh neoiazychnikov)*" [The Experience of Comparative Analysis of the Texts of A.A. Dobrovolsky and H.F. Wirth (On the Question of the Source Base of Russian Neopagans)].

_____ "*Problema genezisa sovremennogo russkogo iazychestva v rabotakh rossiiskikh issledovatelei*" [The Problem of the Genesis of Contemporary Russian Paganism in the Works of Russian Scholars]. In: (see succeeding citation).

395

_____(ed.). *'Rus' iazycheskaia': ethnicheskaia religioznost' v Rossii i Ukraine XX-XXI vv.* [*'Pagan Rus': Ethnic Religiosity in Russia and Ukraine in the 20th-21st Centuries*]. Novgorod: Novgorod State Pedagogical University, 2010.

_____*Pochvennik ot iazychestva: mirovozzrechenskie diskursy volkhva Velimira (N.N. Speranskogo)* [*A Pochvennik from Paganism: The Ideological Discourses of Volkhv Velimir (N.N. Speransky)*]. Nizhnii Novgorod: Volga Typograph, 2014.

Sidorina, T.Iu. and T.L. Poliannikov. *Natsionalizm. Teorii i politicheskaia istoriia* [*Nationalism: Theories and Political History*]. Moscow: State University Higher School of Economics, 2006.

Slauson, Irv. *The Religion of Odin*. Red Wing: Asatru Free Church Committee/Viking House, 1978.

Sokolova, V.K. *Vesenne-letnie kalendarnye obriady russkikh, ukraintsev i belorusov* [*Spring-Summer Calendar Rites of the Russians, Ukrainians, and Belarusians*]. Moscow: Science, 1979.

Soral, Alain. *Poniat' Imperiu: Griadushchee global'noe upravlenie ili vosttanie natsii?* [*Understanding Empire: Impending Global Governance, or an Uprising of Nations?*]. Moscow: Global Revolutionary Alliance, 2012.

Speranskaya, Natella. *Dionis presleduemyi* [*Dionysus Pursued*]. Moscow: Cultural Revolution, 2014.

_____"Interview with Seyyed Hossein Nasr." *Medium*, 2013.

_____ *Put' k Novoi Metafizike* [*The Path to the New Metaphysics*]. Moscow: Eurasian Movement, 2012.

Speransky, N. (Velimir). *Iazychniki otvechaiut: Broshiura No. 13* [*Pagans Respond: Pamphlet # 13*]. Troitsk, 2013.

_____*Volkhvy protiv globalizma* [*Volkhvs against Globalism*]. Samoteka: 2014.

Spiesberger, Karl. *Runenmagie: Handbuch der Runenkunde* [*Rune Magic: A Handbook of Runecraft*]. Burstadt: Paul Hartmann Verlag, 2009.

Steblin-Kamensky, M. *Mir sagi. Stanovlenie literatury* [*The World of the Saga: The Emergence of Literature*]. Moscow: Leningrad: Science, 1984.

_____ *Mif* [*Myth*]. Leningrad: Science, 1976.

Stinson, Mark Ludwig. *Heathen Families: Nine Modern Fables for Heathen Children and a Collection of Essays Regarding Heathen Families*. Liberty: Jotun's Bane Kindred, 2011.

_____*Heathen Gods: A Collection of Essays Concerning the Folkway of Our People*. Liberty: Jotun's Bane Kindred, 2011.

_____*Heathen Tribes: A Collection of Essays Concerning the Tribes of Our Folk*. Liberty: Jotun's Bane Kindred/Temple of Our Heathen Gods, 2009.

Sukhov, A.D. (ed.). *Vvedenie khristianstva na Rusi* [*The Introduction of Christianity in Rus*]. Moscow: Institute of Philosophy of the Academy of Sciences of the USSR/ Mysl [Thought], 1987.

Svarte, Askr (Evgeny Nechkasov). "A-I-U and Stillness: A Commentary on Herman Wirth's Study of the Year-Wheel". Translated by J.M.A. *Warha Europe* 2, 2018-2019: 18-30.

_____"Dobroslav: vzgliad traditsionalista" [*Dobroslav: A Traditionalist View*]. Svarte Aske, 2014.

_____*Gap: At the Left Hand of Odin*. Fall of Man Press, 2019.

_____"An Interview with Wulf Grimsson." Svarte Aske, 19/6/2013.

_____*Identichnost' iazychnika v XXI veke* [*Pagan Identity in the 21st Century*]. Moscow: Veligor, 2020.

_____"The Kalash People and their Identity". Novosibirsk: Svarte Aske, 2019.

_____*Polemos: Iazycheskii traditsionalizm I - Zaria iazychestva* [*Polemos: Pagan Traditionalism I - The Dawn of Paganism*] Moscow: Veligor, 2016.

_____*Polemos: Iazycheskii traditsionalizm II - Perspektivy iazychestva* [*Polemos: Pagan Traditionalism II - Pagan Perspectives*]. Moscow: Veligor, 2016.

_____*Priblizhenie i okruzhenie. Ocherki mysli o Germanskom Logose, Traditsii i Nichto* [*Forthcoming and Encirclement: Thoughts on the Germanic Logos, Tradition, and Nothingness*]. Novosibirsk: Svarte Aske, 2017.

Telegin, S.M. *Volia k mifu: Problema neoiazyschestva* [*The Will to Myth: The Problem of Neopaganism*]. Warha 3, 2016.

Tmenov, V.Kh. "*Osetinskoe iazychestvo v sisteme srednevekovykh religioznykh verovanii narodov Severnogo Kavkaza*" [Ossetian Paganism in the System of the Medieval Religious Beliefs of the Peoples of the North Caucasus]. In: *Problemy etnografii Osetin: Sbornik nauchnykh trudov 2* [*Problems of Ossetian Ethnography: A Compilation of Scholarly Works 2*). Vladikavkaz: SO NII, 1992.

Tokarev, S.A., I.N. Grozdov, Y. V. Ivanov, et. al. (eds). *Kelandarnye obychai i obriady v stranakh zarubezhnoi Evropy* [*Calendric Customs and Rites in the Countries of Exterior Europe*]. Moscow: Science, 1977.

Vasil'chenko, Andrey. *Ariiskii mif III Reikha* [*The Aryan Myth of the Third Reich*]. Moscow: Yauza Press, 2008.

Veleslav (Ilya Cherkasov). *The Great Perfection Doctrine.* Translated by Ilya Koptilin. Fall of Man, 2016.

_____*Kniga Rodnoi Very: Osnovy Rodovogo Vedaniia Rusov i Slavian* [*The Book of Native Faith: The Foundations of the Native Knowledge of the Rus and Slavs*]. Moscow: Veligor, 2009.

_____ *Kniga Velikoi Navi: Khaosofiia i Russkoe Navoslavie* [*The Book of the Great Nav': Chaosophy and Russian Navoslavie*]. Society of Death Consciousness, 2011.

_____ *Liber ABRAXAS: Protiv Boga i Prirody* [*Against God and Nature*]. Society of Death Consciousness, 2011.

_____ "*Obshchestvo i kasty*" [Society and Castes]. Svarte Aske, 2012. [http://askrsvarte.org/blog/post_11/].

_____ *Osnovy Rodnoveriia: Obriadnik. Kologod* [*The Foundations of Native Faith: A Book of Rites and the Year-Circle*]. Saint Petersburg: Vedic Heritage, 2010.

_____ *Shuinyi put': Chernaia kniga Navi* [*The Left-Hand Path: The Black Book of Nav'*]. Moscow: Veligor, 2011.

_____ *Uriadnik malyi* [*The Small Constable*].

Venner, Dominque. "Living in Accordance with Our Tradition". *Counter-Currents*, 8/10/2013.

Warren, Ian B. "The 'European New Right' Defining and Defending Europe's Heritage: An Interview with Alain de Benoist." *New European Conservative*, 2014.

Wirth, Herman. *Der Aufgang der Menschheit: Untersuchungen zur Geschichte der Religion, Symbolik und Schrift der Atlantisch-Nordischen Rasse*. Jena: Eugen Diederich, 1928.

_____ *Die Heilige Urschrift der Menschheit: Symbolgeschichtliche Untersuchungen diesseits und jenseits des Nordatlantik*. Leipzig: Koehler & Amelang, 1936.

_____ *Khronika Ura Linda. Drevneishaiia istoriia Evropy* [*The Ura Linda Chronicle: The Most Ancient History of Europe*]. Moscow: Veche, 2007.

Wotans Krieger. "A New Perspective on Loki as a Left-Hand Path Germanic God." Svarte Aske.

Zhekulin, V.I. and A.N. Rozov. *Obriadovaia poeziia* [*Ritual Poetry*]. Moscow: Sovremennik [Contemporary], 1989.

Devi Gita: The Song of the Goddess. Translated by C. Mackenzie Brown. New York: State University of New York Press, 1998.

The Elder Edda: A Book of Viking Lore. Translated by Andrew Orchard. New York: Penguin, 2011.

The Poetic Edda: Parallel Old Norse-English Edition. Edited by J. Knife. Findelworks, 2017.

The Poetic Edda: Stories of the Norse Gods and Heroes. Translated by Jackson Crawford. Indianapolis: Hackett Publishing, 2015.

The Odinist Anthology. Asatru Free Assembly, 1983.

"Osnovy veroucheniia Asatru" [Foundations of the Asatru Creed]. *Basic Document for the Registration of Asatru Religious Organizations in the Russian Federation.* 2013.

The Rigveda: The Earliest Religious Poetry of India. Translated by Stephanie W. Johnson and Joel P. Brereton. Oxford: Oxford University Press/University of Texas South Asia Institute, 2014.

Rodnoverie [*Native Faith*] Nos. 1-8, 2009-2013.

Severnyi Veter [*Northern Wind*] Nos. 1-7. Kiev/Minsk: 2013-2014.

Shatapatha Brahmana. *Sacred Books of the East.* Translated by Julius Eggeling. Oxford: Oxford University Press, 1894.

Skazki i legendy ingushei i chechentsev [*Tales and Legends of the Ingush and Chechens*]. Moscow: Science/Editorial Board of Eastern Literature, 1983.

The Song Celestial, or Bhagavad-Gita, from the Mahabharata. Translated by Sir Edwin Arnold. New York: Truslove, Hanson & Comba, 1900.

The Thirteen Principal Upanishads. Translated by Robert Hume. Oxford: Oxford University Press, 1921.

Al'manakh "Traditsiia" [*"Tradition" Almanac*] Nos. 3-5. Edited by Alexander Dugin and Natalya Speranskaya. Moscow: Eurasian Movement, 2012-2013.

Al'manakh "Traditsiia i Traditsionalizm" [*Tradition and Traditionalism Almanac*]. Donetsk: 2013.

Warha 1: Al'manakh o Puti Levoi Ruki [*Almanac of the Left-Hand Path*]. Novosibirsk: Svarte Aske, 2015.

Warha 2. Novosibirsk: Svarte Aske, 2016.

Warha 3: Iazychestvo, Traditsionalizm, Put' Levoi Ruki [*Paganism, Traditionalism, and the Left-Hand Path*]. Novosibirsk: Svarte Aske, 2016.

Warha 4: Filosofiia, Traditsionalizm, Tribuna, Poeziia [*Philosophy, Traditionalism, Tribune, and Poetry*]. Novosibirsk: Svarte Aske, 2017.

Warha 5: Traditsiia, Filosofiia, Tribuna, Poeziia [*Tradition, Philosophy, Tribune, Poetry*]. Novosibirsk: Svarte Aske, 2018.

Warha 6: Traditsiia, Filosofiia, Tribuna, Poeziia [*Tradition, Philosophy, Tribune, Poetry*]. Novosibirsk: Svarte Aske, 2019.

Warha Europe 1: Almanac of Pagan Traditionalism and the Left Hand Path. Novosibirsk: Svarte Aske, 2017.

Warha Europe 2: Tradition and Identity. Novosibirsk: Svarte Aske, 2019.